The
ATLAS
of
BRITISH BIRDLIFE

The
ATLAS
of
BRITISH BIRDLIFE
Bob Scott

IVY ❧ LEAF

Atlas of British Birdlife

First published in 1987 by
Country Life Books an imprint of
The Hamlyn Publishing Group Limited

This edition published in 1991 by
Ivy Leaf
Michelin House
81 Fulham Road
London SW3 6RB

This edition produced exclusively for Bookmart Limited

Conceived and produced for The Hamlyn Publishing Group by
Curtis Garrett Limited, The Old Vicarage,
Hornton-cum-Studley, Oxford OX9 1BT, England.

ISBN 0 86363 030 8

Layout by David Hibbert and Jerry Burman Associates
Illustrated checklist maps by Christoph le Blanc
Index by Barbara James
Filmset by SX Composing Limited
Produced by Mandarin Offset **Printed and Bound in China**

Author's Dedication.
To my mAny friends that made this booK possible
I have enjoyeD thier Birdwatching compAny throughout bRitain
(sic)!

ACKNOWLEDGEMENTS
ENGLAND SCENE LIBRARY: 108, 115.
FOTOBANK: 90, 91, 92, 93, 97, 100, 101, 113, 118, 122-23, 125, 127,
130, 132, 139, 140, 143, 148 (top), 151, 152, 154 (bottom),
155 (top & bottom), 159, 160, 161, 166-67, 169, 177, 181, 182, 190,
193, 194, 195, 199.
R A GARRATT: 119.
NATURAL IMAGE/PETER WILSON: 6.
OCTOPUS BOOKS: 144.
BOB SCOTT: 69, 77, 78, 81, 84, 86, 88, 104, 105, 107, 133, 163, 164,
165, 171, 172.
SEAPHOT LIMITED: PLANET EARTH PICTURES: Richard Coomber
183 (bottom); Ivor Edmonds 129; David George 70; John Lythgoe 75, 112,
157; John and Gillian Lythgoe 73, 158; Richard Matthews title page, 178;
David Phillips 141, 146, 147; John Waters and Bernadette Spiegel 79;
ZEFA PICTURE LIBRARY (UK) LTD: 83, 154 (top), 183 (top), 184, 186; E G
Carle 168; Tony Craddock 94, 96; W F Davidson 148 (bottom), 174, 176;
Karl E Deckart 187; F Park 191; H Schmied 198; Simon Warner 138, 173.

CONTENTS

Pied Flycatcher

INTRODUCTION

Interest in the environment, the countryside, and its wildlife continues to grow rapidly in Britain. National and local societies of both general and specific interest carry on expanding or are created, and rarely an evening passes without a television presentation on a natural history topic. At the forefront of this established and still-growing sympathy with all things natural is the popular pastime of birdwatching or 'birding' as it is often called.

Membership of bird clubs and ornithological societies continues to increase – The Royal Society for the Protection of Birds is fast approaching its 500 000th member while its junior branch, the Young Ornithologists Club, has almost 100 000 members. Every weekend, the bird reserves and established birding localities, particularly in southern England, are, if anything, overcrowded with birdwatchers!

It is now possible to buy magazines devoted to the hobby on railway-station bookstalls, to make telephone calls to find out where the most exciting and rare species have been seen in the last few days, to join groups of like-minded enthusiasts on trips to some of the most exciting localities within Britain, or even on holiday visits to exotic sites from Siberia to Antarctica.

One of the great advantages of birdwatching as a hobby is that it is possible to enjoy so much without spending vast sums of money. On the other hand, the sky is the limit if you can afford it. You should treat this part of the book as a guide only, because what is perfect for one birder may be of no use to another. You should try to acquire an identification (field) guide, a pair of binoculars, and suitable clothing. After that, your needs and priorities will vary.

Of course, you must be able to identify the birds you see. One of the most frustrating aspects of birdwatching for a beginner is the apparent ease with which an experienced birder can name the birds glimpsed briefly as they fly overhead or flit behind the bushes even when they seem to show little that could possibly be recognized. There is no short cut to the experience to be gained from regular birdwatching and the steady accumulation of knowledge. The techniques of field identification have been developing steadily since the days when the gun and the taxidermist were the only means of identification. There is still much to be learnt, and whole books have been written on specialized identification problems such as birds of prey in flight or gulls with their confusing array of immature plumages. No birdwatcher, however experienced, can put a name to every bird he or she sees, but the number of occasions when the bird cannot be recognized immediately does decrease as experience is gained.

Field guides and other books
No birder should lack a good identification field guide. The sole function of the guide is to enable the rapid confirmation of the identity of any species seen. Coupled with the rise in interest in birding have been significant developments in the format and contents of field guides. The following guides are all intended to fit the pocket (of jacket or car) and are designed to enable you to identify the birds you see.

Bruun, B, Delin, H, and Svensson, L. 1986. *Country Life Guide to Birds of Britain and Europe.* Hamlyn.

Ferguson-Lees, J, Willis, I, and Sharrock, J T R. 1983. *The Shell Guide to the Birds of Britain and Ireland.* Michael Joseph.

Hayman, P, 1979. *The Birdwatcher's Pocket Guide.* Mitchell Beazley.

Heinzel, H, Fitter, R, and Parslow, J. 1985. *The Birds of Britain and Europe.* Collins.

Holden, P and Sharrock, J T R. 1984. *The RSPB Book of British Birds.* Macmillan.

Perrins, C. 1987. *Collins New Generation Guide to Birds.* Collins.

Peterson, R, Mountfort, G, and Hollom, P A D. 1984. *A Field Guide to the Birds of Britain and Europe.* Collins.

Scott, B and Forrest, D. 1980. *The Birdwatcher's Key.* Warne.

About this book
The Atlas of British Birdlife is not intended to be a field guide – its contents are not specifically designed to help the reader identify the birds seen. The book helps with the second stage for the birder – the bringing of the bird and the birdwatcher together. Different species live in different habitats and occur at different times of the year. The intention of this work is to tell you where and when. Having discovered where and when the birds are to be found – where should the birdwatcher go to coincide? Many of the sites detailed are well-known traditional birding venues, others are less popular and allow the visiting birdwatchers more scope to search and to explore to make their own discoveries. Entries in the county-by-county section of the book, although useable on their own, will prove most informative if consulted in conjunction with the latest Ordnance Survey 'Landranger Series of Great Britain' maps at a scale of 1:50 000 (2 centimetres to 1 kilometre or approximately 1¼ inches to 1 mile).

A book which encompasses the entire British Isles cannot be expected to provide the detail required by the enthusiast who wishes to concentrate on one county or geographical area. It is hoped, however, that as the interest develops, the range of contents provided will lead the reader to more specific information, be it through a local bird club or a more detailed published guide.

Keeping up to date
Information, particularly addresses, do change; new

and updated publications continue to appear; and new reports are published. One of the best ways to keep up to date is to refer to the annual publication: Pemberton, J E (editor). *The Birdwatcher's Yearbook and Diary*. Buckingham Press.

Binoculars and telescopes

In addition to a field guide, a pair of binoculars is a must for the would-be birder. On the market today there is a bewildering array of different models of binoculars made in many different countries, and varying widely in price. The correct pair of binoculars for any birdwatcher is the pair that is optically sound, is comfortable to use, and is also affordable. You should always try to test different models under field conditions before buying. Viewing the high street from the shop doorway is no substitute for a day in the field observing birds under the conditions that will prevail each time the binoculars are taken out. The most recent pair of binoculars acquired by the author needed three complete days of use before they felt 'comfortable' and satisfactory.

Binoculars are designated by two figures. The first indicates the magnification (for example, 8X, 9X, or 10X), the second indicates the diameter of the object lens (the one furthest from the eye) in millimetres (for example, X30, X40, or X50). The combination of these two figures gives a general guideline to the quality of the picture: the larger the object lens the brighter the image; the higher the magnification the duller the image. Therefore, you will need to balance these two features. The most popular binoculars with birdwatchers are usually 8X30, 10X40, and 10X50. The independent journal, *British Birds* (Fountains, Park Lane, Blunham, Bedford MK44 3NJ), undertakes a regular survey of binoculars and telescopes used by birdwatchers and in the latest published results (1985) the following were the five most popular binoculars in increasing order of price: ZEISS JENA Jenoptem 10X50; SWIFT Audubon 8.5X44; OPTOLYTH Alpin 10X50; ZEISS WEST Dialyt 10X40B; LEITZ Trinovid 10X40B.

Most regular birders soon find that they need a telescope (or rather a spotting 'scope in modern parlance), but this should always be acquired after the binoculars, and a 'scope should never be considered a substitute for the binoculars. The knowledge of just when there is a need comes with experience. A sturdy tripod is essential and all this adds to the weight of the equipment to be carried. The *British Birds* survey showed the following four to be the most popular telescopes, again in increasing order of price: BUSHNELL Spacemaster X60; BUSHNELL Discoverer 15-60X60; KOWA TS-1/TS-2 X60; OPTOLYTH 30X75GA.

Clothing

The clothes you wear for birdwatching should be functional and comfortable. Subdued colours – browns, greens, and greys – are a must, and the bright yellows, blues, and reds should be avoided. Sensible footwear is dictated by the weather and terrain; rubber boots are worth wearing to keep feet dry, and stout shoes or walking boots are good for rocky surfaces. How much is carried (a small light-weight backpack is useful) depends upon how far you intend to walk from the car (regretfully, a vehicle is an essential piece of birdwatching equipment if you wish to reach some of the more out-of-the-way sites), but warm jerseys, anoraks, and waterproofs all have their place when birdwatching in the British climate. Being warm and dry makes a day's birding that much more enjoyable.

Fully equipped and ready for a day's birding, the birdwatcher should be very aware of two codes of behaviour or practice that relate to all persons using the countryside or visiting nature reserves. The first of these is *The Country Code*:

1 Guard against all risk of fire
2 Fasten all gates
3 Keep dogs under proper control
4 Keep to the paths across farm land
5 Use gates and stiles to cross fences, hedges, and walls
6 Leave livestock, crops, and machinery alone
7 Take your litter home
8 Help to keep all water clean
9 Protect wildlife, wild plants, and trees
10 Take special care on country roads
11 Make no unnecessary noise

The second code is more specific to the birdwatcher and has been compiled by six different ornithological organizations, *The Birdwatchers' Code of Conduct*:

1 The welfare of birds must come first
2 Habitat must be protected
3 Keep disturbance to birds and their habitat to a minimum
4 When you find a rare bird think carefully about whom you should tell
5 Do not harass rare migrants
6 Abide by the Bird Protection Acts at all times
7 Respect the rights of landowners
8 Respect the rights of other people in the countryside
9 Make your records available to the local bird recorder
10 Behave abroad as you would when birdwatching at home

Remember that birdwatching should be fun but, as time passes and interests develop, so do the more specialized interests of the birdwatcher. You will probably find that these interests grow if you join one or more of the ornithological societies; details of many will be found in the county-by-county sections of this book. Nationally, there are several which can provide information on a range of subjects, and most produce their own magazine or journal:

British Ornithologists' Union, c/o The Zoological Society of London, Regent's Park, London NW1 4RY. Publishes the quarterly journal, *Ibis*.

British Trust for Ornithology, Beech Grove, Station Road, Tring, Herts HP23 5NR. Publishes the journals, *Bird Study* and *Ringing and Migration*.

Royal Society for the Protection of Birds, The Lodge, Sandy, Beds SG19 2DL. Publishes the quarterly magazine, *Birds*.

Wildfowl Trust, Slimbridge, Gloucester GL2 7BT. Publishes the magazine, *Wildfowl World* and journal, *Wildfowl*.

Young Ornithologists' Club, The Lodge, Sandy, Beds SG19 2DL. Publishes the bimonthly magazine, *Bird Life*.

In addition to these societies, there are two monthly magazines that are open to subscription. Both provide information and news for the birdwatcher:

Bird Watching, Bushfield House, Orton Centre, Peterborough PE2 0UW.

British Birds, Fountains, Park Lane, Blunham, Bedford MK44 3NJ.

Keeping records

Keeping detailed records of observations by taking some form of notes can add greatly to the interest of a day's outing, and can eventually form the background to a survey or historical collection of records. The basic notes may be simple lists of species seen, or numbers recorded with where and when. These kinds of data are often very useful for a local bird society that is attempting to compile an annual assessment of bird status in the area. Notes collected can be kept in diary form, card index, loose-leaf book, or, these days, even a home computer. Compiling records can be fascinating in itself, but it will be even more exciting if it is coupled with specialized recording using sketch pad, camera, or sound recorder. This should not be undertaken without seeking the detailed knowledge and advice available through the appropriate organizations, societies, and books:

Busby, J. 1986. *Drawing Birds: An RSPB Guide*. Christopher Helm.

Leslie, C W. 1984. *The Art of Field Sketching*. Prentice-Hall.

Wildlife Sound Recording Society, c/o National Sound Archive, 29 Exhibition Road, London SW7 2AS.

The excitement of birdwatching in the British Isles is enhanced by the fact that we can never be absolutely certain of the species that can be seen on any given day. This stems from our geographical position on the western seaboard of the European land mass – an ideal location to experience the mass migrations of vast numbers of birds every spring and autumn. The 'official' British list contains the names of over 500 species of birds. To qualify as a 'British' bird, a species must either have been recorded in an apparently wild state in Britain or Ireland or alternatively be a species which, although introduced by humans, or escaped from captivity, has now established a wild breeding stock which apparently maintains itself without the need for further introductions to support it. Examples of the latter include the familiar Pheasant and Ruddy Duck together with the less-familiar Egyptian Goose and Ring-necked Parakeet. The Canada Goose and Little Owl could reasonably be expected to appear under this category but, in fact, both have occurred in the British Isles 'in an apparently wild state'.

Migration

Many of the 500 or so British species are only extremely rare visitors, ranging from the Black-browed Albatross from southern oceans, to the Hudsonian Godwit from North America; from Ross's Gull from the high Arctic to the Neddle-tailed Swift from the Far East. To record such a rarity is a red-letter day indeed and to find this type of bird happens few times in any birdwatcher's lifetime. However, the regular comings and goings of the more 'normal' migrants present many opportunities for a range of observations. Every autumn, the summer visitors to Britain must leave for milder southern climates to ensure their survival during the cold northern winters. These are mainly the insect-eating species, and include the familiar Swallow and Cuckoo, as well as most of the breeding warblers and flycatchers, together with several of the wagtails, pipits, and smaller thrushes. Their place is taken by the countless thousands of birds from eastern and northern Europe that move south and west to spend their winter in the relatively milder climate on the Atlantic seaboard away from the frozen land mass of central and eastern Europe. Each winter the British Isles play host to huge concentrations of Starlings, thrushes, finches, and wildfowl that can provide some of the most spectacular of all Britain's birdwatching.

The mysteries surrounding the comings and goings of all these migrant birds have fascinated people for centuries and, in ancient times, many strange theories were developed to explain the seasonal absence of certain birds. Swallows were thought to hibernate in the bottoms of ponds. Cuckoos were considered to change into Sparrowhawks and Barnacle Geese were supposed to have emerged from barnacles. Modern research has answered many questions and corrected many earlier misconceptions. The use of light aluminium-alloy rings inscribed with an address and number, and fitted on birds' legs have produced many exciting recoveries from around the world. The ringing of birds in Britain is very carefully controlled by the British Trust for Ornithology which publishes an annual report highlighting many of the most exciting reports. By the end of 1985, over eighteen million birds had been ringed in Britain and nearly 400 000 had been recovered. In the report for that year was mention of a Storm Petrel from South Africa, a Brent Goose from Canada, a Pochard from Bulgaria, an Osprey from Morocco, a Ruff from Mali, a Redwing from Cyprus, and a Goldcrest from Poland.

Bird migration is always most apparent at coastal localities, but even inland where the spectacular migratory arrivals are absent, and streams of birds following the coastline are not to be seen, the arrival of the first Swallow, the singing of the first Willow Warbler, and the calling of the first Cuckoo are all indications of migratory movements. We are often preoccupied with the first arrivals and forget that the bulk of these returning summer visitors are still to come. The first half of May is always a busy spring period, for this is the time when most of our summer visitors arrive. Many will have been with us for a month or more, but this is the time of peak arrival when the incoming tide of returning birds reaches its highest. Some have only comparatively short journeys across the English Channel, others have travelled from the Mediterranean basin, some from south of the Sahara, while yet others are merely passing through on a mammoth journey from Antarctica to the Arctic.

As with all migratory movements, the weather plays a key role. Flying birds are at the mercy of every gust of wind, every drop of rain, every depression and bank of fog. It is the affects of these weather conditions that can produce the unexpected – the off-course migrant swept across the North Sea to make landfall on the Norfolk coast; the sudden shower of rain just before dawn forcing to ground the huge numbers of nocturnal migrants as they cross the Dorset coastline; the unexpected gale and driving rain causing exhausted migrants to seek shelter on a barren Scottish island. The result: Britain is one of the most exciting countries in the world in which to go birdwatching.

Bird gardening

Far-flung islands and distant coastlines need not be the only birding interest. Much closer to home the humble suburban back garden can provide good birdwatching. Gardening for wildlife is now a favourite pastime of many; encouraging birds by providing suitable food, nesting cover, and artificial nest sites has become a national obsession and an increasing amount of literature is devoted to the subject:

Dennis, J V. 1986. *A Complete Guide to Bird Feeding*. Knopf.
du Feu, C. 1985 *Nestboxes*. British Trust for Ornithology.
Glue, D. 1984. *The Garden Bird Book*. Macmillan.
Soper, T. 1986. *The Bird Table Book*. David & Charles.

Wood, N. 1985. *Birds in Your Garden*. Hamlyn.

Garden birds can be fed in two ways: natural food-bearing plants can be planted or encouraged; or artificial food can be placed on suitable feeding devices. Bird tables and hanging bags of nuts, together with a birdbath, are now very much part of the garden furniture. Without doubt, peanuts are the most popular food provided, usually in mesh baskets or bags hanging from a suitable tree or beneath the bird table. The kernels of other nuts should also be tried. A complete range of kitchen scraps, including bones from the meat, fat, bread, and soft fruit will all be eaten, and a wide range of seeds is usually available from pet-food shops, or even from the grocer and supermarket. For the real bird-feeding enthusiast is the challenge of providing live food by rearing mealworms – or how about maggots? Many kinds of shrubs and bushes can be planted to provide cover and food for birds; among those recommended are Cotoneasters, Berberis, Rowan, Yew, and Pyracanthas. Hawthorn and Buckthorn will provide both shelter and food, and supplement the artificial nest-sites with more natural opportunities.

At one time, the garden nest-box was simply the hole-fronted box suitable for nesting tits but, through experiment and development, a whole range of bird boxes are now available, and are relatively easy to construct. Some are not particularly suitable for gardens but, even so, there is no reason why attempts should not be made to provide boxes for Blue and Great Tits, Robins, Spotted Flycatchers, House Martins, Starlings, Swifts, and even Tawny Owls.

Breeding and nesting

The breeding season is a critical time in the annual cycle of all bird species, and, for the birdwatcher, it is an exciting time to observe. The variation in breeding behaviour, nest construction, egg design, and food requirements seems endless, but enthusiasm to see and learn more must be tempered with concern for the welfare of the breeding birds. Visits to nests can unwittingly provide telltale signs that attract the attention of unwelcome predators.

At one extreme of the variation is the well-secreted Wren's nest hidden where a brick is missing from the wall at the bottom of the garden and tucked in well behind the ivy. At the other extreme, the hundreds of Gannets in a noisy, crowded colony easily visible many miles away. Between these two is the Carrion Crow, isolated on the top of a tall tree yet clearly visible even if it is out of reach; or the colony of ground-nesting terns whose eggs rest on the bare stones but are camouflaged and almost invisible. Tucked away within the hole in a dead tree are the pure white eggs of a woodpecker. These have no need of camouflage and the parent bird must be able to see them in the dark interior of the nesting cavity. In a clump of rushes beside the pond are the dozen or so, pale-coloured duck eggs, but these are well hidden when they are being incubated by the dull-plumaged female, in contrast to her brightly coloured mate. Whenever she leaves the nest, the eggs are carefully covered with the down that lines the nest. The deep cup of a falcon's nest contains relatively small, round eggs that can be turned easily by the sitting bird; waders' eggs are large and pointed and fit neatly in the nest, pointed end inwards to enable the parent to cover all four. On a vertical cliff ledge, auks build no nests but lay pear-shaped eggs which, if knocked, roll in circles to avoid falling over the edge.

The ways of rearing young are as variable as the eggs themselves. Ducklings are active almost from the hatch, swimming well and finding their own food. Pheasant chicks run rapidly after their parents and are capable of flight well before they are fully grown. All waders have active chicks. By contrast, the garden Blackbirds are hatched blind and naked, and are fed in the nest for two weeks with a similar period of parental care after fledging. Of all the British breeding birds, the Cuckoo has the strangest and perhaps best-known breeding behaviour. The adult female can select just the right time at which to lay her egg in the foster-parent's nest, carefully moving one of the host's own eggs at the same time. Evolution has given the Cuckoo a shorter incubation period than that of host species and, upon hatching, the young Cuckoo efficiently throws all the other eggs from the nest. The unsuspecting parents, probably Dunnock, Reed Warbler, or Meadow Pipit, are left with the task of feeding the apparently unsatisfiable youngster well after it has grown larger than themselves. Larger birds frequently require even longer to rear their young. The Grey Heron incubates its eggs for some four weeks; it then feeds the young in the nest for a further eight weeks before fledging. For up to two weeks after flying, the young still return to the nest to be fed – a total of fourteen weeks of parental attention.

Conservation and protection of wild birds

Breeding herons and egrets were the stimulation for the founding of two of the world's major conservation and protection societies. In North America, the National Audubon Society was founded to combat the killing of egrets in the southern states. In the breeding season these birds grow extensive ornamental plumes which take part in their ritualized display patterns. It was for these plumes, used to adorn ladies' hats, that the birds were killed. Similar movements were taking place in Britain and, in 1889, a Fur and Feather Group was founded near Manchester, with the object of protesting about the trade in birds' feathers in the millinery trade. Slowly the group widened its objectives to become the Society for the Protection of Birds and, in 1904, it was granted the Royal Charter and the familiar RSPB was formed.

Since that date the society's work in bird pro-tection and conservation has grown. Campaigns have been fought against oil pollution, egg collecting, illegal trapping and shooting, and the indiscriminate use of poisons. An education programme has involved teachers and schools, the production of films, videos, and magazines, and the formation of a very active junior section, the Young Ornithologists Club. Since it first acquired land, the RSPB has steadily increased its reserve holding and now manages over 120 reserves throughout the United Kingdom. In addition to managing the land for the benefit of the wildlife, visitors are welcomed to many of the reserves where facilities are available for them to view the bird life. In recent years, the RSPB can proudly claim to have been closely involved with the recolonization of Britain by Avocets and Ospreys, to have safeguarded the few remaining pairs of Marsh Harriers and Bitterns, and the organization is now protecting the majority of the Roseate Terns that nest in Britain.

With the current legislation of the 'Wildlife and Countryside Act', together with the general support provided by a public opinion very much in favour of wildlife conservation, the bird population of Britain is perhaps, in many ways, better off now than it has been in the past. Today, the threats are more international, as problems become global. It is the loss of tropical rain forests, the slaughter of millions of birds on their annual migrations, and the indiscriminate use of chemicals in third-world countries that are posing the biggest threats to Britain's birdlife. The conservation and protection movements of Britain and the world must now pay more attention to the international scene.

KEY TO THE MAPS

Note the different colours used in the maps are intended to be a general guide only. Largely, they are confined by county boundaries where possible. They function as an indication of the relative abundances of different bird species during different seasons of the year. Where tints of the main colours used occur, the species concerned is of less frequent occurrence.

 species present only for breeding

 species present (but not breeding) for part or all of the year, usually as a passage migrant or as a winter visitor

 species present throughout the year including breeding

 indicates those counties where there are recent records of vagrant species or those areas in which rare species are likely to be found

Note where arrows are shown on a map, they indicate the direction of any migratory movement for that species.

 for birds breeding in Britain;

for birds which do not breed in Britain.

Also where a boundary is given by a dashed line, this indicates the possible extreme extent of a species' presence in the relevant colour.

There are two bar charts below each map. The letters in each represent the months of the year: J = January to D = December.

For the upper bar chart:

 indicates that the species is either present on its breeding grounds and/or that it is nesting during those months of the year.

 indicates the months of the year when rare or vagrant species are most likely to occur.

For the lower bar chart:

 indicates when the species is present in areas in which it does not normally breed or in which it is present as a non-breeding migrant.

Note where tints of the main colours have been used, this indicates the possible presence of a species.

Habitat bar chart

 woodland (eg woods and scrub)

 heaths (eg heath, moorland, downland, etc)

 wetland (eg bogs, reedbeds, wet meadows, etc)

 fresh water (eg river, lake, gravel pit, etc)

 mountain

 coastal (eg dunes, tidal mud, ocean, cliffs, etc)

farmland (eg fields, hedgerows, etc)

urban (eg buildings, railways, parks, golf courses, etc)

Note within the habitat bar charts, the use of the colours and tints is the same as in the maps etc so that, for example, red indicates that the bird is present in that habitat for breeding only.

Red-throated Diver *LOON*
Gavia stellata
(Gaviidae)

55–65 cm (22–26 in)
Breeds in north, winters in coastal waters. Migrants from north spend winter. Winter vagrant to inland waters.

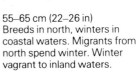

Black-throated Diver *LOON*
Gavia arctica
(Gaviidae)

58–70 cm (23–28 in)
Breeds in north, winters in coastal waters. Migrants from Norway spend winter. Winter vagrants in west and to inland waters.

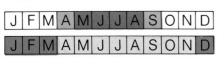

Great Northern Diver *[COMMON LOON]*
Gavia immer
(Gaviidae)

70–85 cm (28–33 in)
Migrants from north-west spend winter. Occasional individuals summer in northern waters, perhaps nesting.

| J | F | M | A | M | J | J | A | S | O | N | D |

| J | F | M | A | M | J | J | A | S | O | N | D |

Little Grebe
Tachybaptus ruficollis
(Podicipedidae)

26 cm (10 in)
Movement to coastal waters in severe winters. Some winter visitors arrive from east.

| J | F | M | A | M | J | J | A | S | O | N | D |

| J | F | M | A | M | J | J | A | S | O | N | D |

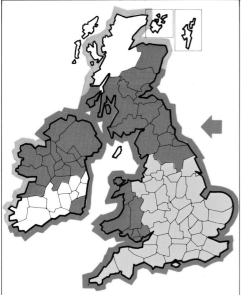

Great Crested Grebe
Podiceps cristatus
(Podicipedidae)

45–50 cm (18–20 in)
Most numerous in south-east.
Movement to coastal waters
in winter. Some winter visitors
arrive from east.

| J | F | M | A | M | J | J | A | S | O | N | D |

| J | F | M | A | M | J | J | A | S | O | N | D |

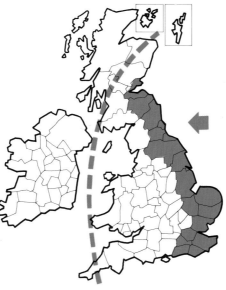
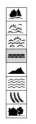

Red-necked Grebe
Podiceps grisegena
(Podicipedidae)

40–50 cm (16–20 in)
Winter population arrives from
east. Numbers vary, when
large, birds move further west.

| J | F | M | A | M | J | J | A | S | O | N | D |

| J | F | M | A | M | J | J | A | S | O | N | D |

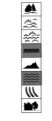

Slavonian Grebe HORNED GREBE)
Podiceps auritus
(Podicipedidae)

34 cm (13 in)
Breeding population small.
Migrants from north spend
winter.

| J | F | M | A | M | J | J | A | S | O | N | D |

| J | F | M | A | M | J | J | A | S | O | N | D |

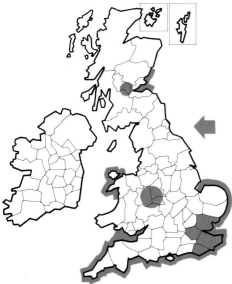

Black-necked Grebe
Podiceps nigricollis
(Podicipedidae)

30 cm (12 in)
Isolated breeding and non-
breeding birds can appear
almost anywhere. Migrants
from east spend winter.

| J | F | M | A | M | J | J | A | S | O | N | D |

| J | F | M | A | M | J | J | A | S | O | N | D |

NORTHERN
Fulmar
Fulmarus glacialis
(Procellariidae)

47 cm (19 in)
May be present at inshore
waters throughout year.

| J | F | M | A | M | J | J | A | S | O | N | D |

| J | F | M | A | M | J | J | A | S | O | N | D |

Cory's Shearwater
Calonectris diomedea
(Procellariidae)

45 cm (18 in)
Non-breeding visitor from
southern colonies. Numbers
vary annually.

| J | F | M | A | M | J | J | A | S | O | N | D |

| J | F | M | A | M | J | J | A | S | O | N | D |

Great Shearwater
Puffinus gravis
(Procellariidae)

48 cm (19 in)
Non-breeding visitor from
south Atlantic nesting islands.

| J | F | M | A | M | J | J | A | S | O | N | D |

| J | F | M | A | M | J | J | A | S | O | N | D |

Sooty Shearwater
Puffinus griseus
(Procellariidae)

45 cm (18 in)
Non-breeding visitor from
south Atlantic nesting islands.

| J | F | M | A | M | J | J | A | S | O | N | D |

| J | F | M | A | M | J | J | A | S | O | N | D |

Manx Shearwater
Puffinus puffinus
(Procellariidae)

35 cm (14 in)
Breeding confined to marine
islands. Severe autumn storms
can result in inland records.

| J | F | M | A | M | J | J | A | S | O | N | D |

| J | F | M | A | M | J | J | A | S | O | N | D |

Storm Petrel
Hydrobates pelagicus
(Hydrobatidae)

16 cm (6 in)
Breeding largely confined to
islands. Severe autumn storms
can result in inland records.

| J | F | M | A | M | J | J | A | S | O | N | D |

| J | F | M | A | M | J | J | A | S | O | N | D |

Leach's Petrel
Oceanodroma leucorhoa
(Hydrobatidae)

20 cm (8 in)
Breeding confined to 5 northern
islands. Severe autumn storms
can result in inland records.

| J | F | M | A | M | J | J | A | S | O | N | D |

| J | F | M | A | M | J | J | A | S | O | N | D |

Gannet
Sula bassana
(Sulidae)

90–100 cm (35–39 in)
Breeding confined to specific
colonies. Some southern
movement post-breeding but
present in British waters
throughout year.

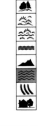

| J | F | M | A | M | J | J | A | S | O | N | D |

| J | F | M | A | M | J | J | A | S | O | N | D |

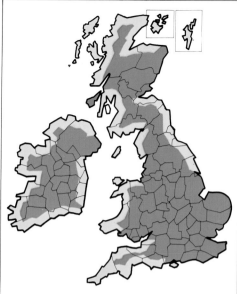

Cormorant
Phalacrocorax carbo
(Phalacrocoracidae)

90 cm (35 in)
Mainly resident. Coastal and
inland dispersal after breeding.

J F M A M J J A S O N D
J F M A M J J A S O N D

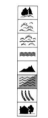

Shag
Phalacrocorax aristotelis
(Phalacrocoracidae)

68 cm (27 in)
Mainly resident. Essentially
marine.

J F M A M J J A S O N D
J F M A M J J A S O N D

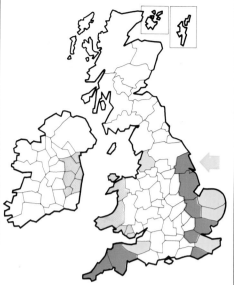

Bittern
Botaurus stellaris
(Ardeidae)

75 cm (30 in)
Less than 50 pairs nest in
Britain. Small arrival from east
in some winters.

J F M A M J J A S O N D
J F M A M J J A S O N D

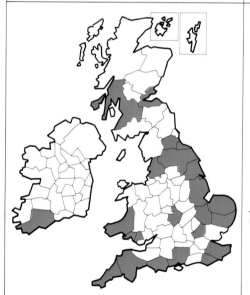

Little Bittern
Ixobrychus minutus
(Ardeidae)

35 cm (14 in)
Map reflects recent 10-year
period. Vagrant from southern
Europe. Rarely more than 10
records per year.

J F M A M J J A S O N D
J F M A M J J A S O N D

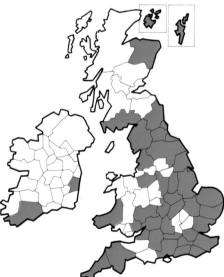
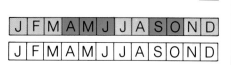

Night Heron
Nycticorax nycticorax
(Ardeidae)

60 cm (24 in)
Map reflects recent 10-year
period. Vagrant from southern
Europe. Rarely more than 10
records per year.

J F M A M J J A S O N D
J F M A M J J A S O N D

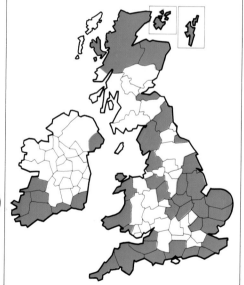

Little Egret
Egretta garzetta
(Ardeidae)

56 cm (22 in)
Map reflects recent 10-year
period. Vagrant from southern
Europe. Rarely more than 20
records per year. Occasionally
winters in south-west.

J F M A M J J A S O N D
J F M A M J J A S O N D

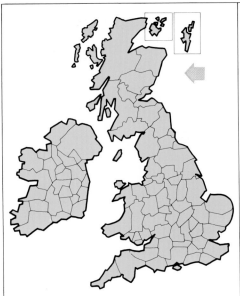

Grey Heron
Ardea cinerea
(Ardeidae)

95 cm (37 in)
Population in excess of 5000 breeding pairs. Small winter arrival in north and dispersal in south.

| J | F | M | A | M | J | J | A | S | O | N | D |
| J | F | M | A | M | J | J | A | S | O | N | D |

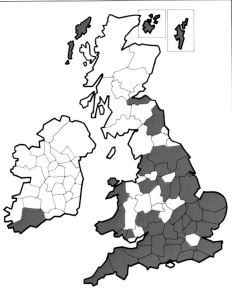

Purple Heron
Ardea purpurea
(Ardeidae)

85 cm (33 in)
Map reflects recent 10-year period. Vagrant from southern Europe. Approximately 20 individuals recorded per year.

| J | F | M | A | M | J | J | A | S | O | N | D |
| J | F | M | A | M | J | J | A | S | O | N | D |

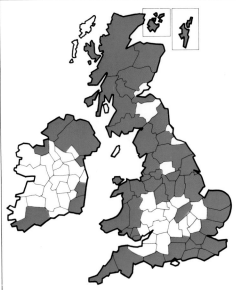

White Stork
Ciconia ciconia
(Ciconiidae)

110 cm (43 in)
Map reflects recent 10-year period. Vagrants from southern Europe. Rarely more than 25 records per year.

| J | F | M | A | M | J | J | A | S | O | N | D |
| J | F | M | A | M | J | J | A | S | O | N | D |

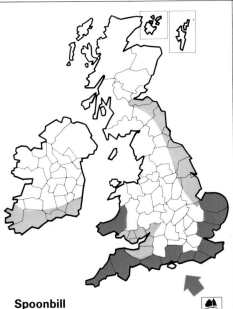

Spoonbill
Platalea leucorodia
(Threskiornithidae)

86 cm (34 in)
Steadily increasing numbers on south and east coasts.

| J | F | M | A | M | J | J | A | S | O | N | D |
| J | F | M | A | M | J | J | A | S | O | N | D |

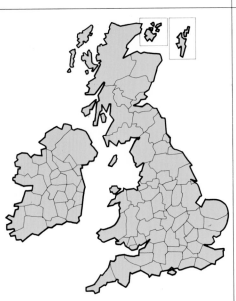

Mute Swan
Cygnus olor
(Anatidae)

150 cm (59 in)
Population some 3000 breeding pairs. Largely sedentary.

| J | F | M | A | M | J | J | A | S | O | N | D |
| J | F | M | A | M | J | J | A | S | O | N | D |

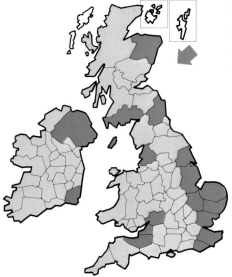

Bewick's Swan
Cygnus columbianus
(Anatidae)

120 cm (47 in)
Winter arrivals from north-east. British population 4500. Distribution dependent on weather.

| J | F | M | A | M | J | J | A | S | O | N | D |
| J | F | M | A | M | J | J | A | S | O | N | D |

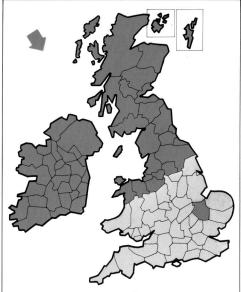
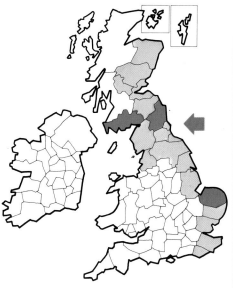
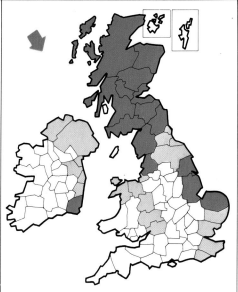

Whooper Swan
Cygnus cygnus
(Anatidae)

155 cm (61 in)
Winter population arrives from
north-west. British population
up to 9000. Distribution
dependent on weather.

J	F	M	A	M	J	J	A	S	O	N	D
J	F	M	A	M	J	J	A	S	O	N	D

Bean Goose
Anser fabalis
(Anatidae)

75 cm (30 in)
Winter population arrives from
east. British population rarely
more than 200.

J	F	M	A	M	J	J	A	S	O	N	D
J	F	M	A	M	J	J	A	S	O	N	D

Pink-footed Goose
Anser brachyrhynchus
(Anatidae)

70 cm (28 in)
Winter population arrives from
north-west. British population
75 000.

J	F	M	A	M	J	J	A	S	O	N	D
J	F	M	A	M	J	J	A	S	O	N	D

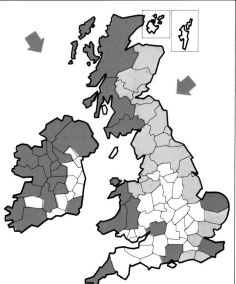

White-fronted Goose
Anser albifrons
(Anatidae)

70 cm (28 in)
2 distinct winter populations
from north-west and north-
east. British population 20 000.

J	F	M	A	M	J	J	A	S	O	N	D
J	F	M	A	M	J	J	A	S	O	N	D

Greylag Goose
Anser anser
(Anatidae)

82 cm (32 in)
Winter population arrives from
north-west. Native population
in Scotland. Feral population in
south. 800+ breeding pairs.
66 000 birds in winter.

J	F	M	A	M	J	J	A	S	O	N	D
J	F	M	A	M	J	J	A	S	O	N	D

Snow Goose
Anser caerulescens
(Anatidae)

70 cm (28 in)
Genuine vagrants largely
confined to west and north.
Position confused by escapes
from captivity.

J	F	M	A	M	J	J	A	S	O	N	D
J	F	M	A	M	J	J	A	S	O	N	D

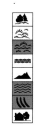

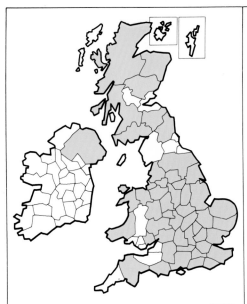

Canada Goose
Branta canadensis
(Anatidae)

95 cm (37 in)
An increasing and spreading
feral population. Over 2000
breeding pairs.

J F M A M J J A S O N D
J F M A M J J A S O N D

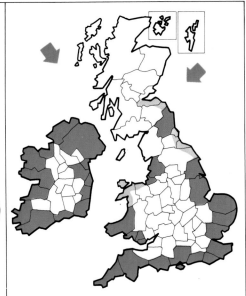

Barnacle Goose
Branta leucopsis
(Anatidae)

63 cm (25 in)
Winter arrivals from north-
west and north-east.
Occasional birds from east to
coastal south-east England.
British population 27 000.

J F M A M J J A S O N D
J F M A M J J A S O N D

Brent Goose
Branta bernicla
(Anatidae)

58 cm (23 in)
Winter arrivals from north-
west and north-east. British
population 52 000.

J F M A M J J A S O N D
J F M A M J J A S O N D

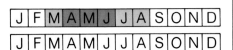
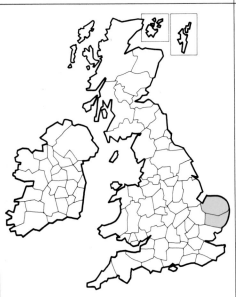

Egyptian Goose
Alopochen aegyptiacus
(Anatidae)

70 cm (28 in)
Feral population of 400.

J F M A M J J A S O N D
J F M A M J J A S O N D

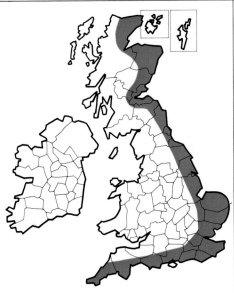

Ruddy Shelduck
Tadorna ferruginea
(Anatidae)

64 cm (25 in)
Most frequent on east and
south coasts but position
confused by large number of
escapes from captivity.

J F M A M J J A S O N D
J F M A M J J A S O N D

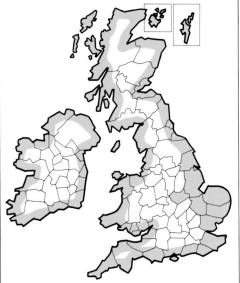

Shelduck
Tadorna tadorna
(Anatidae)

62 cm (24 in)
Many British birds depart east
in late summer, returning in
winter. At peak British
population 60 000.

J F M A M J J A S O N D
J F M A M J J A S O N D

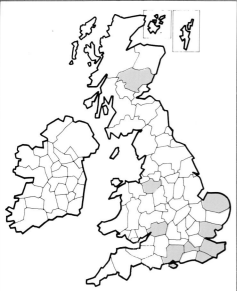

Mandarin
Aix galericulata
(Anatidae)

45 cm (18 in)
British population 500 pairs,
descended from feral stock.

J	F	M	A	M	J	J	A	S	O	N	D

J	F	M	A	M	J	J	A	S	O	N	D

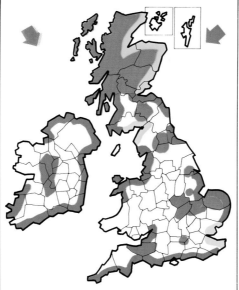

Wigeon
Anas penelope
(Anatidae)

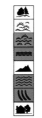

46 cm (18 in)
Migrants from north-west and
north-east spend winter. Nearly
500 pairs nest. Up to 180 000
in winter.

J	F	M	A	M	J	J	A	S	O	N	D

J	F	M	A	M	J	J	A	S	O	N	D

Gadwall
Anas strepera
(Anatidae)

50 cm (20 in)
Migrants from east spend
winter. Breeding population
500 pairs, up to 5000 in winter.

J	F	M	A	M	J	J	A	S	O	N	D

J	F	M	A	M	J	J	A	S	O	N	D

Teal
Anas crecca
(Anatidae)

35 cm (14 in)
Large numbers arrive from
north to spend winter.
Breeding population 4000
pairs, up to 75 000 in winter.

J	F	M	A	M	J	J	A	S	O	N	D

J	F	M	A	M	J	J	A	S	O	N	D

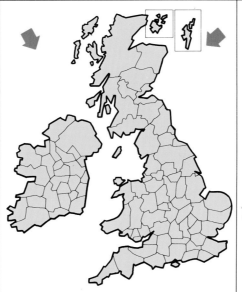

Mallard
Anas platyrhynchos
(Anatidae)

58 cm (23 in)
Large numbers arrive from
north to spend winter.
Breeding population 90 000
pairs, up to 700 000 in winter.

J	F	M	A	M	J	J	A	S	O	N	D

J	F	M	A	M	J	J	A	S	O	N	D

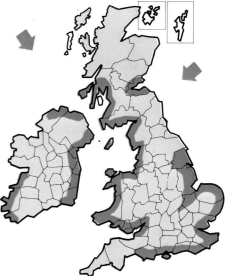

Pintail
Anas acuta
(Anatidae)

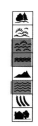

60 cm (24 in)
Over 20 000 arrive from north
to spend winter. Up to 10
pairs may nest.

J	F	M	A	M	J	J	A	S	O	N	D

J	F	M	A	M	J	J	A	S	O	N	D

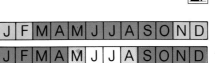

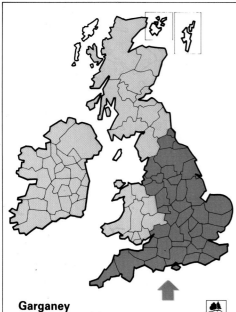

Garganey
Anas querquedula
(Anatidae)

39 cm (15 in)
Summer visitor from south.
Up to 100 pairs may nest.

J	F	M	A	M	J	J	A	S	O	N	D

J	F	M	A	M	J	J	A	S	O	N	D

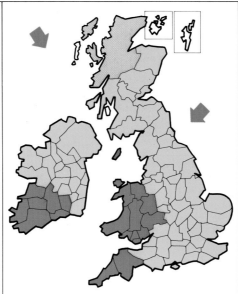

Shoveler
Anas clypeata
(Anatidae)

50 cm (20 in)
Breeding population of 1000
pairs mainly depart for winter.
Up to 10 000 arrive from north
to spend winter.

J	F	M	A	M	J	J	A	S	O	N	D

J	F	M	A	M	J	J	A	S	O	N	D

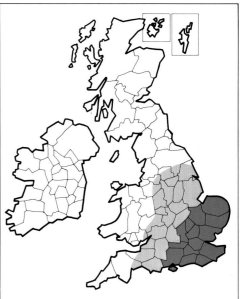

Red-crested Pochard
Netta rufina
(Anatidae)

56 cm (22 in)
Formerly more numerous.
Many records may refer to
escapes from waterfowl
collections.

J	F	M	A	M	J	J	A	S	O	N	D

J	F	M	A	M	J	J	A	S	O	N	D

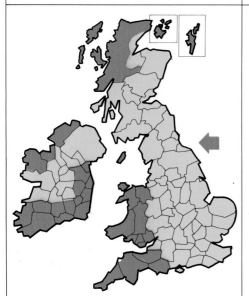
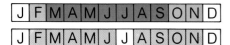

Pochard
Aythya ferina
(Anatidae)

45 cm (18 in)
Large numbers arrive from
east to spend winter. Breeding
population of 400 pairs and
increasing, up to 45 000 in
winter.

J	F	M	A	M	J	J	A	S	O	N	D

J	F	M	A	M	J	J	A	S	O	N	D

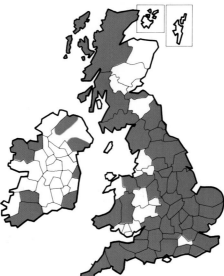

Ring-necked Duck
Aythya collaris
(Anatidae)

42 cm (17 in)
Map reflects recent 10-year
period. Vagrant from North
America. Rarely more than 20
in any one year.

J	F	M	A	M	J	J	A	S	O	N	D

J	F	M	A	M	J	J	A	S	O	N	D

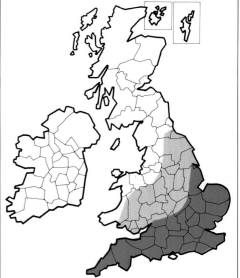

Ferruginous Duck
Aythya nyroca
(Anatidae)

41 cm (16 in)
Annual numbers variable and
position complicated by
escapes from captivity.

J	F	M	A	M	J	J	A	S	O	N	D

J	F	M	A	M	J	J	A	S	O	N	D

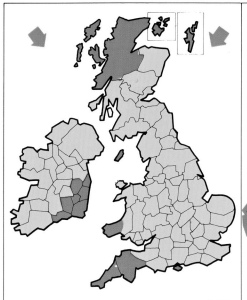

Tufted Duck
Aythya fuligula
(Anatidae)

45 cm (18 in)
Large numbers arrive from
north to spend winter. Breeding
population of 8000 pairs and
increasing, up to 50 000 in
winter.

J	F	M	A	M	J	J	A	S	O	N	D

J	F	M	A	M	J	J	A	S	O	N	D

Scaup
Aythya marila
(Anatidae)

48 cm (19 in)
Up to 10 000 arrive from north
to spend winter. No regular
inland records.

J	F	M	A	M	J	J	A	S	O	N	D

J	F	M	A	M	J	J	A	S	O	N	D

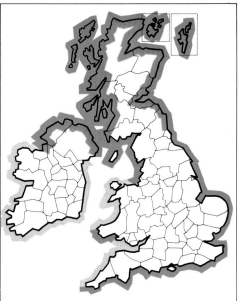

Eider
Somateria mollissima
(Anatidae)

60 cm (24 in)
Population of 60 000 largely
non-migratory. Non-breeding
birds disperse around coast.

J	F	M	A	M	J	J	A	S	O	N	D

J	F	M	A	M	J	J	A	S	O	N	D

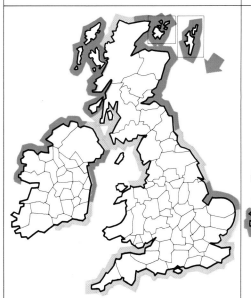

Long-tailed Duck
Clangula hyemalis
(Anatidae)

50 cm (20 in)
Perhaps 20 000 arrive from
north-east to spend winter.
Extremely rare inland.

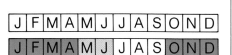

J	F	M	A	M	J	J	A	S	O	N	D

J	F	M	A	M	J	J	A	S	O	N	D

Common Scoter
Melanitta nigra
(Anatidae)

49 cm (19 in)
Breeding population of
approximately 100 pairs. Over
35 000 arrive from north to
spend winter. Large migrations
off south coast.

J	F	M	A	M	J	J	A	S	O	N	D

J	F	M	A	M	J	J	A	S	O	N	D

Surf Scoter
Melanitta perspicillata
(Anatidae)

56 cm (22 in)
Map reflects recent 10-year
period. Vagrant from North
America. Rarely more than 10
per year. Extremely rare inland.

J	F	M	A	M	J	J	A	S	O	N	D

J	F	M	A	M	J	J	A	S	O	N	D

Velvet Scoter
Melanitta fusca
(Anatidae)

54 cm (21 in)
Up to 3000 arrive from north-east to spend winter, mainly on Scottish coast. Extremely rare inland.

| J | F | M | A | M | J | J | A | S | O | N | D |

| J | F | M | A | M | J | J | A | S | O | N | D |

Goldeneye
Bucephala clangula
(Anatidae)

46 cm (18 in)
Breeding population approaching 50 pairs. Up to 15 000 arrive from north-east to spend winter.

| J | F | M | A | M | J | J | A | S | O | N | D |

| J | F | M | A | M | J | J | A | S | O | N | D |

Smew
Mergus albellus
(Anatidae)

41 cm (16 in)
Migrants from north-east spend winter, mainly in south-east but numbers and distribution dependent upon severity of winter.

| J | F | M | A | M | J | J | A | S | O | N | D |

| J | F | M | A | M | J | J | A | S | O | N | D |

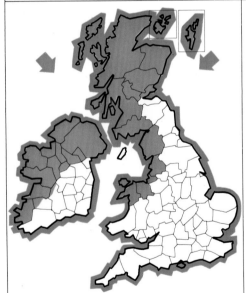

Red-breasted Merganser
Mergus serrator
(Anatidae)

55 cm (22 in)
Breeding population of 2000 pairs and increasing. Migrants from north spend winter when over 7000 in coastal waters.

| J | F | M | A | M | J | J | A | S | O | N | D |

| J | F | M | A | M | J | J | A | S | O | N | D |

Goosander
Mergus merganser
(Anatidae)

62 cm (24 in)
Breeding population of 1000 pairs and increasing. Migrants from north-east spend winter when over 4000 on British waters.

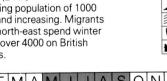

| J | F | M | A | M | J | J | A | S | O | N | D |

| J | F | M | A | M | J | J | A | S | O | N | D |

Ruddy Duck
Oxyura jamaicensis
(Anatidae)

40 cm (16 in)
Breeding population from feral stock. 100 pairs increasing and spreading.

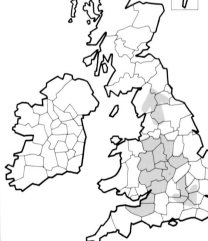
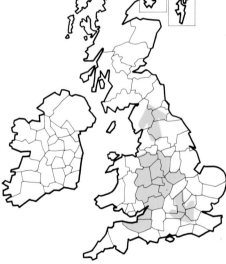

| J | F | M | A | M | J | J | A | S | O | N | D |

| J | F | M | A | M | J | J | A | S | O | N | D |

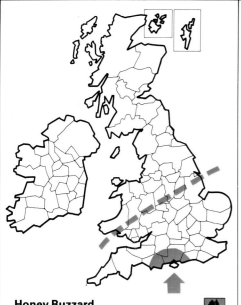

Honey Buzzard
Pernis apivorus
(Accipitridae)

55 cm (22 in)
Summer visitor from south.
Rarely more than 10 breeding
pairs but isolated nesting does
occur.

J F M A M J J A S O N D
J F M A M J J A S O N D

Red Kite
Milvus milvus
(Accipitridae)

63 cm (25 in)
Resident breeding population
of 40 pairs.

J F M A M J J A S O N D
J F M A M J J A S O N D

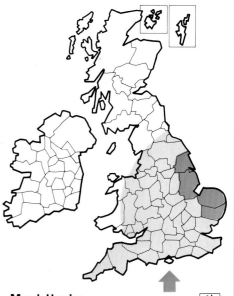

Marsh Harrier
Circus aeruginosus
(Accipitridae)

52 cm (20 in)
Summer visitor from south.
Occasional birds in winter.
Breeding population 30 pairs
and increasing.

J F M A M J J A S O N D
J F M A M J J A S O N D

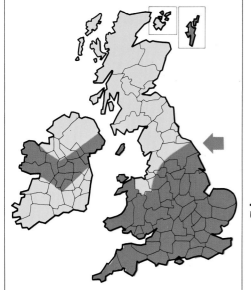

Hen Harrier
Circus cyaneus
(Accipitridae)

48 cm (19 in)
Migrants from east spend
winter. Up to 800 breeding
pairs.

J F M A M J J A S O N D
J F M A M J J A S O N D

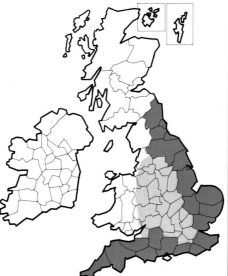

Montagu's Harrier
Circus pygargus
(Accipitridae)

45 cm (18 in)
In some years 2 or 3 pairs may
nest.

J F M A M J J A S O N D
J F M A M J J A S O N D

Goshawk
Accipiter gentilis
(Accipitridae)

50–60 cm (20–24 in)
Small resident population,
perhaps as many as 70 pairs
and increasing.

J F M A M J J A S O N D
J F M A M J J A S O N D

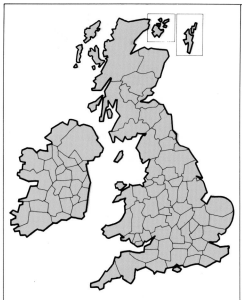

Sparrowhawk
Accipiter nisus
(Accipitridae)

28–38 cm (11–15 in)
Over 20 000 breeding pairs
and increasing.

J F M A M J J A S O N D
J F M A M J J A S O N D

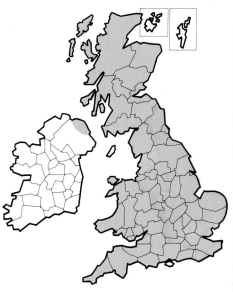

Buzzard
Buteo buteo
(Accipitridae)

54 cm (21 in)
Approximately 10 000 breeding
pairs.

J F M A M J J A S O N D
J F M A M J J A S O N D

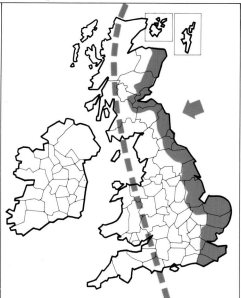

Rough-legged Buzzard
Buteo lagopus
(Accipitridae)

55 cm (22 in)
Birds from north-east spend
winter. Numbers and western
extent vary annually.

J F M A M J J A S O N D
J F M A M J J A S O N D

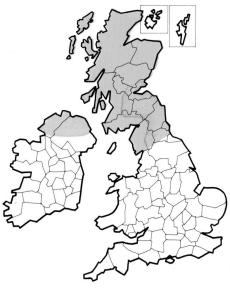

Golden Eagle
Aquila chrysaetos
(Accipitridae)

80 cm (31 in)
Up to 500 breeding pairs.

J F M A M J J A S O N D
J F M A M J J A S O N D

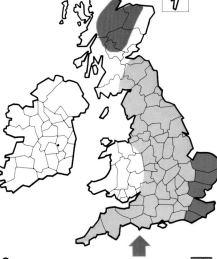

Osprey
Pandion haliaetus
(Pandionidae)

55 cm (22 in)
Summer visitor from south.
Over 30 breeding pairs and
increasing. Frequency of
migrants elsewhere also
increasing.

J F M A M J J A S O N D
J F M A M J J A S O N D

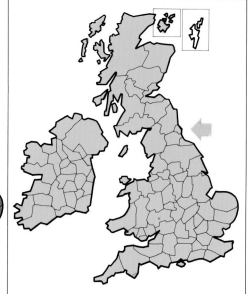

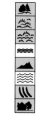

Kestrel
Falco tinnunculus
(Falconidae)

34 cm (13 in)
Small numbers arrive from east
to spend winter. Breeding
population of approximately
100 000 pairs.

J F M A M J J A S O N D
J F M A M J J A S O N D

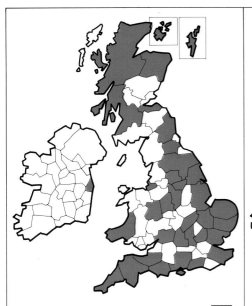

Red-footed Falcon
Falco vespertinus
(Falconidae)

30 cm (12 in)
Map reflects recent 10-year period. Vagrant from south-east Europe. Rarely more than 15 records per year.

| J | F | M | A | M | J | J | A | S | O | N | D |
| J | F | M | A | M | J | J | A | S | O | N | D |

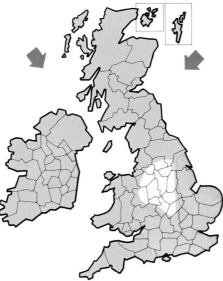

Merlin
Falco columbarius
(Falconidae)

30 cm (12 in)
Migrants from north spend winter but both wintering and breeding populations decreasing markedly.

| J | F | M | A | M | J | J | A | S | O | N | D |
| J | F | M | A | M | J | J | A | S | O | N | D |

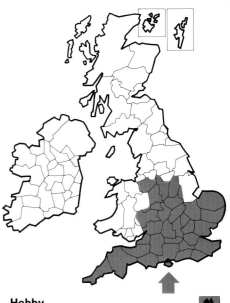

Hobby
Falco subbuteo
(Falconidae)

33 cm (13 in)
Summer visitor from south. Between 100 and 200 pairs nest annually.

| J | F | M | A | M | J | J | A | S | O | N | D |
| J | F | M | A | M | J | J | A | S | O | N | D |

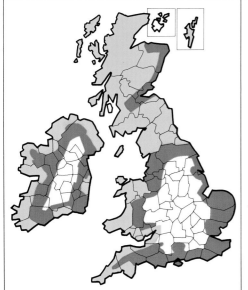

Peregrine
Falco peregrinus
(Falconidae)

43 cm (17 in)
Breeding population of approximately 800 pairs, increasing and spreading.

| J | F | M | A | M | J | J | A | S | O | N | D |
| J | F | M | A | M | J | J | A | S | O | N | D |

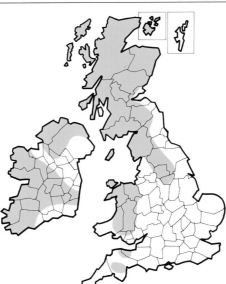

Red Grouse
Lagopus lagopus
(Tetraonidae)

40 cm (16 in)
Decreasing, but fluctuating population, rarely exceeding 500 000 pairs.

| J | F | M | A | M | J | J | A | S | O | N | D |
| J | F | M | A | M | J | J | A | S | O | N | D |

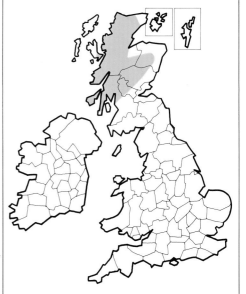

Ptarmigan
Lagopus mutus
(Tetraonidae)

35 cm (14 in)
Population probably declined to less than 10 000 pairs.

| J | F | M | A | M | J | J | A | S | O | N | D |
| J | F | M | A | M | J | J | A | S | O | N | D |

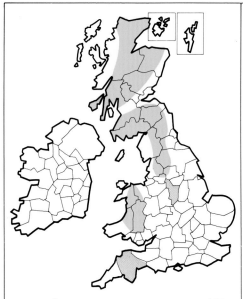

Black Grouse
Tetrao tetrix
(Tetraonidae)

40–50 cm (16–20 in)
Breeding population in excess
of 10 000 pairs.

J F M A M J J A S O N D
J F M A M J J A S O N D

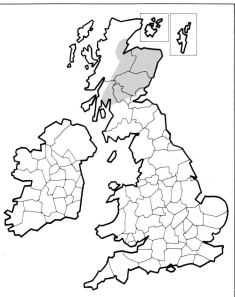

Capercaillie
Tetrao urogallus
(Tetraonidae)

75 cm (30 in)
Following extinction in 1700s,
reintroduced in 1800s, population now in excess of 1000
pairs.

J F M A M J J A S O N D
J F M A M J J A S O N D

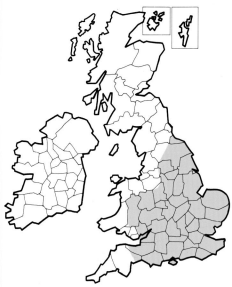

Red-legged Partridge
Alectoris rufa
(Phasianidae)

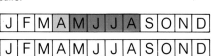

34 cm (13 in)
Introduced in 1600s. More
northerly introductions have
taken place. Breeding population in excess of 100 000
pairs.

J F M A M J J A S O N D
J F M A M J J A S O N D

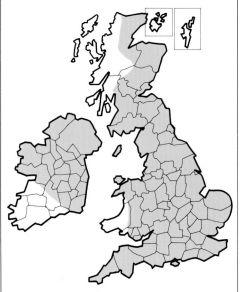

Grey Partridge
Perdix perdix
(Phasianidae)

30 cm (12 in)
Population decreasing, probably less than 500 000 pairs.

J F M A M J J A S O N D
J F M A M J J A S O N D

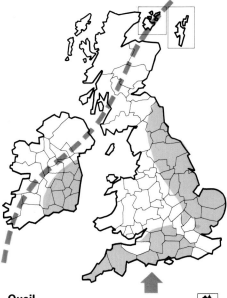

Quail
Coturnix coturnix
(Phasianidae)

18 cm (7 in)
Summer visitor from south,
numbers and distribution
varying annually.

J F M A M J J A S O N D
J F M A M J J A S O N D

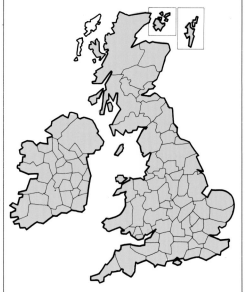

Pheasant
Phasianus colchicus
(Phasianidae)

50–90 cm (20–35 in)
Population   augmented   by
annual release of reared birds.

J F M A M J J A S O N D
J F M A M J J A S O N D

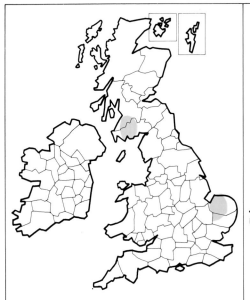

Golden Pheasant
Chrysolophus pictus
(Phasianidae)

60–110 cm (24–43 in)
Successful introductions in 2 areas. Perhaps over 500 breeding pairs.

J F M A M J J A S O N D
J F M A M J J A S O N D

Lady Amherst's Pheasant
Chrysolophus amherstiae
(Phasianidae)

60–120 cm (24–47 in)
Successful colonization in 1 area, with up to 200 pairs, but hybridizes with released Golden Pheasants.

J F M A M J J A S O N D
J F M A M J J A S O N D

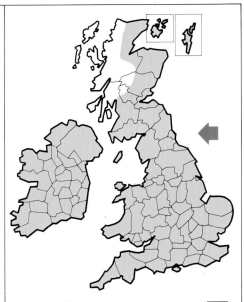

Water Rail
Rallus aquaticus
(Rallidae)

25 cm (10 in)
Some migrants arrive from east to spend winter. Breeding distribution patchy, perhaps over 2000 pairs.

J F M A M J J A S O N D
J F M A M J J A S O N D

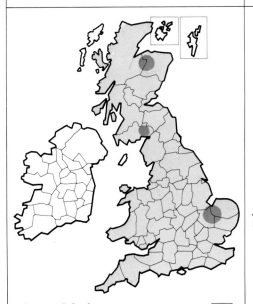

Spotted Crake
Porzana porzana
(Rallidae)

23 cm (9 in)
Small numbers appear annually, with breeding occurring in some years, but often at widely scattered sites.

J F M A M J J A S O N D
J F M A M J J A S O N D

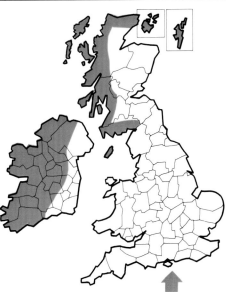

Corncrake
Crex crex
(Rallidae)

29 cm (11 in)
Decreasing summer visitor. Under 2000 calling birds.

J F M A M J J A S O N D
J F M A M J J A S O N D

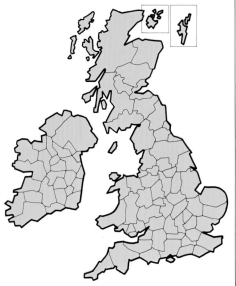

Moorhen
Gallinula chloropus
(Rallidae)

33 cm (13 in)
Breeding population estimated at 300 000 pairs and perhaps increasing.

J F M A M J J A S O N D
J F M A M J J A S O N D

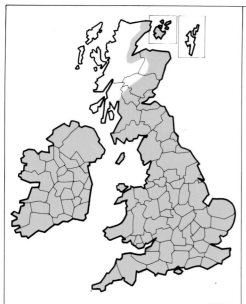

Coot
Fulica atra
(Rallidae)

37 cm (15 in)
Increasing population, perhaps
as many as 100 000 pairs.

| J | F | M | A | M | J | J | A | S | O | N | D |
| J | F | M | A | M | J | J | A | S | O | N | D |

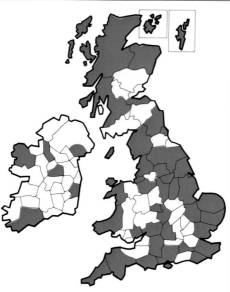

Crane
Grus grus
(Gruidae)

110–120 cm (43–47 in)
Map reflects recent 10-year
period. Vagrant from south-
east. Numbers vary annually,
rarely more than 50.

| J | F | M | A | M | J | J | A | S | O | N | D |
| J | F | M | A | M | J | J | A | S | O | N | D |

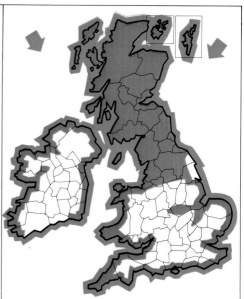

Oystercatcher
Haematopus ostralegus
(Haematopodidae)

43 cm (17 in)
Breeding population perhaps
as high as 30 000 pairs and
increasing. Migrants from north
spend winter, with 200 000
present.

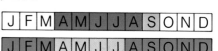

| J | F | M | A | M | J | J | A | S | O | N | D |
| J | F | M | A | M | J | J | A | S | O | N | D |

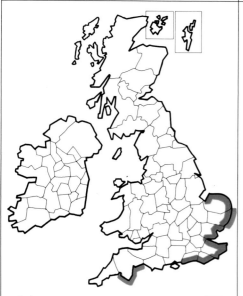

Avocet
Recurvirostra avosetta
(Recurvirostridae)

44 cm (17 in)
Breeding population 250 pairs
and increasing, resulting in
spread from traditional wintering sites.

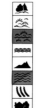

| J | F | M | A | M | J | J | A | S | O | N | D |
| J | F | M | A | M | J | J | A | S | O | N | D |

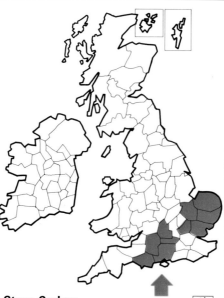

Stone Curlew
Burhinus oedicnemus
(Burhinidae)

42 cm (17 in)
Summer visitor, probably less
than 250 pairs and decreasing.

| J | F | M | A | M | J | J | A | S | O | N | D |
| J | F | M | A | M | J | J | A | S | O | N | D |

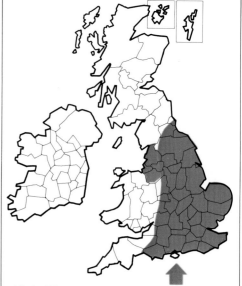

Little Ringed Plover
Charadrius dubius
(Charadriidae)

14 cm (6 in)
Summer visitor. Breeding
population of some 500 pairs.

| J | F | M | A | M | J | J | A | S | O | N | D |
| J | F | M | A | M | J | J | A | S | O | N | D |

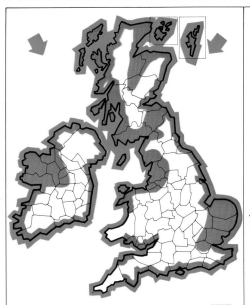

Ringed Plover
Charadrius hiaticula
(Charadriidae)

19 cm (7 in)
Breeding population of some 10 000 pairs, largely resident. Migrants from north pass through on route to southern wintering grounds.

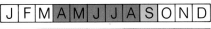

| J | F | M | A | M | J | J | A | S | O | N | D |
| J | F | M | A | M | J | J | A | S | O | N | D |

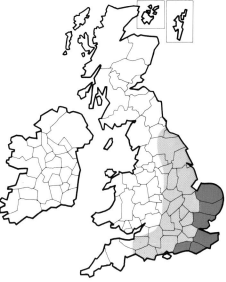

Kentish Plover
Charadrius alexandrinus
(Charadriidae)

16 cm (6 in)
Annual each spring and summer in small numbers. Occasional breeding attempt.

| J | F | M | A | M | J | J | A | S | O | N | D |
| J | F | M | A | M | J | J | A | S | O | N | D |

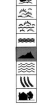

Dotterel
Charadrius morinellus
(Charadriidae)

21 cm (8 in)
Less than 100 pairs nesting annually.

| J | F | M | A | M | J | J | A | S | O | N | D |
| J | F | M | A | M | J | J | A | S | O | N | D |

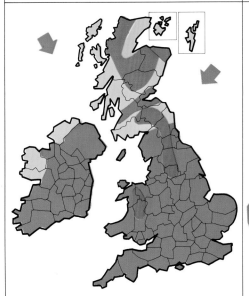

Golden Plover
Pluvialis apricaria
(Charadriidae)

28 cm (11 in)
Breeding population less than 30 000 pairs. Migrants from north spend winter when roughly 400 000 birds are present.

| J | F | M | A | M | J | J | A | S | O | N | D |
| J | F | M | A | M | J | J | A | S | O | N | D |

Grey Plover
Pluvialis squatarola
(Charadriidae)

28 cm (11 in)
Migrants from north-east may remain throughout year, but most numerous in winter when up to 12 000. Commonest in south-east.

| J | F | M | A | M | J | J | A | S | O | N | D |
| J | F | M | A | M | J | J | A | S | O | N | D |

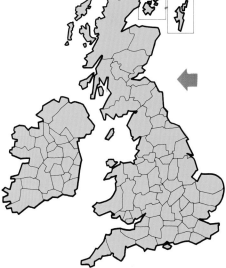

Lapwing
Vanellus vanellus
(Charadriidae)

30 cm (12 in)
Breeding population estimated at 200 000 pairs but decreasing. Migrants from east spend winter when perhaps 1 million birds present.

| J | F | M | A | M | J | J | A | S | O | N | D |
| J | F | M | A | M | J | J | A | S | O | N | D |

Knot
Calidris canutus
(Scolopacidae)

24 cm (9 in)
Migrants from north-east total
over 300 000 at winter peak.

| J | F | M | A | M | J | J | A | S | O | N | D |

| J | F | M | A | M | J | J | A | S | O | N | D |

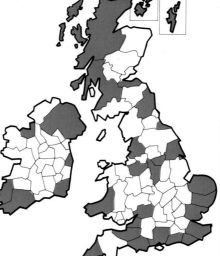

Sanderling
Calidris alba
(Scolopacidae)

20 cm (8 in)
Migrants from north pass
through and remain for winter.
Over 10 000 birds at winter
peak.

| J | F | M | A | M | J | J | A | S | O | N | D |

| J | F | M | A | M | J | J | A | S | O | N | D |

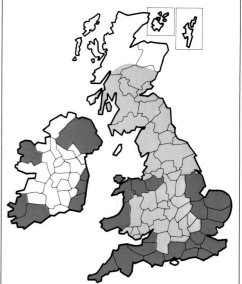

Little Stint
Calidris minuta
(Scolopacidae)

13 cm (5 in)
Migrants from north-east pass
through, small numbers remain
for winter.

| J | F | M | A | M | J | J | A | S | O | N | D |

| J | F | M | A | M | J | J | A | S | O | N | D |

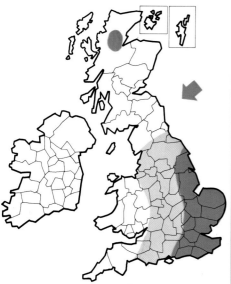

Temminck's Stint
Calidris temminckii
(Scolopacidae)

14 cm (6 in)
Migrants from north-east pass
through in small numbers:
Breeding now annual, up to 6
pairs, in Scotland.

| J | F | M | A | M | J | J | A | S | O | N | D |

| J | F | M | A | M | J | J | A | S | O | N | D |

White-rumped Sandpiper
Calidris fuscicollis
(Scolopacidae)

16 cm (6 in)
Map reflects recent 10-year
period. Vagrant from North
America. Rarely more than 30
per year, usually less than 10.

| J | F | M | A | M | J | J | A | S | O | N | D |

| J | F | M | A | M | J | J | A | S | O | N | D |

Pectoral Sandpiper
Calidris melanotos
(Scolopacidae)

21 cm (8 in)
Commonest North American
vagrant wader, up to 40
recorded per year.

| J | F | M | A | M | J | J | A | S | O | N | D |

| J | F | M | A | M | J | J | A | S | O | N | D |

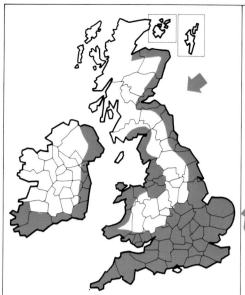

Curlew Sandpiper
Calidris ferruginea
(Scolopacidae)

19 cm (7 in)
Migrants from north-east pass through annually. Numbers variable, but over 3000 extremely unusual.

J F M A M J J A S O N D
J F M A M J J A S O N D

Purple Sandpiper
Calidris maritima
(Scolopacidae)

21 cm (8 in)
Migrants from north spend winter, perhaps as many as 25 000 birds. Isolated breeding attempts have occurred in Scotland.

J F M A M J J A S O N D
J F M A M J J A S O N D

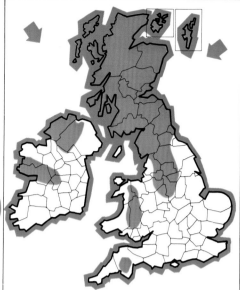

Dunlin
Calidris alpina
(Scolopacidae)

18 cm (7 in)
Migrant and wintering birds frequently occur inland. Migrants from north spend winter and pass through. Up to 8000 pairs nest and 600 000 at winter peak.

J F M A M J J A S O N D
J F M A M J J A S O N D

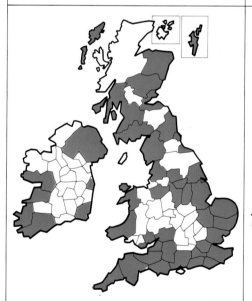

Buff-breasted Sandpiper
Tryngites subruficollis
(Scolopacidae)

19 cm (7 in)
Map reflects recent 10-year period. Vagrant from North America. Up to 20 per year, exceptionally as many as 70.

J F M A M J J A S O N D
J F M A M J J A S O N D

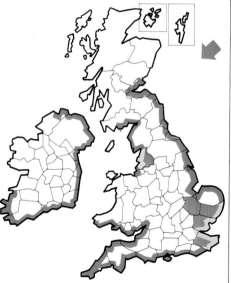

Ruff
Philomachus pugnax
(Scolopacidae)

23–29 cm (9–11 in)
Migrants from north-east pass through. Increasing numbers now winter, probably over 2000. Breeding at isolated sites in small numbers.

J F M A M J J A S O N D
J F M A M J J A S O N D

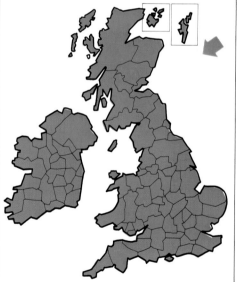

Jack Snipe
Lymnocryptes minimus
(Scolopacidae)

18 cm (7 in)
Migrants from north-east arrive to spend winter.

J F M A M J J A S O N D
J F M A M J J A S O N D

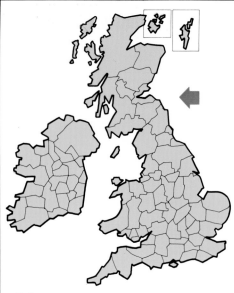

Snipe
Gallinago gallinago
(Scolopacidae)

26 cm (10 in)
Breeding population in marked decline and becoming restricted in distribution. Migrants from east spend winter.

J	F	M	A	M	J	J	A	S	O	N	D
J	F	M	A	M	J	J	A	S	O	N	D

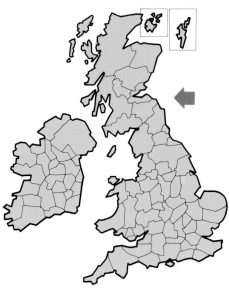

Woodcock
Scolopax rusticola
(Scolopacidae)

34 cm (13 in)
Breeding population probably increasing. Numbers augmented by migrants from east in winter.

J	F	M	A	M	J	J	A	S	O	N	D
J	F	M	A	M	J	J	A	S	O	N	D

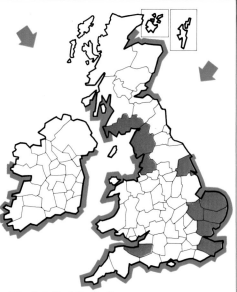

Black-tailed Godwit
Limosa limosa
(Scolopacidae)

41 cm (16 in)
Breeding population of some 50 pairs and decreasing. Migrants from north-west spend winter, from north-east pass through. Up to 15 000 present in winter.

J	F	M	A	M	J	J	A	S	O	N	D
J	F	M	A	M	J	J	A	S	O	N	D

Bar-tailed Godwit
Limosa lapponica
(Scolopacidae)

38 cm (15 in)
Migrants from north-east spend winter and pass through. At peak over 50 000 on coast.

J	F	M	A	M	J	J	A	S	O	N	D
J	F	M	A	M	J	J	A	S	O	N	D

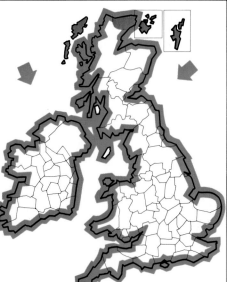

Whimbrel
Numenius phaeopus
(Scolopacidae)

41 cm (16 in)
Breeding population over 100 pairs and increasing. Migrants from north pass through. Although largely coastal not infrequent inland.

J	F	M	A	M	J	J	A	S	O	N	D
J	F	M	A	M	J	J	A	S	O	N	D

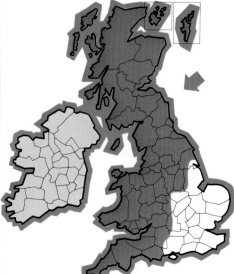

Curlew
Numenius arquata
(Scolopacidae)

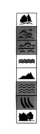

55 cm (22 in)
Breeding population in excess of 40 000 pairs and probably increasing. Migrants from north-east spend winter when peak of 200 000 birds.

J	F	M	A	M	J	J	A	S	O	N	D
J	F	M	A	M	J	J	A	S	O	N	D

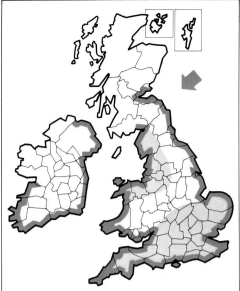

Spotted Redshank
Tringa erythropus
(Scolopacidae)

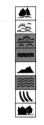

30 cm (12 in)
Migrants from north-east pass
through, with up to 100
wintering.

J	F	M	A	M	J	J	A	S	O	N	D

J	F	M	A	M	J	J	A	S	O	N	D

Redshank
Tringa totanus
(Scolopacidae)

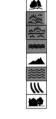

28 cm (11 in)
Breeding population in excess
of 40 000 pairs. Migrants from
north-west spend winter when
peaks of nearly 100 000 birds.
Migrants from north-east pass
through.

J	F	M	A	M	J	J	A	S	O	N	D

J	F	M	A	M	J	J	A	S	O	N	D

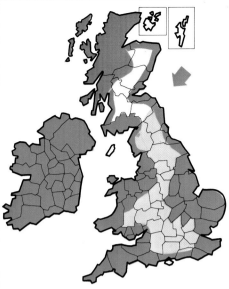

Greenshank
Tringa nebularia
(Scolopacidae)

32 cm (13 in)
Breeding population of 500–
1000 pairs. Migrants from
north-east pass through, small
wintering population of over
500.

J	F	M	A	M	J	J	A	S	O	N	D

J	F	M	A	M	J	J	A	S	O	N	D

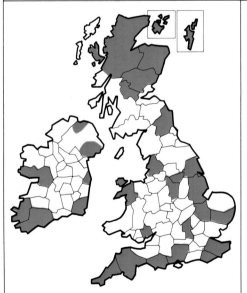

Lesser Yellowlegs
Tringa flavipes
(Scolopacidae)

24 cm (9 in)
Map reflects recent 10-year
period. Vagrant from North
America. Rarely more than 10
per year.

J	F	M	A	M	J	J	A	S	O	N	D

J	F	M	A	M	J	J	A	S	O	N	D

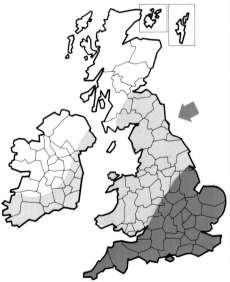

Green Sandpiper
Tringa ochropus
(Scolopacidae)

23 cm (9 in)
Migrants from north-east pass
through, small numbers remain
for winter.

J	F	M	A	M	J	J	A	S	O	N	D

J	F	M	A	M	J	J	A	S	O	N	D

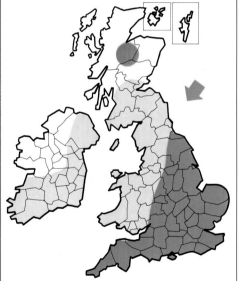

Wood Sandpiper
Tringa glareola
(Scolopacidae)

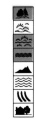

20 cm (8 in)
Up to 10 pairs nest annually.
Migrants from north-east pass
through, numbers vary greatly.

J	F	M	A	M	J	J	A	S	O	N	D

J	F	M	A	M	J	J	A	S	O	N	D

Common Sandpiper
Actitis hypoleucos
(Scolopacidae)

20 cm (8 in)
Breeding population less than
50 000 pairs. Summer visitor
from south, small numbers
winter on south coast.

| J | F | M | A | M | J | J | A | S | O | N | D |

| J | F | M | A | M | J | J | A | S | O | N | D |

Turnstone
Arenaria interpres
(Scolopacidae)

23 cm (9 in)
Migrants from north-east pass
through, those from north-
west remain for winter, when
population peaks at 12 000.

| J | F | M | A | M | J | J | A | S | O | N | D |

| J | F | M | A | M | J | J | A | S | O | N | D |

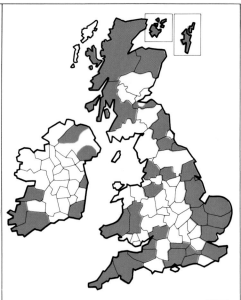

Wilson's Phalarope
Phalaropus tricolor
(Scolopacidae)

23 cm (9 in)
Map reflects recent 10-year
period. Vagrant from North
America. Rarely more than 10
per year.

| J | F | M | A | M | J | J | A | S | O | N | D |

| J | F | M | A | M | J | J | A | S | O | N | D |

Red-necked Phalarope
Phalaropus lobatus
(Scolopacidae)

19 cm (7 in)
Breeding population of some
30 pairs. Rare autumn records
at almost any coastal locality.

| J | F | M | A | M | J | J | A | S | O | N | D |

| J | F | M | A | M | J | J | A | S | O | N | D |

Grey Phalarope
Phalaropus fulicarius
(Scolopacidae)

21 cm (8 in)
Migrants from north blown on
to western shores in winter.
Numbers vary annually, some
years inland records.

| J | F | M | A | M | J | J | A | S | O | N | D |

| J | F | M | A | M | J | J | A | S | O | N | D |

Pomarine Skua
Stercorarius pomarinus
(Stercorariidae)

51 cm (20 in)
Migrants from north-east
appear in coastal waters in
varying numbers dependent
upon weather conditions.

| J | F | M | A | M | J | J | A | S | O | N | D |

| J | F | M | A | M | J | J | A | S | O | N | D |

Arctic Skua
Stercorarius parasiticus
(Stercorariidae)

44 cm (17 in)
Breeding population
approaching 3000 pairs and
increasing. Migrants from
north-east pass through.

J F M A M J J A S O N D
J F M A M J J A S O N D

Long-tailed Skua
Stercorarius longicaudus
(Stercorariidae)

50 cm (20 in)
Rarely more than 25 records
per year.

J F M A M J J A S O N D
J F M A M J J A S O N D

Great Skua
Stercorarius skua
(Stercorariidae)

58 cm (23 in)
Breeding population in excess
of 6000 pairs and increasing.
Migrants from north-west pass
through.

J F M A M J J A S O N D
J F M A M J J A S O N D

Mediterranean Gull
Larus melanocephalus
(Laridae)

37 cm (15 in)
More than 50 records in some
years but colonization very
slow. Rarely more than 3 pairs
nesting per year. Inland records
increasing.

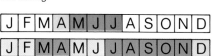

Little Gull
Larus minutus
(Laridae)

28 cm (11 in)
Migrants from north-east pass
through, but migratory pattern
not fully understood.

J F M A M J J A S O N D
J F M A M J J A S O N D

Sabine's Gull
Larus sabini
(Laridae)

33 cm (13 in)
Numbers vary annually
dependent upon weather
conditions. Most records in
west, some years up to 100
birds. Occasionally inland.

J F M A M J J A S O N D
J F M A M J J A S O N D

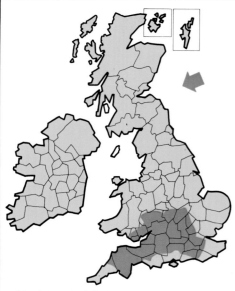

Black-headed Gull
Larus ridibundus
(Laridae)

37 cm (15 in)
Migrants from north-east spend winter. Breeding population in excess of 100 000 pairs and increasing.

J F M A M J J A S O N D
J F M A M J J A S O N D

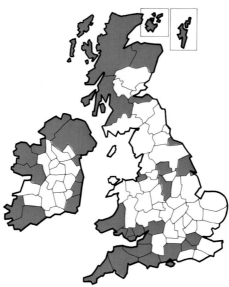

Ring-billed Gull
Larus delawarensis
(Laridae)

45 cm (18 in)
Map reflects recent 10-year period. Vagrant from North America. First recorded in 1973, well over 300 records by end 1983.

J F M A M J J A S O N D
J F M A M J J A S O N D

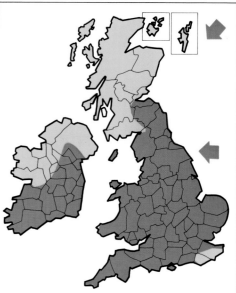

Common Gull
Larus canus
(Laridae)

41 cm (16 in)
Breeding population over 30 000 pairs and increasing. Isolated breeding outside normal range. Migrants from east and north-east spend winter.

J F M A M J J A S O N D
J F M A M J J A S O N D

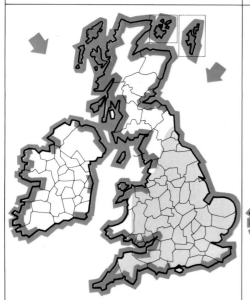

Lesser Black-backed Gull
Larus fuscus
(Laridae)
53 cm (21 in)
Breeding population increasing. Numbers wintering and occurring inland increasing. Migrants from north pass through.

J F M A M J J A S O N D
J F M A M J J A S O N D

Herring Gull
Larus argentatus
(Laridae)

60 cm (24 in)
Breeding population some 300 000 pairs and increasing. Migrants from north arrive to spend winter.

J F M A M J J A S O N D
J F M A M J J A S O N D

Iceland Gull
Larus glaucoides
(Laridae)

56 cm (22 in)
Migrants from north-west arrive to spend winter, up to 100 per year in Scotland and Ireland. Inland records unusual.

J F M A M J J A S O N D
J F M A M J J A S O N D

Glaucous Gull
Larus hyperboreus
(Laridae)

70 cm (28 in)
Migrants from north-east arrive
to spend winter. Numbers
highly variable and flocks of up
to 100 have been recorded.

J F M A M J J A S O N D
J F M A M J J A S O N D

Great Black-backed Gull
Larus marinus
(Laridae)

71 cm (28 in)
In excess of 25 000 breeding
pairs with small numbers of
migrants from north-east
spending winter. Unusual
inland.

J F M A M J J A S O N D
J F M A M J J A S O N D

Kittiwake
Rissa tridactyla
(Laridae)

39 cm (15 in)
Breeding population probably
in excess of 500 000 pairs and
probably slowly increasing.
Migrants from north pass
through and winter in British
waters.

J F M A M J J A S O N D
J F M A M J J A S O N D

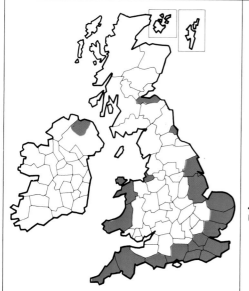

Gull-billed Tern
Gelochelidon nilotica
(Sternidae)

38 cm (15 in)
Map reflects recent 10-year
period. Vagrant from southern
Europe. As many as 10 per
year is unusual.

J F M A M J J A S O N D
J F M A M J J A S O N D

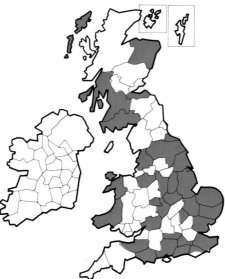

Caspian Tern
Sterna caspia
(Sternidae)

53 cm (21 in)
Map reflects recent 10-year
period. Vagrant from south-
east Europe. Rarely more than
10 records per year.

J F M A M J J A S O N D
J F M A M J J A S O N D

Sandwich Tern
Sterna sandvicensis
(Sternidae)

41 cm (16 in)
Summer visitor from south.
Over 16 000 pairs nesting,
population increasing.

J F M A M J J A S O N D
J F M A M J J A S O N D

Guillemot
Uria aalge
(Alcidae)

42 cm (17 in)
Breeding population 600 000
pairs and probably increasing.

| J | F | M | A | M | J | J | A | S | O | N | D |

| J | F | M | A | M | J | J | A | S | O | N | D |

Razorbill
Alca torda
(Alcidae)

38 cm (15 in)
Breeding population in excess
of 140 000 pairs.

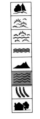

| J | F | M | A | M | J | J | A | S | O | N | D |

| J | F | M | A | M | J | J | A | S | O | N | D |

Black Guillemot
Cepphus grylle
(Alcidae)

34 cm (13 in)
Breeding population of less
than 10 000 pairs, largely
resident.

| J | F | M | A | M | J | J | A | S | O | N | D |

| J | F | M | A | M | J | J | A | S | O | N | D |

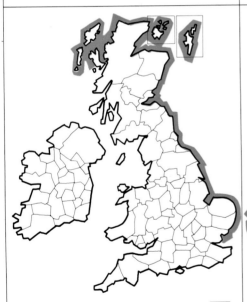

Little Auk
Alle alle
(Alcidae)

20 cm (18 in)
Numbers vary annually
dependent upon weather.
Occasional inland records.

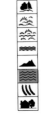

| J | F | M | A | M | J | J | A | S | O | N | D |

| J | F | M | A | M | J | J | A | S | O | N | D |

Puffin
Fratercula arctica
(Alcidae)

28 cm (11 in)
Breeding population probably
over 500 000 pairs.

| J | F | M | A | M | J | J | A | S | O | N | D |

| J | F | M | A | M | J | J | A | S | O | N | D |

Rock Dove
Columba livia
(Columbidae)

33 cm (13 in)
Some apparently genuine birds
remain on western and
northern coasts. Feral population throughout.

| J | F | M | A | M | J | J | A | S | O | N | D |

| J | F | M | A | M | J | J | A | S | O | N | D |

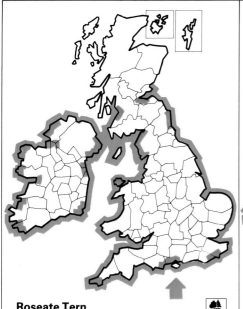

Roseate Tern
Sterna dougalii
(Sternidae)

33 cm (13 in)
Summer visitor with breeding
population less than 500 pairs
and decreasing.

| J | F | M | A | M | J | J | A | S | O | N | D |
| J | F | M | A | M | J | J | A | S | O | N | D |

Common Tern
Sterna hirundo
(Sternidae)

33 cm (13 in)
Summer visitor with breeding
population in excess of 16 000
and reasonably stable.

| J | F | M | A | M | J | J | A | S | O | N | D |
| J | F | M | A | M | J | J | A | S | O | N | D |

Arctic Tern
Sterna paradisaea
(Sternidae)

34 cm (13 in)
Summer visitor with breeding
population under 80 000 pairs
and decreasing.

| J | F | M | A | M | J | J | A | S | O | N | D |
| J | F | M | A | M | J | J | A | S | O | N | D |

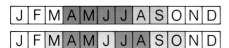

Little Tern
Sterna albifrons
(Sternidae)

23 cm (9 in)
Summer visitor with breeding
population approximately 2000
pairs and stable.

| J | F | M | A | M | J | J | A | S | O | N | D |
| J | F | M | A | M | J | J | A | S | O | N | D |

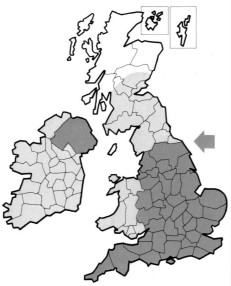

Black Tern
Chlidonias niger
(Sternidae)

24 cm (9 in)
Migrants from east pass
through in spring and autumn.

| J | F | M | A | M | J | J | A | S | O | N | D |
| J | F | M | A | M | J | J | A | S | O | N | D |

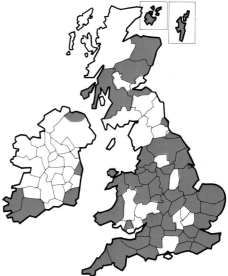
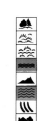

White-winged Black Tern
Chlidonias leucopterus
(Sternidae)

22 cm (9 in)
Map reflects recent 10-year
period. Vagrant from south-
east Europe. More than 30
records per year is unusual.

| J | F | M | A | M | J | J | A | S | O | N | D |
| J | F | M | A | M | J | J | A | S | O | N | D |

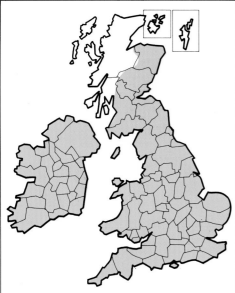

Stock Dove
Columba oenas
(Columbidae)

33 cm (13 in)
Breeding population in excess
of 100 000 pairs and increasing.

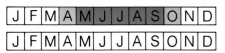

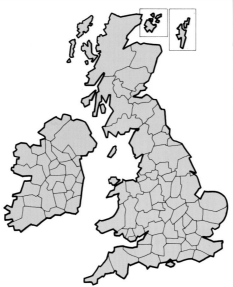

Woodpigeon
Columba palumbus
(Columbidae)

41 cm (16 in)
Breeding population perhaps
in excess of 5 million pairs and
increasing.

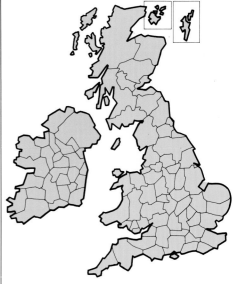

Collared Dove
Streptopelia decaocto
(Columbidae)

32 cm (13 in)
Following colonization in 1955,
breeding population now
probably under 50 000 pairs
and stable.

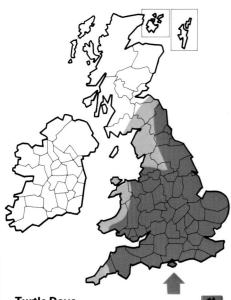

Turtle Dove
Streptopelia turtur
(Columbidae)

27 cm (11 in)
Summer visitor with breeding
population probably over
125 000 pairs with range
expanding.

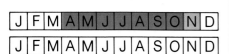

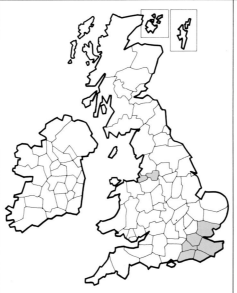

Ring-necked Parakeet
Psittacula krameri
(Psittacidae)

40 cm (16 in)
Since first regular breeding in
1969, population now exceeds
500 pairs.

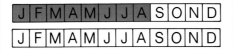

Cuckoo
Cuculus canorus
(Cuculidae)

33 cm (13 in)
Summer visitor, widespread
but perhaps decreasing.

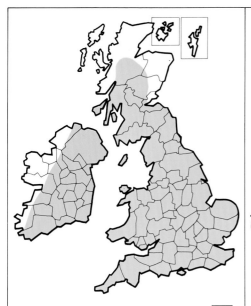

Barn Owl
Tyto alba
(Tytonidae)

36 cm (14 in)
Population fluctuates, but probably decreasing with less than 7000 breeding pairs.

J	F	M	A	M	J	J	A	S	O	N	D

J	F	M	A	M	J	J	A	S	O	N	D

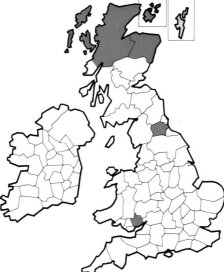

Snowy Owl
Nyctea scandiaca
(Strigidae)

60 cm (24 in)
Map reflects recent 10-year period, when very few records, although resident but not breeding in Shetland. Vagrant from north.

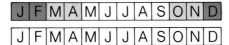

J	F	M	A	M	J	J	A	S	O	N	D

J	F	M	A	M	J	J	A	S	O	N	D

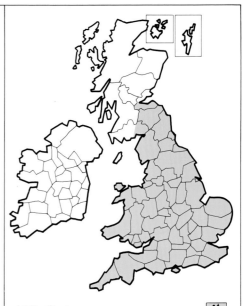

Little Owl
Athene noctua
(Strigidae)

22 cm (9 in)
An introduced species, total population probably less than 10 000 pairs.

J	F	M	A	M	J	J	A	S	O	N	D

J	F	M	A	M	J	J	A	S	O	N	D

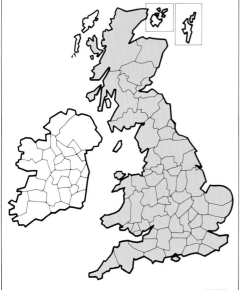

Tawny Owl
Strix aluco
(Strigidae)

38 cm (15 in)
Breeding population is perhaps as high as 100 000 pairs.

J	F	M	A	M	J	J	A	S	O	N	D

J	F	M	A	M	J	J	A	S	O	N	D

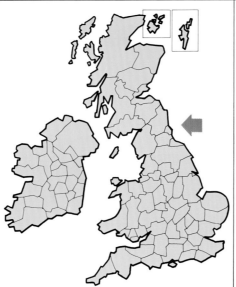

Long-eared Owl
Asio otus
(Strigidae)

36 cm (14 in)
A changing breeding population, usually over 3000 pairs, joined by migrants from east in winter.

J	F	M	A	M	J	J	A	S	O	N	D

J	F	M	A	M	J	J	A	S	O	N	D

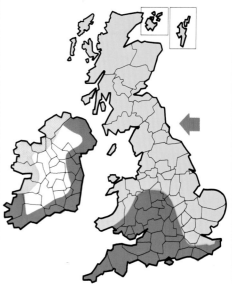

Short-eared Owl
Asio flammeus
(Strigidae)

38 cm (15 in)
Breeding population extremely variable, dependent upon food supply, 1000–10 000 pairs. Migrants from east spend winter.

J	F	M	A	M	J	J	A	S	O	N	D

J	F	M	A	M	J	J	A	S	O	N	D

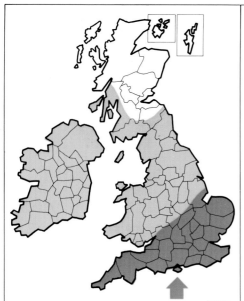

Nightjar
Caprimulgus europaeus
(Caprimulgidae)

27 cm (11 in)
Breeding population of some 2000 pairs probably decreasing.

J F M A M J J A S O N D
J F M A M J J A S O N D

Swift
Apus apus
(Apodidae)

17 cm (7 in)
Breeding population roughly 100 000 pairs.

J F M A M J J A S O N D
J F M A M J J A S O N D

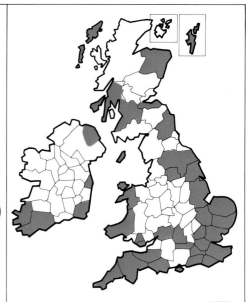

Alpine Swift
Apus melba
(Apodidae)

22 cm (9 in)
Map reflects recent 10-year period. Vagrant from southern Europe. More than 10 records per year unusual.

J F M A M J J A S O N D
J F M A M J J A S O N D

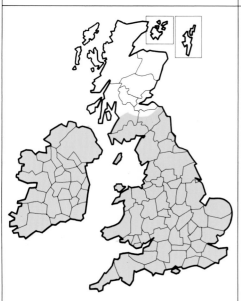

Kingfisher
Alcedo atthis
(Alcedinidae)

17 cm (7 in)
Breeding population fluctuates with severity of winter. Probably over 5000 pairs.

J F M A M J J A S O N D
J F M A M J J A S O N D

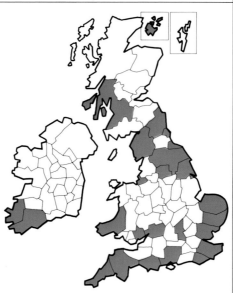

Bee-eater
Merops apiaster
(Meropidae)

28 cm (11 in)
Map reflects recent 10-year period. Vagrant from southern Europe. More than 20 per year unusual, more often less than 10.

J F M A M J J A S O N D
J F M A M J J A S O N D

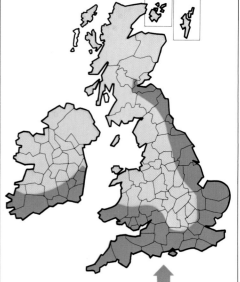

Hoopoe
Upupa epops
(Upupidae)

28 cm (11 in)
Most numerous as spring visitor in south. Over 100 per year is unusual.

J F M A M J J A S O N D
J F M A M J J A S O N D

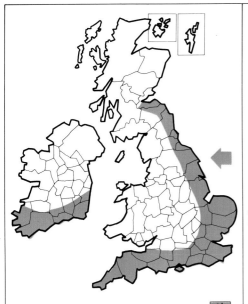

Wryneck
Jynx torquilla
(Picidae)

16 cm (6 in)
Probably now extinct as a
breeding species. Annual on
spring and autumn migrations.

| J | F | M | A | M | J | J | A | S | O | N | D |
| J | F | M | A | M | J | J | A | S | O | N | D |

Green Woodpecker
Picus viridis
(Picidae)

32 cm (13 in)
Breeding population perhaps
20 000 pairs, with northward
spread of distribution.

| J | F | M | A | M | J | J | A | S | O | N | D |
| J | F | M | A | M | J | J | A | S | O | N | D |

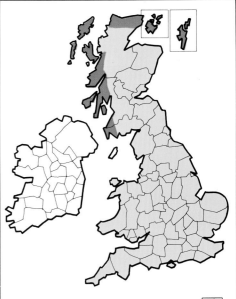

Great Spotted
Woodpecker
Dendrocopos major
(Picidae)

23 cm (9 in)
Breeding population in excess
of 30 000 pairs, spreading and
increasing.

| J | F | M | A | M | J | J | A | S | O | N | D |
| J | F | M | A | M | J | J | A | S | O | N | D |

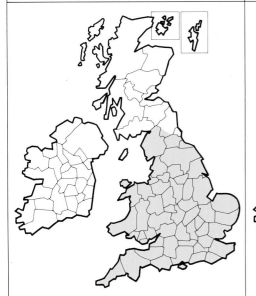

Lesser Spotted
Woodpecker
Dendrocopos minor
(Picidae)

15 cm (6 in)
Breeding population estimated
at approximately 5000 pairs.

| J | F | M | A | M | J | J | A | S | O | N | D |
| J | F | M | A | M | J | J | A | S | O | N | D |

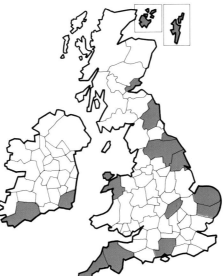

Short-toed Lark
Calandrella brachydactyla
(Alaudidae)

14 cm (6 in)
Map reflects recent 10-year
period. Vagrant from southern
Europe. More than 20 per year
unusual. Annual in Shetland.

| J | F | M | A | M | J | J | A | S | O | N | D |
| J | F | M | A | M | J | J | A | S | O | N | D |

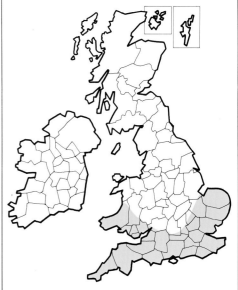

Woodlark
Lullula arborea
(Alaudidae)

15 cm (6 in)
Breeding population probably
less than 200 pairs and
decreasing.

| J | F | M | A | M | J | J | A | S | O | N | D |
| J | F | M | A | M | J | J | A | S | O | N | D |

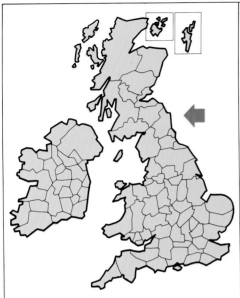

Skylark
Alauda arvensis
(Alaudidae)

18 cm (7 in)
Extremely common, probably
in excess of 2 million breeding
pairs. Migrants from east
spend winter.

| J | F | M | A | M | J | J | A | S | O | N | D |

| J | F | M | A | M | J | J | A | S | O | N | D |

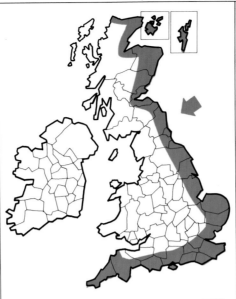

Shore Lark
Eremophila alpestris
(Alaudidae)

16 cm (6 in)
Winter visitor from north-east.
Commonest on south-east
coast. Numbers vary annually.

| J | F | M | A | M | J | J | A | S | O | N | D |

| J | F | M | A | M | J | J | A | S | O | N | D |

Sand Martin
Riparia riparia
(Hirundinidae)

12 cm (5 in)
Dramatic decrease in breeding
population.

| J | F | M | A | M | J | J | A | S | O | N | D |

| J | F | M | A | M | J | J | A | S | O | N | D |

Swallow
Hirundo rustica
(Hirundinidae)

19 cm (7 in)
Breeding population probably
less than 1 million and
decreasing.

| J | F | M | A | M | J | J | A | S | O | N | D |

| J | F | M | A | M | J | J | A | S | O | N | D |

House Martin
Delichon urbica
(Hirundinidae)

13 cm (5 in)
Breeding population in excess
of 300 000 pairs.

| J | F | M | A | M | J | J | A | S | O | N | D |

| J | F | M | A | M | J | J | A | S | O | N | D |

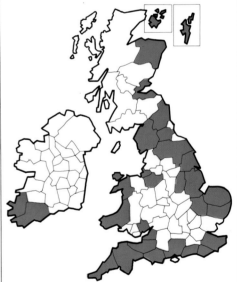

Richard's Pipit
Anthus novaeseelandiae
(Motacillidae)

18 cm (7 in)
Map reflects recent 10-year
period. Vagrant from eastern
Europe. Up to 100 records per
year, but numbers vary greatly.

| J | F | M | A | M | J | J | A | S | O | N | D |

| J | F | M | A | M | J | J | A | S | O | N | D |

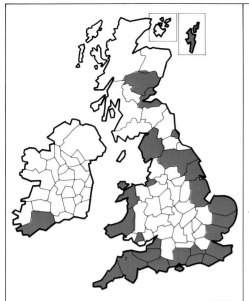

Tawny Pipit
Anthus campestris
(Motacillidae)

17 cm (7 in)
Map reflects recent 10-year period. Vagrant from southern Europe. Up to 40 records per year.

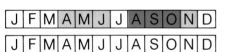

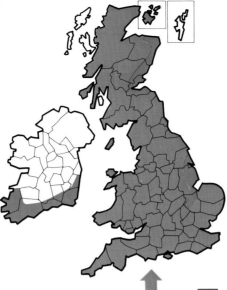

Tree Pipit
Anthus trivialis
(Motacillidae)

15 cm (6 in)
Breeding population perhaps as high as 100 000 pairs.

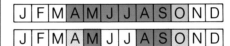

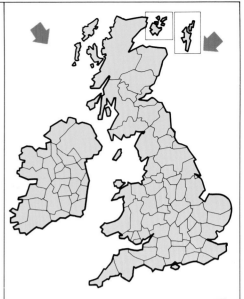

Meadow Pipit
Anthus pratensis
(Motacillidae)

15 cm (6 in)
Breeding population probably exceeds 3 million pairs, of which many move south in winter. Migrants from north spend winter.

| J | F | M | A | M | J | J | A | S | O | N | D |
| J | F | M | A | M | J | J | A | S | O | N | D |

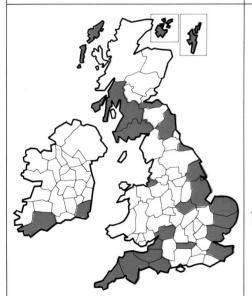

Red-throated Pipit
Anthus cervinus
(Motacillidae)

15 cm (6 in)
Map reflects recent 10-year period. Vagrant from north-east Europe. Rarely 10 records per year.

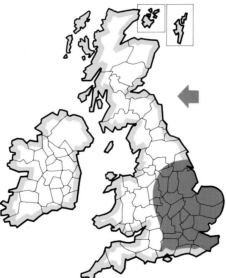

Rock Pipit
Anthus spinoletta
(Motacillidae)

17 cm (7 in)
Breeding population exceeds 50 000 pairs with migrants from east spending winter.

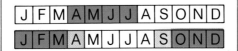

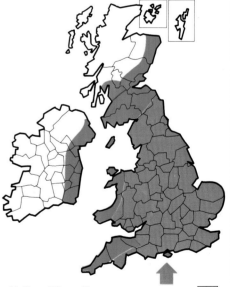

Yellow Wagtail
Motacilla flava
(Motacillidae)

16.5 cm (6 in)
Breeding population probably under 25 000 pairs and decreasing.

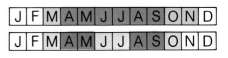

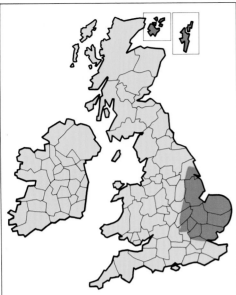

Grey Wagtail
Motacilla cinerea
(Motacillidae)

18 cm (7 in)
Breeding population probably
in excess of 20 000 pairs.

| J | F | M | A | M | J | J | A | S | O | N | D |

| J | F | M | A | M | J | J | A | S | O | N | D |

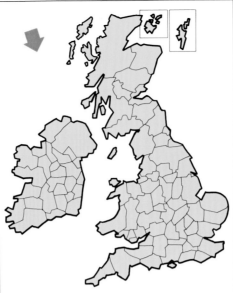

Pied Wagtail
Motacilla alba
(Motacillidae)

18 cm (7 in)
Breeding population of
approximately 500 000 pairs.
Migrants from north-west pass
through in spring and autumn.

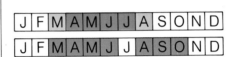

| J | F | M | A | M | J | J | A | S | O | N | D |

| J | F | M | A | M | J | J | A | S | O | N | D |

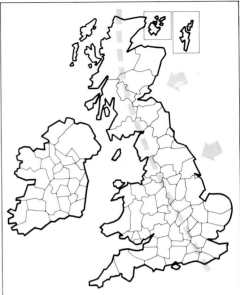

Waxwing
Bombycilla garrulus
(Bombycillidae)

18 cm (7 in)
An invasion species from east,
annual numbers vary greatly.

| J | F | M | A | M | J | J | A | S | O | N | D |

| J | F | M | A | M | J | J | A | S | O | N | D |

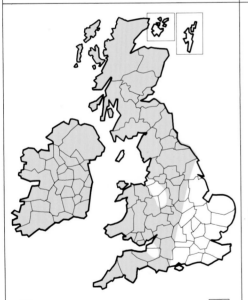

Dipper
Cinclus cinclus
(Cinclidae)

18 cm (7 in)
Breeding population probably
approaching 30 000 pairs but
varies with severity of winter.

| J | F | M | A | M | J | J | A | S | O | N | D |

| J | F | M | A | M | J | J | A | S | O | N | D |

Wren
Troglodytes troglodytes
(Troglodytidae)

9.5 cm (4 in)
Breeding population very
dependent upon winter
weather. Peaking as high as
10 million pairs.

| J | F | M | A | M | J | J | A | S | O | N | D |

| J | F | M | A | M | J | J | A | S | O | N | D |

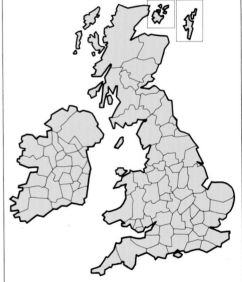

Dunnock
Prunella modularis
(Prunellidae)

14.5 cm (6 in)
Breeding population perhaps
in excess of 5 million pairs.

| J | F | M | A | M | J | J | A | S | O | N | D |

| J | F | M | A | M | J | J | A | S | O | N | D |

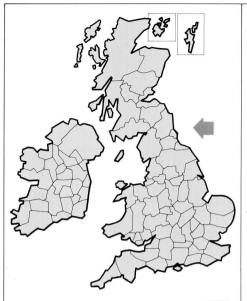

Robin
Erithacus rubecula
(Turdidae)

14 cm (6 in)
Breeding population approximately 5 million pairs, and
perhaps increasing. Migrants
from east spend winter.

J F M A M J J A S O N D
J F M A M J J A S O N D

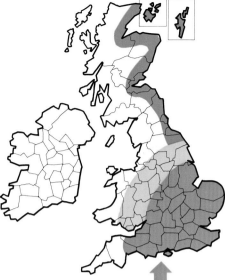

Nightingale
Luscinia megarhynchos
(Turdidae)

16.5 cm (6 in)
Breeding population probably
in excess of 4000 pairs and
increasing.

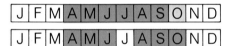

J F M A M J J A S O N D
J F M A M J J A S O N D

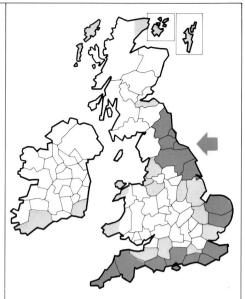

Bluethroat
Luscinia svecica
(Turdidae)

14 cm (6 in)
Passage migrant from east.
Spring and autumn numbers
dependent upon prevailing
weather.

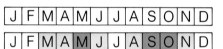

J F M A M J J A S O N D
J F M A M J J A S O N D

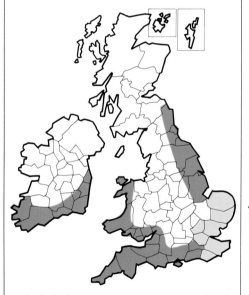

Black Redstart
Phoenicurus ochruros
(Turdidae)

14 cm (6 in)
Breeding population less than
100 pairs and decreasing.
Complicated migratory move-
ments through southern
Britain.

J F M A M J J A S O N D
J F M A M J J A S O N D

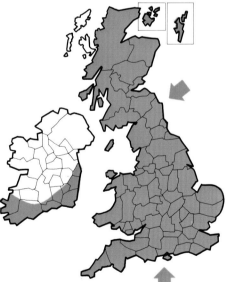

Redstart
Phoenicurus phoenicurus
(Turdidae)

14 cm (6 in)
Breeding population perhaps
over 50 000 pairs but decreasing. Passage migrants from
east pass through spring and
autumn.

J F M A M J J A S O N D
J F M A M J J A S O N D

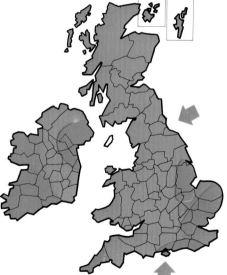

Whinchat
Saxicola rubetra
(Turdidae)

12.5 cm (5 in)
Breeding population less than
40 000 pairs and decreasing.
Passage migrants from east
pass through spring and
autumn.

J F M A M J J A S O N D
J F M A M J J A S O N D

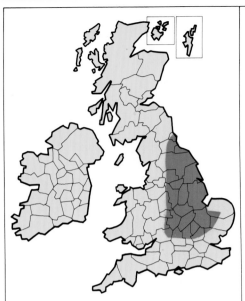

Stonechat
Saxicola torquata
(Turdidae)

12.5 cm (5 in)
Breeding population varies in
response to severity of winter,
approximately 10 000 pairs.

| J | F | M | A | M | J | J | A | S | O | N | D |

| J | F | M | A | M | J | J | A | S | O | N | D |

Wheatear
Oenanthe oenanthe
(Turdidae)

15 cm (6 in)
Summer visitor with breeding
population in excess of 50 000
pairs. Migrants from north pass
through spring and autumn.

| J | F | M | A | M | J | J | A | S | O | N | D |

| J | F | M | A | M | J | J | A | S | O | N | D |

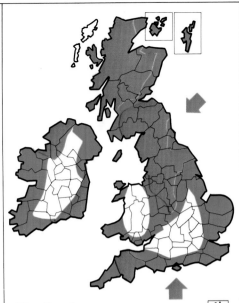

Ring Ouzel
Turdus torquatus
(Turdidae)

24 cm (9 in)
Breeding population in region
of 10 000 pairs. Migrants from
north-east pass through spring
and autumn.

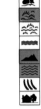

| J | F | M | A | M | J | J | A | S | O | N | D |

| J | F | M | A | M | J | J | A | S | O | N | D |

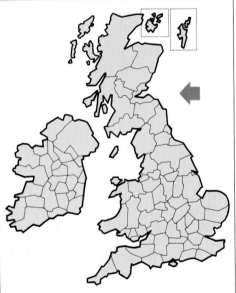

Blackbird
Turdus merula
(Turdidae)

25 cm (10 in)
Breeding population perhaps
exceeds 7 million pairs.
Migrants from east pass
through and spend winter.

| J | F | M | A | M | J | J | A | S | O | N | D |

| J | F | M | A | M | J | J | A | S | O | N | D |

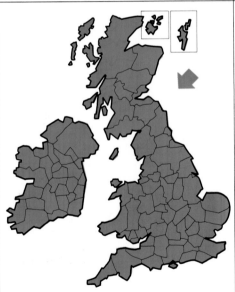

Fieldfare
Turdus pilaris
(Turdidae)

25.5 cm (10 in)
Winter visitor from east.
Occasional pairs breed in
north.

| J | F | M | A | M | J | J | A | S | O | N | D |

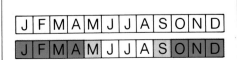

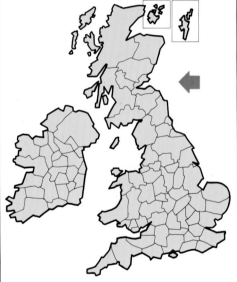

Song Thrush
Turdus philomelos
(Turdidae)

23 cm (9 in)
Breeding population approximately 2 million pairs, but
numbers vary. Migrants from
east pass through and remain
for winter.

| J | F | M | A | M | J | J | A | S | O | N | D |

| J | F | M | A | M | J | J | A | S | O | N | D |

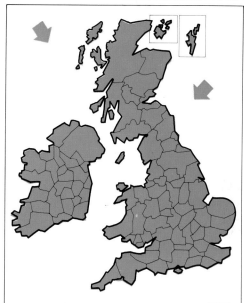

Redwing
Turdus iliacus
(Turdidae)

21 cm (8 in)
Winter visitor from north, some birds passing through. Up to 30 pairs may remain to nest, mostly northern Scotland.

| J | F | M | A | M | J | J | A | S | O | N | D |

| J | F | M | A | M | J | J | A | S | O | N | D |

Mistle Thrush
Turdus viscivorus
(Turdidae)

27 cm (11 in)
Breeding population approximately 500 000 pairs.

| J | F | M | A | M | J | J | A | S | O | N | D |

| J | F | M | A | M | J | J | A | S | O | N | D |

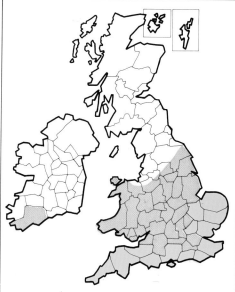

Cetti's Warbler
Cettia cetti
(Sylviidae)

14 cm (6 in)
Breeding population probably exceeds 300 pairs and is increasing and spreading.

| J | F | M | A | M | J | J | A | S | O | N | D |

| J | F | M | A | M | J | J | A | S | O | N | D |

Grasshopper Warbler
Locustella naevia
(Sylviidae)

13 cm (5 in)
Breeding population perhaps as high as 25 000 pairs.

| J | F | M | A | M | J | J | A | S | O | N | D |

| J | F | M | A | M | J | J | A | S | O | N | D |

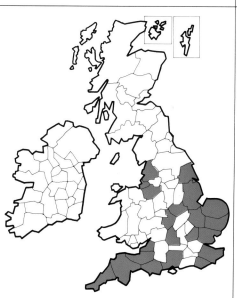

Savi's Warbler
Locustella luscinioides
(Sylviidae)

14 cm (6 in)
Map reflects recent 10-year period. Vagrant from south and east Europe. A few pairs nest annually in east.

| J | F | M | A | M | J | J | A | S | O | N | D |

| J | F | M | A | M | J | J | A | S | O | N | D |

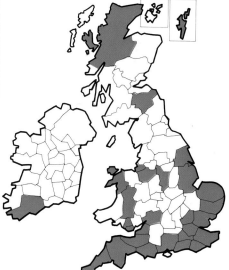

Aquatic Warbler
Acrocephalus paludicola
(Sylviidae)

13 cm (5 in)
Map reflects recent 10-year period. Vagrant from eastern Europe. Up to 100 records per year.

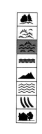

| J | F | M | A | M | J | J | A | S | O | N | D |

| J | F | M | A | M | J | J | A | S | O | N | D |

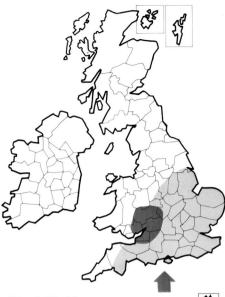

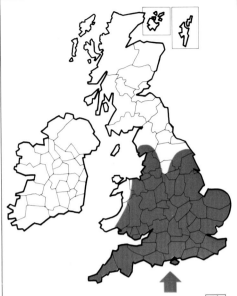

Sedge Warbler
Acrocephalus schoenobaenus
(Sylviidae)

13 cm (5 in)
Breeding population probably
less than 500 000 pairs.

J	F	M	A	M	J	J	A	S	O	N	D

J	F	M	A	M	J	J	A	S	O	N	D

Marsh Warbler
Acrocephalus palustris
(Sylviidae)

12.5 cm (5 in)
Breeding population small and
local, with scattered isolated
attempts in some years.

J	F	M	A	M	J	J	A	S	O	N	D

J	F	M	A	M	J	J	A	S	O	N	D

Reed Warbler
Acrocephalus scirpaceus
(Sylviidae)

12.5 cm (5 in)
Breeding population probably
exceeding 50 000 pairs.

J	F	M	A	M	J	J	A	S	O	N	D

J	F	M	A	M	J	J	A	S	O	N	D

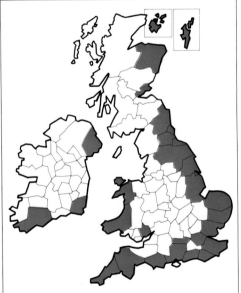

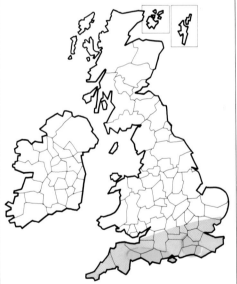

Icterine Warbler
Hippolais icterina
(Sylviidae)

13.5 cm (5 in)
Regular passage migrant from
south-east with over 50 records
annually, mainly on east coast.

J	F	M	A	M	J	J	A	S	O	N	D

J	F	M	A	M	J	J	A	S	O	N	D

Melodious Warbler
Hippolais polyglotta
(Sylviidae)

13 cm (5 in)
Regular passage migrant from
south with nearly 50 records
annually, mainly on west coast.

J	F	M	A	M	J	J	A	S	O	N	D

J	F	M	A	M	J	J	A	S	O	N	D

Dartford Warbler
Sylvia undata
(Sylviidae)

12.5 cm (5 in)
Small resident population very
variable in numbers, dependent upon severity of winter.

J	F	M	A	M	J	J	A	S	O	N	D

J	F	M	A	M	J	J	A	S	O	N	D

Barred Warbler
Sylvia nisoria
(Sylviidae)

15 cm (6 in)
Regular autumn passage
migrant from east, up to 100
recorded annually.

J	F	M	A	M	J	J	A	S	O	N	D

J	F	M	A	M	J	J	A	S	O	N	D

Lesser Whitethroat
Sylvia curruca
(Sylviidae)

13.5 cm (5 in)
Probably less than 50 000
breeding pairs.

J	F	M	A	M	J	J	A	S	O	N	D

J	F	M	A	M	J	J	A	S	O	N	D

Whitethroat
Sylvia communis
(Sylviidae)

14 cm (6 in)
Breeding population less than
500 000 pairs, and decreasing.

J	F	M	A	M	J	J	A	S	O	N	D

J	F	M	A	M	J	J	A	S	O	N	D

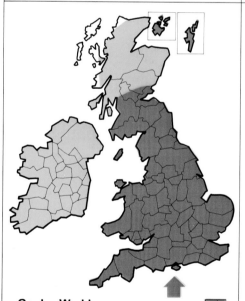
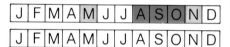

Garden Warbler
Sylvia borin
(Sylviidae)

14 cm (6 in)
Breeding population less than
100 000 pairs, but probably
increasing.

J	F	M	A	M	J	J	A	S	O	N	D

J	F	M	A	M	J	J	A	S	O	N	D

Blackcap
Sylvia atricapilla
(Sylviidae)

14 cm (6 in)
Breeding population in excess
of 200 000 pairs. Increasing
numbers remain during winter.

J	F	M	A	M	J	J	A	S	O	N	D

J	F	M	A	M	J	J	A	S	O	N	D

Greenish Warbler
Phylloscopus trochiloides
(Sylviidae)

11 cm (4 in)
Map reflects recent 10-year
period. Vagrant from east.
Rarely more than 10 records
per year.

J	F	M	A	M	J	J	A	S	O	N	D

J	F	M	A	M	J	J	A	S	O	N	D

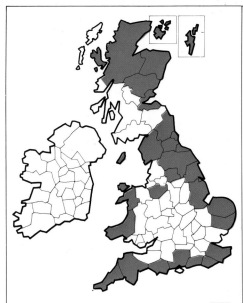

Pallas's Warbler
Phylloscopus proregulus
(Sylviidae)

11 cm (4 in)
Map reflects recent 10-year
period. Vagrant from east.
Most years less than 10
records, exceptionally up to
100.

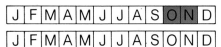

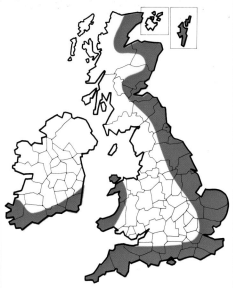

Yellow-browed Warbler
Phylloscopus inornatus
(Sylviidae)

10 cm (4 in)
Annual passage migrant from
the east, often over 100
records per year.

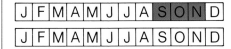

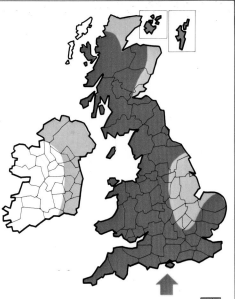

Wood Warbler
Phylloscopus sibilatrix
(Sylviidae)

12.5 cm (5 in)
Breeding population in excess
of 30 000 pairs.

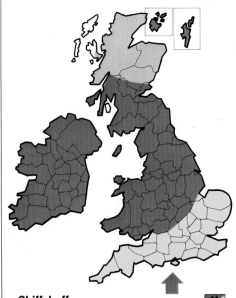

Chiffchaff
Phylloscopus collybita
(Sylviidae)

11 cm (4 in)
Breeding population approximately 300 000 pairs. Increasing numbers wintering in
south.

Willow Warbler
Phylloscopus trochilus
(Sylviidae)

11.5 cm (4 in)
Breeding population probably
in excess of 3 million pairs.

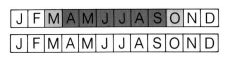

Goldcrest
Regulus regulus
(Sylviidae)

9 cm (3.5 in)
Breeding population dependent upon severity of winter,
probably in excess of 1 million
pairs. Migrants from east
spend winter.

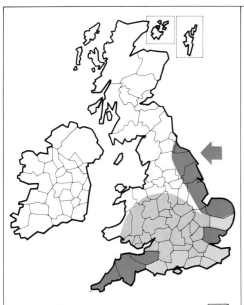

Firecrest
Regulus ignicapillus
(Sylviidae)

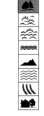

9 cm (3.5 in)
Winter visitor and passage
migrant from east. Small
breeding population in excess
of 100 pairs.

J	F	M	A	M	J	J	A	S	O	N	D
J	F	M	A	M	J	J	A	S	O	N	D

Spotted Flycatcher
Muscicapa striata
(Muscicapidae)

14 cm (6 in)
Summer visitor with breeding
population in excess of
100 000 pairs.

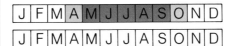

J	F	M	A	M	J	J	A	S	O	N	D
J	F	M	A	M	J	J	A	S	O	N	D

Red-breasted Flycatcher
Ficedula parva
(Muscicapidae)

11.5 cm (5 in)
Regular passage migrant from
east, over 50 per year.

J	F	M	A	M	J	J	A	S	O	N	D
J	F	M	A	M	J	J	A	S	O	N	D

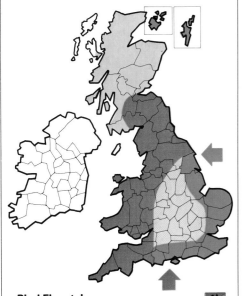

Pied Flycatcher
Ficedula hypoleuca
(Muscicapidae)

13 cm (5 in)
Summer visitor with breeding
population in excess of 10 000
pairs. Migrants from east pass
through, mainly in autumn.

J	F	M	A	M	J	J	A	S	O	N	D
J	F	M	A	M	J	J	A	S	O	N	D

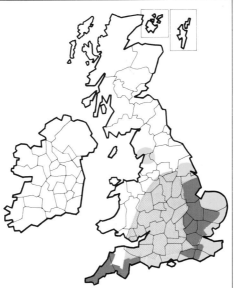

Bearded Tit
Panurus biarmicus
(Timaliidae)

16.5 cm (6 in)
Breeding population very
dependent upon severity of
winter.

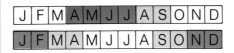

J	F	M	A	M	J	J	A	S	O	N	D
J	F	M	A	M	J	J	A	S	O	N	D

Long-tailed Tit
Aegithalos caudatus
(Aegithalidae)

14 cm (6 in)
Breeding population in excess
of 100 000 pairs.

J	F	M	A	M	J	J	A	S	O	N	D
J	F	M	A	M	J	J	A	S	O	N	D

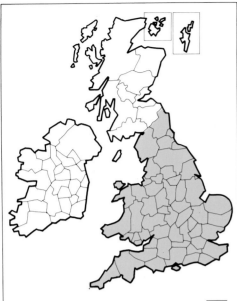

Marsh Tit
Parus palustris
(Paridae)

11.5 cm (5 in)
Breeding population approximately 100 000 pairs.

J F M A M J J A S O N D
J F M A M J J A S O N D

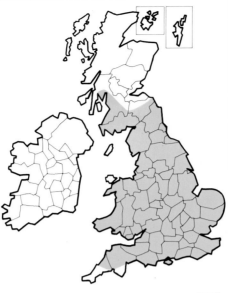

Willow Tit
Parus montanus
(Paridae)

11.5 cm (5 in)
Breeding population less than 100 000 pairs.

J F M A M J J A S O N D
J F M A M J J A S O N D

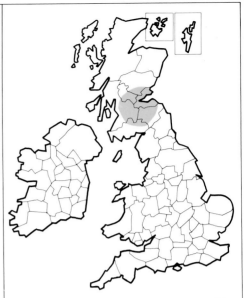

Crested Tit
Parus cristatus
(Paridae)

11.5 cm (5 in)
Breeding population perhaps exceeding 1000 pairs.

J F M A M J J A S O N D
J F M A M J J A S O N D

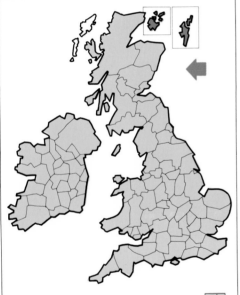

Coal Tit
Parus ater
(Paridae)

11.5 cm (5 in)
Breeding population increasing, perhaps in excess of 1 million pairs.

J F M A M J J A S O N D
J F M A M J J A S O N D

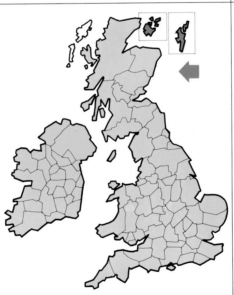

Blue Tit
Parus caeruleus
(Paridae)

11.5 cm (5 in)
Breeding population probably in excess of 5 million pairs.

J F M A M J J A S O N D
J F M A M J J A S O N D

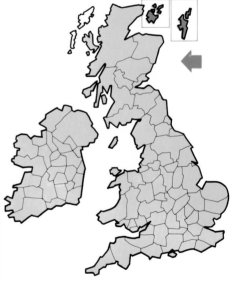

Great Tit
Parus major
(Paridae)

14 cm (6 in)
Breeding population in excess of 3 million pairs and probably increasing.

J F M A M J J A S O N D
J F M A M J J A S O N D

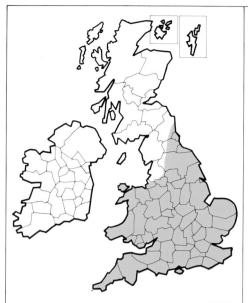

Nuthatch
Sitta europaea
(Sittidae)

14 cm (6 in)
Breeding population
approaching 25 000 pairs.

| J | F | M | A | M | J | J | A | S | O | N | D |
| J | F | M | A | M | J | J | A | S | O | N | D |

Treecreeper
Certhia familiaris
(Certhiidae)

12.5 cm (5 in)
Breeding population in excess
of 150 000 pairs.

| J | F | M | A | M | J | J | A | S | O | N | D |
| J | F | M | A | M | J | J | A | S | O | N | D |

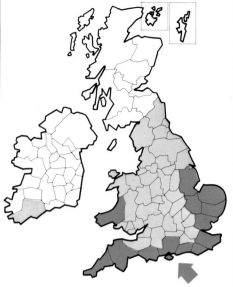

Golden Oriole
Oriolus oriolus
(Oriolidae)

24 cm (9 in)
Annual spring visitor, particularly in south-east, where small
breeding population.

| J | F | M | A | M | J | J | A | S | O | N | D |
| J | F | M | A | M | J | J | A | S | O | N | D |

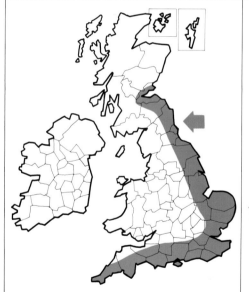

Red-backed Shrike
Lanius collurio
(Laniidae)

17 cm (7 in)
Very small numbers still breed.
Mainly passage migrant from
east.

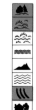

| J | F | M | A | M | J | J | A | S | O | N | D |
| J | F | M | A | M | J | J | A | S | O | N | D |

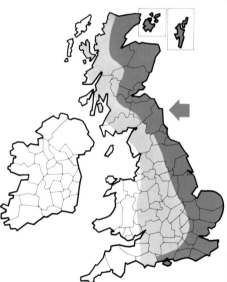

Great Grey Shrike
Lanius excubitor
(Laniidae)

24 cm (9 in)
Passage migrant and winter
visitor from east, numbers vary
annually.

| J | F | M | A | M | J | J | A | S | O | N | D |
| J | F | M | A | M | J | J | A | S | O | N | D |

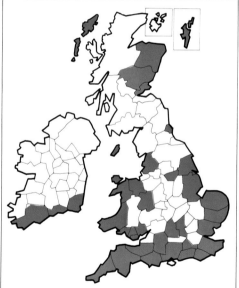

Woodchat Shrike
Lanius senator
(Laniidae)

17 cm (7 in)
Map reflects recent 10-year
period. Vagrant from south.
Up to 20 records per year.

| J | F | M | A | M | J | J | A | S | O | N | D |
| J | F | M | A | M | J | J | A | S | O | N | D |

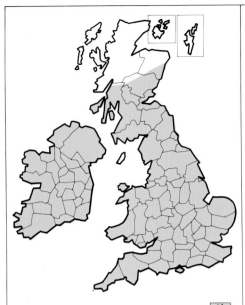

Jay
Garrulus glandarius
(Corvidae)

34 cm (13 in)
Breeding population approximately 100 000 pairs and probably increasing.

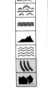

| J | F | M | A | M | J | J | A | S | O | N | D |
| J | F | M | A | M | J | J | A | S | O | N | D |

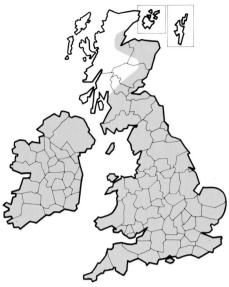

Magpie
Pica pica
(Corvidae)

46 cm (18 in)
Breeding population probably in excess of 250 000 pairs and increasing.

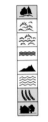

| J | F | M | A | M | J | J | A | S | O | N | D |
| J | F | M | A | M | J | J | A | S | O | N | D |

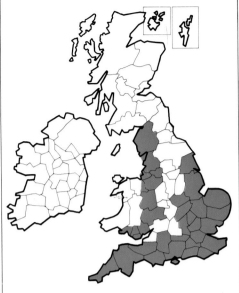

Nutcracker
Nucifraga caryocatactes
(Corvidae)

33 cm (13 in)
Not an annual vagrant. Position distorted by over 300 records in 1 year.

| J | F | M | A | M | J | J | A | S | O | N | D |
| J | F | M | A | M | J | J | A | S | O | N | D |

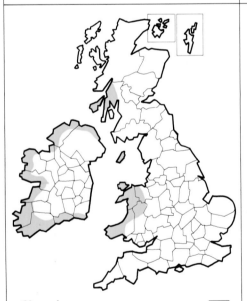

Chough
Pyrrhocorax pyrrhocorax
(Corvidae)

39 cm (15 in)
Breeding population less than 1000 pairs and decreasing.

| J | F | M | A | M | J | J | A | S | O | N | D |
| J | F | M | A | M | J | J | A | S | O | N | D |

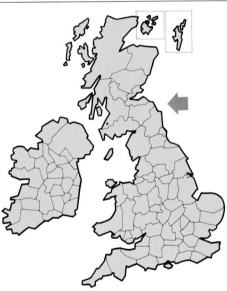

Jackdaw
Corvus monedula
(Corvidae)

33 cm (13 in)
Breeding population probably in excess of 500 000 pairs. Migrants from east spend winter.

| J | F | M | A | M | J | J | A | S | O | N | D |
| J | F | M | A | M | J | J | A | S | O | N | D |

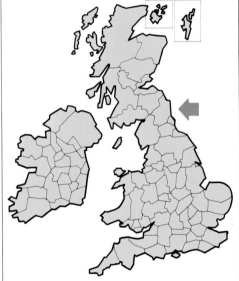

Rook
Corvus frugilegus
(Corvidae)

46 cm (18 in)
Breeding population perhaps 1 million pairs, but decreasing. Migrants from east spend winter.

| J | F | M | A | M | J | J | A | S | O | N | D |
| J | F | M | A | M | J | J | A | S | O | N | D |

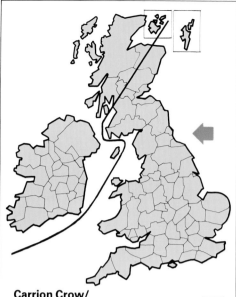

Carrion Crow/ Hooded Crow
Corvus corone
(Corvidae)

46 cm (18 in)
Breeding population perhaps 1 million pairs. Hooded Crow north of line, Carrion Crow south. Some migrants from east spend winter.

J	F	M	A	M	J	J	A	S	O	N	D
J	F	M	A	M	J	J	A	S	O	N	D

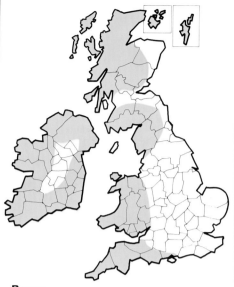

Raven
Corvus corax
(Corvidae)

63 cm (25 in.)
Breeding population approximately 5000 pairs.

J	F	M	A	M	J	J	A	S	O	N	D
J	F	M	A	M	J	J	A	S	O	N	D

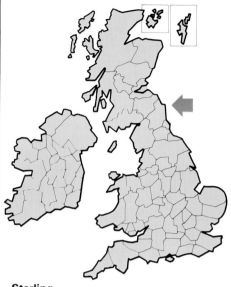

Starling
Sturnus vulgaris
(Sturnidae)

21.5 cm (8 in)
Breeding population probably exceeds 4 million pairs. Huge numbers migrate from east to spend winter.

J	F	M	A	M	J	J	A	S	O	N	D
J	F	M	A	M	J	J	A	S	O	N	D

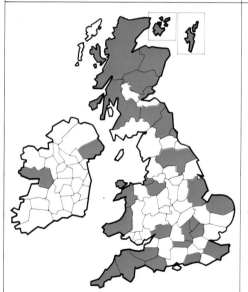

Rose-coloured Starling
Sturnus roseus
(Sturnidae)

21.5 cm (8 in)
Map reflects recent 10-year period. Vagrant from eastern Europe. Rarely more than 10 records per year.

J	F	M	A	M	J	J	A	S	O	N	D
J	F	M	A	M	J	J	A	S	O	N	D

House Sparrow
Passer domesticus
(Passeridae)

14.5 cm (6 in)
Breeding population possibly in excess of 5 million pairs.

J	F	M	A	M	J	J	A	S	O	N	D
J	F	M	A	M	J	J	A	S	O	N	D

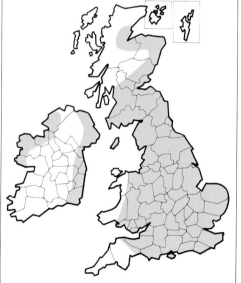

Tree Sparrow
Passer montanus
(Passeridae)

14 cm (6 in)
Breeding population possibly well in excess of 100 000 pairs.

J	F	M	A	M	J	J	A	S	O	N	D
J	F	M	A	M	J	J	A	S	O	N	D

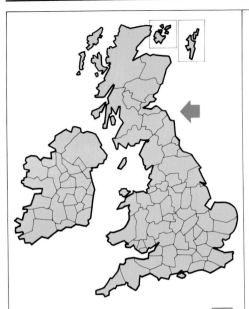

Chaffinch
Fringilla coelebs
(Fringillidae)

15 cm (6 in)
Breeding population perhaps
as high as 7 million pairs.
Large numbers of migrants
from east spend winter.

| J | F | M | A | M | J | J | A | S | O | N | D |

| J | F | M | A | M | J | J | A | S | O | N | D |

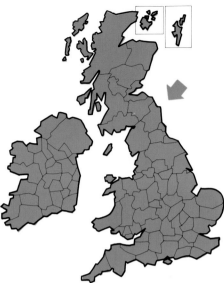

Brambling
Fringilla montifringilla
(Fringillidae)

14.5 cm (6 in)
Winter visitor from north-east,
numbers vary annually. In
some years occasional
breeding pair in north.

| J | F | M | A | M | J | J | A | S | O | N | D |

| J | F | M | A | M | J | J | A | S | O | N | D |

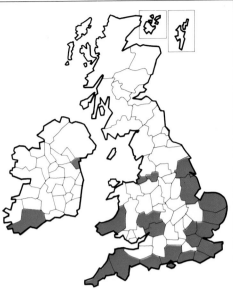

Serin
Serinus serinus
(Fringillidae)

11.5 cm (5 in)
Map reflects recent 10-year
period. Vagrant from southern
Europe. Over 40 records per
year unusual. Small numbers
may nest near south coast.

| J | F | M | A | M | J | J | A | S | O | N | D |

| J | F | M | A | M | J | J | A | S | O | N | D |

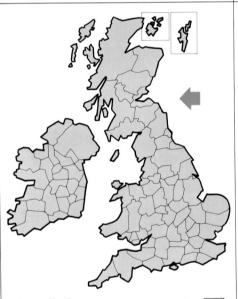

Greenfinch
Carduelis chloris
(Fringillidae)

14.5 cm (6 in)
Breeding population probably
in excess of 1 million pairs.
Migrants from east spend
winter.

| J | F | M | A | M | J | J | A | S | O | N | D |

| J | F | M | A | M | J | J | A | S | O | N | D |

Goldfinch
Carduelis carduelis
(Fringillidae)

12 cm (5 in)
Breeding population probably
in excess of 300 000 pairs and
increasing. Many breeding
birds depart south in winter,
others arrive from east.

| J | F | M | A | M | J | J | A | S | O | N | D |

| J | F | M | A | M | J | J | A | S | O | N | D |

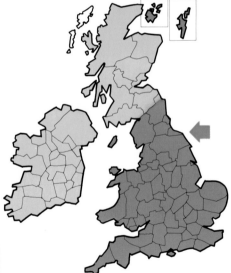

Siskin
Carduelis spinus
(Fringillidae)

12 cm (5 in)
Breeding population fluctuates,
often pairs south of normal
range, total usually in excess
of 20 000 pairs. Migrants from
east spend winter.

| J | F | M | A | M | J | J | A | S | O | N | D |

| J | F | M | A | M | J | J | A | S | O | N | D |

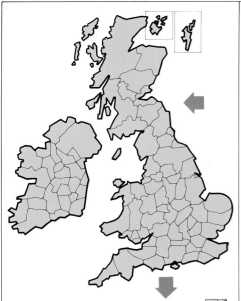

Linnet
Carduelis cannabina
(Fringillidae)

13.5 cm (5 in)
Breeding population probably in excess of 1 million pairs. Many breeding birds depart south in winter, others arrive from east.

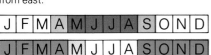

| J | F | M | A | M | J | J | A | S | O | N | D |
| J | F | M | A | M | J | J | A | S | O | N | D |

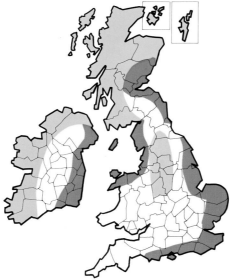

Twite
Carduelis flavirostris
(Fringillidae)

13.5 cm (5 in)
Breeding population in excess of 20 000 pairs. Movement south and towards coast in winter.

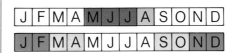

| J | F | M | A | M | J | J | A | S | O | N | D |
| J | F | M | A | M | J | J | A | S | O | N | D |

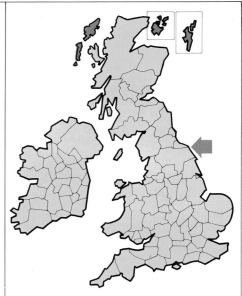

Redpoll
Carduelis flammea
(Fringillidae)

12.5 cm (5 in)
Breeding population perhaps approaching 500 000 pairs and increasing. Migrants from east spend winter.

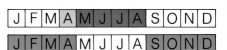

| J | F | M | A | M | J | J | A | S | O | N | D |
| J | F | M | A | M | J | J | A | S | O | N | D |

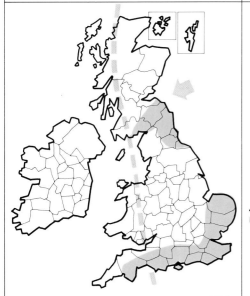

Crossbill
Loxia curvirostra
(Fringillidae)

16.5 cm (6.5 in)
Breeding population highly variable, dependent upon variable autumn invasions.

| J | F | M | A | M | J | J | A | S | O | N | D |
| J | F | M | A | M | J | J | A | S | O | N | D |

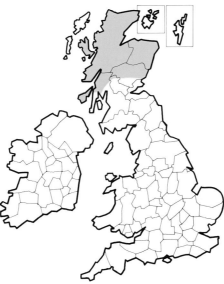

Scottish Crossbill
Loxia scotica
(Fringillidae)

17 cm (7 in)
Breeding population perhaps as high as 1000 pairs.

| J | F | M | A | M | J | J | A | S | O | N | D |
| J | F | M | A | M | J | J | A | S | O | N | D |

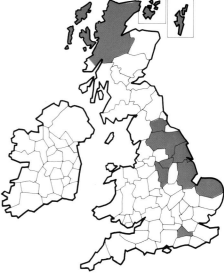

Parrot Crossbill
Loxia pytyopsittacus
(Fringillidae)

17.5 cm (7 in)
Map reflects recent 10-year period. Vagrant from north-east Europe.

| J | F | M | A | M | J | J | A | S | O | N | D |
| J | F | M | A | M | J | J | A | S | O | N | D |

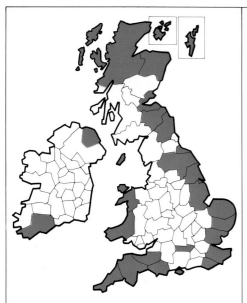

Scarlet Rosefinch
Carpodacus erythrinus
(Fringillidae)

14.5 cm (6 in)
Map reflects recent 10-year period. Vagrant from eastern Europe. As many as 50 records per year.

| J | F | M | A | M | J | J | A | S | O | N | D |
| J | F | M | A | M | J | J | A | S | O | N | D |

Bullfinch
Pyrrhula pyrrhula
(Fringillidae)

15 cm (6 in)
Breeding population in excess of 500 000 pairs.

| J | F | M | A | M | J | J | A | S | O | N | D |
| J | F | M | A | M | J | J | A | S | O | N | D |

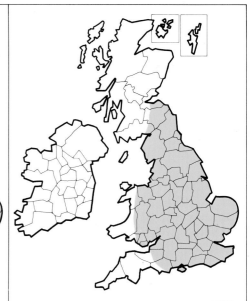

Hawfinch
Coccothraustes coccothraustes
(Fringillidae)

18 cm (7 in)
Breeding population less than 10 000 pairs, most numerous in south.

| J | F | M | A | M | J | J | A | S | O | N | D |
| J | F | M | A | M | J | J | A | S | O | N | D |

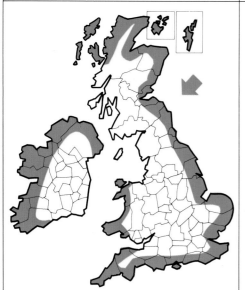

Lapland Bunting
Calcarius lapponicus
(Emberizidae)

15 cm (6 in)
Migrants from north-east spend winter, numbers vary annually. Occasional breeding records in Scotland.

| J | F | M | A | M | J | J | A | S | O | N | D |
| J | F | M | A | M | J | J | A | S | O | N | D |

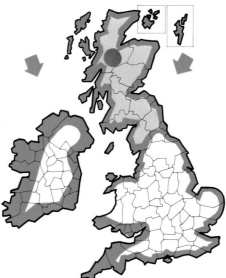

Snow Bunting
Plectrophenax nivalis
(Emberizidae)

16.5 cm (6.5 in)
In excess of 10 pairs breed annually. Migrants from north spend winter.

| J | F | M | A | M | J | J | A | S | O | N | D |
| J | F | M | A | M | J | J | A | S | O | N | D |

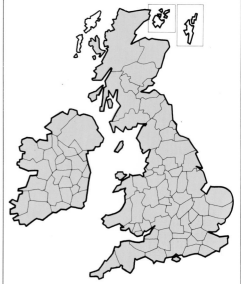

Yellowhammer
Emberiza citrinella
(Emberizidae)

16.5 cm (6.5 in)
Breeding population approximately 1 million pairs.

| J | F | M | A | M | J | J | A | S | O | N | D |
| J | F | M | A | M | J | J | A | S | O | N | D |

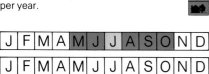
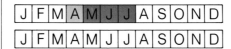

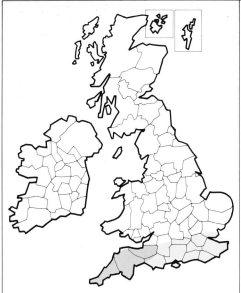

Cirl Bunting
Emberiza cirlus
(Emberizidae)

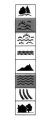

16.5 cm (6.5 in)
Breeding population perhaps
as high as 100 pairs.

J F M A M J J A S O N D
J F M A M J J A S O N D

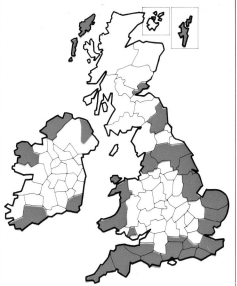

Ortolan Bunting
Emberiza hortulana
(Emberizidae)

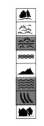

16.5 cm (6.5 in)
Regular passage migrant from
east with in excess of 50
records per year.

J F M A M J J A S O N D
J F M A M J J A S O N D

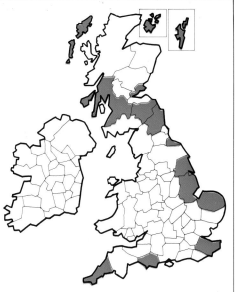

Rustic Bunting
Emberiza rustica
(Emberizidae)

14.5 cm (6 in)
Map reflects recent 10-year
period. Vagrant from north-
east Europe. Over 10 records
per year is unusual.

J F M A M J J A S O N D
J F M A M J J A S O N D

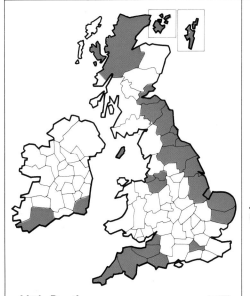

Little Bunting
Emberiza pusilla
(Emberizidae)

13.5 cm (5 in)
Map reflects recent 10-year
period. Vagrant from north-
east Europe. Over 15 records
per year is unusual.

J F M A M J J A S O N D
J F M A M J J A S O N D

Reed Bunting
Emberiza schoeniclus
(Emberizidae)

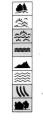

15 cm (6 in)
Breeding population in excess
of 500 000 pairs.

J F M A M J J A S O N D
J F M A M J J A S O N D

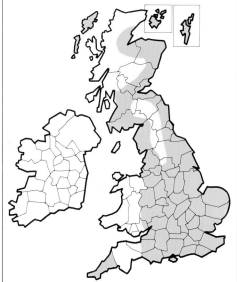

Corn Bunting
Miliaria calandra
(Emberizidae)

18 cm (7 in)
Breeding population in excess
of 10 000 pairs but perhaps
decreasing.

J F M A M J J A S O N D
J F M A M J J A S O N D

VAGRANT SPECIES

The following eighty-five species have been recorded between ten and 125 times in the twenty-five year period up to 1983. Each species is detailed as follows:

English name
Scientific name (family)
Length
Area of origin (no. records in twenty-five years up to 1983; total British records)
period mainly recorded
Habitat; region of British Isles where most likely to occur.

White-billed Diver
Gavia adamsii (Gaviidae)
80-90 cm (31-35 in)
Arctic (65, 91) January-May
Coastal; Scotland and eastern England.

Black-browed Albatross
Diomedea melanophris (Diomedeidae)
80-95 cm (31-37 in)
Southern oceans (23, 25) March-October
Coastal; northern Scotland and Ireland.

Little Shearwater
Puffinus assimilis (Procellariidae)
25-30 cm (10-12 in)
Atlantic islands (53, 58) August-October
Coastal; western Ireland.

Squacco Heron
Ardeola ralloides (Ardeidae)
45 cm (18 in)
Southern Europe (22, 118) May-July and September-October
Wetlands; southern England.

Cattle Egret
Bubulcus ibis (Ardeidae)
50 cm (20 in)
Southern Europe (31, 34) April-May and July-September
Wetlands; western Europe and southern Ireland.

Great White Heron
Egretta alba (Ardeidae)
85-100 cm (33-39 in)
South-east Europe and Asia (14, 25) May-June
Wetlands; scattered throughout Scotland, England, and Wales.

Black Stork
Ciconia nigra (Ciconiidae)
100 cm (39 in)
Eastern Europe (21, 50) May-June
Wetland and farmland; eastern Scotland and England.

Glossy Ibis
Plegadis falcinellus (Threskiornithidae)
60 cm (24 in)
South-east Europe (25, 'large numbers')
August-December
Wetlands; western Scotland, coastal England and Wales, southern Ireland.

Lesser White-fronted Goose
Anser erythropus (Anatidae)
58 cm (23 in)
North-east Europe and Siberia (64, 115)
December-March
Wetland and farmland; Gloucestershire, and other regular goose-wintering areas.

Red-breasted Goose
Branta ruficollis (Anatidae)
55 cm (22 in)
Siberia (10, 28) December-February
Coastal and farmland; southern England.

American Wigeon
Anas americana (Anatidae)
50 cm (20 in)
North America (97, 130) October-May
Coastal, wetlands, and water; south-west England and south-west Ireland.

American Black Duck
Anas rubripes (Anatidae)
59 cm (23 in)
North America (11, 12) no pattern
Wetland and water; single birds establish residence, no pattern.

Blue-winged Teal
Anas discors (Anatidae)
39 cm (15 in)
North America (89, 113) April-June and September-November
Wetland and water; throughout, no pattern.

King Eider
Somateria spectabilis (Anatidae)
56 cm (22in)
Arctic (107, 170) March-June
Coastal; Scotland and northern Ireland

Black Kite
Milvus migrans (Accipitridae)
55 cm (22 in)
South and east Europe (53, 66) April-June
Woodland, wetland, and farmland; southern England.

Gyr Falcon
Falco rusticolus (Falconidae)
50-55 cm (20-22 in)
Arctic (68, 'large numbers') March-May and November-January
Coastal and farmland; Scotland, south-west England, and Ireland.

Little Crake
Porzana parva (Rallidae)
19 cm (7.5 in)
South and east Europe (26, 95) April-May and August-November
Wetland and farmland; southern England and southern Ireland.

Little Bustard
Tetrax tetrax (Otididae)
43 cm (17 in)
Southern Europe and north Africa (10, 'over 100') October-January
Farmland; southern England.

Great Bustard
Otis tarda (Otididae)
75-100 cm (30-39 in)
Southern and eastern Europe (10, 'large numbers') December-March
Farmland; eastern England.

Black-winged Stilt
Himantopus himantopus (Recurvirostridae)
38 cm (15 in)
Southern Europe (69, 172) April-May and August-September
Wetland and water; southern England and Wales.

Collared Pratincole
Glareola pratincola (Glareolidae)
25 cm (10 in)
Southern Europe (32, 69) May-July
Wetland, farmland, and water; southern and eastern England.

Black-winged Pratincole
Glareola nordmanni (Glareolidae)
25 cm (10 in)
South-east Europe (13, 19) August-September
Farmland and wetland; south-east England.

Killdeer
Charadrius vociferus (Charadriidae)
25 cm (10 in)
North America (27, 38) November-March
Coastal and farmland; south-west England, Wales, and southern Ireland.

Lesser Golden Plover
Pluvialis dominica (Charadriidae)
25 cm (10 in)
North America (79, 91) September-October
Farmland and wetland; southern England and southern Ireland.

Sociable Plover
Chettusia gregaria (Charadriidae)
29 cm (11 in)
Asia (19, 24) no pattern
Farmland; southern England.

Semipalmated Sandpiper
Calidris pusilla (Scolopacidae)
14.5 cm (6 in)
North America (31, 35) September-October
Wetland and coastal; southern England and south-west Ireland.

Least Sandpiper
Calidris minutilla (Scolopacidae)
14 cm (5.5 in)
North America (17, 24) August-September
Wetland and water; south-west England and south-west Ireland.

Baird's Sandpiper
Calidris bairdii (Scolopacidae)
15 cm (6 in)
North America (97, 109) September-October
Water and wetlands; southern England and southern Ireland.

Sharp-tailed Sandpiper
Calidris acuminata (Scolopacidae)
18 cm (7 in)
Northern Siberia (11, 17) August-October
Wetland; no pattern.

Broad-billed Sandpiper
Limicola falcinellus (Scolopacidae)
16.5 cm (6.5 in)
North-east Europe (50, 79) May-June and August-September
Wetland; no pattern.

Stilt Sandpiper
Micropalama himantopus (Scolopacidae)
20 cm (8 in)
North America (12, 14) July-September
Wetland; south-east England and southern Ireland.

Great Snipe
Gallinago media (Scolopacidae)
28 cm (11 in)
North-east Europe (47, 229) September-October
Wetland and farmland; Shetland, south-east England, and Scilly.

Long-billed Dowitcher
Limnodromus scolopaceus (Scolopacidae)
25 cm (10 in)
North America (73, 86) September-November
Wetland and coastal; southern England and south-west Ireland.

Upland Sandpiper
Bartramia longicauda (Scolopacidae)
27 cm (11 in)
North America (20, 37) September-October
Farmland; south-west England, Wales, and southern Ireland.

Marsh Sandpiper
Tringa stagnatilis (Scolopacidae)
23 cm (9 in)
Eastern Europe and Asia (29, 45) May and July-August
Wetland; south-east England.

Greater Yellowlegs
Tringa melanoleuca (Scolopacidae)
30 cm (12 in)
North America (12, 26) July-October
Wetland; Ireland.

Solitary Sandpiper
Tringa solitaria (Scolopacidae)
20 cm (8 in)
North America (14, 21) August-September
Wetland; southern England and southern Ireland.

Terek Sandpiper
Xenus cinereus (Scolopacidae)
23 cm (9 in)
North-east Europe and Siberia (18, 22) May-June
Wetland; southern England.

Spotted Sandpiper
Actitis macularia (Scolopacidae)
20 cm (8 in)
North America (58, 69) May-June and August-November
Wetland and water; no pattern.

Laughing Gull
Larus atricilla (Laridae)
39 cm (15 in)
North America (30, 35) no pattern
Coastal and water; no pattern.

Bonaparte's Gull
Larus philadelphia (Laridae)
35 cm (14 in)
North America (31, 46) January-March and August-October
Coastal and water; southern England and Irish sea.

Ross's Gull
Rhodostethia rosea (Laridae)
32 cm (12.5 in)
Northern Siberia, Greenland, and Canada (32, 40) December-February
Coastal; Scotland and northern England.

Ivory Gull
Pagophila eburnea (Laridae)
44 cm (17.5 in)
Arctic (24, 104) November-February
Coastal, Scotland, north-east England and Ireland.

Whiskered Tern
Chlidonias hybridus (Sternidae)
25 cm (10 in)
South-east Europe (51, 79) April-June
Water; southern England.

Brünnich's Guillemot
Uria lomvia (Alcidae)
42 cm (16.5 in)
Arctic (14, 18) no pattern
Coastal; Scotland and northern England.

Great Spotted Cuckoo
Clamator glandarius (Cuculidae)
39 cm (15 in)
Southern Europe (20, 27) March-May and August
Woodland and farmland; no pattern.

Yellow-billed Cuckoo
Coccyzus americanus (Cuculidae)
30 cm (12 in)
North America (19, 41) September-November
Woodland and farmland; western Scotland, southern England, and western Ireland.

Scops Owl
Otus scops (Strigidae)
20 cm (8 in)
Southern Europe (13, 78) April-May and September-November
Woodland and farmland; southern England.

Roller
Coracias garrulus (Coraciidae)
30 cm (12 in)
South and east Europe (69, 208) May-October
Heaths, woodland, and farmland; widespread.

Red-rumped Swallow
Hirundo daurica (Hirundinidae)
18 cm (7 in)
South and east Europe (75, 85) April-May
Wetland and farmland; England and Wales.

Olive-backed Pipit
Anthus hodgsoni (Motacillidae)
14.5 cm (6 in)
Asia (25, 27) September-October
Wetland and urban; Shetland and Scilly.

Pechora Pipit
Anthus gustavi (Motacillidae)
15 cm (6 in)
Siberia (11, 23) September-October
Heaths; Shetland.

Citrine Wagtail
Motacilla citreola (Motacillidae)
16.5 cm (6.5 in)
Asia (32, 36) September-October
Wetlands and coastal; Shetland and eastern England.

Thrush Nightingale
Luscinia luscinia (Turdidae)
16.5 cm (6.5 in)
Eastern Europe (45, 52) May and September-October
Woodland; Scotland and eastern England.

Black-eared Wheatear
Oenanthe hispanica (Turdidae)
14.5 cm (6 in)
Southern Europe (20, 36) September-October
Heaths and farmland; Shetland and southern England.

Desert Wheatear
Oenanthe deserti (Turdidae)
14.5 cm (6 in)
North Africa (10, 21) no pattern
Coastal and farmland; eastern England.

Rock Thrush
Monticola saxatilis (Turdidae)
19 cm (7 in)
Central and southern Europe (10, 16) May-June
Coastal and farmland; no pattern.

White's Thrush
Zoothera dauma (Turdidae)
27 cm (11 in)
Siberia (10, 39) November
Farmland; no pattern.

Gray-cheeked Thrush
Catharus minimus (Turdidae)
16 cm (6 in)
North America (15, 17) October-November
Woodland; northern Scotland, Wales, south-west England, and Ireland.

Black-throated Thrush
Turdus ruficollis (Turdidae)
23 cm (9 in)
Asia (10, 13) October
Farmland; no pattern.

American Robin
Turdus migratorius (Turdidae)
25 cm (10 in)
North America (15, 27) November-February
Farmland; northern Scotland, south-west England, and Ireland.

Lanceolated Warbler
Locustella lanceolata (Sylviidae)
11.5 cm (4.5 in)
Asia (22, 31) September-October
Coastal; Shetland.

Great Reed Warbler
Acrocephalus arundinaceus (Sylviidae)
19 cm (7 in)
Europe (107, 130) May-June
Wetland; southern England.

Olivaceous Warbler
Hippolais pallida (Sylviidae)
13.5 cm (5 in)
Southern Europe (10, 12) September-October
Woodland; southern England.

Booted Warbler
Hippolatis caligata (Sylviidae)
11.5 cm (4.5 in)
Asia (16, 17) September
Woodland; Shetland and southern England.

Subalpine Warbler
Sylvia cantillans (Sylviidae)
12 cm (5 in)
Southern Europe (96, 119) April-June
Woodland; coastal counties, no pattern.

Sardinian Warbler
Sylvia melanocephala (Sylviidae)
13.5 cm (5 in)
Southern Europe (11, 12) April-May
Woodland; eastern England.

Arctic Warbler
Phylloscopus borealis (Sylviidae)
12 cm (5 in)
Northern Scandinavia and Siberia (106, 128) August-October
Woodland; Shetland, eastern Scotland, and eastern England.

Radde's Warbler
Phylloscopus schwarzi (Sylviidae)
12.5 cm (5 in)
Asia (43, 44) October
Woodland; eastern Scotland and eastern England.

Dusky Warbler
Phylloscopus fuscatus (Sylviidae)
12.5 cm (5 in)
Asia (37, 39) October-November
Woodland; eastern England.

Bonelli's Warbler
Phylloscopus bonelli (Sylviidae)
11.5 cm (4.5 in)
Central and southern Europe (73, 79) August-October
Woodland; England, Wales, and southern Ireland.

Isabelline Shrike
Lanius isabellinus (Laniidae)
17 cm (7 in)
Southern Asia (16, 17) October-November
Heath and woodland; eastern England.

Lesser Grey Shrike
Lanius minor (Laniidae)
20 cm (8 in)
South and east Europe (88, 121) May-June and September-October
Woodland and farmland; Shetland, southern and eastern England.

Red-eyed Vireo
Vireo olivaceus (Vireonidae)
16 cm (6 in)
North America (18, 21) October
Woodland; south-west England, western Wales, and southern Ireland.

Arctic Redpoll
Carduelis hornemanni (Fringillidae)
13 cm (5 in)
Arctic (62, 92) October-February
Heath, woodland, and farmland; eastern Scotland and eastern England.

Two-barred Crossbill
Loxia leucoptera (Fringillidae)
14.5 cm (6 in)
Northern Europe and Asia (23, 64) July-February
Heath and woodland; Scotland, northern, and eastern England.

Yellow-rumped Warbler
Dendroica coronata (Parulidae)
14 cm (5.5 in)
North America (10, 11) October
Woodland and farmland; south-west England.

Blackpoll Warbler
Dendroica striata (Parulidae)
14 cm (5.5 in)
North America (17, 18) October
Woodland and farmland; south-west England.

White-throated Sparrow
Zonotrichia albicollis (Emberizidae)
17 cm (7 in)
North America (11, 13) April-June
Woodland and farmland; coastal counties, no pattern.

Dark-eyed Junco
Junco hyemalis (Emberizidae)
16 cm (6 in)
North America (11, 12) May
Woodland and urban; Shetland and southern England.

Yellow-breasted Bunting
Emberiza aureola (Emberizidae)
14 cm (5.5 in)
North-east Europe and northern Asia (92, 111) September-October
Heath and farmland; Shetland, east and south-west England.

Black-headed Bunting
Emberiza melanocephala (Emberizidae)
16.5 cm (6.5 in)
South-east Europe (49, 54) May-June
Heath, woodland, and farmland; coastal counties, no pattern.

Rose-breasted Grosbeak
Pheucticus ludovicianus (Emberizidae)
21 cm (8 in)
North America (13, 14) October
Woodland and farmland; south-west England, west Wales, and southern Ireland.

RARE SPECIES

List of thirty-six 'rare species' recorded in the British Isles between five and nine times in the twenty-five-year period 1958-83. There are a further seventy-seven species recorded on less than five occasions in that twenty-five-year period, plus of course others that have not been recorded since before 1958.

Bobolink
Dolichonyx oryzivorus (Icteridae)
18 cm (7 in)
North America (10, 10) October
Farmland; Scilly and southern Ireland.

Northern Oriole
Icterus galbula (Icteridae)
19 cm (7 in)
North America (13, 14) October
Woodland; south-west England.

Pied-billed Grebe
Podilymbus podiceps

Wilson's Petrel
Oceanites oceanicus

American Bittern
Botaurus lentiginosus

Steller's Eider
Polysticta stelleri

White-tailed Eagle
Haliaeetus albicilla

Sora
Porzana carolina

Baillon's Crake
Porzana pusilla

Cream-coloured Courser
Cursorius cursor

Greater Sand Plover
Charadrius leschenaultii

Franklin's Gull
Larus pipixcan

Bridled Tern
Sterna anaethetus

Sooty Tern
Sterna fuscata

Rufous Turtle Dove
Streptopelia orientalis

Black-billed Cuckoo
Coccyzus erythrophthalmus

Tengmalm's Owl
Aegolius funereus

Common Nighthawk
Chordeiles minor

Little Swift
Apus affinis

Lesser Short-toed Lark
Calandrella rufescens

Crested Lark
Galerida cristata

Alpine Accentor
Prunella collaris

Rufous Bush Robin
Cercotrichas galactotes

Red-flanked Bluetail
Tarsiger cyanurus

Pied Wheatear
Oenanthe pleschanka

Swainson's Thrush
Catharus ustulatus

Eye-browed Thrush
Turdus obscurus

Dusky Thrush
Turdus naumanni

River Warbler
Locustella fluviatilis

Paddyfield Warbler
Acrocephalus agricola

Collared Flycatcher
Ficedula albicollis

Short-toed Treecreeper
Certhia brachydactyla

Penduline Tit
Remiz pendulinus

Black-and-White Warbler
Mniotilta varia

Northern Parula
Parula americana

American Redstart
Setophaga ruticilla

Song Sparrow
Zonotrichia melodia

Pine Bunting
Emberiza leucocephalos

DEVON AND CORNWALL

CORNWALL

Cornwall is situated at the south-west corner of England. It is a county that, in the last twenty years, has attracted the attention of thousands of birdwatchers, especially during the annual pilgrimage to the Isles of Scilly. In the 1950s, a group of dedicated birders established a regular programme of watching the migration through the islands and began to record a small number of rare visitors. In particular, they noted North American species that had either been blown across the Atlantic in a series of weather depressions or, more likely, had landed on board an east-bound ship somewhere off the east coast of North America and survived the journey to depart at the first land sighted. These days, the Isles of Scilly, with their large numbers of birders, contribute a steady stream of rare and unusual birds in a profusion that is probably only paralleled by the north Norfolk coast on Fair Isle in the Shetlands. Increasingly, it is being discovered that the Cornish mainland can be equally productive for rare birds. This mainland provides a wealth of habitats, ranging from nearly 250 miles of coastline, much of it rocky and exposed, via the more sheltered estuaries, to artificial reservoirs, and expanses of moorland to extensive woods. Cornwall plays an important part in British ornithology when much of the remainder of the country is frozen in cold winters, for here the milder Atlantic climate keeps areas of water free from ice, and estuaries open. At these times, hundreds-of-thousands of birds can move into the county. By the end of 1983, 425 species had been recorded in Cornwall, including some sixty of North American origin.

Birdwatching sites

ISLES OF SCILLY

Five inhabited islands, together with a collection of hundreds of rocks and islets, make up what is now a famous birdwatching locality. Access is by sea or air from Penzance and the erstwhile 'flower-and-tourist' islands are now invaded annually by hundreds, probably thousands of birdwatchers, the majority seeking the rare and unusual in late autumn when the islands can boast an impressive list of exotic species. Breeding seabirds, notably Storm Petrel and Roseate Tern, occur in nationally important numbers with Puffin and Manx Shearwater in sizeable colonies. These birds are all found on the smaller uninhabited islands where their security is asssured by the controlled access of the Nature Conservancy Council which has a management agreement with the Duchy of Cornwall Estate, the owner of the islands. Geographically, the islands are situated perfectly to receive visits by a wide range of migrant species, together with seabirds and shore birds in abundance throughout the year.

PORTHGWARRA – LAND'S END (OS SW367216)

This area is almost as rewarding as the Isles of Scilly, and does not necessitate a boat or air journey to reach it. It comprises an exposed area of coast in the very south-west corner of Britain and it is a site which can boast an impressive list of rare birds, as well as some exciting possibilities for watching seabirds. The days following severe south-westerly gales are likely to produce the largest numbers of

seabirds blown close inshore and, in late autumn, these can include Great and Sooty Shearwaters together with the Balearic Shearwater (the Mediterranean race of the more familiar Manx). Passing skuas can include both Great and Arctic, as well as the rarer (and more difficult to identify), Pomarine. For land birds, spring and autumn migrants can be extremely abundant following a night of heavy cloud and rain, especially if the wind is from the south.

MARAZION MARSH (OS SW510313)

This is the site of the largest reedbed in Cornwall although it is still small by east-coast standards. The area is now the home for the recently arrived Cetti's Warbler, and also provides a base for species, such as Bittern and Snipe, in cold winters when they are forced to leave more regular sites to the east. Other arrivals from the east can include the Bearded Tit and a small but regular number of various wildfowl, including some notable counts of Shoveler. In March each year, this is an excellent site in which to search for the earliest-arriving summer migrants, the Sand Martins, Wheatears, and Redstarts.

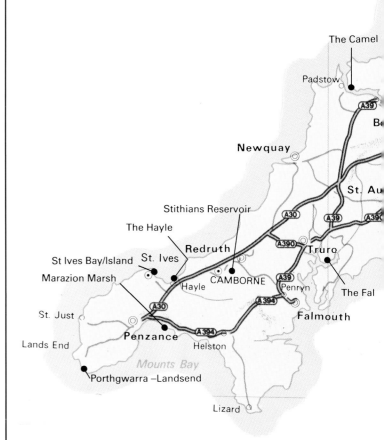

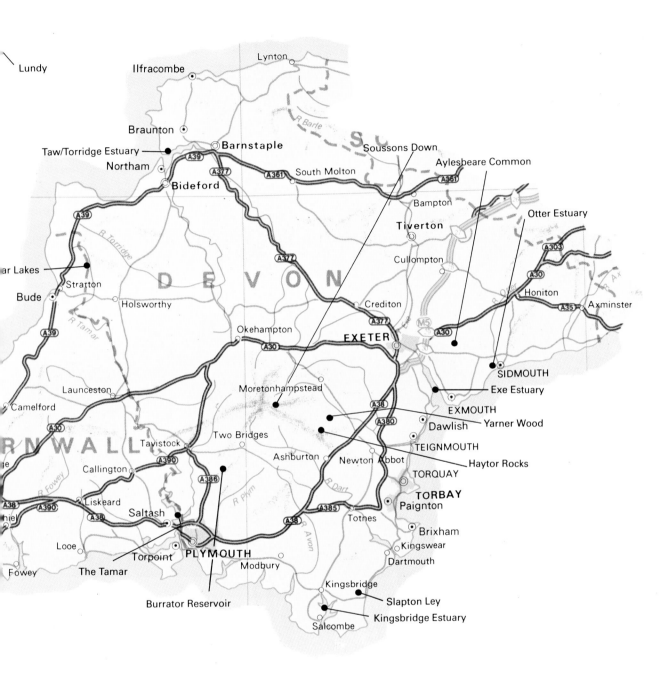

STITHIANS RESERVOIR (OS SW714364)

This is an autumn and winter site for the birdwatcher – an exposed, shallow reservoir (the largest area of open fresh water in Cornwall) with muddy margins and no major disturbance. From late summer onwards, large numbers of waders, including many rarities, are to be found, and, among the flock of regularly occurring Golden Plover, the rarer North American Lesser Golden Plover is an almost annual visitor.

ST IVES BAY/ISLAND (OS SW521411)

The reputation of St Ives Bay has been justly earned for sightings of seabirds following severe autumn storms when species normally to be encountered far out to sea are blown inshore and become 'trapped' in the bay. Enthusiastic seabird watchers have become expert in the most suitable weather conditions and will travel great distances to be on 'the island' when striking movements of tens-of-thousands of shearwaters, gannets, skuas, and so on can be witnessed. On one lucky day, observers at this site added the South Polar Skua to the British list.

CORNISH ESTUARIES

To the birds, the estuaries of the south-west are of extreme importance in the severest of winters when much of Britain becomes frozen and the birds are forced to move to the milder climate. There is interest at other times, however; for, within a county that has a predominantly rocky coastline, the low land and mud that surround the river mouths provide a unique habitat.

Hayle (OS SW546365) is a relatively small, highly industrialized estuary that holds no nationally important bird populations. For the birdwatcher, however, it is one of the most easily accessible estuaries. The main road runs beside the tidal mud and, at the south end of the estuary, is a public observation hide provided by the RSPB. Wigeon and Golden Plover occur in good numbers and there is an excellent list of rare species – probably a reflection of the large numbers of birders that stop here on their way to the Isles of Scilly!

The Fal (OS SW8440) estuary is a complex of rivers near Falmouth that provides a wide variety of tidal mud and a wintering site for nationally important populations of Black-tailed Godwit, Curlew, Spotted Redshank, and Greenshank. Three species of diver and five of grebe can be encountered while, in late spring, the occasional Little Egret or Spoonbill is not unusual.

The Camel (OS SW920770) estuary is the largest on the north coast of Cornwall and includes tidal mud and grass meadows. This is one of the few sites in the county where White-fronted Geese winter regularly. Nationally important numbers of Golden Plover and Curlew occur, and small numbers of wild swans, rarer geese, and waders, such as Little Stint, are also features of winter. The Cornwall Birdwatching and Preservation Society has two hides on the site.

The Tamar (OS SX4360) estuary forms the boundary between Cornwall and Devon and is one of the most important and productive of the south-west estuaries. It is nationally important for a range of wintering species including Wigeon, Golden Plover, Dunlin, and Redshank – all of which occur in populations totalling several thousands. Probably this estuary is best known for its traditional and increasing wintering population of Avocets which migrate here from their East Anglian nesting sites. Migrant waders, including some of the rarer North American species, are a feature of the site.

Organizations in Cornwall
Cornwall Birdwatching and Preservation Society (CBWPS), 39 Fairfield Road, Bude
Cornwall Trust for Nature Conservation (CTNC), Dairy Cottage, Trelissick, Feock, Truro TR3 6QL
RSPB Members' Groups based at: 'North Cornwall' and 'Cornwall (except north)' (details from RSPB, The Lodge, Sandy, Beds SG19 2DL)

Annual reports
'Birds in Cornwall' 5 Newquay Road, St Coumb Major TR9 6RW
'Isles of Scilly Bird Report' 4 Pentlands Flats, St Marys, Isles of Scilly TR21 0HY

Books
Hunt, D. *A Guide to Birdwatching in the Isles of Scilly*. J Sanders, 1978.
Norman, D & Tucker, V. *Where to Watch Birds in Devon and Cornwall*. Croom Helm, 1984.
Penhallurick, R D. *Birds of the Cornish Coast*. Bradford Barton, 1969.
Penhallurick, R D. *The Birds of Cornwall and the Isles of Scilly*. Headland Publications, 1978.

The discovery of two old Cornish records
The first British record of a **Blue-cheeked Bee-eater** was of a bird seen at St Agnes on the Isles of Scilly on 22 June 1951, and this Middle Eastern species has not been recorded in the British Isles since. It was to remain as the first and only British record for a further ten years, however, and then become the second. In 1962, the collection of stuffed birds in the Tresco Abbey Museum on the islands was being closely examined and there (labelled as a bee-eater) was a Blue-cheeked Bee-eater that had been shot on St Marys, Isles of Scilly on 13 July 1921 – some thirty years earlier than the St Agnes bird. Thus this was the first of two British records although it had to wait more than forty years to be revealed.
A **Green-backed Heron** that was shot by a gamekeeper near St Austell on 27 October 1889 had to wait over eighty years before becoming the first to be recorded in Britain. Its credentials were not thought to be genuine until 1972. The specimen is now in the Truro museum.

Some firsts from the Isles of Scilly
With justification, the islands are accepted as an excellent part of Britain to discover and watch rare birds. Here is a list of species recorded for the first time in the British Isles, all on the Isles of Scilly and all in recent years.
Northern Waterthrush (North America), September/October 1958
American Purple Gallinule (North America), November 1958
Bobolink (North America), September 1962
Parula Warbler (North America), October 1966
Blackpoll Warbler (North America), October 1968
Hooded Warbler (North America), September 1970
Scarlet Tanager (North America), October 1970
Yellow-bellied Sapsucker (North America), September/October 1975
Semipalmated Plover (North America), October/November 1978
Magnolia Warbler (North America), September 1981
Green Warbler (Asia), September/October 1983
Cliff Swallow (North America), October 1983

The 'Cornish' Chough
The Chough has a close association with the county of Cornwall; indeed, many early writers believed that it was the only site where the species could be found although, in truth, it occurred and still does, on much of the rocky Atlantic seaboard of western Europe. As a result of this close association, the bird featured on many Cornish designs and insignia. Undoubtedly, it was once very common in the county but its numbers declined throughout the 1800s and into the 1900s. It was lost completely from the south coast and from Land's End by 1900, although a few pairs remained at traditional sites on the north coast until the very last of the 'Cornish' Choughs died in 1973. Once, it was a bird that had been kept as a pet throughout Cornwall to the extent that, at the end of the eighteenth century, it was reported that it was very common to see tame birds in many gardens. And, now, sadly, the 'Cornish' Chough has disappeared from Cornwall.
So much a feature of the county's past, the Chough was given many local names: Cornish Daw; Cornish Kae; Killigrew; Palores; Cornish Jack; Hermit Crow; Market Jew Crow; Tshau-ha.

The Isles of Scilly are perfectly situated for visiting migrants.

DEVON

Devon is the only English county with a split coastline – along the Bristol and English Channels. Generally, Devon is dominated by the large central granite block of Dartmoor, and the other upland mass of Exmoor spreads across the Somerset border in the north. Although it is perhaps over-shadowed ornithologically by Cornwall, its western neighbour, the county has much variety and includes such birdwatching meccas as the island of Lundy or some of the exciting rivers and estuaries which break up the rocky coastline. The sheer cliffs and wilderness of the northern coast contrast with the gentler, more developed coastline of the south. Areas of natural fresh water are scarce, but increasing demands for water supplies have led to an extensive network of reservoirs, particularly on the higher ground among the open country of Exmoor and Dartmoor. Still possessing some excellent woodland, Devon's river valleys boast splendid oakwoods while, increasingly, upland sites are being planted with conifers.

Birdwatching sites

DARTMOOR NATIONAL PARK

The exposed moorland is home for a limited number of species that can live among the sparse vegetation of the windswept open mass of granite with its heather and gorse. Dartmoor consists of nearly 400 square miles where the Red Grouse survives in small numbers and can be seen throughout the year. Most birds are only present in the summer months and include Ring Ouzel, Wheatear, and Whinchat, together with the more familiar Meadow Pipit and Skylark which are all widespread. The upland reservoirs, with the associated streams and rivers, attract Grey Wagtail and Dipper, and, in the winter months, Goosander.

Yarner Wood (OS SX780788) A National Nature Reserve wardened by the Nature Conservancy Council, this mixed woodland site is dominated by oaks. A wealth of summer bird life can be seen and heard from the pathways through the woodland. Good numbers of warblers nest, and, each summer, Redstart, Pied Flycatcher, and Wood Warbler are all abundant, the former two making use of the nestboxes provided. On the surrounding open country, Nightjar, Grasshopper Warbler, and Ring Ouzel can be found. Birds are few in the winter months.

Haytor Rocks (OS SX758770) is more of a view point than a place to walk and search for birds. Circling Buzzards are very much a feature while, in the winter months, a Hen Harrier or Merlin may hunt nearby. It is worth looking out for early spring migrants, particularly Ring Ouzel or Wheatear, while Ravens can be seen at all times of the year.

Soussons Down (OS SX6779) consists of open hillsides with their associated views of woodland and forestry. For the birdwatcher, the site is probably most productive in the winter evenings when the roosting species begin to congregate. Fieldfare and Redwing, sometimes accompanied by large numbers of Starlings, often harried by a hunting Merlin, are all regular features. Wintering Hen Harrier and Short-eared Owl are not uncommon and, in some years, a Great Grey Shrike will set up a winter territory. There are Resident Buzzard, Raven, and Dipper.

Burrator Reservoir (OS SX555685), like many upland areas of water surrounded by steep rocky sides, attracts relatively small numbers of birds. In the winter months, the

The Taw-Torridge estuary provides a site for gatherings of waders.

highlight is the Goosander flock which may be seen throughout the day, although additional birds flight in at dusk. At this time of the day, the surrounding woodland can also be productive, with Woodcock, and Tawny and Barn Owls. In summer, there is little to be seen on the water but the woods hold interesting populations of Redstart, Tree Pipit, and woodpeckers.

SLAPTON LEY (OS SX823421)

This is one of the best-known Devon birdwatching sites. A successful field study centre provides accommodation for many residential courses on all aspects of the natural history of the area, while the Devon Birdwatching and

Organizations in Devon

Devon Birdwatching and Preservation Society (DBWPS), 14 Parkers Way, Bridgetown, Totnes TQ9 5UF

Devon Trust for Nature Conservation (DTNC), 35 New Bridge Street, Exeter EX4 3AH

RSPB Members' Groups based at: Exeter, North Devon, Plymouth, and South Devon (details from RSPB, The Lodge, Sandy, Beds SG19 2DL)

Annual reports

'Devon Bird Report' Brook Cottage, Sampford Spiney, Yelverton, Devon

'Lundy Field Society Annual Report' 26 High Street, Spetisbury, Blandford, Dorset

Books

Dymond, J N. *The Birds of Lundy.* Devon Birdwatching and Preservation Society, 1980.

Moore, R. *The Birds of Devon.* David & Charles, 1969.

Norman, D and Tucker, V. *Where to Watch Birds in Devon and Cornwall.* Croom Helm, 1984.

Peak wader counts on Devon estuaries

Some recent peak winter counts of waders from all Devon estuaries:

Oystercatcher	5750
Ringed Plover	1230
Golden Plover	3050
Grey Plover	475
Dunlin	9250
Black-tailed Godwit	800
Bar-tailed Godwit	615
Curlew	3185
Redshank	1935
Turnstone	460

Some firsts from Lundy

Species recorded for the first time in the British Isles that were found on the island of Lundy:

American Robin (North America), October/ November 1952

Yellowthroat (North America), November 1954

Sardinian Warbler (southern Europe), May 1955

Northern Oriole (North America), October 1958

Bimaculated Lark (Middle East), May 1962

Rufous-sided Towhee (North America), June 1966

Spanish Sparrow (southern Europe), June 1966

Devon ringing recoveries

Siskin: ringed Exmouth, Devon, March 1981; caught Rostov, Russia, November 1981.

Greylag Goose: ringed Slonsk, Poland, June 1980; found dead Paignton, Devon, November 1980.

Mandarin: ringed Guernsey, July 1980; found dead Ottery St Mary, Devon, December 1980.

Swallow: ringed Blaxton, Devon, July 1980; found dead Cape, South Africa, December 1980.

Fieldfare: ringed Cullompton, Devon, February 1982; found dead Vaasa, Finland, August 1982.

Cirl bunting ♀ ♂

Preservation Society is closely involved with a ringing programme as part of a bird migration study at the site. A freshwater lagoon fringed with reeds and sallow bushes, separated from the coast of Start Bay by a narrow strip of beach, is bound to be productive for birds. In the winter months, large numbers of ducks, grebes, and occasionally divers occur, especially if severe weather forces them to leave the open sea for more sheltered waters. Slapton is, however, a site for all-year-round birdwatching with an impressive list of breeding, wintering, migrating, and vagrant species. Recent colonists include the Cetti's Warbler with the rarer Savi's Warbler occurring in some years. The sheltered situation attracts wintering warblers and Firecrest, while suitable weather conditions can bring vagrants from almost every corner of the globe, ranging from Ring-necked Duck and Ring-billed Gull from North America to Purple Heron and Little Bittern from southern Europe. Not far to the south of Slapton are Start Point and Prawle Point, two areas noted for their migrant birds, and sites likely to hold an interesting selection of seabirds offshore in the late autumn.

AYLESBEARE COMMON (OS SY057898)
The RSPB reserve on Aylesbeare and Harpford Common forms part of what remains of the Woodbury Pebblebed Commons that are now so fragmented. Birds are few in the winter months but the wet and dry heaths, with their associated clumps of conifer trees, can provide excellent summer birdwatching for those specialist heathland species. This is one of the few sites in Devon where the Dartford Warbler nests, although the strength of the population is very dependent upon the severity of the preceeding winter. Nightjar, Curlew, Tree Pipit, and Stonechat all nest, while Buzzard and Hobby are seen regularly, with occasional pairs nesting in the area. May and June are the ideal months for birdwatching here.

TAMAR LAKES (OS SS295110 and 287210)
Close to the Tamar estuary and the border with Cornwall, these lakes form part of an important complex of tidal mud, riverine habitat, and estuary. Most interesting for the flocks of migrant and wintering waders, the sheltered position of the two tidal 'lakes' results in concentrations of birds at times of gale and storm. Similarly, these conditions will often result in the occurrence of several marine birds on the lakes; species such as divers, grebes, and Brent Geese. Wildfowl occur in good numbers and wintering Peregrine are often present to prey on these and on the congregations of waders.

LUNDY
Although there is no longer a bird observatory operating on the island, Lundy, off the North Devon coast and sitting in the entrance to the Bristol Channel, is a familiar name in British ornithology. For some twenty-five years, regular recording of the bird migration through the island was undertaken by a series of resident ornithologists, and an impressive list of bird species was completed. Over 270 species of birds have been recorded on this largely barren granite island which is a mere 3 miles in length by half-a-mile in width. The small amount of habitation, cultivation, gardens, and ponds provides the attraction to many of the birds which make probably an unscheduled stop on the island. Breeding seabirds include Fulmar, Manx Shearwater, and Shag. The Gannet formerly bred but has not done so since 1903, while the Puffin, very much the symbol of Lundy, has declined dramatically. A crossing to the island by boat from the port at Ilfracombe or now, Bideford, will often produce some interesting views of seabirds, including the possibility of Leach's and Storm Petrels, but, to coincide with large numbers of arrivals or the occasional rare bird on the island is a very chancy business. As with so many birding localities where the interest is centred upon the migrants, the visiting birdwatcher is entirely dependent upon the prevailing weather.

DEVON ESTUARIES
As in the case of the neighbouring county of Cornwall, the estuaries of Devon contrast with the rocky coastline and provide a wintering ground for large numbers of waders and wildfowl. Numbers vary annually with the severity of weather in northern and eastern England.

Kingsbridge (OS SX745415) Several extensive creeks combine to form this large south-coast estuary. Large numbers of Wigeon and Golden Plover occur but no populations of national importance are recorded.

Exe (OS SX9881) This extensive site, with its associated marshes, is probably the most important of the Devon estuaries. The mouth of the river is bounded by a shingle and dune system that has become well known for its migrant birds, and some thirteen species of wintering wildfowl and wader occur in nationally important numbers – three of which, the Wigeon, Ringed Plover, and Black-tailed Godwit, are present at internationally important levels. This is one of the main wintering sites for the British breeding Avocets with well over 100 present in most winters.

Otter (OS SY075821) This is one of the smaller estuaries, but it is surrounded by some excellent birdwatching country that regularly produces views of Kingfisher, Heron, and woodpeckers. Because the estuary is so narrow, the birds suffer considerable disturbance, but high-tide roosts of waders in mid-winter are worth observing.

Taw-Torridge (OS SS465315) This extensive estuarine system is the only major example of this habitat on the north coast. In addition to the estuarine mud, the flanking sands are the site of an internationally important gathering of Sanderling, while other populations of note include Oystercatcher, Ringed Plover, Golden Plover, and Curlew. Red-breasted Merganser, Eider, Common Scoter, and the occasional Scaup all appear in the river mouth. On the north shore is Braunton Burrows National Nature Reserve administered by the Nature Conservancy Council.

SOMERSET AND AVON

SOMERSET

Largely a rural county, Somerset consists of a rich alluvial
central plain drained by the rivers Axe and Parrett flowing
northwards into the Bristol Channel at Bridgwater Bay – the
entrance to the Severn estuary. To the north, the plain is
bounded by the Mendip Hills and, to the south and west,
by the Blackdown Hills and the Quantocks. In the extreme
west is the highest point in the county, the 518-metre (1705-
foot) peak of Dunkery Beacon in the Exmoor National Park.
The habitat in the county lacks variety; natural woodland is
in short supply, and, although pastures are decreasing,
agriculture is still primarily grazing with relatively small
meadows. Bird populations have been seriously affected by
the loss of marginal land, improved drainage,
and by the rapid disappearance of old orchards that
once held numerous nesting sites and produced the famous Somerset cider.

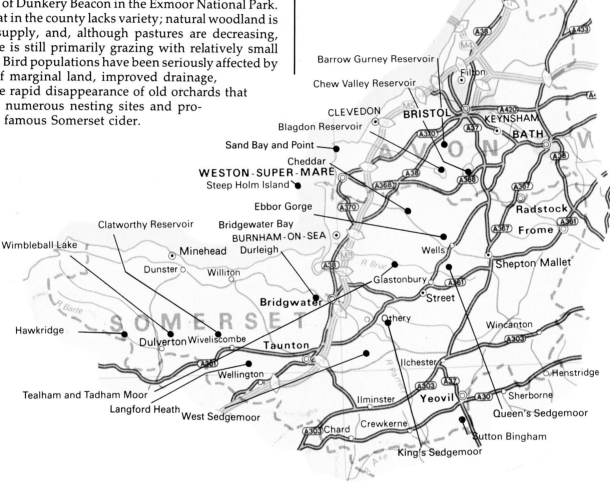

Birdwatching sites

BRIDGWATER BAY

Stretching from Weston-super-Mare to Minehead, the bay
forms the outer limits of the Severn estuary, and contains
some major wader roosts and vast concentrations of
wildfowl. Among the latter, nearly 3000 moulting Shelduck
in late summer make this site unique while, in midwinter,
more than 2000 Wigeon and up to 100 Shoveler demonstrate
that the area is of national importance. Most interesting
among the waders is the spring concentration of Whimbrel
and the autumn gathering of Black-tailed Godwit. The most
productive birdwatching is at the Parrett estuary on a rising
tide when the birds congregate on the mud and excavated
pools, both of which are overlooked by hides on the Nature
Conservancy Council reserve.

SOMERSET LEVELS

Although the levels or moors of central Somerset are in-
dividually named, they collectively comprise one of the

largest areas of low-lying ground in England. Seasonal
flooding is now less likely to occur as improved drainage
with pump-operated schemes have significantly lowered
the water levels on some sites, allowing arable farming to
replace the more traditional pastures with their summer
grazing and winter abandonment to floods and birds.

In other areas commercial peat extraction has resulted
in the loss of grassland but a replacement with pools may
have some value for bird life. Various areas on the levels
have been made reserves by the Royal Society for the
Protection of Birds (West Sedgemoor) and Somerset Trust
for Nature Conservation (Tealham Moor). The Nature Conservancy Council is also closely involved in the area.

All the different moors are readily visible from the
boundary roads or the droves/trackways that criss-cross
the site. The numbers of birds breeding, wintering, or
migrating, are very dependent upon the amount of flooding and the persistence with which the water remains.
Common nesting waders are Lapwing, Redshank, Snipe,
and Curlew, with a few pairs of Black-tailed Godwit on

West Sedgemoor. Wintering species may include up to 30000 Wigeon, over 1000 Golden Plover, and up to 8000 Dunlin. In summer, Whinchat and Yellow Wagtail abound, with flocks of Whimbrel a feature of all the moors in May.

The surrounding woodlands should not be overlooked for they contain nesting Buzzard, Hobby, and Sparrowhawk, as well as Grey Heron and a wide range of other woodland species. Woodland visiting is possible by the RSPB reserve at **West Sedgemoor** (OS ST361238). Other levels that should be visited are **King's Sedgemoor** (ST410335), **Queen's Sedgemoor** (ST530410), and **Tealham** and **Tadham Moor** (ST410445).

EBBOR GORGE (OS ST523485)

This is a scenically spectacular National Nature Reserve run by the Nature Conservancy Council and set in the Mendip Hills. The gorge is best visited in the spring and early summer when the maximum bird song can be heard and all of the visiting summer migrants have arrived. As well as containing many typical western woodland species, during dusk in early June you should find roding Woodcock, hooting Tawny Owl, and singing Grasshopper Warbler, and there is even a chance of glimpsing a fox or badger. A series of paths and nature trails leads from the reserve car park.

The birds on the Somerset levels depend upon the water which persists.

LANGFORD HEATH (OS ST100236)

This is a small, wet heathland reserve of the Somerset Trust for Nature Conservation containing areas of scrub and mature dry woodland. A nature trail passes through the variety of habitats, and on a summer visit, one might encounter such migrant species as Hobby, Tree Pipit, and Nightingale.

EXMOOR

Situated in the north-west of the county and stretching across the Devon border, the Exmoor National Park covers over 250 square miles of woodland and high moorland with fertile valleys and fast-flowing streams. In the north, the park reaches to the Somerset coast where the steep cliffs support seabird colonies on the Devon side of the border, but Fulmars colonized within the county near Glenthorne in the late 1970s.

Very much a feature of Exmoor is the Buzzard; its mewing cry can be heard throughout the park, and this bird is just one of the 250 or so species recorded within the boundary. Of these, over 110 species nest and a further fifty or so are regular in winter or on migration.

Wimbleball Lake (OS SS968307) is a reserve of the Somerset Trust for Nature Conservation and is a site for wintering wildfowl, particularly Mallard and Wigeon. The

Organizations in Somerset

Somerset Ornithological Society (SOS), 109 Highbridge Road, Burnham-on-Sea
Somerset Trust for Nature Conservation (STNC), Fyne Court, Broomfield, Bridgwater TA5 2EQ
RSPB Members' Groups based in Crewkerne and Taunton (details from RSPB, The Lodge, Sandy, Beds SG19 2DL)

Annual reports

'Somerset Birds' Barnfield, Tower Hill Road, Crewkerne TA18 8BJ
'Exmoor Naturalist' 12 King George Road, Minehead TA24 5JD

Books

Allen, N V. *The Birds of Exmoor.* Exmoor Press, 1971.
Palmer, E M and Ballance, D K. *The Birds of Somerset.* Longman, 1968.

Ancient bird records from Somerset

The Mendip Hills, with their caves and caverns, have supplied a surprising array of bird remains from the Pleistocene Epoch (up to 400 000 years ago). Many of these species can no longer be expected in Somerset, but their occurrence at that time gives some clues as to bird distribution before the ice ages:
Dalmatian Pelican *Pelecanus crispus* at Glastonbury
Golden Eagle *Aquila chrysaetos* at Burrington
White-tailed Eagle *Haliaeetus albicilla* at Meare Lake
Ptarmigan *Lagopus mutus* at Cheddar

Crane *Grus grus* at Glastonbury
Eagle Owl *Bubo bubo* at Chelm's Combe
Richard's Pipit *Anthus novaeseelandiae* at Burrington

Wallcreepers in Somerset

Surprisingly, for a species so rare in Britain that it has only been recorded on nine occasions, the **Wallcreeper,** *Tichodroma muraria*, a spectacular non-migratory bird from the mountains of southern Europe, has appeared in Somerset on three separate occasions. The two records in the 1970s, however, probably refer to the same individual returning to a suitable wintering ground. The first was at Mells in September 1901 but, in early November 1976, a bird was discovered in rocky, mountain-like habitat near Cheddar and remained throughout the winter until it was seen for the last time on 6 April 1977. In November of that year, the bird was back, this time staying until 9 April 1978. There have been no British records since that date.

Grouse survive on Exmoor?

The **Red Grouse** is not a native of Somerset, but unsuccessful attempts were made to introduce the species on to Exmoor in the 1820s. Further releases in 1961, however, were more successful and the species became established and spread throughout the heather moorland with a maximum population of unknown numbers in about 1940. For reasons not known, there followed a quite dramatic decline, and the present population is extremely small. Although a few birds are recorded every year, proven breeding is a very rare event.

In contrast, the **Black Grouse** is a native of the county and, at one time, was very common throughout the marginal lands of many of Somerset's uplands. In the second half of the nineteenth century over 4000 were shot on one estate alone, with as many as 200 in a single year. Since the early years of the twentieth century, the species has undergone a marked decline and there are now just a few birds confined to Exmoor. If hand-reared birds had not been released occasionally, the species would almost certainly have become extinct and, indeed, it may have done so anyway.

Eagle owl

---

surrounding farmland has now developed into extensive scrubland where a range of species may be found.

Hawkridge (OS SS870291) is an area of great variety with a network of well-signed paths maintained by the Exmoor National Park. This is probably one of the best birdwatching sites on Exmoor and all the classic Exmoor species can be found in the area. On the tops, there are the Buzzards and Ravens, with Wood Warbler and Pied Flycatcher in the oakwoods, and Dipper and Grey Wagtail along the fast- flowing streams.

SOMERSET RESERVOIRS
None of the county's reservoirs is particularly attractive to large numbers of waterbirds. The largest concentrations occur on Cheddar reservoir but this is a very artificial site and is greatly disturbed by water-sport activities. Some viewing is possible from public access areas at all sites, but permission may be necessary to gain entry to the sites. Some of the peak winter populations to be expected on the three main 'birding' reservoirs are shown in the table:

	Cheddar (ST442538)	Durleigh (ST270363)	Sutton Bingham (ST550110)
Teal	1000	350	400
Mallard	500	500	400
Shoveler	80	10	60
Pochard	750	150	200
Tufted Duck	300	80	200
Goldeneye	50	2	10

Clatworthy Reservoir (OS ST042315) holds few waterbirds but the surrounding woodland can provide excellent birdwatching for both Great and Lesser Spotted Wood-

peckers as well as for the resident Buzzards, and, out on the water, Canada Geese.

AVON

Situated north of the Mendip Hills, and formed from parts of Somerset and Gloucestershire, Avon is very much centred on the urban areas that surround Bath, Bristol, Avonmouth, and Weston-super-Mare. Ornithologically, the main interest is in the south of the county and the Severn coastline which stretches from the mouth of the Exe in the south to near Berkeley in the north. Being an urban county, the birdwatching is focused on artificial sites which include the reservoirs, docks, and sewage disposal works. Much of the county's bird history is split between Somerset and Gloucestershire but, in recent years, the Avon Ornithological Group, in conjunction with natural history and ornithological societies in Bristol have brought together a consistent county recording.

Birdwatching sites

RESERVOIRS
The reservoirs (or lakes as they are referred to locally) occur in the south of the county and attract the attention of many birdwatchers so that, over the years, a wide variety of species, including many rarities, has been recorded.

The oldest of the three is **Barrow Gurney** (OS ST544679) which consists of three separate reservoirs constructed in the late 1800s and is now of less importance than the two newer sites, although the Barrow Gurney lakes still attract a variety of species and can be viewed from public roads. The remaining two lakes are under the control of the Bristol Waterworks Company (Recreation Department, Woodford Lodge, Bristol BS18 8XH) and, although limited viewing from public footpaths and adjoining roads is possible, a permit is required for complete access.

Blagdon (OS ST515597), over 160 hectares (400 acres) in area, is best viewed from the A368 and the dam; while **Chew Valley** (OS ST570600), the newest of the three and over 400 hectares (1000 acres) in area, has public roads on many sides with good views from the north. A nature reserve has been established at the southern extremity. Since its official opening in 1956, Chew Valley has recorded more than 250 species including, in addition to the impressive list of wildfowl, a range of breeding species, such as Sedge and Reed Warblers, and passage migrants, such as Little Stint and Ruff. Recent rarities have included a Marbled Teal (still awaiting official entry to the List of British Birds), Marsh Sandpiper, and Whiskered Tern.

STEEP HOLM ISLAND (OS ST229608)

Access to this island is by boat on certain days from Weston-super-Mare. Steep Holm is administered by the Kenneth Allsop Memorial Trust, from whom details are available at: Milborne Port Post Office, Sherborne, Dorset.

It is possible to stay on the island. Some 3½ miles off the Avon coast, Steep Holm, with its rugged cliffs, sits halfway between the English and Welsh coastlines in the middle of the Bristol Channel. The island is best known for its breeding colonies of gulls, with recent counts made up of: Great Black-backed Gull 30 pairs; Lesser Black-backed Gull 500 pairs; Herring Gull 1500 pairs.

Other breeding species include up to forty pairs of Cormorants, together with a high density of Wren, Dunnock, Robin, and Blackbird in the extensive scrub areas. The Peregrine is now recorded annually.

SAND BAY AND POINT (OS ST320659)

This headland and sandy bay north of Weston-super-Mare are reached via Kewstoke. This site has not produced spectacular records of seabirds, although Manx Shearwater can appear in midsummer and Fulmar at any time of the year. More importantly, the bay functions as a feeding site for wader concentrations, including good numbers of Dunlin, Bar-tailed Godwit, Curlew, and Redshank.

Here only a small number of willows can be seen on West Sedgemoor.

Organizations in Avon
Bristol Ornithological Club (BOC), 37 Spring Hill, Milton, Weston-super-Mare BS22 9AX
Bristol Naturalists' Society (BNS), 23 Netherways, Yeo Park, Clevedon
Avon Wildlife Trust (AWT), 32 Jacobs Well Road, Bristol BS8 1DR
RSPB Members' Groups based at: Bath, Bristol, and Weston-super-Mare (details from RSPB, The Lodge, Sandy, Beds SG19 2DL)

Annual reports
'Avon Bird Report' 12 Birbeck Road, Bristol BS9 1BD

Ruddy Duck in Avon
The colonization of Britain by this North American species is a story in which the Avon reservoirs play a large part. The first birds to escape into the wild did

so from the Wildfowl Trust collection at Slimbridge in Gloucestershire in the winter of 1952-53. During the following twenty years, more than seventy birds are thought to have flown from that site as a result of successful captive breeding. The first record of wild living birds in Avon was of four drakes at Chew Valley in 1957, with the first recorded breeding in the wild in Britain taking place at this reservoir in 1960. As many as four pairs may still nest in the county each year, but it is not as a breeding species that the Ruddy Duck has moved into Avon. Numbers on the reservoirs are small in midsummer – often less than ten in June and July; but a large winter influx at both Blagdon and Chew Valley can produce a maximum flock of over 400 at both sites with a recent peak of 526 at Chew Valley in December 1983. These wintering congregations are almost certainly birds from the highly successful West Midland breeding sites that have established

a regular winter migration.

Some peak waterbird counts at Chew Valley 1982-84

Little Grebe	107
Great Crested Grebe	510
Cormorant	34
Mute Swan	113
Canada Goose	233
Wigeon	655
Gadwall	365
Teal	5600
Mallard	1900
Shoveler	490
Pochard	1285
Tufted Duck	355
Goldeneye	127
Goosander	64

DORSET AND WILTSHIRE

DORSET

Not surprisingly, the birdwatchers of Dorset are drawn towards the coastline for, ornithologically, the county has a justifiably good reputation from Christchurch Harbour and the migration watchpoint of Hengistbury Head in the east via Poole Harbour and Portland to Chesil Beach and beyond in the west – all sites famous for their breeding, wintering, and migrating birds. Running northwards like layers on a cake, the county can boast some of Britain's best remaining heathlands, the western limit of the New Forest, a belt of open chalkland, and the wooded vales to the north. Two major rivers flow into two major harbours: the Frome into Poole Harbour and the Avon into Christchurch Harbour. This variety of habitat gives rise to the diversity of species – more than 360 have been recorded in the 1000 square miles that make up Dorset. In fact, the only habitats missing from the county seem to be mountains and large expanses of natural fresh water – and even the latter has been provided in recent years by the steadily increasing amount of gravel extraction. A measure of the county's importance can be judged from the significance of some of the nationally rare breeding species that occur. Stone Curlew and Montagu's Harrier just manage to maintain a population on the chalklands, while Dartford Warblers are able to survive even the coldest of winters on the heaths. Little Terns nest on the shingle beaches and Cetti's Warblers have colonized the coastal fringe, particularly in the Weymouth area.

Birdwatching sites

WEYMOUTH AREA
Weymouth can boast two RSPB reserves, **Radipole Lake** (OS SY675796) and **Lodmoor** (OS SY690811). Both have easy access, are open for visiting at all times, and include excellent facilities for disabled visitors.

For Radipole Lake and the reserve information centre, access is best achieved from the swannery car park in the town centre; while for Lodmoor, the newest of the two reserves and still developing its visitor facilities, parking is adjacent to the sealife centre on the coast road towards Wareham. Both sites have very spacious observation hides and a full day's birdwatching can be enjoyed throughout the year, with the largest number of species to be encountered at high tide or towards dusk when roosting birds begin to congregate.

At Radipole some 240 species have been recorded, including a dramatic population of Cetti's Warblers that shout loudly at passers-by from the scrub-lined pathways, while the reedbeds are famous for the large numbers of Reed and Sedge Warblers, together with the almost annual appearance of the rarer Aquatic Warbler. In autumn and winter, the reeds provide a secure roosting site for large numbers of Swallows, Sand Martins, and Starlings, as well as a mixed wagtail roost often including several hundred Yellow Wagtails. The open water attracts a range of wintering wildfowl.

Lodmoor is a very different habitat, consisting largely of open grassland interspersed with drainage ditches. Over the years, the site has been threatened in many ways, ranging from extensive drainage schemes to rubbish dumping as a form of reclamation. Its future now seems secure. A well-documented ornithological history of the site provides some interesting reading. Water Pipits were first recorded in Dorset in 1925 at Lodmoor; they are now noted here every year. Water Rail, Bearded Tit, and Cetti's Warbler are regular breeding species, while Marsh and Savi's Warblers appear, but as yet have not stayed to nest. Recent rare visitors include Wilson's Phalarope, Shore Lark, and Richard's Pipit.

Portland Bill (OS SY677681) became an established site at which to observe bird migration in Dorset thanks to the enthusiasm of a small band of amateur birdwatchers in the early 1950s. Following their success and a national interest in bird migration studies, the establishment of the Portland Bill Observatory took place in 1955 with a formal opening of its present home in the Old Lighthouse in 1961. The observatory is permanently staffed and continuous observations, spanning more than twenty-five years, have now been gathered; approaching 75 000 birds have been ringed as part of the detailed migration studies. The observatory provides overnight, hostel-type accommodation and intending visitors should contact the warden at the Old Lighthouse, Portland, Dorset.

Organizations in Dorset
Dorset Bird Club, 53 Weymouth Bay Avenue, Weymouth DT3 5AD
Dorset Naturalists' Trust, 39 Christchurch Road, Bournemouth BH1 3NS
RSPB Members' Groups based at; Gillingham, Bournemouth, Poole, and Dorchester (details from RSPB, The Lodge, Sandy, Beds SG19 2DL)

Annual reports
'Dorset Bird Report', Dorset County Museum, High Street West, Dorchester
'Birds of Christchurch Harbour', 27 Waltham Road, Boscombe, Bournemouth BH7 6PE
'Portland Bird Observatory Report', The Old Lighthouse, Portland, Dorset

Books
Prendergast, E D V and Boys, J V. *The Birds of Dorset*. David & Charles, 1983

Gulls in Dorset
For an unknown reason, and perhaps simply because an enthusiastic band of Dorset birdwatchers enjoys the challenge of locating rare and unusual species among the vast congregations of gulls that occur on the Dorset coast, the county can boast more than its fair share of unusual occurrences. A total of sixteen species of gulls has been recorded in Dorset, with perhaps the seventeenth still to be confirmed.
Mediterranean Gull *Larus melanocephalus*: first recorded in 1958, now annual in small numbers and may be seen throughout the year.
Laughing Gull *L. atricilla*: three records, 1969, 1980, and 1983.
Franklin's Gull *L. pipixcan*: one record, 1982.
Little Gull *L. minutus*: a regular autumn visitor; scarce at other times.
Sabine's Gull *L. sabini*: Rarely more than ten per annum; usually associated with autumn gales.
Bonaparte's Gull *L. philadelphia*: three records, 1970, 1975, and 1981.
Black-headed Gull *L. ridibundus*: very common.
Ring-billed Gull *L. delawarensis*: first recorded in 1976; over ten now recorded annually.
Common Gull *L. canus*: very common, particularly as a migrant and winter visitor.
Lesser Black-backed Gull *L. fuscus*: very common, particularly as a migrant.
Herring Gull *L. argentatus*: very common.
Iceland Gull *L. glaucoides*: rarely as many as ten per winter.
Glaucous Gull *L. hyperboreus*: small numbers each winter.
Great Black-backed Gull *L. marinus*: common.
Ross's Gull *Rhodostethia rosea*: two records, 1967 and 1974.
Kittiwake *Rissa tridactyla*: very common offshore.
Ivory Gull *Pagophila eburnea*: eight records, only two this century, 1931 and 1980.
In addition, there are two unconfirmed records of the Slender-billed Gull, *L. genei*, in 1955 and 1979, a species that has yet to be admitted to the official Dorset list.

Portland Bill presents a rather bleak vista and, indeed, it can be a disappointment to visiting birdwatchers on a day when few birds turn up. A visit that coincides with a marked off-shore passage of seabirds, however, can bring the excitement of large numbers of shearwaters, skuas, and divers. In suitable weather conditions, large numbers of migrants may be forced to land or, alternatively, a very obvious visible passage may take place with birds arriving or departing at the very tip of the Bill. In addition to the migration, the rocky cliffs supply nesting sites for Guillemot, Razorbill, Puffin, and Rock Pipit while, in the winter months, a small flock of Purple Sandpipers take up residence.

The Fleet (OS SY5784 to SY6675) extends from Portland Harbour in the east, along the landward side of the 8 miles of Chesil Beach to Abbotsbury and its famous swannery in the west. Some of the best birdwatching is from the car park at Ferrybridge from where it is possible to search the waters of the harbour on a calm winter's day in the hope of finding

The Fleet behind the 8 miles of Chesil Beach offers excellent birdwatching from the car park at Ferrybridge.

Arne is important for heathland birds such as Dartford Warbler.

grebes, divers, or the sea ducks, Common and Velvet Scoters. At low tide, many waders are on the mud of East Fleet, including Grey Plover, Knot, and Turnstone, and these can also be viewed from the car park.

The Dorset Coast Path follows the northern shore of the Fleet and provides excellent views of areas which contain as many as 8000 Wigeon or up to 200 Pintail and Goldeneye. Birdwatchers should avoid the Chesil Beach itself in summer to avoid disturbance to the threatened colony of up to fifty nesting pairs of Little Terns. The swannery at Abbotsbury is recorded to have existed for some 900 years, during which time the population has varied considerably. In the late 1960s the numbers were as low as nineteen pairs but, more typically in recent years, a population of forty to fifty pairs has nested annually. During the winter months the swan population on the Fleet can increase to nearly 1000.

POOLE HARBOUR/PURBECK

Durlstone Head (OS SZ035773) is a well-established country park with visitor facilities that make it very easy to view the nesting seabirds which make use of the cliffs, from the Head itself westwards towards St Aldhelm's Head. Accurate counts of the number of pairs are difficult to obtain, but Guillemot and Razorbill are apparently maintaining their numbers, although it must be questionable whether the Puffins still survive. Fulmar and Kittiwake have colonized and increased their numbers, while other cliff-nesting species, such as Jackdaw, Rock Pipit, and Stock Dove, are all numerous. At migration times, the clifftop paths can provide excellent opportunities for locating passage birds, such as Wheatear and Whinchat, around the areas of close-cropped grass, or Whitethroat and Garden Warbler among the bramble and hawthorn bushes.

Poole Harbour is bounded by two important heathland reserves: to the south is the National Nature Reserve at **Studland** (OS SZ025845), administered by the Nature Conservancy Council; and to the west is the **Arne** reserve (OS SY973879) of the RSPB. Both are very important sites for the typical heathland species of birds, especially Dartford Warbler, Nightjar, and Stonechat, as well as many of the other key animals associated with this specialized habitat – Sand Lizard, Smooth Snake, and several species of dragonflies. Both sites have facilities for visitors by way of nature trails and observation hides, and both areas offer excellent views across the harbour towards Brownsea Island (Arne) and over Studland Bay (Studland). It is possible, therefore, to combine a visit for the heathland species (very much confined to the spring and early summer) with a chance of seeing migrant waders or late-departing winter wildfowl within Poole Harbour itself.

Even better views of Poole Harbour can be obtained on a visit to **Brownsea Island** (OS SZ020880). Boats leave regularly from Poole Quay and, by special arrangement, journeys to various parts of the harbour can be organized, in addition to the direct journey to Brownsea Island. The Dorset Naturalists' Trust has a reserve on the north shore of the island where a series of lagoons holds nesting Sandwich and Common Terns, and the associated woodlands house the county's largest Grey Heronry, now numbering nearly 100 pairs; the Herons exploit the excellent feeding throughout the harbour. Outside the reserve area, the island holds many surprises, including a population of red squirrels and some remarkably tame Peacocks! High tide is an exciting time on the island with the lagoons providing a roost for congregations of over 1000 Oystercatcher and Redshank. A programme of ringing waders on the island has produced recoveries of Oystercatchers from Greenland and the Faeroes, Curlew Sandpipers from the USSR and France, and Curlews from Finland and Sweden.

CHRISTCHURCH HARBOUR

In 1974, the administrative changes to the county boundaries removed this excellent birdwatching site from Hampshire, and that county's loss became Dorset's gain. The local nature reserve at **Stanpit Marshes** (OS SZ168920) is under the control of the Christchurch District Council. Access is from Stanpit Lane car park in Christchurch, and visiting is best in mid-winter when large congregations of waders can be expected with well over 1000 Dunlin at times. The Avon valley, which leads into the harbour, provides a suitable guideline for passing migrants, many of which stay briefly on the reserve. To see migrants, however, the visiting birdwatcher should go to the other side of the harbour where **Hengistbury Head** (OS SZ178904) provides a splendid view point as well as excellent walks and woodland areas for grounded migrants. A wide range of seabirds can be expected offshore, including a regular flock of Eider, while the trees should be closely watched for Sparrowhawk and Firecrest – not forgetting to keep a careful watch on the harbour itself to observe the bird movements that take place with the tidal changes.

WILTSHIRE

A land-locked county, Wiltshire is unfortunately rather impoverished, ornithologically, compared with its coastal neighbours. The Cotswold Water Park in the north falls mainly in Gloucestershire, and the New Forest in the extreme south-east is confined largely to Hampshire. Both of these sites are referred to under the appropriate counties. The dominant feature of Wiltshire is the central upland of Salisbury Plain and Marlborough Downs. Much of it is now under intensive agriculture but vast tracks of the natural downland have been preserved as a result of the military presence and its use as an extensive training ground. To the north the low-lying land borders the Cotswolds and, in the south, the Avon river and its tributaries provide another area of low-lying land around Salisbury.

Birdwatching sites

COATE WATER COUNTRY PARK (OS SU178820)
The Park is situated on the southern edge of Swindon, and only about 2 miles from Exit 15 on the M4 motorway. Originally an extensive reservoir, the site has been developed by the construction of a separate water area and is now a local nature reserve administered by the Thamesdown Borough Council. The second lake is shallower, well vegetated, and a small selection of wildfowl occurs, together with breeding warblers and migrant waders.

Some of the old beechwoods of Savernake Forest remain despite replanting with conifers by the Forestry Commission.

SAVERNAKE FOREST (OS SU2665)
To the east of Marlborough, Savernake Forest is a considerable area of woodland under the control of the Forestry Commission. Much of the area has been replanted with conifers, but some of the old trees remain. Access is possible on many of the paths and rides, and good populations of typical woodland species can be found, including Redstart and Sparrowhawk.

BRITFORD WATER MEADOWS (OS SU170280)
Situated on the banks of the Avon and opposite the town of Petersfinger, the water meadows are, together with other meadows along this stretch of the Avon river, probably among the richest bird habitats in the county. Although there is more interesting birdwatching across the Hampshire border, the White-fronted Geese and Bewick's Swans pass through and sometimes remain within Wiltshire. Small numbers of nesting Redshank and Snipe occur, with winter wildfowl totalling several hundred Wigeon and Teal, a feature of each year if the winter flood conditions are suitable. The river attracts Kingfishers and Little Grebes, with Grey Wagtails as regular winter visitors.

Organizations in Wiltshire
Wiltshire Ornithological Society (WOS), Westdene, The Ley, Box, Corsham SN14 9JZ
Wiltshire Trust for Nature Conservation (WTNC), 19 High Street, Devizes SN10 1AT
RSPB Members' Groups based at North Wilts and South Wilts (details from RSPB, The Lodge, Sandy, Beds SG19 2DL)

Annual reports
'Hobby' (annual report of WOS) Westdene, The Ley, Box, Corsham SN14 9JZ

Books
Buxton, J. *The Birds of Wiltshire*. Wiltshire Library and Museum Service, 1981

The Great Bustard in Wiltshire
Historically, Salisbury Plain was the breeding site for the Great Bustard in England. Probably never common, it was certainly widespread and more numerous than at most other sites in Britain. It was regularly hunted and featured in special menus prepared for the Mayor of Salisbury. Even though increased protection was afforded the species from the mid-1500s until nearly 1800, the decline continued, probably as much the result of changing agricultural practices as the continued persecution of the birds. The last proven breeding was in 1806, and a series of records during the remainder of that century all referred to birds being shot. The last records of a wild Great Bustard in Wiltshire was of a female shot in 1891. In recent years, attempts have been made to reintroduce the species to Salisbury Plain but, as yet, with little success.

HAMPSHIRE AND THE ISLE OF WIGHT

HAMPSHIRE

Hampshire can boast an exciting coastline, with the Solent, Southampton Water, and Spithead in the centre of the county, and Portsmouth and Langstone Harbours, Hayling Island, and Chichester Harbour (on the boundary with Sussex) in the east. The county is divided by four north-south-flowing rivers: the western two, the Avon and the Test provide the boundaries for the New Forest; the eastern two, the Itchen and the Meon flow from the extensive chalklands that make up the bulk of inland Hampshire – open rolling down and farmland. Parts of the extreme north of the county have been used as military training grounds but, as a result of new roads and communications, it is now within easy access of London and has in places developed a strong resemblance to suburbia, although the gardens and parks are extensive and well vegetated.

Birdwatching sites

LANGSTONE HARBOUR AND FARLINGTON MARSHES (OS SU6903 and 6804)

These two adjoining reserves complement each other perfectly. Langstone Harbour, a reserve of the RSPB, is largely tidal mud, rich in feeding for a wide range of waders and wildfowl, but completely covered each high tide. A series of islands in the harbour provides secure roost sites but, more importantly, the neighbouring Farlington Marshes, safely behind the sea wall and a reserve of the Hampshire and Isle of Wight Naturalists' Trust, provide an extensive feeding and resting area where the birds are not disturbed by tide and from where the visiting birdwatcher can look out over the extensive mudflats. Farlington Marshes consist of wet grassland and a reed-fringed lagoon; the surrounding sea wall provides an excellent base from which to watch the birds, particularly some of the more unusual passage migrants, such as Little Stint, Spotted Redshank, or Jack Snipe. In winter the flocks of Wigeon and Brent Geese are regular features of the grassland. This is very much a winter birdwatching site. Looking out across the harbour from the southern end of Farlington, in midwinter and on a rising tide, huge flocks of waders can be seen wheeling and massing in the sky as their feeding grounds are lost to the incoming water. At high tide, grebes and mergansers are frequently to be seen.

TITCHFIELD HAVEN (OS SU536025)

This is a reserve of the Hampshire County Council, situated between Portsmouth and Southampton on the eastern shore of Southampton Water. This site can provide interest throughout the year, but is probably best in the winter months when concentrations of waders, including Black-tailed Godwit, can be seen and when Bittern occur regularly. A combination of open water, muddy banks, reedbeds, and flooded meadows provides a good selection of species, including breeding Bearded Tit and Cetti's Warbler. Observation hides, nature trail, and information centre are all features of the reserve.

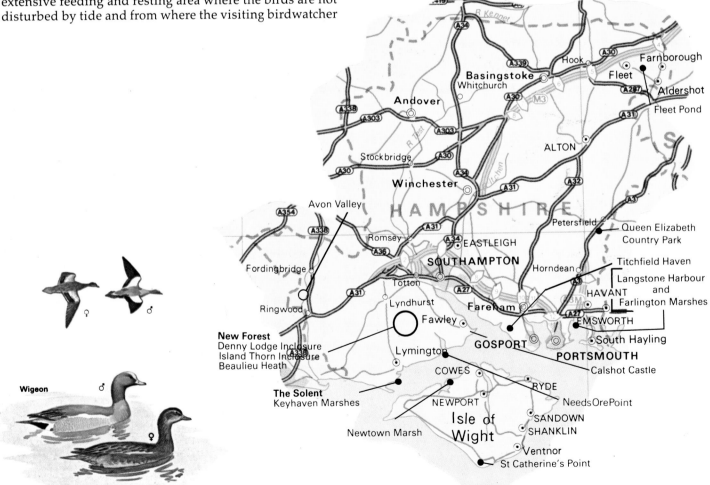

Wigeon

NEW FOREST

Over 140 square miles in extent, the New Forest has many areas of interest to the birdwatcher, and from the wealth of car parks and walking routes available throughout the forest, there is much to be seen, from the Redstarts of the old oakwoods, to the Stonechats and perhaps Dartford Warblers of the more open heath. May and June are the best months for visiting, when the bird song is at its peak and the summer migrants are all in residence. An evening walk at this time could well provide sight and sound of Hobby, Nightjar, and Grasshopper Warbler. Former regular breeding species, such as Woodlark, Red-backed Shrike, and Montagu's Harrier, are now extremely rare but they are still recorded occasionally. Among the many places worth visiting in the Forest, **Denny Lodge Inclosure** (OS SU340045), **Island Thorn Inclosure** (OS SU220150), and **Beaulieu Heath** (OS SU350000) between them provide examples of the wide range of habitat available. Buzzard and Sparrowhawk can be found around the woodland with Kestrels hovering over the more open country. Look for woodpeckers and Hawfinches near the oakwoods, Wood Warblers where there are beach trees, Grey Wagtails by the streams, and Coal Tits, Goldcrests, and Crossbills in the conifers. In recent years small numbers of Siskins have stayed to nest.

AVON VALLEY (OS SU146100 and SU157075)

North of Ringwood, the River Avon passes through an area of gravel workings that have given rise to some excellent sites for nesting Little Ringed Plover as well as winter flocks of Pochard and Tufted Duck. In cold weather, the numbers of waterfowl can reach several thousands while, in spring and autumn, migrant waders, such as Green Sandpiper and Little Stint, are regularly to be seen. Further north, at Ibsley,

The RSPB's Langstone Harbour reserve provides rich feeding grounds for many waders and wildfowl.

the river flows through a series of flood meadows where nesting Redshank, Snipe, and Yellow Wagtail are very much a highlight of the summer months, while Bewick's Swan, White-fronted Goose, and Wigeon occur each winter.

THE SOLENT

The north shore of the Solent, from **Keyhaven Marshes** (OS SZ310910) via **Needs Oar Point** (OS SZ428977) to **Calshot Castle** (OS SU488025), presents a complete contrast to the heavily industrialized shore of Southampton Water. The mudbanks at the mouth of the Lymington and Beaulieu rivers provide intertidal feeding areas for flocks of wintering waders and Brent Geese. At Needs Oar Point, there is a nesting colony of Black-headed Gulls and Common Terns, a colony that gained national recognition as the first site in Britain for the nesting of the Mediterranean Gull. Although

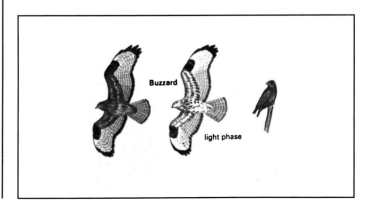

Organizations in Hampshire

Hampshire Ornithological Society (HOS), Greenbanks, Broad Road, Monxton, Andover SP11 8AT

Hampshire and Isle of Wight Naturalists' Trust (HNT), 8 Market Place, Romsey SO5 8NB

RSPB Members' Groups based at: Basingstoke, north-east Hants, Portsmouth, Southampton, and Winchester (details from RSPB, The Lodge, Sandy, Beds SG19 2DL)

Annual reports

'Hampshire Bird Report', Teal Cottage, Salisbury Lane, Over Wallop SO20 8JJ

'Hants/Surrey Border Bird Report', 4 Cygnet Court, Old Cove Road, Fleet, Hants

Books

Clark, J M. *Birds of the Hants/Surrey Border.* Hobby Books, 1984

Cohen, E and Taverner, J. *A Revised List of Hampshire and Isle of Wight Birds.* Oxford Illustrated Press, 1972.

Taverner, J H. *Wildfowl in Hampshire.* Warren & Son, 1962.

Some peak counts from Hampshire harbours

	Chichester	Langstone	Portsmouth
Brent Goose	11 849	7536	2236
Shelduck	4552	2432	680
Wigeon	925	2000	300
Goldeneye	75	84	85
Red-breasted Merganser	92	194	60
Oystercatcher	1872	1700	665
Ringed Plover	824	610	382
Grey Plover	2648	1320	638
Knot	1000	1010	765
Dunlin	30 084	30 250	8110
Curlew	2652	1633	498
Redshank	3405	2698	981

American land birds in Southampton

It has been known for many years that North American land birds can cross the Atlantic by means of a ship-assisted passage. In the past, the large passenger liners that regularly plied between New York and Southampton provided a temporary safe haven, with many people on board prepared to care for or feed stranded birds. In October or November 1958 four White-throated Sparrows, *Zonotrichia albicollis*, arrived in Southampton on a Cunard ship. The birds were caught and placed in an aviary in East Park, Southampton where the last one died in 1964. A bird of the same species at Needs Oar Point in May 1961 almost certainly had just completed a crossing on the *Queen Elizabeth* which passed nearby with a bird on board only four days before the sighting. Most remarkable of all was the arrival in Southampton of the RMS *Mauretania* on 14 October 1962. Shortly after leaving New York, it was estimated that there were some 130 individual land birds on board but, on arrival at Southampton, only four remained on the vessel: two White-throated Sparrows, one Song Sparrow, *Melospiza melodia*, and one Slate-coloured Junco, *Junco hyemalis*. A Parula Warbler, *Parula americana*, had survived an earlier crossing the same year, but had died two days after arrival at Southampton; while in

1961, a Blackpoll Warbler, *Dendroica striata*, had successfully crossed on the *Queen Elizabeth*, remained on board in Southampton, and eventually died on board on the return crossing to New York.

Organizations in the Isle of Wight

Isle of Wight Natural History & Archaeological Society, Ivy Cottage, New Barn Lane, Shorwell, PO30 3JQ

RSPB Members' Group for Isle of Wight (details from RSPB, The Lodge, Sandy, Beds SG19 2DL) *See* also under Hampshire.

Annual reports

'Isle of Wight Bird Report', Westering, Moor Lane, Brightstone, Newport PO30 4DL

Books

See under Hampsshire.

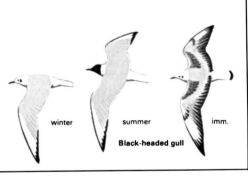

winter   summer   imm.

Black-headed gull

Mediterranean Gulls did not establish themselves fully, they are still recorded regularly from the area and, occasionally, they hybridize with the very common Black-headed Gulls. Offshore, grebes, Red-breasted Merganser, occasional Eider, and divers are seen regularly in winter. There are many access points to the coastline from the southern edge of the New Forest, and there is car parking at the Calshot and Lepe Country Parks as well as at Lymington and Keyhaven.

QUEEN ELIZABETH COUNTRY PARK (OS SU715205)

The park is run by the Hampshire County Council and contains a variety of habitats that include woodland and open downland. At peak holiday times, the area immediately surrounding the visitors' centre attracts too many people for many birds to be seen, but a relatively short walk to some of the quieter parts of the park will produce a good variety of bird life, including typical downland species, such as Yellowhammer, Whitethroat, and Kestrel. Avoid the site during the winter. This is one of the few sites in Britain where it is relatively easy to see Golden Pheasants; look for them among the conifers.

FLEET POND (OS SU820550)

So much of the interest in the county is centred on the coastal strip that few inland sites attract large numbers of birdwatchers. Fleet Pond, in the north-eastern part of the county is a small reserve of the Hart District Council and, in addition to the water itself, the surrounding woodland and heathland attract a range of species. Both Great Crested Grebe and Canada Goose nest, while, in the past, diligent birdwatchers have found rarities, such as the Great Reed

Warbler from southern Europe and Blue-winged Teal from North America.

ISLE OF WIGHT

The ornithological history of the Isle of Wight is very much tied to Hampshire and only in recent years has it developed its own identity. Although small, the county includes a considerable variety of habitats; the only major omissions are areas of open fresh water.

Birdwatching sites

NEWTOWN MARSH (OS SZ425914)

Newtown Marsh is a reserve of the Isle of Wight County Council. Since it was flooded in 1954, the numbers and variety of species recorded have been most impressive. From Newtown, a public right of way follows the wall of the old harbour which gives excellent views across the reserve. Breeding species include Black-headed Gulls and occasional terns, with Oystercatchers and Shelduck. Non-breeding waders summer at the site and, in winter, both species of godwit, as well as Brent Geese, are common. This is the most exciting birdwatching on the island.

ST CATHERINE'S POINT (OS SZ499753)

At migration time, during spring and autumn, St Catherine's Point is an excellent watching place, both for grounded land birds as well as migrating seabirds passing along the Channel. In addition to large concentrations of grounded night migrants – once attracted by the lighthouse – occasional rarities have been recorded. In recent years, these have included Black Kite and Melodious Warbler.

WEST AND EAST SUSSEX AND KENT

WEST AND EAST SUSSEX

The administrative division of Sussex into two counties has not been well received by birdwatchers. The county has an ornithological history based upon the observations by some of Britain's leading ornithologists and, in this century, Sussex can boast three comprehensive county avifaunas. Surprisingly, it was not until 1962 that the county formed its ornithological society but, thanks to the energies of the Sussex birdwatchers, there had been a county annual report for many years before this. With some 350 species recorded, this must be one of the richest bird counties in Britain; there is an excellent range of habitats stretching west to east like layers of a cake. In the south, the coastal plain eventually gives way to the chalk of the South Downs which reach the sea at Beachy Head. The land then falls away to the north, through the Greensand and Wealden Clay, but rises again to the Hastings Beds which reach the sea in the east of the county at Fairlight. There are no large areas of natural fresh water, but the growth in human population and industry has resulted in extensive reservoirs and gravel excavations, mainly in the east; while the saltmarsh and tidal mud of the harbours and estuaries are mainly in the west.

Birdwatching sites

CHICHESTER AREA
In the west of the county and bordering Hampshire is Sussex's greatest expanse of tidal mud. Consequently, here are some of the largest concentrations of winter waders and wildfowl. This area can provide an exciting day's bird-watching at any time of the year for, within easy reach of the town of Chichester, is a wide range of habitats.

Beachy Head, at the eastern end of the chalk cliffs of the Seven Sisters seen here, provides Sussex with a famous migration watchpoint.

Thorny Deeps (OS SU755040) on the northern end of Thorny Island provides grazing marsh, reedbed, and mud-fringed channels. Breeding Redshank, Yellow Wagtail, and Bearded Tit are typical species, with wintering Hen Harrier and Wigeon flocks as regular features. Freshwater waders, such as Spotted Redshank and Wood Sandpiper, are usual autumn migrants beside the open water.

Across the harbour on the eastern shore, between West Itchenor and **West Wittering** (OS SZ767990), is one of the best places to observe the concentrations of winter species in the harbour (for figures *see* Hampshire), and a public footpath follows the shoreline between these two towns. This is very much a winter walk, preferably on a rising tide. A careful watch should be kept for Avocets at this site.

Further east is the point of **Selsey Bill** (OS SZ858921) and, in spring and autumn, a careful watch offshore, preferably when the wind is blowing from the south-east, can reveal some spectacular movements of seabirds passing along the Channel. The April and May passage can include large numbers of terns, Common Scoter, and skuas, the latter now including a well-established movement of Pomarine Skuas. The autumn passage is less dramatic but may include an equally large variety of species.

To the north of Selsey is the **Pagham Harbour** reserve (OS SZ8796) of the West Sussex County Council. The area is best viewed from the nature trails which start at the reserve car park on the Siddlesham-Selsey road, or from Church Norton which is only a short walk from the coast and the harbour mouth. Breeding Little Terns and migrant waders are features of the site and, offshore in the winter months, Eider and Slavonian Grebes are regular visitors.

On the immediate eastern outskirts of Chichester itself are the **Chichester gravel pits** (OS SU8703), a complex of gravel workings easily viewed from the surrounding roads. Tufted Duck and Pochard concentrate in the winter months and Ruddy Duck are present throughout the year. Both Ringed and Little Ringed Plovers are regular.

Arundel (OS TQ020080) is a Wildfowl Trust reserve and, in addition to the normal visitor facilities including a collection of captive wildfowl, the reserve has hides overlooking a series of ponds and flooded meadows which attracts a range of species, including large numbers of Snipe and Water Rail. Cetti's Warblers have colonized and Kingfishers are regularly present. Almost opposite the entrance to the reserve is Arundel Park and Swanbourne Lake with the surrounding areas of woodland and scrub. In complete contrast to the wildfowl reserve, this site contains a good selection of typical southern English woodland species, such as Nuthatch, woodpeckers, and tits.

MIDHURST COMMONS AND HEATHS
Heathland was once more extensive in the county but, during the last 150 years, a dramatic decline has taken place and only small remnants now remain on the Greensand. In West Sussex these remaining heaths are in the Midhurst area and, of these, two are worth visiting for birdwatching: **Ambersham Common** (OS SU9119) and **Lavington Common** (OS SU946188). Late spring and early summer are most productive and, although the Woodlark and Redbacked Shrike no longer occur, Tree Pipit, Nightjar, and Stonechat still nest, as do Hobby and Dartford Warbler.

AMBERLEY AREA
On the northern edge of the South Downs escarpment and just north of the village of Amberley, the River Arun passes through a floodplain of water meadows. The **Amberley Wild Brooks** (OS TQ0314) have been partially drained but, in a wet season, still attract numbers of wildfowl, including occasional geese and wild swans; but, just to the north at Greatham Bridge, the Sussex Trust for Nature Conservation has established a reserve at **Waltham Brooks** (OS TQ026159) where floodwater is maintained on the meadows and this is now the most regular site for the Bewick's Swans, large numbers of Snipe, and wintering

The South Downs are an important feature in Sussex's rich landscape.

Ruff. In summer, Yellow Wagtail and Redshank nest. On the slightly higher ground surrounding the floodplain are several wooded hillsides, and **Rackham Woods** (OS TQ046146) immediately to the east of the Wild Brooks contain a good selection of woodland species, including all three woodpeckers, Redstart, and Wood Warbler.

EAST SUSSEX RESERVOIRS
The largest and newest of the four main Sussex reservoirs is **Bewl Bridge** (OS TQ683348) which straddles the border with Kent, covers over 300 hectares (750 acres), and was constructed in 1978. In the short period since its completion, the reservoir has established a sizeable bird community which includes a count of over 1100 Canada Geese (the largest count ever recorded in Sussex), and over 6000 gulls are regularly recorded roosting at the site.

At just over 100 hectares (250 acres) and constructed in 1954, the **Weir Wood Reservoir** (OS TQ402348) can be viewed from the road between East Grinstead and West Hoathly. At this site, as many as twenty pairs of Greatcrested Grebes nest annually, in excess of 100 young Mallard are reared, and wintering flocks of Tufted Duck and Pochard can exceed 100. The two smaller reservoirs, both of just over 60 hectares (150 acres), are at **Darwell** (OS TQ715212) and **Arlington** (OS TQ533074). Access to the former is not easy because the reservoir is some way from the nearest road, but Arlington can be reached from the B2108 north of Alfriston. Both reservoirs attract wintering flocks of Pochard and Tufted Duck, while more than 1000 Wigeon have been recorded at Arlington.

FORE WOOD (OS TQ756128)
Fore Wood was a neglected coppice woodland when it was acquired by the RSPB as a reserve in 1976. Extensive management work, including the creation of nature trails from the village of Crowhurst, has resulted in a marked increase in the bird population, and all species typical of a southern woodland site now nest. The best time to visit is from late April through into early June when bird song is at its maximum. In addition to six species of tits and three of woodpeckers, in most years, Sparrowhawk, Woodcock, and Hawfinch all nest. Warblers are now attracted to the managed areas, and Green Sandpiper and Kingfisher visit the newly constructed pond.

Organizations in Sussex

Sussex Ornithological Society (SOS), 69 Farhalls Crescent, Horsham RH12 4BT

Sussex Trust for Nature Conservation (STNC), Woods Mill, Henfield BN5 9SD

RSPB Members' Groups based at: Battle, Brighton, Chichester, Crawley, East Grinstead, Eastbourne, Hastings, Heathfield, Lewes, and Worthing (details from RSPB, The Lodge, Sandy, Beds SG19 2DL)

Annual reports

'Sussex Bird Report', 3 Hurst Way, Hastings TN35 4PW

'Friends of Rye Harbour Nature Reserve Annual Report', 2 Watch Cottages, Nook Beach, Winchelsea TN36 4LU

'Pagham Harbour LNR Annual Report', Selsey Road, Sidlesham, Chichester PO20 7NE

'Shoreham and District OS Annual Report', Rock Cottage, Common Hill, West Chiltington, Pulburough RH20 2NS

Books

des Forges, G and Harber, D D. *A Guide to the Birds of Sussex*. Oliver and Boyd, 1963.

Shrubb, M. *The Birds of Sussex*. Phillimore, 1979.

Walpole-Bond, J. *A History of Sussex Birds*. Witherby, 1938.

'Hastings Rarities'

During the early years of the twentieth century, a large number of extremely rare birds was reported from the Hastings area of East Sussex and neighbouring Kent. Indeed, in some years, more than twenty-five nationally extremely rare birds were reported, almost all of them passing through the hands of George Bristow a taxidermist from St Leonards. Over the years, controversy raged about the validity of these birds as genuine migrants to Britain - some authorities maintaining their authenticity, others expressing doubts, and yet others labelling them as complete forgeries imported for sale to collectors prepared to pay high prices for the skins of 'British-taken' birds. Many of the early books included these records as genuine, but the debate continued until eventually a discussion took place in print in the journal, *British Birds*, during the 1960s. The outcome was that, with very few notable exceptions, ornithological authorities considered that the 'Hastings Rarities' were false and not genuine vagrants to Britain and should, therefore, be deleted from the official list. As a result, Sussex immediately lost forty species from the county list, although more than eight of these have now been re-established, including the Cetti's Warbler which now breeds in the county and the Whiskered Tern that has been recorded on six separate occasions.

Cetti's warbler

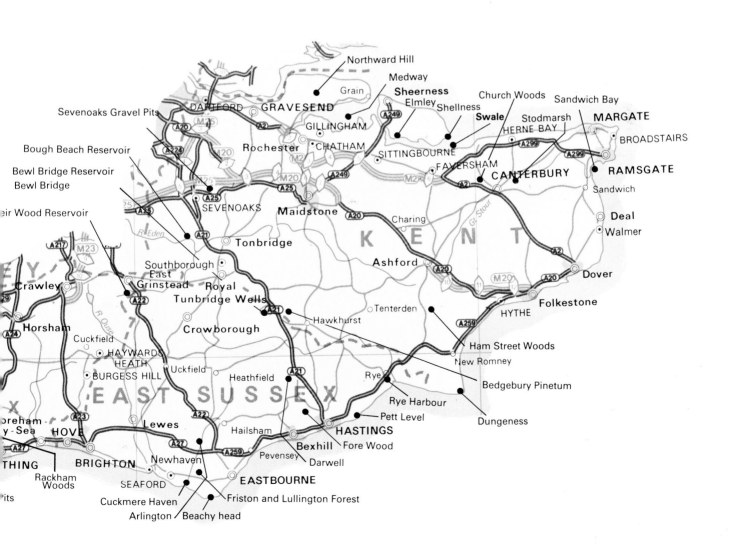

BEACHY HEAD (OS TV582952)

The cliffs of Beachy Head are largely chalk and hold very few breeding seabirds. A few Herring Gulls nest and, at one time, this was a regular breeding station for the Peregrine which has yet to recolonize the Sussex coast. Beachy Head is famous as a migration watchpoint with various well-established areas in which to search for grounded migrant birds. In the east, just south of Eastbourne is Whitbread Hollow where, for many years, regular counts of migrants, including the trapping and ringing of birds, has taken place. Further west, near the now disused Belle Tout light-house, is a small wood which is equally worth searching, as is the scrub cover near Birling Gap due south of Eastdean. Over the years, the migrants reported from these and other sites on the Head have been many and varied and, in spring and autumn, the bird population is changing almost daily. Icterine and Melodious Warblers are almost annual while, in recent years, other unusual species have included Lesser Grey Shrike. Pallas's Warbler, and Sussex's first record of a Thrush Nightingale.

CUCKMERE HAVEN (OS TV515993)

The haven is part of a much larger country park administered by the East Sussex County Council. An information centre and car park are situated where the A259 coast road crosses the Cuckmere river and, from here, it is possible to walk to the river mouth and eastwards towards the Seven Sisters Country Park. The river lacks an estuary with tidal mud so that wading birds are not a feature. Breeding Ringed Plover and Common Tern nest on islands in the lagoon behind the shingle beach, while Redshank and Yellow Wagtail nest further inland on the meadows. Bird populations are not high, but unexpected and exciting birds, such as the Little Crake, do turn up; in this case, it attracted many hundreds of birdwatchers after being shown on television.

Kent's Northward Hill reserve, here clothed in the bluebells of spring, provides home for Britain's largest Grey Heron rookery.

FRISTON AND LULLINGTON FOREST (OS TQ5500)

The extensive area of Friston Forest is managed by the Forestry Commission and includes many public rights of way from which the typical woodland species can be seen. It is best to avoid the coniferous areas and concentrate on a spring visit early or late in the day. Immediately north of the forest is the Nature Conservancy Council's Lullington Reserve, a more open area and again well seen from the many public footpaths. Bird life is varied, including both species of partridge; Kestrel and Sparrowhawk; Cuckoo and Turtle Dove. Nightingale and Grasshopper Warbler nest.

PETT LEVEL (OS TQ903147)

The pools at Pett Level lie immediately behind the sea wall and beside the coast road from Pett to Rye. Viewing is easy, and birds can be numerous and exciting although, at other times, the pools are empty. The site is best visited in the winter following some severe gales in the Channel when several species, including divers, Velvet Scoter, and Scaup take shelter on the site. In recent years, the Sussex Ornithological Society has arranged for one of the pools to be drained in autumn to provide an attractive feeding area for migrant waders. This practice has been a great success; many waders visit the site and they are very easy to see. Recently these have included a Least Sandpiper and up to three Pectoral Sandpipers from North America as well as an almost annual Temminck's Stint from northern Europe. Around the pools, the grass fields of the Levels provide feeding for large flocks of Golden Plover, Curlew, and Lapwing while, in wet winters, geese and Wigeon feed on the site. At dusk, this is a popular feeding area for Short-eared and Barn Owls.

RYE HARBOUR (OS TQ942189)

This is a mixed area of shingle, old gravel extractions, meadows, and some saltmarsh; the area is run as a reserve by the East Sussex County Council. The site has access footpaths and observation hides and is best known for its highly successful colony of Little Terns, while other breeding birds include Ringed Plover, Oystercatcher, Shelduck, and Wheatear. In the winter months the islands in the gravel pits provide a secure high-tide roost for congregations of Dunlin, Curlew, and Redshank while, on the beach, look for Turnstone and Sanderling. Migrant species may be located in the many patches of gorse and bramble scrub which also provide nesting cover for Whitethroat and Linnet.

KENT

Forming the south-east corner of the British Isles, and supporting a wide variety of habitats as well as a relatively large human population, Kent can provide for a wide diversity of bird species. The extensive coastline ranges from sandy beaches to high cliffs and from tidal estuary to freshwater marshes (now sadly largely drained). The county can still boast extensive woodland, much of it deciduous in structure, and a range of agricultural activities is still maintained although the Kentish orchards and hop fields have declined in recent years. Industrial influence in the county has resulted in the formation of a large number of areas of water, ranging from clay and gravel extraction pits to the creation of drinking-water reservoirs. The contrast between the urbanized north and west, where the county butts Greater London, and the more rural south and east is striking, but, because of the Channel ports, Kent is bisected by a series of motorways.

Birdwatching sites

NORTH KENT MARSHES

This extensive area covers the estuaries of the Rivers Thames, Medway, and Swale, and includes several sites of birding interest.

Thames: Cliffe Marshes (OS TQ730770) with its cattle-grazed meadows comprise the only non-arabilized area left beside the Thames. It provides breeding haunts for Redshank, Lapwing, and Yellow Wagtail. With flooding, these same fields attract high-tide roosts of waders from the Thames mud, and large concentrations of Curlew are not unusual. The nearby pools, the result of clay diggings, are particularly exciting for flocks of wintering duck, while the muddy margins regularly attract spring and autumn waders such as Little Stint and Curlew Sandpiper, with the occasional rarities such as Pectoral and Buff-breasted Sandpipers.

Further east, the now-drained marshes of **High Halstow** (OS TQ7878) still occasionally attract the wintering White-fronted Geese, but rising above them to the south is the RSPB reserve at **Northward Hill** (OS TQ784764) [a National Nature Reserve] and home of the largest Grey Heron colony in the British Isles, now exceeding 200 pairs. Views of the heronry, which is deep in the oak trees, are not easy, but the reserve supports a wide variety of woodland species that can be seen and heard from the visitor paths that traverse the site. An evening visit in late May is the best time for the Nightingale while, in winter, large numbers of birds arrive to use the dense hawthorn bushes as secure roosting sites.

Medway (OS TQ874720) This is an estuary of extensive tidal mud flats and saltings. It is internationally important for its wintering wildfowl and waders. It is not an easy area for the birdwatcher to observe, and you must visit the site on a rising tide when the birds are being forced to leave their feeding grounds. Viewing from any sea wall or bank will prove successful. Look out for the flocks of Brent Geese and Black-tailed Godwit.

Swale On the north shore lies the Isle of Sheppey with the RSPB reserve at **Elmley** (OS TQ960675) and the Nature Conservancy Council reserve at **Shellness** (OS TQ050680). These areas of flooded grazing marsh provide some of the most exciting birding in Kent with high populations of breeding, wintering, and migrating waterbirds. At times, nearly 2000 White-fronted Geese may be seen in the area, and this site holds the largest concentration of breeding Pochard in the British Isles.

STODMARSH (OS TR215610)

Stodmarsh is a National Nature Reserve of lagoons, reed-beds, and scrub with a splendid birders' walk from Stodmarsh village to Grove Ferry. This is the area of colonization in Britain by the Cetti's Warbler. Large numbers of wintering wildfowl are joined by roosting Hen Harriers while, in the summer months, Bearded Tits are joined by large numbers of Reed, Sedge, and Grasshopper Warblers.

DUNGENESS (OS TR080180)

Dungeness is famous for its bird observatory and RSPB reserve. It is an open, windswept shingle headland with a rather inhospitable appearance and yet with its own distinctive beauty. Large numbers of migrant birds pass through this site and seabirds can be watched from the shore. The numbers and intensity of passage will vary daily according to the prevailing weather, however. Colonies of gulls and terns nest on the reserve while, in winter months, wildfowl, including roosting Bewick's Swans, are regular features. Gales can regularly drive grebes, divers, and other seabirds on to the shelter of the freshwater pits.

CHURCH WOODS (OS TR110600) near CANTERBURY; HAM STREET WOODS (OS TR010340) near ASHFORD

The RSPB reserve (approach from the village of Rough Common) and the National Nature Reserve at Ham Street provide some of the most extensive deciduous woodland in south-east England. It is a particularly good site for spring/early summer visits when the woodland species are in full song, including Nightingale, Redstart, Tree Pipit, and a wide range of warblers.

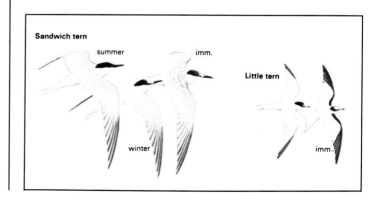

Sandwich tern — summer — imm.

Little tern

winter — imm.

Organizations in Kent

Kent Ornithological Society (KOS), 9 Greenfinches, New Barn, Longfield DA3 7ND

Kent Trust for Nature Conservation (KTNC), 1a Bower Mount Road, Maidstone ME16 8AX

Dungeness Bird Observatory (DBO), Romney Marsh, Kent TN29 2NA

Sandwich Bay Bird Observatory (SBBO), Guildford Road, Sandwich Bay CT13 9PF

RSPB Members' Groups based at: Canterbury, Folkestone, Gravesend, Maidstone, Medway, Sevenoaks, Thanet and Tonbridge (details from RSPB, The Lodge, Sandy, Beds SG19 2DL)

Annual reports

'Kent Bird Report' Perry Fields Cottage, Wingham, Canterbury CT3 1ER

Books

Taylor, D. *Birdwatching in Kent.* Meresborough Books, 1985.

Taylor, D W et al. *The Birds of Kent* (2nd ed.) Meresborough Books, 1984.

Rare birds in Kent

Geographically, Kent is uniquely positioned and abounds in enthusiastic birders. Consequently, the county can boast a long list of visiting rare birds including many first timers for the official British list:

Cream-coloured Courser **Wingham** 1785
Spotted Sandpiper **Sheerness** July 1863
Bridled Tern **Dungeness** 19 November 1931
Royal Tern **Sandwich Bay** 28 July 1965
Pallid Swift **Stodmarsh** 13 May 1978
Short-toed Treecreeper **Dungeness** 27 September 1969

A Pallas's Sandgrouse seen flying over the reedbeds at Stodmarsh on 28 December 1964 was the first to be noted in western Europe since 1909! Two Glossy Ibis, which have resided in the county since 1975 and 1979 respectively, spend most of their time at Stodmarsh during the winter and then move to the Isle of Sheppey for the summer months. During these several years spent in Kent, they have occasionally sallied northwards as far as Suffolk and Norfolk but, so far, they have always returned.

Kent specialities

Breeding

Fulmars on the cliffs of Folkestone and Dover.

Mediterranean Gulls and Roseate Terns on the islands at Dungeness

Common Gulls in the Dungeness area (the only regular English nesting site).

Nightingales in many of the woods, particularly numerous in east Kent near Canterbury.

Cetti's and Savi's Warblers in the Stour Valley, especially at Stodmarsh (the former is now common, the latter still rare).

Ring-necked Parakeets which, following successful colonization by escaped birds, are now most numerous near Gravesend and on the Isle of Thanet.

Migrating

Common Scoters offshore in large numbers in late March/April.

Pomarine Skuas off Dungeness in early May.

Large numbers of small birds pass through Kent each spring and autumn, with concentrations at coastal localities such as Sandwich Bay, St Margarets, and Dungeness. The peak period for spring is late April/early May, while, in autumn, warblers are commonest in August/September with thrushes and finches in October/November.

Wintering

White-fronted and Brent Geese in the North Kent Marshes.

Large numbers of duck on the many areas of water, including Smew at Dungeness (now one of the few regular wintering sites for this species).

Thrushes and finches on the farmland, the numbers depending upon the severity of the winter and available food supply.

Birds with Kent names

Kent is unique among British counties in having three species of birds named after the county or one of its towns. Unfortunately, all three were to disappear as breeding birds in Kent, although one has now recolonized. The Dartford Warbler last bred in 1891 and, with the loss of its favoured gorse-clad heaths, it is unlikely to be re-established. There has been a small number of late autumn records at coastal sites which probably reflect years of high breeding success and possibly involve passage birds from continental European nesting localities. The Kentish Plover is still an annual spring visitor in small numbers, and nesting attempts are occasionally recorded although no regular breeding has taken place since 1928 in the Dungeness area and 1890 in the Sandwich area. With suitable coastal reserves preventing disturbance, this is a species that could well reappear as a regular British breeding species. The third species to bear a local name is the Sandwich Tern, named after the town where the first specimen was obtained in 1784. Little is known of its early nesting in the county, but it had ceased to nest regularly in the mid-1800s. Suitable nesting islands have been provided and, on the Dungeness reserve in 1979, the area was recolonized. Numbers are now steadily increasing and have exceeded 150 pairs.

SANDWICH BAY (OS TR345610)

This is yet another site in Kent famous for a bird observatory and reserve. The extensive sand-dunes and tidal beach provide for a rich variety of gulls and waders, many of which gather into a massive roost at high tide. Over many years the observatory has recorded an extensive list of migrant species, including several firsts for the county.

SEVENOAKS GRAVEL PITS (OS TR520570)

The Sevenoaks Experimental Wildfowl Reserve is operated by the Jeffery Harrison Memorial Trust and is a prime example of conservation after use for commercial gravel extraction. Among the breeding birds is the Little Ringed Plover, but the site is best known for its wintering wildfowl. Access is by arrangement c/o Tadorna, Bradbourne Vale Road, Sevenoaks TN13 3DH.

BOUGH BEECH (OS TQ490475) AND
BEWL BRIDGE (OS TQ67535) RESERVOIRS

These are two relatively new reservoirs formed by flooding, and have extensive natural banks. Good views are readily obtained at both sites from points of vehicle access, and good numbers of wintering wildfowl can be expected in the undisturbed sections.

BEDGEBURY PINETUM (OS TQ725335)

This is one of the few woodland sites worthy of a winter visit. The keen birder can expect to find evening gatherings of Crossbill, Hawfinch, and Siskin as the birds collect for roosting.

The National Nature Reserve at Stodmarsh in Kent has an excellent walk for visiting birdwatchers.

GREATER LONDON, SURREY, AND HERTFORDSHIRE

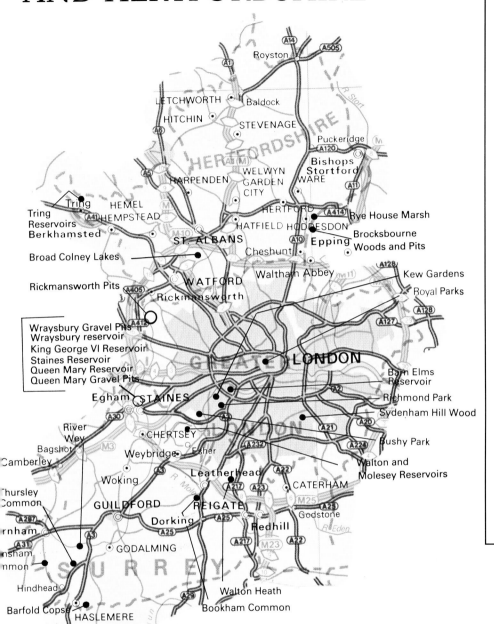

Rarities at Staines Reservoir

The Staines Reservoir beside the A3044 is probably the easiest of all the reservoirs to visit. There is public access along the central causeway which provides excellent views across both sections and, in the early 1980s, the reservoirs were drained for maintenance work which added to their attractiveness. The list of rare birds at this site is impressive and, in a three-year period the following were recorded:

Black-throated Diver	Kentish Plover
Great Northern Diver	Baird's Sandpiper
Manx Shearwater	Pectoral Sandpiper
Leach's Petrel	Wilson's Phalarope
Red-crested Pochard	Red-necked Phalarope
Long-tailed Duck	Arctic Skua
Marsh Harrier	Great Skua
Peregrine	Mediterranean Gull
Osprey	Ring-billed Gull
Avocet	Iceland Gull
Collared Pratincole	Caspian Tern

northern race

southern race

Great grey shrike

LONDON

Political changes make an ornithological definition of 'London' difficult. The Ornithological Section of the London Natural History Society compiles its observations from within a radius of 20 miles from St Paul's, but this area includes a considerable proportion of the 'Home Counties'. The central core of the Greater London area is, at first glance, unlikely to contain much of interest to the birdwatcher – largely, a concrete jungle with a high density of human population. However, the few reservoirs and, more importantly, the Royal Parks, despite their high levels of disturbance, are very attractive to many species.

Birdwatching sites

BARN ELMS RESERVOIR (OS TQ3377)

Nestling beside the Thames near Hammersmith, this collection of four different areas of water not only attracts a selection of winter waterfowl but, because of the proximity of the river, often provides the birdwatcher with unexpected arrivals that have obviously been following the Thames until they are attracted to the greater expanse of water at Barn Elms. At one time, this was a major wintering ground for Smew and Goosander but, although these species still occur regularly, their numbers are now greatly

In London's concrete jungle, the reservoirs are attractive to many birds.

Ringing recoveries from Surrey
Coot: a young bird ringed at Reigate in July 1982
    was found shot in France in December 1982.
Mallard: a bird ringed in Poland in June 1981 was
    shot at Godalming in November 1982.
Lapwing: a chick ringed at Effingham in 1980 was
    found shot in Portugal in February 1981.
Snipe: a bird ringed at Horsham in August 1963 was
    shot in Eire in March 1964.
Nightingale: an adult ringed at Witley in June 1979
    was recorded back at the same site in June 1984.
Lesser Whitethroat: a bird ringed near Staines in
    August 1979 was found dead in Switzerland in
    May 1981.
Blackcap: a migrant ringed at Queen Mary
    Reservoir in September 1981 was found dead in
    Algeria in October 1983.
Siskin: an adult ringed near Virginia Water in April
    1980 was trapped and released in Lithuania,
    USSR in October 1981; it was then trapped and
    released again at Virginia Water in January 1982
    and was then found dead in Finland in April 1984.

Organizations in Surrey
Surrey Bird Club (SBC), Applegarth House, The
    Hildens, Westacott RH4 3JX
Surrey Trust for Nature Conservation (STNC),
    Hatchlands, East Clandon, Guildford GU4 7RT
RSPB Members' Groups based at: Dorking, East
    Surrey, Epsom, Guildford, and Weybridge (details
    from RSPB, The Lodge, Sandy, Beds SG19 2DL)

Annual reports
'Surrey Bird Report', Flat C, Avington, 31 London
    Road, Guildford GU1 1SH

Books
Parr, D. *Birds in Surrey 1900-1970*. Batsford, 1972.

reduced. Tufted Duck and Pochard can exceed 600 individuals, while small parties of Gadwall are regular with occasional pairs nesting among the uncut vegetation on the reservoir banks. In recent years, sightings of more typically marine species have included Scaup, Common Scoter, Turnstone, Kittiwake, Iceland Gull, and Little Auk – all tending to favour the late autumn for their appearance.

ROYAL PARKS
London's Royal Parks have, of late, tended to show a small but steady increase in the numbers of species occurring and breeding. This has been particularly apparent in the Central London sites, such as Hyde Park and Kensington Gardens, St James's and Green Park, Regent's Park and Greenwich Park. There are probably two main reasons for this increase: the growing tendency to create and encourage undisturbed 'bird sanctuary zones' within the parks; and the general reduction in pollution of the London atmosphere and waterways resulting in an increase in the availability of food. Bird records from the Central London parks include over ninety different species each year with more than thirty species nesting. The greatest concentrations are in Kensington Gardens and Regent's Park. The more outlying parks, such as Richmond, Hampton Court, Bushy, and Kew Gardens, have always held a greater variety of birds than other parts of London, and annually produce some unexpected visitors. Over 100 species are recorded annually with some sixty breeding. Recent sightings have included: **Hyde Park** – Slavonian Grebe and Shag; **Kensington Gardens** – Lesser Spotted Woodpecker; **St James's Park** – Ruddy Duck; **Regent's Park** – Mediterranean Gull and Firecrest; **Richmond Park** – Red-throated Diver; **Bushy Park** – Hoopoe and Dartford Warbler; **Kew Gardens** – White-fronted Goose and Hawfinch.

SYDENHAM HILL WOOD (OS TQ346726)
This is a small woodland site managed as a reserve by the London Wildlife Trust. Although it is close to Central London and in an extensive residential area, the reserve contains as wide a range of species as would be found in any south-eastern English deciduous wood, including woodpeckers, warblers, tits, and so on. Early and late in the day during May and June are the best times for visiting, when bird song is at its peak, although the reserve is always open.

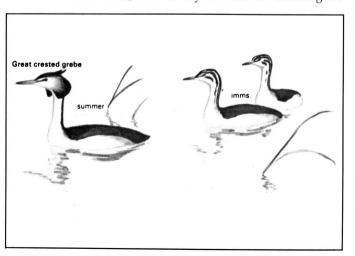

Great crested grebe

summer

imms.

SURREY

The clays, Greensand, and chalk that make up the base rocks of Surrey, coupled with its proximity to London and the high level of urbanization between them, govern the bird habitats of the county. A combination of heaths, commons, woods, and the results of industry in the form of gravel pits, reservoirs and sewage farms broadly summarize the birdwatching habitats in Surrey. Two major rivers, the Wey and the Mole, flow north to the Thames which forms the northern boundary of the county. Ornithologically, the London boundary has always been slightly complicated by the recording area of the London Natural History Society; the latter is concerned with bird observations within 20 miles of St Paul's Cathedral – which includes nearly one-third of Surrey. With the reorganization of county boundaries, several additional birdwatching sites (formerly in Middlesex) fell within the new county boundary, but the Surrey Bird Club continues to operate in the old 'vice county of Surrey' which is bounded by the Thames in the north and Kent in the east.

The proximity of London resulted in Surrey supplying many of the birds needed for Britain's capital in the nineteenth century when keeping cagebirds, particularly Surrey-caught Nightingales, was highly fashionable. The woods and heaths of the county also provided the street markets of the day with such edible delicacies as Skylark, Wheatear, and Green Woodpecker! A change in attitudes from the beginning of the twentieth century produced a growing interest in the recording of birds rather than the trapping – even so, by the 1980s, the county still does not have a major bird reserve, old or new, within its boundaries.

Such exotics as Slavonian Grebes have been spotted recently in Hyde Park.

Birdwatching sites

HEATHS AND COMMONS

Many of the Surrey commonlands, particularly near London, have been lost, and, in parts of the county, large tracts of land are under the control of the military. Well in excess of 10 000 hectares (25 000 acres) of commonland with public access still exist, however, and many of the heathland sites within this total are important for the breeding bird communities of the county. Several sites now include reserves or protected areas: at **Thursley Common** (OS SU8941) is a Nature Conservancy Council reserve; **Frensham Common** (OS SU8440) has a country park run by the Waverley District Council; **Bookham Common** (OS TQ1256) and the nearby **Walton Heath** (OS TQ2253) have a series of nature trails arranged by the National Trust.

Bookham Common is a unique site in that the London Natural History Society has been carrying out detailed observations and recordings of all aspects of its wildlife for over forty years. Thus, the Society has accumulated a valuable series of bird observations showing annual variations in populations. The commons tend to lack birds in the winter months, although parties of Fieldfares and Redwings will exploit any berry crops, while occasional Great Grey Shrikes or Hen Harriers occur in most years.

Late May or June are most productive for the visiting birdwatcher, with Tree Pipit, Grasshopper Warbler, Stonechat, and, in some areas, Nightjar and Hobby. The Dartford Warbler nests regularly but numbers are very dependent upon the severity of the preceding winter.

The few remaining heathlands of Surrey, such as Frensham Common, are important breeding sites.

BARFOLD COPSE (OS SU928318)
This is a small RSPB mixed woodland reserve situated south-west of Haslemere off the B2131. The oak tree is dominant, with an understorey of hazel and two small woodland streams. The bird population is mixed with typical species, such as Nuthatch, woodpeckers, and a range of warblers in summer. Tawny Owls nest and Sparrowhawks occur regularly.

RIVER WEY
Between Guildford and Woking, the River Wey has a navigation channel owned by the National Trust. Near Woking there are several small gravel extractions in the valley, and the river and its navigation continues through this area to join the Thames at Weybridge. There are several access points to the river and it is possible to walk along the bank for several miles. The small gravel pits at Papercourt can be viewed from several roads near the town of Send. The river area should be searched thoroughly for views of Kingfisher, Grey Wagtail, and Little Grebe while, in the winter months, occasional Green Sandpiper and Water Rail can be encountered. The Papercourt area is a site for winter visiting, with over 100 Pochard and Tufted Duck, and up to forty-five Goosander. Occasional migrant waders, such as Spotted Redshank, Jack Snipe, and Ruff may make a brief stop.

RESERVOIRS
In the Thames Valley, stretching from Sunbury to Wraysbury is an almost continuous line of gravel pits and reservoirs which, although artificial and largely embanked with concrete, have produced a wealth of bird records over the years and have become sites of major importance for their wintering wildfowl populations. At times, when it has been necessary to drain them for maintenance work, they have also attracted migrant waders, including several rare visitors. Some sites have public viewing while, at others, there is strict control of access. Information on visiting is available from the Thames Water Authority. This network of water areas is very much on the boundary of Berkshire, Surrey, and the old county of Middlesex but, for completeness, they are all listed here, from west to east, together with some recent sightings: **Queen Mother Reservoir:** Leach's Petrel; two Black-throated Divers; and Red-necked Grebe. **Wraysbury Gravel Pits:** Night Heron; up to 1000 Pochard; and Alpine Swift. **Wraysbury Reservoir:** Great Northern Diver; Little Auk; and Ferruginous Duck. **King George VI Reservoir:** up to nine Black-necked Grebes; sixty-five Goosander; and Great Skua. **Staines Reservoir:** up to twenty Black-necked Grebes; seventy Goosander; together with many rarities (*see* below). **Queen Mary Reservoir:** peak of over 350 Great Crested Grebes; and Leach's Petrel. **Queen Mary Gravel Pits:** over 300 Canada Geese; and twenty-seven Goosander. **Walton and Molesey Reservoirs:** 300 Canada Geese; and up to eighty-three Goldeneye. **Queen Elizabeth II Reservoir:** Red-throated Diver; and over 100 Cormorants. **Island Barn Reservoir:** up to four Black-necked Grebes; and Long-tailed Duck.

HERTFORDSHIRE
Being so close to London, Hertfordshire, stretching from the clay of London suburbs at Watford and Barnet in the south to the Chiltern chalk at Luton and Stevenage in the north, has become a very urbanized county. The highest ground, the edge of the Chilterns, is in the west with the most rural areas in the east where the county borders Cambridgeshire and the fens. Two main rivers and their tributaries drain the county southwards, the Colne in the west and Lee in the east. Both rivers have their associated gravel workings which, together with a limited number of reservoirs (the main complex being at Tring), provide the only sizeable areas of open water in the county. Much of the north is arable farmland, with grassland and urban development concentrated in the south. Woodland is widely scattered and is now in short supply with only a small fraction of the historically extensive woods to be found in the county. Natural or seminatural woods are extremely rare. Some 275 species have been recorded in Hertfordshire, approximately 130 of which have bred.

Birdwatching sites

TRING RESERVOIRS (OS SP9113)
This complex of reservoirs, which undoubtedly forms one of the most important bird sites in the county, was originally constructed in the early years of the nineteenth century to ensure the availability of water for the Grand Union Canal which, at that time, was of major commercial importance for Hertfordshire. The site is now a National Nature Reserve under the control of the Nature Conservancy Council and includes a series of car parks, nature trails, footpaths, and observation hides, all of which provide excellent facilities for visiting birdwatchers at any time of the year. Among the regularly recorded species are Great Crested Grebes with as many as eighty birds present in the autumn and up to twelve breeding pairs; there may be many hundreds of wintering wildfowl, principally Mallard, Teal, Shoveler, Tufted Duck, and Pochard; several species

of waders occur during the spring and autumn migrations; and, also to be seen are large roosts of gulls, often containing as many as 25 000 individuals. Two breeding records are of national importance: a pair of Black-necked Grebes in 1919 constituted the first English breeding record; and a pair of Little Ringed Plovers in 1938 provided the first British breeding record. Little Ringed Plovers still nest occasionally, but Black-necked Grebes have now been relegated to irregular migrants.

BROAD COLNEY LAKES (OS TL175033)
This is a small reserve of river banks, disused gravel pit, and young woodland under the control of the Hertfordshire and Middlesex Trust for Nature Conservation. A series of paths and a hide can be used throughout the year. The woodland and scrub attract a range of species, including summer warblers, while the reed-fringed areas of water attract grebes, coot, and a small number of winter wildfowl.

RYE HOUSE MARSH (OS TL386100)
This RSPB reserve forms part of the Lee Valley Regional Park and has a staffed educational centre involved in a wide range of field courses and other activities. Public visiting is possible on certain days when a nature trail and hides can provide excellent views of a wide range of species in an otherwise very urban setting. Several species nest: a selection of warblers, including the recently colonized Cetti's Warbler; Mallard and Tufted Duck. In winter, Kingfisher, Water Rail, and Snipe are all of regular occurrence.

BROXBOURNE WOODS AND PITS (OS TL3706)
Under the control of the Lee Valley Regional Park, like Rye House, this site is at the northern end of the Lee Valley complex before the river flows southwards into the London area. Access to the site is from the Broxbourne Old Mill Meadows car park, and the habitat range includes woods, river, and open water. A wide range of species can be seen throughout the year with Kingfisher, Nuthatch, and Tree-creeper regularly to be seen.

RICKMANSWORTH PITS (OS TQ0587 to TQ0593)
These pits are the result of gravel extraction in the valley of the River Colne, and they provide a suitable site for a wide range of wintering wildfowl, breeding grebes, and so on, in a county lacking sites of open water.

Organizations in Hertfordshire
Hertfordshire Natural History Society (HNHS) – Ornithological Section – 9 Devonshire Close, Stevenage SG2 8RY
Hertfordshire and Middlesex Trust for Nature Conservation (HMTNC), Grebe House, St Michael's Street, St Albans AL3 4SN
RSPB Members' Groups based at: Chorleywood, Harpenden, Hemel Hempstead, Hertford, Hitchin, Potters Bar, St Albans, South-east, Stevenage, Watford, and Welwyn Garden (details from RSPB, The Lodge, Sandy, Beds SG19 2DL)

Annual reports
'Birds in Hertfordshire', 6 Castle Hill, Berkhampstead HP4 1HE

Books
Holdsworth, M et al. The Birds of Tring Reservoirs. HNHS, 1978.
Mead, C and Smith, K. The Hertfordshire Breeding Bird Atlas. HBBA, 1982.
Sage, B L. A History of the Birds of Hertfordshire.

Barrie & Rockliffe, 1959.
Sage, B L. The Species of Birds Recorded in Hertfordshire. HNHS, 1979.

Rare birds in Hertfordshire
Like all inland counties, Hertfordshire cannot boast a regular series of off-course migrants, and rare birds arriving in the county for the first time are rather few and far between. The following list details species recorded in Hertfordshire on one occasion only together with the year of its occurrence:
Squacco Heron (1979)
Bean Goose (1979)
American Wigeon (1971)
Blue-winged Teal (1978)
Little Crake (1953)
Baillon's Crake (1891)
Sociable Plover (1961)
Long-billed Dowitcher (1977)
Marsh Sandpiper (1887)
Lesser Yellowlegs (1953)
Solitary Sandpiper (1967)

Spotted Sandpiper (1956)
Long-tailed Skua (1937)
Roseate Tern (1969)
Razorbill (1934)
White-winged Lark (1955)
Rock Thrush (1843)
Aquatic Warbler (1960)
Great Reed Warbler (1946)
Paddyfield Warbler (1981)
Ortolan Bunting (1953)
Rustic Bunting (1882)
Little Bunting (1960)

Changes in the breeding birds of Hertfordshire
Species that have begun regular breeding since 1950: Greylag Goose, Canada Goose, Tufted Duck, Little Ringed Plover, Common Tern, Collared Dove, and Meadow Pipit.
Species that have ceased regular breeding since 1950:
Barn Owl, Nightjar, Wryneck, Redstart, Whinchat, Red-backed Shrike, Crossbill, Cirl Bunting.

BERKSHIRE, BUCKINGHAMSHIRE, AND OXFORDSHIRE

BERKSHIRE

The woodlands that once covered the extreme east of the county are now largely lost, but they are represented by some fine stands of timber in Windsor Great Park. In the south only remnants of the heathlands remain on the Surrey and Hampshire borders while the solid block of rolling Berkshire downland that forms the northern boundary of the county is now largely rolling cereal fields. The Thames provides the eastern boundaries, and its main tributaries, the Lambourn and the Kennet, drain the county in an eastward direction. As with so many areas of inland southern Britain, sites of open water are largely artificial. In Berkshire they are confined to the reservoirs of Datchet and Wraysbury in the extreme east, Virginia Water in Windsor Great Park, and the collection of gravel pits in the valleys of the major rivers. Open water is largely absent in the north of the county. Over 280 species of birds have been recorded in Berkshire, up to 190 of which may occur in any one year and over 100 breed annually.

Birdwatching sites

DINTON PASTURES COUNTRY PARK (OS SU7871)

Based on a series of disused gravel pits and managed by the Wokingham District Council, this country park attracts a wide range of woodland and waterbirds, although it is close to the busy M4 motorway. A published guide to the park's nature trail is available from the information centre. Typical species include Kingfisher, Great Crested Grebe, Tufted Duck, and, over the more open country, Kestrel.

WINDSOR GREAT PARK

Under the control of the Crown Estate Commissioners, part of the former Royal Hunting Forest has been declared a reserve by the Nature Conservancy Council. The range of habitats within the park makes this one of the most varied birdwatching areas in the county. Ancient woodland with high forest and open parkland contrast with the more recent coniferous woods. Sparrowhawk, warblers, Tree-creepers, woodpeckers, and Redstart are recorded in the former, while Coal Tit, Goldcrest, and, at times, Crossbill in the latter. Birds of more open country, the Stonechat, Hobby, occasional Woodlark, and Nightjar, are to be found in the open heathland sites with their patches of bracken.

Water has a great attraction for the birds and, likewise birdwatchers and other visitors are also drawn towards **Virginia Water** on the southern edge of the park. In addition to a wide range of wintering wildfowl, Gadwall, Teal, Wigeon, and so on, this is the site at which the Mandarin Duck has successfully colonized Britain. Although small numbers are well established at various other sites in Britain, Windsor Great Park, with a breeding population dependent upon the old oak trees, and flocks often exceeding 100 birds, is the easiest place to view the species. For the birdwatcher, Virginia Water is worth visiting at any time of the year, and a circular walk around the 'Water' and through the adjoining woodland and parkland provides an excellent day's observations.

MAIDENHEAD THICKET (OS SU856811)

This is a small woodland reserve under the control of the National Trust and, although it is close to the busy A4 road, a spring or early summer visit will reveal a wide variety of breeding summer migrants. This is a favoured site for the Nightingale and a dusk visit is likely to find them at their most vocal when other singing species should include Lesser Whitethroat, Blackcap, and Garden Warbler as well as the more familiar Chiffchaff and Willow Warbler. In the winter months a range of tits, woodpeckers, and finches can be expected.

GRAVEL PITS

The river valleys of southern Berkshire contain a considerable number of gravel pits of varying age and size. The extraction programme continues so that the birdwatching potential is always changing. Any gravel pits are worth looking at but you should always make sure that you have permission to go there, and active workings and machinery must be avoided.

Three major sites in Berkshire are **Wraysbury Gravel Pit** (OS TQ0173) on the Surrey border near Slough (together with the nearby reservoir), **Theale Gravel Pit** (OS SU6470) near Reading, and **Thatcham Gravel Pit** near Newbury. All these sites are very productive for birds, concentrations of winter wildfowl, visiting migrants, and rarities, together with a range of other species attracted to the vegetation that has developed on the older, well-established pits. Close by the Thatcham pits are the **Thatcham Reedbeds** (OS SU501673), which form a reserve under the control of the Newbury District Council, and are among the most important reedbeds in southern England. Large numbers of birds are found here throughout the year including passage migrants and rarer visitors, such as Cetti's Warbler and Spotted Crake.

Natural meadows, with their wild flowers, can still be found in Berkshire.

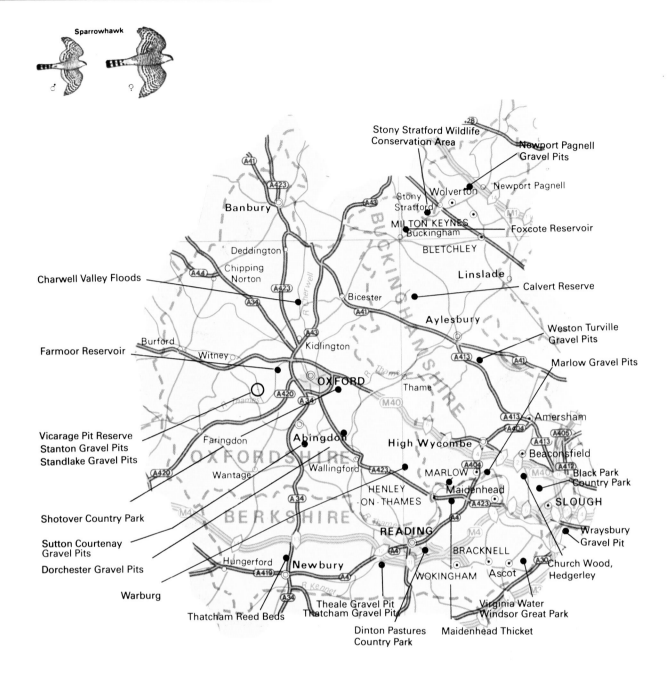

Sparrowhawk

Stony Stratford Wildlife Conservation Area

Newport Pagnell Gravel Pits

Newport Pagnell

Wolverton

Stony Stratford

MILTON KEYNES

Buckingham

Foxcote Reservoir

BLETCHLEY

Banbury

Deddington

Chipping Norton

Charwell Valley Floods

Bicester

Linslade

Calvert Reserve

Aylesbury

Weston Turville Gravel Pits

Farmoor Reservoir

Burford

Witney

Kidlington

Marlow Gravel Pits

OXFORD

Thame

Thame

Amersham

Vicarage Pit Reserve
Stanton Gravel Pits
Standlake Gravel Pits

Faringdon

Abingdon

High Wycombe

Beaconsfield

Wantage

Wallingford

MARLOW

Black Park Country Park

SLOUGH

Shotover Country Park

HENLEY -ON-THAMES

Maidenhead

Wraysbury Gravel Pit

Sutton Courtenay Gravel Pits

READING

BRACKNELL

Ascot

Church Wood, Hedgerley

Dorchester Gravel Pits

Hungerford

Newbury

WOKINGHAM

Warburg

Thatcham Reed Beds

Theale Gravel Pit
Thatcham Gravel Pit

Dinton Pastures Country Park

Virginia Water
Windsor Great Park

Maidenhead Thicket

Organizations in Berkshire

Newbury District Ornithological Club (NDOC), Brimstone Cottage, Little Lane, Upper Bucklebury, Reading RG7 6QX

Reading Ornithological Club (ROC), 18 Harcourt Close, Henley-on-Thames RG9 1UZ

Berkshire, Buckinghamshire and Oxfordshire Naturalists' Trust (BBONT), 3 Church Cowley Road, Rose Hill, Oxford OX4 3JR

RSPB Members' Group based at: East Berkshire (details from RSPB, The Lodge, Sandy, Beds SG19 2DL)

Annual reports

'Birds of Berkshire', 7 Llanvair Drive, South Ascot SL5 9HS

'Newbury Bird Report', 33 Rowan Drive, Newbury

Books

Fitter, Richard (ed.). *The Wildlife of the Thames Counties*. Robert Dugdale, 1985.

Radford, MC. *The Birds of Berkshire and Oxfordshire.* Longman, 1966.

Earliest arrival dates of migrants in Berkshire

For some years, the annual report on the bird life in the county has reported the earliest recorded dates for arriving summer migrants. The following list gives a recent selection:

Turtle Dove – 25 April	Nightingale – 20 April
Cuckoo – 11 April	Sedge Warbler – 2 April
Swift – 21 April	Reed Warbler – 23 April
Sand Martin – 8 March	
Swallow – 13 March	Willow Warbler – 23 March
House Martin – 13 March	
Tree Pipit – 2 April	Spotted Flycatcher – 15 April
Yellow Wagtail – 4 April	

Turtle dove

imm.

BUCKINGHAMSHIRE

From the Thames Valley at its southern boundary, Buckinghamshire stretches northwards and is crossed by a series of distinctive features. The Chilterns and their escarpment form the core of the county, followed by the River Thame that flows westwards through the Vale of Aylesbury. The north of the county is principally agricultural on a limestone base but still retains some of the best examples of woodland in the area. At its northern border, Buckinghamshire drains eastwards via the river Ouse. Ornithological interest in the county is largely confined to woodland, from Burnham Beeches in the south to the edge of Salcey Forest in the north, and the wetland areas. The latter are few, artificial, and confined to the river valleys. Some 270 species have been recorded in the county of which just under 100 breed annually.

Birdwatching sites

CALVERT RESERVE (OS SP683248)

This is a small reserve under the control of the Berkshire, Buckinghamshire and Oxfordshire Naturalists' Trust (BBONT) and based upon disused brick pits. The site attracts a range of winter wildfowl as well as breeding birds in the surrounding scrubland. The reserve can be easily viewed from the road and is best approached via Steeple Claydon, south of Buckingham.

Opposite: *The River Thames winds through Oxfordshire, receiving its water from the chalk and limestone hills. A riverside walk can always be enjoyable for birdwatchers in the county.*

Below: *Woodland and the typical large, arable fields of today's farms meet in this scene which is typical of parts of rural Buckinghamshire. There is little wetland in the county, and what there is is largely artificial.*

CHURCH WOOD, HEDGERLEY (OS SU973873)

This is a small, but very mixed 14-hectare (34-acre) wood owned by the RSPB and containing a varied bird community that includes woodpeckers, tits, occasional Sparrowhawks, and Tawny Owl. In winter the population includes Woodcock, Siskin, and Goldcrest. Because of its extremely varied plant life, the wood contains an excellent variety of butterfly species.

FOXCOTE RESERVOIR (OS SP712364)

This BBONT reserve can be viewed easily from the roadside and is worthy of a visit at any time of the year. In summer, Yellow Wagtails are regular and a good variety of migrant waders occur. In winter it is one of the key sites in the county for winter wildfowl, including a regular occurrence of Goosander and large concentrations of Mallard and Teal. The site is easily viewed from the road leading to Leckhampsted north-east of Buckingham.

STONY STRATFORD WILDLIFE CONSERVATION AREA (OS SP786411)

During the construction of the extensive new road network around Milton Keynes, especially the new A5, a lot of gravel was needed, pits were dug, and, with help from the Milton Keynes Development Corporation, this completely new reserve was constructed. In addition to a car park, nature trail, and observation hide for visitors (it is possible to visit the reserve throughout the year), a good deal of work was undertaken to create a range of sites for breeding and feeding birds. A variety of islands has produced undisturbed sites where winter wildfowl can feed, while specially constructed banks provide suitable breeding areas for Kingfisher and Sand Martin.

BLACK PARK COUNTRY PARK (OS TQ006832)

Within the Country Park, the Buckinghamshire County Council has created a nature reserve that includes part of the lake where nesting rafts have been constructed for species such as Mallard and Great Crested Grebe. A nature trail has been installed which passes through some of the park's mixed woodland which is attractive to a range of species including Nuthatch, several warblers, and Goldcrest.

GRAVEL PITS

Among some of the gravel pits scattered through the county are those at **Marlow** (in the Thames Valley), **Weston Turville** (in the Thame valley), and **Newport Pagnell** (in the Ouse valley). Although many of the older workings are now well vegetated and contain good breeding populations of such species as Reed Bunting and Sedge Warbler, the sites are still best known for the winter duck flocks that are regular features.

Nuthatch

Goldcrest

imm.

Organizations in Buckinghamshire

Buckinghamshire Bird Club (BBC), 319 Bath Road, Cippenham, Slough SL1 5PR

Middle Thames Natural History Society (MTNHS), 113 Holtspur Top Lane, Beaconsfield HP9 1DT

Berkshire, Buckinghamshire and Oxfordshire Naturalists' Trust (BBONT), 3 Church Cowley Road, Rose Hill, Oxford OX4 3JR

RSPB Members' Groups based at: Aylesbury and North (details from RSPB, The Lodge, Sandy, Beds SG19 2DL)

Annual reports

'Buckinghamshire Bird Report', 319 Bath Road, Cippenham, Slough SL1 5PR

'North Bucks Bird Report', 15 Jubilee Terrace, Stony Stratford MK11 1DU

Books

Fitter, Richard (ed.). *The Wildlife of the Thames Counties*. Robert Dugdale, 1985.

Fraser, A C and Youngman, R E. *The Birds of Buckinghamshire and East Berkshire*. Middle Thames Natural History Society, 1976.

Some old records from the county

Some of the more unusual bird records from the last century have never been repeated and are perhaps unlikely to be. Occasionally, the unexpected does happen and a species that has not been recorded for nearly 100 years is noted again. Among these old records, there are always some that must be viewed with a certain amount of suspicion:

Glossy Ibis – one shot near Wendover in October 1886

Guillemot – one seen near Simpson in November 1852

Pallas's Sandgrouse – a flock seen at Farnham Royal in 1888

Scops Owl – one shot near Brill in spring 1833

White-tailed Eagle – one at Fawley in 1895, and then in early 1984 a bird arrived and stayed for some while at Brill

Great Auk – this is perhaps the most amazing of all the old claimed records. The Great Auk was a flightless seabird from the extreme North Atlantic. Yarrel in his *British Birds* states: 'Mr Bullock told Dr. Fleming some years ago that a specimen was taken in a pond of fresh water, two miles from the Thames, on the estate of Sir William Clayton, near Marlow in Buckinghamshire.'

Organizations in Oxfordshire
Oxford Ornithological Society (OOS), Edward Grey
  Institute of Field Ornithology, Department of
  Zoology, South Parks Road, Oxford OX1 3PS
Banbury Ornithological Society (BOS), 20
  Chacombe Road, Middleton Cheney, Banbury
  OX17 2QS
Berkshire, Buckinghamshire and Oxfordshire
  Naturalists' Trust, 3 Church Cowley Road, Rose
  Hill, Oxford OX4 3JR
RSPB Members' Groups based at: Vale of White
  Horse and Oxford (details from RSPB, The Lodge,
  Sandy, Beds SG19 2DL)

Annual reports
'Birds of Oxfordshire', Old Mill Cottage, Avon
  Dassett, Leamington Spa, Warwickshire
'Banbury Ornithological Society Annual Report',
  Tadmarton Manor, Banbury OX15 5TD

Books
Easterbrook, T G. *Birds of the Banbury Area.*

Banbury Ornithological Society, 1983.
Fitter, R (ed.). *The Wildlife of the Thames Counties.*
  Robert Dugdale, 1985.
Radford, M C. *The Birds of Berkshire and
  Oxfordshire.* Longman, 1966.

Birds of Oxfordshire's woods
Most mixed deciduous woods of any size in the
county can be expected to produce something
approaching fifty different species of breeding
birds. This figure will obviously vary depending upon
the wood's location, size, structure, and so on. The
following species can always be expected as the
most numerous:

**Over 50 breeding pairs per square
kilometre (128/sq mi)**

Woodpigeon	Robin
Wren	Goldcrest
Blackbird	Chaffinch

**Between 25 and 50 breeding pairs per
square kilometre (64-128/sq mi)**

Great Tit	Blackcap
Blue Tit	Chiffchaff
Song Thrush	Starling

**Between 10 and 25 breeding pairs per
square kilometre (25-64/sq mi)**

Stock Dove	Marsh Tit
Turtle Dove	Long-tailed Tit
Tawny Owl	Treecreeper
Great Spotted Woodpecker	Garden Warbler
Rook	Willow Warbler
Magpie	Dunnock
Jay	Greenfinch
Coal Tit	

OXFORDSHIRE

The River Thames winds through much of the county,
receiving its waters from the large number of tributaries
that drain the chalk and limestone hills which make up the
bulk of the county. Towards the east, the clay basin of the
Thames becomes more dominant. Very much an agricultural county, the rolling hills of the Cotswolds, Berkshire
Downs, and Chilterns overlook the more fertile vales.

For the birdwatcher, the county can offer open
countryside, varied woods, and riverside walks, but little
extensive water apart from the familiar gravel pits of
modern industry and one major reservoir at Farmoor. A few
flood meadows remain. Oxford has a long association with
British bird study which is still maintained today. The
university nurtured many enthusiastic ornithologists and
is still the home of the Edward Grey Institute which is
primarily concerned with field ornithology. Through its
teams of students and professional staff, the bird life of one
particular site, Wytham Wood, has probably been studied
in greater depth than any other area in the country.
Information obtained at Wytham has revealed extensive
details of the breeding biology of many woodland species.
Far from the coast, and denied a considerable number of
species because of it, Oxfordshire can still produce nearly
200 different species of birds each year.

Birdwatching sites

WARBURG (OS SU720880)
This is one of BBONT's largest and most important reserves, with a wide range of woodland and open grassland
habitats. Although perhaps Warburg is more important for
its varied plant and insect life, the summer months can
produce an interesting selection of breeding birds, including among the migrant warblers, small numbers of
Wood Warblers. Woodcock, Sparrowhawk, and Willow Tit
all occur and an early morning visit to the nature trail in
spring or early summer can be most interesting. The car
park is reached by turning off the A423 at Bix along the road
signposted to Bix Bottom.

CHERWELL VALLEY FLOODS (OS SP4822 northwards)
Although it is no longer as important for bird life as it once

was, at certain times of the year the remaining meadows
beside the Cherwell can attract a range of interesting birds.
Recent weather conditions must be taken into account
when planning a visit to the site because, if the site is dry,
there will be few birds, if any. During winter and early
spring when flooding is present, a variety of waterfowl can
be expected but, even under apparently ideal conditions,
the reservoir and gravel pits of the county now give a better
day's birdwatching. Whooper Swans occur regularly in
small numbers, and parties of Pintail, Wigeon, and Teal
frequently number hundreds. Occasional geese are
recorded while Lapwing flocks often exceed 1000 birds.

FARMOOR RESERVOIR (OS SP4506)
Farmoor is the main site in the county for numbers of
wintering duck, with occasional visits from migrant
waders in spring and autumn. Observing is best from the
access point off the B4044 west of Oxford. In recent years
sightings have included Great Northern and Red-throated
Divers, Slavonian and Black-necked Grebes, Shag, Scaup,
and Velvet and Common Scoters.

SHOTOVER COUNTRY PARK (OS SP5706)
Under the control of the Oxford City Council and very close
to the city centre at Headington, this woodland site can
offer a surprising mixture of woodland, marsh, heath, and
grassland with extensive networks of nature trails.
Historically, this was a Royal hunting forest, and deer are
still to be seen, together with a wide range of bird species.

GRAVEL PITS
For the birdwatcher, the best gravel pits in the county are
located south and west of Oxford, with the **Vicarage Pit
Reserve** (BBONT) near Stanton Harcourt (OS SP400057)
perhaps the main site, with others at **Dorchester, Stanton,
Standlake** (which is near Farmoor reservoir), and **Sutton
Courtenay**. All these sites contribute to the winter wildfowl
population in the county, and some recent maximum
counts are: Great Crested Grebe 167; Mute Swan 121;
Canada Goose 1234; Wigeon 1331; Gadwall 80; Teal 301;
Mallard 2674; Shoveler 137; Pochard 1070; Tufted Duck 931;
Goldeneye 81; Goosander 94.

ESSEX

The predominant clay of Essex is relieved only by areas of chalk in the extreme north-west of the county and the coastal strip of reclaimed silt and alluvium in the south-east. Although geologically rather uniform, the habitat variation is such that, ornithologically, the county holds a variety of exciting birds. The 310 miles or more of coastline is indented by the estuaries of several rivers which provide expanses of tidal mud and saltmarsh that attract huge flocks of migrant and wintering wildfowl and waders. Inland waters are all artificial, but two major reservoirs and a network of gravel pits in the river valleys bring in large numbers of birds.

The north of Essex is intensively cultivated, while the south-west, nearest to London, is the most urban with an extended commuter belt stretching out from the capital to Southend. Paradoxically, it is the south that retains most of the remaining woodland, including the famous Epping Forest. The county is extremely well supplied with a net-work of nature reserves. Five National Nature Reserves have been established by the Nature Conservancy Council, an extensive series is under the control of the Essex Naturalists' Trust, and national bodies such as the Woodland Trust, RSPB, and National Trust all own land in the county. On a more local scale, several district councils have declared 'local nature reserves'. When the total area of all these sites is added up, some 3 per cent of the county's land surface is protected in one way or another. Nearly 340 species of birds have been recorded in Essex, of which almost 120 breed each year.

Birdwatching sites

EPPING FOREST

The 2500 hectares (6250 acres) of ancient woodland that go to make up Epping Forest so close to London owe their survival to King Henry I who declared the area a Royal Forest for the protection of deer. This is a popular public place and can be greatly disturbed by visitors, but early or late in the day the birdwatching can often be excellent, and there are many quiet corners waiting to be discovered. If it is at all possible, avoid visiting the forest during mid-summer weekends when the human population is at its highest. There are many walkways and paths through the woodland, with several car parks and access points. In addition to the mixed deciduous woodland with its pollarded beech and hornbeam, there are areas of open grassland, wet marshes, and bogs.

Throughout the year Stock Dove, woodpeckers, Tawny Owl and Woodcock occur while, in winter, the resident tits flock with the Treecreepers, Nuthatches, and Goldcrests to form wandering parties often accompanied by Redpolls and Siskins. In some years, the Brambling is a common winter visitor, joining the local Chaffinches to exploit any beechmast crop. Small winter flocks of Hawfinches, living in the hornbeams, disperse to breed throughout the forest and, by this time, the summer visitors have arrived, including the Redstart – Epping Forest is one of the few places in Essex where it still nests. An excellent selection of summering warblers is present

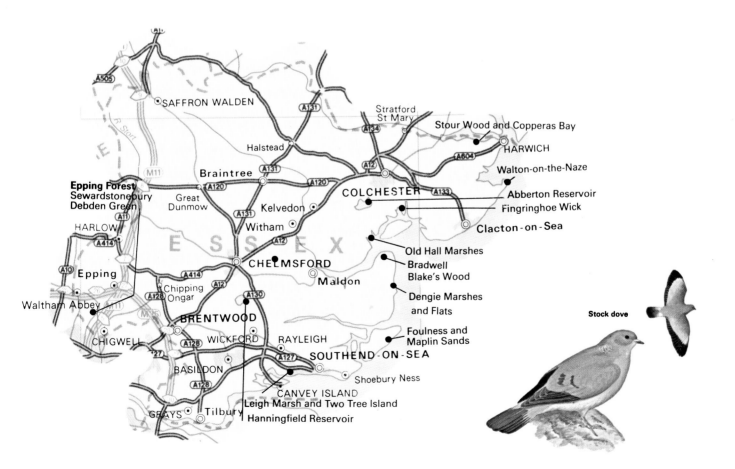

Stock dove

each year. Two areas within the forest worthy of preliminary exploration are at **Sewardstonebury** (OS TQ3995) in the south and **Debden Green** (OS TQ4398) towards the north.

LEIGH MARSH AND TWO TREE ISLAND (OS TQ835850)
A reserve under the control of the Essex Naturalists' Trust and the Nature Conservancy Council, the intertidal mud and rich saltmarsh of this site, together with the offshore island, combine to make it very much a place for winter birdwatching. A hide and nature trail allow observation of the birds without causing disturbance but, at this site, they are particularly tolerant of people, anyway, because they share the area with anglers and yachting people. Famous for its wintering Brent Geese, Leigh can produce a total of 10 000 in most years with numbers in exceptional years rising as high as 20 000. In addition, as many as 2500

Early or late in the day, birdwatching in Epping Forest can be very rewarding.

Wigeon are present among the other wildfowl and the rich mud provides food for a range of waders including as many as 10 000 Dunlin. Access to the reserve is from Leigh-on-Sea, and the footpaths are marked.

ABBERTON RESERVOIR (OS TZ9617)
This is one of the most important reservoirs in Britain for its wintering wildfowl populations with internationally and nationally important numbers of several species including Shoveler, Gadwall, and Goldeneye. Red-crested Pochard are annual arrivals and this is perhaps the one site in Britain where truly wild examples of this species appear regularly. Abberton Reservoir may also boast the unique claim of the only British breeding record of a Gull-billed Tern. At times of migration, several species pass through each year, including Black Terns, many wagtails, and a range of waders –

Some maximum wildfowl counts at Abberton and Hanningfield

	Abberton	Hanningfield
Wigeon	12 000	670
Gadwall	310	202
Teal	12 230	2000
Mallard	7390	1715
Pintail	450	530
Shoveler	1390	390
Pochard	5000	600
Tufted Duck	3390	1590
Goldeneye	765	50
Goosander	114	98

Organizations in Essex
Essex Bird Watching and Preservation Society (EBWPS), 41 Repton Avenue, Gidea Park, Romford RM2 5LT
Essex Naturalists' Trust (ENT), Fingringhoe Wick Nature Reserve, South Green Road, Fingringhoe, Colchester CO5 7DN
RSPB Members' Groups based at: Chelmsford, Colchester, and Southend (details from RSPB, The Lodge, Sandy, Beds SG19 2DL)

Annual reports
'Essex Bird Report', 17 Ingrave Road, Brentwood CM15 8AP

Books
Cox, S. *A New Guide to the Birds of Essex*. Essex Bird Watching and Preservation Society, 1984.

Some rare migrants on the Essex coast
American Wigeon – one shot at Foulness Island on 20 December 1962.
King Eider – one at Colne Point on 18 July 1977.
Oriental Pratincole – one at Hold Hall Marshes, August-October 1981.

dark-breasted   light-breasted

Brent goose

Citrine Wagtail – one at Walton-on-the-Naze, 4-24 July 1976.
Desert Wheatear – one at East Mersea, January-February 1958.
Desert Warbler – one at Frinton-on-Sea, 20-21 November 1975.
Pallas's Warbler – one at The Naze on 16 October 1960.
Scarlet Rosefinch – one at Fingringhoe Wick on 10 September 1981.
Rustic Bunting – one at Bradwell-on-Sea on 18 September 1966.
Black-headed Bunting – one at West Mersea on 7 May 1979.
Rose-breasted Grosbeak – one at Leigh-on-Sea, December-January 1975-76.

Some maximum numbers recorded on the Essex coast

Brent Goose	30 000	Ringed Plover	3000
Shelduck	21 000	Grey Plover	7000
Teal	11 000	Bar-tailed Godwit	14 000
Goldeneye	700	Curlew	12 000
Oystercatcher	15 000	Redshank	15 000

The Crouch estuary is the southernmost of the three estuaries (Crouch/Blackwater/Colne) which create such rich feeding grounds for a variety of birds.

Red-crested pochard

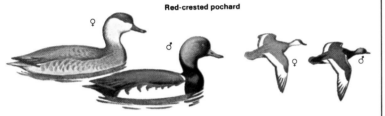

several of which are rare visitors to Britain. For many years, the site has been used for the study of bird migration, particularly wildfowl, with the trapping, ringing, and releasing programme involving over 70000 ducks. An unusual colony of tree-nesting Cormorants has become established.

Abberton is controlled by the Essex Water Company and, although access to much of the site is restricted, there is a birdwatching area that includes observation hides. In addition, excellent birdwatching is available from the causeway that crosses the water as well as from the surrounding roads.

HANNINGFIELD RESERVOIR (OS TQ7398)

The 'other' reservoir in Essex is never as productive as Abberton but regularly attracts a diverse bird population. Access is similarly restricted, but views can be obtained from the roads that surround the site.

CROUCH/BLACKWATER/COLNE

Arguably, the Essex coast between Shoeburyness and Clacton-on-Sea can be one of the most exciting stretches of birdwatching coastline in Britain. The three estuaries create a vast expanse of tidal mud, saltmarsh, and reclaimed coastal grazing marsh which, between them, support a vast bird population and make the total site one of the most important in south-east England. Birds occur in abundance at all times of the year. In the breeding season, Redshank, Common Terns, and colonies of Black-headed Gulls are found on the saltmarsh and islands, while the shingle and shell beaches provide homes for the Little Tern, Ringed Plover, and Oystercatcher. The greatest density of nesting birds is found on the reclaimed marshes behind the seawall. Here Lapwing, Skylark, and Yellow Wagtail abound with smaller numbers of Garganey and Redshank. Heron and Kingfisher are found along the water course and, in most years, Ruff, Black-tailed Godwit, and Avocet are to be seen throughout the summer months. Populations change

almost daily during the spring and autumn migration seasons, with the comings and goings of many passage birds, but, with the onset of winter, numbers increase to dramatic levels. On the mudflats, Brent Geese, Shelduck, and Wigeon dominate the wildfowl, while huge concentrations of waders disperse over the mud at low tide only to congregate in tight packs at times of high water. Along the seawalls Twite, Rock Pipit, Merlin, Short-eared Owl, and Hen Harrier are regular and, in the mouths of the rivers, divers, Slavonian Grebe, Red-breasted Merganser, and Common Scoter all occur. Birdwatching is good throughout, and any coastal site in the area should be examined; however, key sites exist:
Foulness and Maplin Sands – access restricted; **Dengie Marshes and Flats** – Nature Conservancy Council reserve, (OS TM0302), access via Dengie village or Bradwell-on-Sea; **Bradwell** – Bird Observatory (OS TM0308), access via Bradwell-on-Sea; **Old Hall Marshes** – RSPB reserve (OS TL9712), access via Tollesbury; **Fingringhoe Wick** – Essex Naturalists' Trust reserve (OS TM0419), access via Fingringhoe.

WALTON-ON-THE-NAZE (OS TM266245)

If the overnight weather has been such that migrating birds are forced to land, the Naze can be most productive. The scrubland bushes along the cliff path can contain many small migrants, including warblers, flycatchers, and Redstarts. In the winter, the seawall should be searched carefully for Purple Sandpiper and Snow Bunting. At the northern end, Stone Point and the tidal mud of Hamford Water, can produce a range of wildfowl and waders. Access is north of the town, and part of the site includes the Essex Naturalists' Trust reserve. As with so many coastal sites, it is important to check the tides, and no attempt to cross the tidal creeks should be made unless the return journey is known to be possible.

STOUR WOOD AND COPPERAS BAY (OS TM192311)

These two areas combine to provide a reserve of great variety. Both sites are under the management of the RSPB, but Stour Wood is owned by the Woodland Trust. Facilities for visitors, in the form of nature trails and hides, have been installed and the area is worth a visit at any time of the year. The woodland and associated scrub are most productive in summer when, in addition to the resident woodpeckers (three species), there are several warblers, including the Lesser Whitethroat, and Nightingales. The tidal mud and saltmarsh of the bay are most important for the Black-tailed Godwits which may number as many as 1000. Brent Geese, Pintail, and Shelduck also occur in good numbers. Visitor access is from the B1352 near Wrabness.

BLAKE'S WOOD (OS TL775064)

This area of coppiced woodland is just one small reserve within a complex of several near the town of Danbury. Ownership is divided between the National Trust and the Essex Naturalists' Trust and, between them, the sites cover a wide range of woodland habitat, including oak, birch, hornbeam, and chestnut. Breeding birds include Nightingale, Wood Warbler, Hawfinch, Treecreeper, and three species of woodpeckers. Other sites in the vicinity are **Lingwood Common, Danbury Common,** and **Woodham Walter Common**. Access is from the Little Baddow road north of Danbury.

NORFOLK AND SUFFOLK

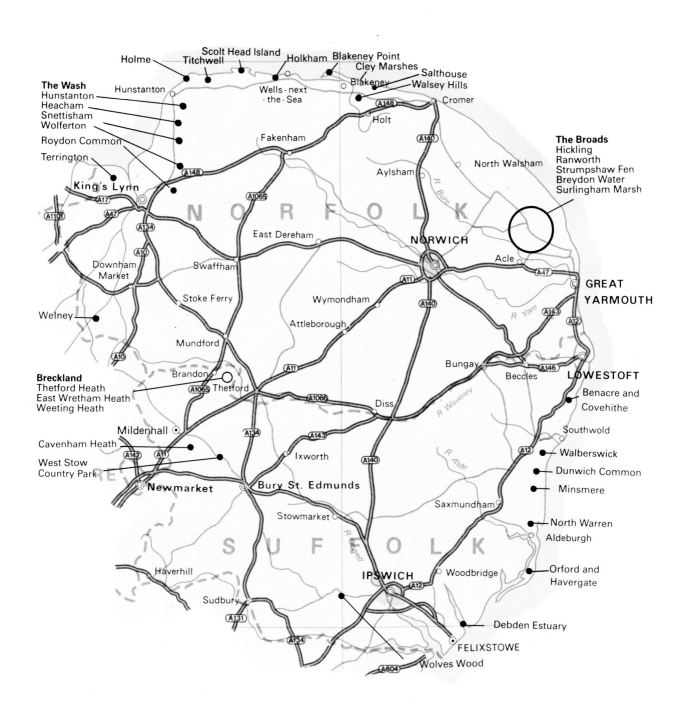

The Wash
Hunstanton
Heacham
Snettisham
Wolferton

Roydon Common

Terrington

Holme
Titchwell
Scolt Head Island
Holkham
Blakeney Point
Cley Marshes
Salthouse
Walsey Hills
Hunstanton
Wells-next-the-Sea
Blakeney

Breckland
Thetford Heath
East Wretham Heath
Weeting Heath

Cavenham Heath

West Stow
Country Park

The Broads
Hickling
Ranworth
Strumpshaw Fen
Breydon Water
Surlingham Marsh

Cromer
Holt
Fakenham
Aylsham
North Walsham
East Dereham
NORWICH
Acle
GREAT YARMOUTH
Swaffham
Downham Market
King's Lynn
Stoke Ferry
Wymondham
Attleborough
Welney
Mundford
Bungay
Beccles
LOWESTOFT
Brandon
Thetford
Diss
Benacre and Covehithe
Southwold
Mildenhall
Walberswick
Dunwich Common
Ixworth
Minsmere
Newmarket
Bury St. Edmunds
Saxmundham
North Warren
Aldeburgh
Stowmarket
Haverhill
Woodbridge
Orford and Havergate
IPSWICH
Sudbury
Debden Estuary
FELIXSTOWE
Wolves Wood

NORFOLK   SUFFOLK

NORFOLK

For many people, Norfolk is considered the 'ultimate' birdwatching county. From the fenlands and flood plains in the west, where the rivers flow westward to the river Ouse to enter the sea at Kings Lynn, the county varies to the drier, higher brecklands with their heaths and sandy soils that occupy its centre. In the east is Broadland with the lakes and meres (or 'broads'), the result of past peat diggings; here, the drainage is eastwards, via rivers that enter the sea at Great Yarmouth. The great sweep of the north Norfolk coast, from the county boundary on the Wash near Kings Lynn to just south of Great Yarmouth, covers some 81 miles. The major proportion of this coastline faces the north and

this is the reason for much of the county's diverse avifauna – certainly many of the extreme rarities. Migrating birds, be they marine or small land birds following the coast or crossing the North Sea, will frequently find the Norfolk coastline suddenly appearing at right-angles to their direction of flight – in many cases, a life-saving situation for an exhausted migrant. In addition, this is probably one of the best-protected coastlines in Britain. Its reserves cover a range of habitats from woodland and gravel pits to salt-marsh and sand-dunes, and stretch from Snettisham in the west to the migration watchpoint of Walsey Hills in the east, after which the holiday/tourist influence of Sheringham and Cromer take over.

Norfolk is mainly an arable county, the flat countryside lending itself to mechanization with the regrettable result of extensive hedgerow loss in the search for bigger, more economic fields. By contrast, the very rural nature of the county has produced an array of land owners prepared to devote a considerable part of their land to game rearing; consequently, many Pheasant coverts have produced excellent bird habitats that, in part, offset the loss of hedges. The Norfolk bird list is impressive, often reaching 280 or more species recorded each year. Even with such large numbers, the county can still add new species to its list, and has even recently added a new breeding species to the British list!

Birdwatching sites

NORTH NORFOLK COAST

A day visit can in no way do justice to the birdwatching potential of this area. Indeed, over the years, several well-known ornithologists have devoted their lives to the changing bird populations of this most famous of coastlines. There are no criteria to suggest the best times to visit – there are always birds to see, and only the numbers and variety will vary with the seasons. Access to most sites is free or available for a small charge although, with so many bird-watchers at some times of the year, certain areas (for example tern-breeding colonies) must have restrictions placed on them. Facilities are excellent, with many walks, observation hides, car parks, and so on, that provide the visiting birdwatcher with all that is needed for a spectacular day's birding – and, in this part of the world, the ornithological surprise is always just around the corner!

Holme (OS TF7044) The bird observatory and nature reserve are managed by the Norfolk Ornithologists' Association and have a full-time warden on site who is in control of the migration studies and bird-ringing programme. There is a nature trail and observation hide, with access from Holme village. Over 280 species of birds have been recorded at this site. To give a better idea of the variety of birds to be found here, some 29000 individuals of 135 species have been ringed at the observatory. Subsequent recoveries have included a Blackbird to Finland, a Swallow to Italy, and a Linnet to Spain.

Titchwell (OS TF7543) This is an RSPB reserve with car park, information centre, and observation hides. Access is from the A149 road west of Titchwell village. The reserve consists of reedbed, saltmarsh, and sand-dune with shingle beach, together with artificial lagoons where water levels can be controlled. Breeding birds include Little Tern, Oystercatcher, and Avocet in the more open areas, while Marsh Harrier, Bittern, and Bearded Tit occur in the reedbeds. Large numbers of migrant waders use Titchwell as a resting and feeding stop and, in winter, ducks are in good numbers on the lagoons, with scoter, Eider, and Long-tailed Duck offshore. Snow Bunting and Purple Sandpiper are regular visitors in small numbers.

Scolt Head Island (OS TF8146) A National Nature Reserve under the control of the Nature Conservancy Council, access to the island is only possible by boat. The main interest is in the extensive breeding colonies of Common Terns (200 pairs) and Sandwich Terns (1700 pairs) with an occasional pair of Arctic Terns. There is a nature trail on the island but the breeding bird area is closed during the nesting season.

Holkham (OS TF8945) A National Nature Reserve controlled by the Nature Conservancy Council, this site may be visited at any time, with access from Holkham village or north of Wells-next-the-Sea. The extensive pine woods regularly attract Goldcrest and Siskin, with Crossbill often visiting – indeed this is the site where Parrot Crossbills bred in Britain for the first time. Extensive sand-dunes and sandflats attract large numbers of winter waders and, on the marsh fields, winter geese (Pink-footed and White-fronted) are regular, together with the resident and, now well-established, Egyptian Geese.

Blakeney Point (OS TF9946) There are two ways of visiting this National Trust site: by boat from Blakeney Quay (which is dependent upon the tides) or by walking a little over 3 miles along the beach from Cley. Although this walk can be tiring, it can also provide good birdwatching and, for the more energetic and those with time to spare, this must be the recommended route. In winter, Shore Lark, Glaucous Gull, and many duck occur; in summer Blakeney rivals Scolt Head for breeding terns; and, at migration times, the bushes on the point can attract large numbers of

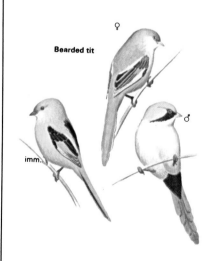

Bearded tit

♀

♂

imm.

Strumpshaw Fen is an RSPB reserve with a circular nature walk overlooking different habitats.

common migrants as well as the more unusual ones. Recent records have included Red-throated Pipit, Little Bunting, Pallas's Warbler, and Rose-coloured Starling.

Cley Marshes (OS TG0544) Cley remains one of the most famous of the Norfolk reserves and is managed by the Norfolk Naturalists' Trust. The car park and visitors' centre is just east of Cley village and, although from here it is possible to walk in a circuit around the reserve, access to the observation hides and internal nature trail is by permit only. Breeding birds include Avocet, Bittern, and Bearded Tit, but it is for the unusual waders that visit this site that the reserve is best known. Recent records have included Buff-breasted, Marsh, Terek, and Spotted Sandpipers.

Walsey Hills (OS TG062441) This site is a migration watchpoint run by the Norfolk Ornithologists' Association. It is interesting not only for the birds that may be present at migration time, but also as a source of information for the best Norfolk coast birdwatching.

Salthouse (OS TG0844) The small pools behind the coastal ridge attract a range of species in winter and at migration time. This is probably the best Snow Bunting haunt, and the surrounding fields attract the Brent Geese flocks. Access is north of the A149, east and west of Salthouse village.

THE BROADS
Understandably the Norfolk Broads are perhaps best known as a holiday area, but the increasing numbers of water-borne holidaymakers, coupled with the high-intensity farming around, have led to high levels of pollution, drainage of the adjoining marshes and flood-meadows, and extensive introduction of piling to replace the eroding natural banks. One major result has been a

marked decrease in the breeding Bitterns and Marsh Harriers. Certain key areas have been established as nature reserves, however, while other sites retain at least some of their former interest.

Hickling (OS TG4222) A mixture of water, reedbeds, marshland, and oak woodland make this Norfolk Naturalists' Trust reserve one of the richest sites in Broadland. The three rare Broadland species, Marsh Harrier, Bittern, and Bearded Tit, all nest and, in common with other sites in the area, Cetti's Warblers have now colonized. Migrant species, such as Spoonbill and Black Tern, occur regularly and, in the breeding season, a wide range of warblers, including Sedge and Reed, nest in the dense vegetation. This can be a popular area for holidaymakers, so visits late or early in the day are likely to be the most productive and it is best to avoid peak holiday weekends.

Ranworth (OS TG356148) Ranworth is not one of the best birdwatching areas, but it is of interest because it is the site of the 'Broadland Conservation Centre' which, not only provides information on the various sites within Broadland, but also has a splendid view across Ranworth Broad. A good selection of wildfowl, including Bewick's Swan, occur in winter. Access is via Ranworth village.

Strumpshaw Fen (OS TG342063) This is an RSPB reserve with car park, information centre, and observation hides. The circular nature trail overlooks a wide variety of habitats. At nearby Buckenham Fen, there is a regular wintering flock of Bean Geese. Access is via Low Road from Brundall.

Much of the Norfolk Brecklands, an unusual heathland area, has been lost to forestry.

Breydon Water (OS TG5007) Just west of Great Yarmouth, this almost forms the eastern limit of the Broads. With its expanse of mud at low tide and closeness to the sea, it will often attract species in addition to those normally associated with Broadland. Curlew, Bar-tailed Godwit, Shelduck, Brent Goose, Knot, and Grey Plover are some of the typically coastal birds to be seen here. In winter, there are also Hen Harrier and Short-eared Owl, together with the possibility of Twite, Snow and Lapland Buntings. The closeness to Great Yarmouth means that this is a site for winter visiting because it is much disturbed in the holiday season.

Surlingham Marsh (OS TG305065) This is a relatively new RSPB reserve, where visitors can find a circular walk with observation points giving views across the flooded marshlands. Waders and wildfowl are the key species to look for, but harriers and owls occur with a range of typical woodland birds in the surrounding area. Access is via Surlingham village with car parking by the church.

BRECKLAND
The Breckland is a very unusual heathland area covering much of central Norfolk. It has its own distinctive bird communities, but much of the area has been lost to agriculture and forestry. The presence of the military has saved some areas, and nature reserves others. The avifauna tends to be specialized and, unfortunately, several of the typical species are in serious decline: Stone Curlew, Wheatear, Red-backed Shrike, Nightjar, Woodlark, and Montagu's Harrier. A small population of some, at least, do manage to maintain a precarious foothold.

Thetford Heath (OS TL8782) The general area around Thetford gives the flavour of Breckland. Here it is possible, on the numerous forestry walks and rides, to encounter breeding Tree Pipit, Stonechat, and occasional Whinchat. Coal Tit, Goldcrest, and Crossbill inhabit the coniferous areas. Winter birdwatching has less to offer, but birds of prey, including the Rough-legged Buzzard, occur, and Great Grey Shrikes occur annually.

East Wretham Heath (OS TL910885) This Norfolk Naturalists' Trust reserve of some 150 hectares (370 acres) includes heath, meres, and woodland. There is an information centre and nature trail. Visits are best in spring and early summer when the main species to look for are Crossbill, Long-eared Owl, Hawfinch, Nightingale, Nightjar, and Grasshopper Warbler. Access is from the A1075 south of East Wretham village.

Weeting Heath (OS TL755880) Here there is a Norfolk Naturalists' Trust/Nature Conservancy Council reserve located due east of Weeting village. It is a very specialized site for Stone Curlew and Wheatear which can be viewed with ease from the observation hides. A good selection of commoner species, such as Red-legged Partridge, Crossbill, and Coal Tit, can also be seen.

WELNEY (OS TL548946)
This Wildfowl Trust centre is part of the Ouse Washes' complex which is largely within the county of Cambridgeshire, and dealt with in more detail under that county. An information centre and observation hides provide excellent viewing of the spectacular numbers of winter wildfowl, including Bewick's and Whooper Swans.

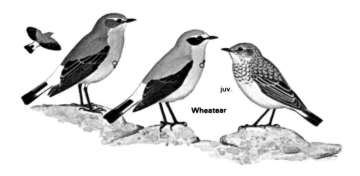

ROYDON COMMON (OS TF685225)
Access to this Norfolk Naturalists' Trust reserve is by public right of way from the road between Grinston and South Wootton. In summer, there are breeding Curlew and Nightjar.

THE WASH
This extensive area, crossing the boundary of Lincolnshire and Norfolk, is one of the largest expanses of intertidal mud and saltmarsh in Britain. Ornithologically, it is of great international importance, with large numbers of wintering and breeding birds. For the visiting birdwatcher, there are several access points, at each of which a different selection of species can be expected.

Hunstanton (OS TF6741) The cliffs provide breeding sites for small numbers of Fulmar, while the views from the clifftop make watching for passing Gannet, divers, grebes, and Eider relatively easy.

Heacham (OS TF6636) Heacham is best known for its high-tide roost, particularly for Knot and Sanderling.

Snettisham (OS TF6431) This is an RSPB reserve based on a series of old gravel extractions immediately behind the sea bank, and provides views across the saltmarsh and mudflats. Access is along the beach, south from Shepherd's Post. Observation hides are available throughout the year, but the best time to come here is in winter when the most spectacular sight is at high tide as the vast congregations of birds start to gather in front of the hides. These may include as many as 70000 waders with some peak counts including: Knot 35000; Grey Plover 1500; Bar-tailed Godwit 5000; Oystercatcher 13000; Dunlin 10000; Redshank 3500; Curlew 1500; Turnstone 1000; and smaller numbers of Sanderling and Ringed Plover. Up to 10000 geese and ducks use the area with counts of: Pink-footed Goose 8000; Brent Goose 1400; Shelduck 2000; and Mallard 1000. The gravel pits attract a range of other species, especially after storms in the North Sea, and, in summer, they hold colonies of Common Tern and Black-headed Gull.

Wolferton (OS TF6228) East of the village is another access point which takes the visiting birdwatcher to the seawall. The view across the saltmarsh and tidal mud is best in winter.

Terrington (OS TF5426) North of the village of Terrington St Clement, it is possible by road and public right of way to reach the coast opposite a mound set out among the mud of the Wash. This was constructed as a trial for a possible Wash barrage. A careful check of the tides and a walk across to the bund can be very productive. Twite and Short-eared Owl are regular in winter and, with a rising tide, birds fly very close to the bund, often providing excellent views of a wide range of wildfowl, waders, and even seabirds blown into the Wash.

SUFFOLK
No doubt the many enthusiastic Suffolk birdwatchers would disagree, but, to a visitor from outside East Anglia, the 390000 hectares (almost 1000000 acres) that make up the county are perhaps overshadowed by their northern neighbour of Norfolk. Suffolk consists of gently undulating arable countryside, mainly based on clay, but varied by the sandy edge of Breckland in the north-west and the gravels and silts of the river valleys. Drainage is mainly eastwards to the 50 miles of North Sea coastline with some seven rivers providing estuaries, including the Stour on the southern boundary and the Waveney in the north. Birdwatchers tend to concentrate on the coastal sites with their associated reedbeds, fens, and lagoons, for this is where bird migration is most apparent and species diversity at its greatest. Some 340 species have been recorded in the county, of which about 130 breed regularly.

Birdwatching sites

COASTLINE
The north of the county can claim the most easterly point in Britain at Ness Point near Lowestoft. Much of the coastline is sand and shingle, often in the form of a high bank protecting the low-lying marshlands immediately inland. The line of the coast runs in a relatively straight north-south direction and there are few dramatic movements of seabirds except when there has been a period of strong onshore easterly winds. Spectacular migratory arrivals can take place, however, such as in September 1965 when the exciting counts included: 10000 Wheatear, 15000 Redstart, and 5000 Pied Flycatcher at Minsmere; 8000 Wheatear, 15000 Redstart, and 4000 Pied Flycatcher at Walberswick; while, at Lowestoft, there were over 30000 examples of these three species combined. Such arrivals are entirely dependent upon climatic conditions.

Benacre and Covehithe (OS TM5383) are small coastal lagoons separated from the sea by high shingle ridges and bounded by areas of rough grassland. In winter months small collections of wildfowl occur, while breeding birds include good populations of both Reed and Sedge Warblers. Low cliffs on the beach at Covehithe are suitable for seawatching at times of easterly weather.

Walberswick (OS TM466737) is a Nature Conservancy Council reserve which contains a wide range of habitats including lagoons, extensive reedbeds, woods, and heaths. On its northern boundary are the tidal mudflats at Blythburgh. Car parking, a hide, and nature trails are provided. The diversity of habitat results in a broad range of species, with breeding birds including the Suffolk specialities of Marsh Harrier, Bittern, Bearded Tit, and Nightjar. In the winter months a variety of wildfowl and waders occurs.

Dunwich Common (OS TM4768) is a large area of heathland owned by the National Trust and sandwiched between the reserves at Walberswick and Minsmere. The cliff-top car parking provides excellent views across the nearby marshes, the access point to the public observation hides on Minsmere beach, and it is an excellent place from which to search the sea for possible bird migration. The heath supports populations of Nightjar, Stonechat, Linnet, and Whitethroat.

The RSPB reserve of **Minsmere** (OS TM4767) is perhaps one of the best-known reserves in Britain, with a reputation that reaches far beyond the British Isles. It is a very popular site for visiting birdwatchers, so that it can often be rather crowded with people at peak times (early May, for example), and it is best to visit at other seasons when visitor pressure is low but birdwatching is just as varied. Recent

The RSPB reserve at Minsmere attracts a wide range of birds including breeding birds, such as Avocets.

Organizations in Suffolk

Suffolk Naturalists' Society (SNS), c/o The Museum, High Street, Ipswich IP1 3QH

Suffolk Ornithologists' Group (SOG), 1 Holly Road, Ipswich IP1 3QN

Suffolk Trust for Nature Conservation (STNC), Park Cottage, Saxmundham IP17 1DQ

RSPB Members' Groups based at: Bury St Edmunds, Ipswich, and Lowestoft (details from RSPB, The Lodge, Sandy, Beds SG19 2DL)

Annual reports

'Suffolk Birds', The Museum, High Street, Ipswich IP1 3QH

Books

Payn, W H. *The Birds of Suffolk*. Ancient House Publishing, 1978.

Suffolk's Loss, Gain, and Loss

In January 1902, a bird settled on a fishing boat at sea off Hopton near Lowestoft. It was taken alive to a taxidermist at Great Yarmouth and, although it was kept alive for two days, it eventually died and was preserved as a specimen. The bird was identified as an immature Allen's Gallinule

(*Porphyrula alleni*), a species normally found south of the Sahara and extremely rare in Europe. Ornithological opinions were divided, but the 'official authorities' decided that the bird was probably an escape from captivity (although no trace or evidence of a lost bird could be found). Thus, the species was not admitted to the official British list and Suffolk had lost its claim for a new bird for Britain. Over seventy years later, Robert Hudson investigated fully the events of 1902, and examined all the claimed European and North African occurrences of the species, including birds in Morocco and Tunisia, at the same time as the Suffolk record. After due consideration of all the evidence, the official British Records Committee admitted Allen's Gallinule to the British list and the Suffolk record was declared genuine. This information was published in 1974, the year that the new county boundaries were introduced into Britain and there was just one small change that affected Suffolk. In the extreme north of the county, the redrawn border meant that a small area passed to Norfolk – that small area included the village of Hopton. For just a brief moment, Suffolk could claim this record, but now (at least politically) the glory passes to Norfolk!

More recently, Suffolk claimed the first White-crowned Black Wheatear (*Oenanthe leucopyga*) for Britain, at Kessingland between 2 and 5 June 1983.

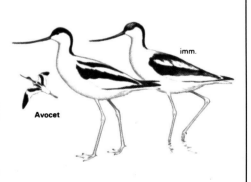

imm.

Avocet

improvements to the visitor facilities have included a new car park from which nature trails lead to the observation hides overlooking the 'scrape'. This area attracts a wide range of birds including breeding species such as terns and Avocets as well as many migrant waders. The reserve also includes some old woodland and extensive heaths, both of which are crossed with public footpaths and, in early summer, a dawn or dusk visit could well be rewarded with Nightingales, Redstarts, Grasshopper Warblers, and several owls. In most years, about 100 species breed at Minsmere and well in excess of 200 species are recorded annually.

Orford and Havergate (OS TM4348) The Orfordness National Nature Reserve includes the RSPB reserve of Havergate Island which sits in the mouth of the river Alde. Access to this reserve is difficult and is by boat so that only official visits to Havergate should be considered. The area contains a large gull colony, as well as breeding Little, Common, and Sandwich Terns. Regular pairs of Arctic Terns are the most southerly nesting in Britain. This is the site where the Avocet re-established itself as a British breeding species and, in addition to the successful colony, there is now a regular wintering flock of over 200 individuals. In winter, Brent and White-fronted Geese, duck, and a range of waders use the area and, after storms at sea, the river mouth will frequently provide shelter for grebes, divers, and sea duck such as Red-breasted Merganser.

In comparison with many of the other sites on the Suffolk coast, **Deben Estuary** (OS TM3238) is rather neglected by birdwatchers but it frequently contains a range of waders and other migrants. Avocets can usually be seen here in most months of the year.

NORTH WARREN (OS TM455587)
This RSPB reserve is a mixture of heathland, fen, and varied woodland and scrub. A short nature trail passes through a good variety of habitats and, during the summer months,

The Deben estuary often provides feeding grounds for waders, including Avocets at most times of the year.

several warblers can be encountered, including Blackcap, Garden Warbler, Whitethroat, Lesser Whitethroat, Willow Warbler, and Chiffchaff. Near the fen, the Grasshopper Warbler is a regular breeding species while, on the heath, Linnet and Yellowhammer are common.

WOLVES WOOD (OS TM055440)
Access to this RSPB reserve is from the car park beside the A1071 east of Hadleigh. This is probably one of the best sites in Britain at which to enjoy the spring and early summer song of Nightingales. The mixed woodland and coppice scrub is particularly suitable for this and a wide range of other woodland species. Three species of woodpeckers, six of tits, and several warblers all nest, and Woodcock and Hawfinch are seen regularly. The reserve has a small information centre and woodland nature trail.

CAVENHAM HEATH (OS TL758728)
This Nature Conservancy Council reserve consists predominantly of heathland but it also has woodland and fen. The reserve car park is by Temple Bridge, east of Mildenhall on the A1101. A wide range of bird species, mainly associated with the heath, includes Nightjar, Grasshopper Warbler, Wheatear, and Whinchat; on the woodland fringe Redpoll, Yellowhammer, Woodcock, and Tree Pipit occur; in the woodland, three species of woodpeckers, Nuthatch, and Treecreeper can be seen. Sparrowhawks are recorded regularly.

WEST STOW COUNTRY PARK (OS TL801715)
On the edge of Breckland, this park of grassland, woods, and old gravel workings is under the control of the St Edmundsbury Borough Council. Grebes and a selection of wildfowl inhabit the water, while owls and Nightjar can be located in the more open areas.

NORTHAMPTONSHIRE, BEDFORDSHIRE, AND CAMBRIDGESHIRE

NORTHAMPTONSHIRE

Much of the county of Northamptonshire is dominated by the River Nene which flows north-eastwards through its flat floodplain that now contains a series of gravel pits stretching from Northampton to Oundle. Many of these are still being actively worked, while others are being re-claimed or lost as a result of new road systems for the county. In the south and extreme west, the landscape is predominantly rolling agriculture, and the hills are the source of several river systems flowing eastwards and westwards. In effect, Northamptonshire is a crossroads in central England, and this is enhanced by the presence of several major road and rail systems together with extensive canals. Natural waters are few and small, but several reservoirs have been constructed, and small woods remain scattered throughout the county. Nearly 280 species have been recorded within the county boundary.

Birdwatching sites

COUNTRY PARKS

There are three country parks established in Northamptonshire, all very different in character, and providing varied interest for the birdwatcher. Country parks, unlike nature reserves, are intended for everyone to enjoy the countryside and are not created just for the specialist naturalist. Many parks do contain sanctuary or reserve areas, but visiting birdwatchers should remember that the parks will be more productive outside peak visiting times. Early and late in the day, when birds are most active and vocal, are the best times for visiting country parks.

Irchester Country Park (OS SP913660) is a woodland area, much of it plantations of larch and pine, but there are also stretches of scrub and open grassland. Disused open-cast ironstone workings add distinctive features which have enhanced the scrubland while, in the wetter zones, alders have become dominant and attractive to winter flocks of Siskin and Redpoll. Typical species of the park include Goldcrest, Coal Tit, and a range of finches and woodpeckers. Sparrowhawks are regularly seen. Access is via the B570 road south-east of Wellingborough.

Compared with Irchester, **Barnwell Country Park** (OS TL035873) is very much a wetland site of disused gravel workings within a loop of the River Nene. There are adjoining meadows and marshland, together with scattered trees and scrub. Bird life is plentiful with nearly 150 species recorded from the site, including Yellow Wagtail and Great Crested Grebe as breeding species. In the winter months, a range of wildfowl occurs and there are regular visits from Water Rail, Heron, and Kingfisher. Because the Park is located centrally in the Nene valley, migrants such as Black, Common, and Arctic Terns pass through annually. Access is from the A605 road south of Oundle.

Owned by the Daventry District Council and situated off the B4036 road north of Daventry, **Daventry Country Park** (OS SP578637) is based around a reservoir with a perimeter walkway that passes through associated areas of willow, scrub, and reedbed. Winter bird populations include a range of wildfowl, and, at migration time, waders, such as Ruff and Little Stint, have been recorded. Breeding birds are varied with Reed and Sedge Warblers in the fringe vegetation, Yellow Wagtails on the more open areas, and Great Crested Grebes on the water's edge.

TITCHMARSH HERONRY RESERVE (OS TL008804)

One of the most extensive gravel workings in the Nene valley is at Thrapston and, on the eastern side of the pits, is the Northamptonshire Trust for Nature Conservation's reserve which contains a heronry of some twenty to twenty-five pairs. The diverse habitat of the area includes woods, water, scrub, and rough pastures and, as such, holds one of the most varied bird populations in the county. Historically, the site was used as a duck decoy. It has produced an impressive array of vagrants which, in recent years, has included Bittern, Osprey, Grey Phalarope, and Spotted Crake. Breeding birds include Little Ringed Plover, Redshank, and Sand Martin. Access is from the A605 road south of Thrapston.

RESERVOIRS

Apart from the series of gravel pits and a few small natural lakes, Northamptonshire is dependent upon its reservoirs to provide areas of open water of sufficient size to be attractive to birds. There are twelve reservoirs scattered through the county, mainly concentrated in the west. Of these, two have become established as key bird sites – particularly in the winter months.

Owned by the Anglian Water Authority and administered by the Northamptonshire Trust for Nature Conservation, **Pitsford Reservoir** (OS SP783710) has recorded over 200 species of birds, including several thousand waterfowl in the winter months. The fringes are sheltered by new plantations of mixed woodland which will steadily enhance and diversify the area as they become established. The reservoir is worth visiting at any time of the year and there are good views across it from the surrounding roads and paths. Some recent peak counts of waterfowl include: Great Crested Grebe 223; Canada Goose 358; Wigeon 1249; Teal 1349; Mallard 1548; Pochard 400; Tufted Duck 985; Coot 1789.

Stanford Reservoir (OS SP605805) is administered by the Northamptonshire Trust for Nature Conservation and owned by the Severn-Trent Water Authority. This reserve is smaller and less varied than the Pitsford site and, as a result, bird populations are lower, with a recorded list of species reduced to 140. Migrant waders occur; there is a gull roost in winter; and this is one of the best sites in the county for viewing Ruddy Ducks. Access is east of Rugby off the B5914 road.

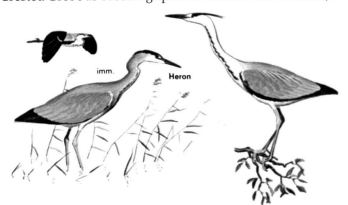

imm.

Heron

SALCEY FOREST (OS SP8051)

Owned by the Forestry Commission, the forest straddles the county boundary with Buckinghamshire, and the reserve area, which protects some of the ancient oak woodland that once made up this forest, is controlled by the two county naturalists' trusts. This is a site for spring and summer visiting, and there are several car parks and walkways along forest rides and tracks. Redstart, Spotted Flycatcher, a range of warblers, and Tree Pipit all nest, while the Nightingale is thought of as a speciality of this reserve.

Organizations in Northamptonshire

Northamptonshire Bird Club (NBC), 7 Manor Road, Pitsford NN6 9AR

Northamptonshire Natural History Society and Field Club (NNHS), 41 Spinney Hill Road, Northampton NN3 1DH

Northamptonshire Trust for Nature Conservation (NTNC), Lings House, Billing Lings, Northampton NN3 4BE

RSPB Members' Groups based at: Mid-Nene and Northampton (details from RSPB, The Lodge, Sandy, Beds SG19 2DL)

Annual reports

'Northamptonshire Bird Report', 25 Westcott Way, Favell Green, Northampton NN3 3BE

Books

Webster, B. *Birds of Northamptonshire*. Northamptonshire Natural History Society and Field Club, 1966.

Escaped birds in Northamptonshire

The recording of escaped birds has now become established as a regular feature in many counties. Historically, several of these species have successfully colonized (eg Ruddy Duck, Mandarin, Ring-necked Parakeet), and so on and it is only by recording the early observations that the full story becomes available. Most common of all escapes are the ornamental waterfowl and pheasants but, in recent years, Northamptonshire has had an interesting selection of other escapes.

Rough-legged Buzzard – one at Northampton in February 1982 was recaptured by its owner.

Lanner Falcon – one at Billing in January 1984 was wearing falconer's jesses.

Blacksmith Plover – one at Ditchford in July 1982 (an African wader not recorded north of the Sahara).

Barbary Dove – one at Coton in June 1984 (a domesticated form of the African Collared Dove).

Black-rumped Waxbill – one at Hardwick Wood in August 1984 (a Central African finch).

Red-collared Whydah – one at Stanford in August/September 1984 (a widespread African finch).

Black-headed Oriole – one at Chacombe in July 1984 (a Central American species).

BEDFORDSHIRE
Chalk, Greensand, and clay dominate Bedfordshire, one of the smallest English counties. Urban areas prevail on the southern chalk, while the lower-lying clays of the north are drained northwards and eastwards by the meandering River Ouse and its tributaries, the Flitt and Ivel. Quarrying for the range of materials available (chalk, clay, and gravel) has resulted in several abandoned water-filled pits; these are particularly noticeable south-west of Bedford and in the valley of the Ouse near the Cambridgeshire border. Areas of natural water are very few, as are woods. Many of the latter are plantations or are associated with open parkland, and are mainly confined to the extreme north or to the central Greensand belt that passes through the county. Some 260 species of birds have been recorded in Bedfordshire.

Birdwatching sites

FLITWICK MOOR (OS TL046354)
This is a Bedfordshire and Huntingdonshire Naturalists' Trust reserve based upon old peat diggings; now it is a varied wetland area with woods and grassland. Some 100 species of birds have been recorded, including breeding populations of Water Rail and Grasshopper Warbler. The alder clumps attract Siskin and Redpoll and, in the summer, a variety of breeding warblers occurs. Access to the reserve car park is off the A507 road at Maulden south of Bedford.

THE LODGE, SANDY (OS TL188478)
The headquarters of the RSPB, the impressive building is set in some 40 hectares (100 acres) of woodland, parkland, and remnant heath. Access to the car park is via the B1042 road east of Sandy. Breeding birds include the three woodpeckers, Nuthatch, Treecreeper, Tree Pipit, Sparrowhawk, and several warblers. The artificial lake is occasionally visited by Heron and Kingfisher, and the old pine trees around the car park attract Crossbill.

FELMERSHAM RESERVE (OS SP988583)
This is a disused gravel pit reserve with bordering pasture and scrub. The site is under the control of the Bedfordshire and Huntingdonshire Naturalists' Trust. Although it is only some 21 hectares (52 acres) in area, the site attracts a good range of breeding, wintering, and passage birds. Access is via the Felmersham-Sharnbrook road north of Bedford.

HARROLD-ODELL COUNTRY PARK (OS SP956567)
Access to this Bedfordshire County Council park is from the village of Harrold, north-west of Bedford. Visitor facilities include a car park and nature trail. Based on a series of disused gravel workings, much of the site has been landscaped and includes grazing meadows stretching down to the River Ouse. Birdwatchers will find it relatively easy to escape the more popular parts of the park. Sparrowhawks and Kingfishers are regular and the hedgerows contain Long-tailed Tits, Sedge Warblers, and Bullfinches. Winter wildfowl and migrant waders occur, with nesting Great Crested Grebe and Canada Goose.

GRAVEL PITS
In common with many inland counties, the gravel-pit complexes of Bedfordshire have become focal points for birdwatchers, attracting an array of water-associated species that would not otherwise occur. Two sites that have proved particularly attractive are: **Wyboston Gravel Pits** (OS TL1757) access from the A1 south of St Neots; **Stewartby Gravel Pits** (OS TL0042) access from the A5140 south of Bedford.

Organizations in Bedfordshire
Bedfordshire Natural History Society (BNHS), 7 Little Headlands, Putnoe, Bedford MK41 8JT

Bedfordshire and Huntingdonshire Wildlife Trust Ltd (BHWT), Priory Country Park, Barkers Lane Bedford

RSPB Members' Groups based at: Bedford, East and South (details from RSPB, The Lodge, Sandy, Beds SG19 2DL)

Annual reports
'The Bedfordshire Naturalist' (includes the county bird report), 4 Oakley Road, Bromham, Bedford MK43 8HY

Books
Harding, B D. *Bedfordshire Bird Atlas*. Bedfordshire Natural History Society, 1979

Lady Amherst's Pheasant in Bedfordshire
First introduced into Britain (from the mountains of China/Burma) in 1828, this attractive pheasant was the subject of several introduction attempts during the 1800s. One of these releases was at Woburn, Bedfordshire in 1890, with further birds released in Whipsnade Park in the 1930s. From these introductions (several others in southern England were not successful) has come the established population that now warrants the species being included in the official British list. The birds are largely confined to the woods in the south of the county where an estimated population of between 100 and 200 pairs breed annually, although confirmed breeding is confined to twenty pairs.

Recent additions to the Bedfordshire list
Mediterranean Gull – a first-winter bird at Luton in February 1982.

Eider – an immature male at Brogborough in December 1982.

White Stork – one at Potton in May 1983.

Collared Pratincole – one at Girtford in May 1983.

Serin – a first-year female caught by a cat at Biggleswade in February 1984.

Some recent peak counts on the Ouse and Nene washes

	Ouse	Nene
Mute Swan	643	164
Bewick's Swan	4549	334
Wigeon	25 456	4987
Teal	2513	1629
Mallard	6377	925
Pintail	769	948
Golden Plover	2885	176
Lapwing	6679	2653
Snipe	891	582

CAMBRIDGESHIRE

The chalky uplands of southern Cambridgeshire, that still retain small numbers of breeding Stone Curlew and Quail, give way, via belts of clay and Greensand, to the extensively drained fens in the north of the county. Drainage throughout is north-eastwards via the rivers Ouse and Cam, towards the Wash and the North Sea. Ornithologically, the northern fenland is dominated by the Nene and Ouse Washes, two areas of flood plains. Although strictly Cambridgeshire is an inland county, it benefits from its low-lying features which stretch across Norfolk and Lincolnshire to the sea. Historically, the undrained fens were influenced by the tides – as indeed are some areas today – and the county's avifauna is strongly influenced by this ready access to the east coast. Some 300 species of birds have been recorded in Cambridgeshire.

With local government reorganization, Cambridgeshire swallowed up its smaller neighbour, Huntingdonshire, and this has presented a slight complication for the natural history world. The Bedfordshire and Huntingdonshire Naturalists' Trust now covers part of the modern county of Cambridgeshire; the Cambridgeshire and Isle of Ely Naturalists' Trust also covers part! Cambridgeshire and Huntingdonshire still retain separate annual bird reports!

Birdwatching sites

FOWLMERE (OS TL407461)

This RSPB reserve was formerly part of the Grand Fen Mere whose size was steadily reduced by drainage until the existing site – now mainly old watercress beds – is a small oasis in the midst of extensive arable farmland. The present habitat consists of reedbeds, open water, and extensive scrub which provides a secure roosting site for many hundreds of birds that feed on the surrounding farmland, and flight into the reserve each evening. In mid-winter, the roosts can contain thousands of birds, including Fieldfare, Redwing, Corn Bunting, and Pied Wagtail, together with the occasional Hen Harrier. Bearded Tits have bred at the site as do Water Rails, Kingfishers, Reed Buntings, and Grasshopper Warblers. Reed and Sedge Warblers are both very common as are several other warblers in the surrounding scrub. Access is off the A10 road just west of Fowlmere village, and facilities include hides and a nature trail.

GRAFHAM WATER (OS TL1468)

Construction of what was to be the largest reservoir in England began in 1962 and, upon completion, the Anglian Water Authority arranged for the western end of the site to be a nature reserve administered by the Bedfordshire and Huntingdonshire Naturalists' Trust. Access to the site is via the various car parks, and it is possible to walk around much of the reservoir's margin. The main interest is with the winter wildfowl and passage waders, with some peak counts: Great Crested Grebe 550; Mallard 1400; Teal 600; Wigeon 1300; Tufted Duck 1500; Goldeneye 150. Among the more unusual records have been Wilson's Phalarope, Richard's Pipit, and Great Grey Shrike. Visiting at any time of the year can be productive.

LITTLE PAXTON GRAVEL PITS (OS TL195630)

This site is a gravel pit complex just north of St Neots; it is still in active use, but the older areas can provide good birdwatching from the network of public footpaths, including a riverside walk. Access is from the A1 road and through Little Paxton village. The site includes a small heronry, breeding Gadwall and Kingfisher, migrant Green Sandpipers, Greenshank, and other waders, together with a range of wintering wildfowl and many small birds in the surrounding scrub.

OUSE WASHES (OS TL471861)

This extensive washland is intended to hold flood water from the River Ouse at times of heavy rain and high tides when water is prevented from escaping to the North Sea. Three organizations have reserves in the area: the RSPB; the Cambridgeshire and Isle of Ely Naturalists' Trust; and the Wildfowl Trust whose Welney reserve is across the county boundary in Norfolk. Car parks and hides make this an excellent site for winter birdwatching when the large congregations of Bewick's and Whooper Swans are present, together with thousands of Wigeon and other wildfowl. Breeding specialities include Black-tailed Godwit, Ruff, and Spotted Crake. Access to the various reserves is well signposted on the surrounding roads.

NENE WASHES (OS TL277992)

This RSPB reserve lies north of Whittlesey town, off the B1040 road. It is a drier site than the Ouse Washes, although recent management work has provided some flooding. Typical breeding species include Snipe, Yellow Wagtail, and Redshank. In some years, wintering Short-eared Owls stay and nest, while Garganey, Teal, and Shoveler breed in the reed-fringed ditches. Huge concentrations of finches (including Goldfinch, Greenfinch, and Linnet) together with Hen Harriers and Merlins occur in the late autumn and winter.

The washland of the River Ouse can be excellent for winter birdwatching.

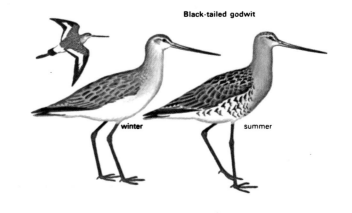

Black-tailed godwit

winter   summer

Organizations in Cambridgeshire
Cambridge Bird Club (CBC), 15 Highfield Road, Impington, Cambridge CB4 4PF
Huntingdonshire Fauna and Flora Society (HFFS), 94 High Street, Upwood, Huntingdom PE17 1QE
Cambridgeshire and Isle of Ely Naturalists' Trust (CAMBIENT), 5 Fulbourn Manor, Fulbourn
Bedfordshire and Huntingdonshire Wildlife Trust (BHWT), Priory Country Park, Barkers Lane, Bedford
RSPB Members' Groups based at: Cambridge, Huntingdon, and Peterborough (details from RSPB, The Lodge, Sandy, Beds SG19 2DL)

Annual reports
'Cambridge Bird Club Report', 95 Hemingford Road, Cambridge
'Huntingdonshire Fauna and Flora Society Annual Report', 94 High Street, Upwood, Huntingdon PE17 1QE

Books
Lack, D. *The Birds of Cambridgeshire*. Cambridge Bird Club, 1934.
Research Committee, Cambridge Bird Club. *A Checklist of the Birds of Cambridgeshire*. Cambridge Bird Club, 1978.

Tebbutt, C F. *The Birds of Huntingdonshire*. Private printing, 1967.

Wisbech sewage farm – a site lost
One of the most famous birdwatching sites in Cambridgeshire, one that has provided a wealth of rare and unusual records, passed into decline in 1985, to be lost as a major wader site in Fenland. Changes in the sugar beet operations meant that settling beds were no longer required, and Wisbech sewage farm must now be a 'fond' memory to many birdwatchers. During 1984, twenty-seven different species of waders were recorded, including Temminck's Stint, White-rumped Sandpiper, Pectoral Sandpiper, and Great Snipe. Counts of up to seventy Ruff, twenty Little Stint, and thirteen Curlew Sandpiper were all noted. In addition to the waders, up to 200 Pintail, a North American Blue-winged Teal, Spotted Crake, as many as sixty Yellow Wagtail, and a Hobby were all recorded. The name of Wisbech will be sadly missed from the bird reports.

Gadwall

Bewick's swan

imm.

FERRY MEADOWS COUNTRY PARK (OS TL147977)
This large park of some 200 hectares (500 acres) is run by the Peterborough Development Corporation. The site includes gravel excavations, wet meadows, woods, and a range of scrubland and young plantations. Included within the park is a nature reserve with observation hides overlooking an area of managed floodland which provides excellent conditions for a range of migrant waders following the Nene Valley (the River Nene flows through the park). Nearly 200 species of birds have been recorded, almost half of which remain to nest, including Redshank, Snipe, Water Rail, and Yellow Wagtail. Even at the height of the holiday season, a visiting birdwatcher can find a secluded spot away from disturbance. Islands within the gravel pits provide safe nesting sites for Ringed Plover, Little Ringed Plover, and Common Tern. Access is well signposted off the A605 road west of Peterborough.

One of the drainage dykes through typical Cambridgeshire fenland.

WICKEN FEN (OS TL563705)
This National Trust reserve is generally considered to be the oldest and perhaps the most famous of all British reserves. The on-site windmill, once used to drain the area, is now employed to maintain water levels within a fen that is surrounded by drained agricultural land. The reed- and sedge-beds, interspersed with stands of open water, ditches, and damp woodland, provide a habitat for a range of species that includes many breeding warblers, wintering owls, and harriers, as well as a variety of wildfowl. The reserve is best viewed from the tower hide, but a network of nature trails explores the great variety of vegetation at this site.

WOODWALTON FEN AND HOLME FEN
(OS TL2384 and TL2089)
These two Nature Conservancy Council reserves are relict fenland now left isolated within an area of intensive arable agriculture. Woodwalton is largely wet grassland, bog, and areas of water, while Holme is predominantly wet birch woodland. As a result, the bird populations of the sites are very different, although the two areas complement each other for a day's birdwatching. Holme is less diverse in its bird species, but includes several breeding warblers, owls, and woodpeckers; while Woodwalton provides sites for Nightingale, Grasshopper Warbler, and Little Grebe. Access to Woodwalton is west of Ramsey Heights off the B1040 road west of Ramsey; for Holme, north of the B660 road in Holme village.

GLOUCESTERSHIRE AND HEREFORD AND WORCESTER

GLOUCESTERSHIRE

From west to east, Gloucestershire divides naturally into four distinct regions. The Wye Valley, with its associated Forest of Dean, adjoins the Welsh border and, from the high points in the forest, the area looks eastwards across the valley of the River Severn and its tidal mud towards the open areas of the Cotswold Hills. In the extreme east, there are gravel deposits in the lowlands at the source of the River Thames where excavations have created pits that form the basis of the Cotswold Water Park. This range in habitat, from dense oakwood and rolling downland, to tidal mud-flats and open water, has produced a county list of more than 280 species and, as such, Gloucestershire can rival several more easterly counties for its birdwatching. The river valleys also tend to funnel migratory species into the county. In spring migrant birds that follow the Bristol Channel eastwards and northwards continue along the valley of the Severn and Avon until eventually they reach the North Sea via the River Ouse and the Wash. The return migration in the autumn is probably even more dramatic, and Gloucestershire sits squarely in the path of probably Britain's largest overland migration route.

Birdwatching sites

COTSWOLD WATER PARK

The concept of constructing such a park was established in the late 1960s after some forty years of gravel excavation had produced a series of pits that straddled the Gloucestershire and Wiltshire border. Nearly 100 different areas of water are now included within the park's 5500 hectares (13600 acres), which is administered by the two county councils. Although a wide range of recreational activities is catered for, several sections have been devoted to wildlife, and the idea of reserves within the park is being pursued – the Gloucestershire Trust for Nature Conservation has a series of sites.

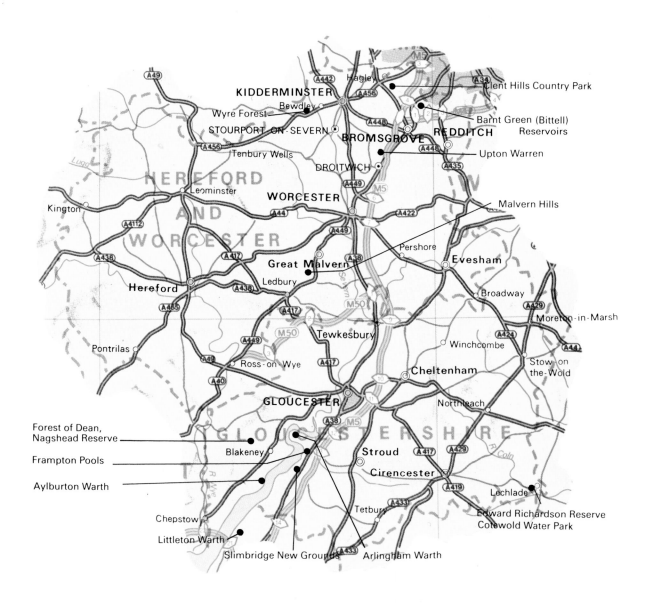

One such reserve is the **Edward Richardson Reserve** (OS SU215007) which is reached via the A361 road south of Lechlade. Here, there is car parking and an observation hide. This is a relatively recently established site but the birdwatching is already impressive. Almost 200 species have been recorded and there is something of interest to be seen throughout the year. Many of the older excavations are well vegetated and large populations of small breeding birds occur: these include both Reed and Sedge Warblers, together with increasing numbers of Nightingales and an occasional Marsh Warbler. The muddy margins attract waders, and the open water is attracting a steadily increasing number of winter wilfowl. Among the more unusual species that can be seen regularly are Red-crested Pochard, Hobby, and Little Ringed Plover; in any one year as many as twenty-six different species of waders may be recorded. This site is rapidly becoming a key locality for birdwatching in Gloucestershire.

FOREST OF DEAN

The Forest of Dean was England's first National Forest Park; it is owned by the Forestry Commission but its reserves are administered by the RSPB, the Gloucestershire Trust for Nature Conservation, and the Nature Conservancy Council. For the birdwatcher, the forest is best visited in spring and early summer when the migrants have arrived and bird song is at its peak. The most attractive areas are the old oak woodlands – and the best is the RSPB's **Nagshead reserve** (OS SO611079) where some forty woodland species nest annually, and facilities for the visitor include a car park, information centre, and observation hide. Large numbers of nestboxes sited throughout the wood are used in the long-term, very detailed study of the breeding Pied Flycatchers and, in some years, as many as 100 pairs may nest. Other breeding species include Redstart, Hawfinch, Firecrest, Whinchat, Sparrowhawk, and Wood Warbler.

SLIMBRIDGE NEW GROUNDS (OS SO723048)

This is an 800-hectare (2000-acre) reserve of the Wildfowl Trust which includes the Trust's headquarters and a comprehensive collection of captive birds. Although Slimbridge is very much a tourist attraction in the holiday season, it is during the winter months when birdwatchers will find it most interesting, with the large numbers of White-fronted Geese and Bewick's Swans. Every year, small numbers of the more unusual wildfowl occur, and these have included Britain's first Ring-necked Duck, several Lesser White-fronted Geese, and the occasional Red-breasted Goose. Small numbers of migrant waders also feature at the site. Access to the reserve, west of the A38 road, is well signposted.

The oak woodlands of the Forest of Dean should be visited in late spring and early summer when bird song has reached its peak.

FRAMPTON POOLS (OS SO755075)

These disused gravel pits, close to the River Severn, can provide excellent birdwatching from the pathways around their boundary. Access is from the B4071 road east of Frampton-on-Severn. The proximity of the river provides the attraction for passing migrants, and Black Terns, Little Gulls, and several waders occur regularly. Among the breeding birds, Water Rails are probably annual, as are Gadwall and Great Crested Grebe. The more unusual visitors to have been reported include Osprey, Temminck's Stint, and Grey Phalarope.

AYLBURTON WARTH (OS SO6199)

This is just one of the numerous 'warths' on both banks of the River Severn from which it is possible to watch feeding waders and wildfowl on the tidal mud. Numbers are highest during the winter and in migration seasons. Access to many of the sites is possible by public footpath, and current Ordnance Survey maps should be consulted.

Other sites are at: **Arlingham Warth** (SO7012) and **Littleton Warth** (ST5890).

Organizations in Gloucestershire

Gloucestershire Naturalists' Society (GNS), Filkins, Awre, Newnham GL14 1EJ

Gloucestershire Trust for Nature Conservation (GTNC), Church House, Standish, Stonehouse, Gloucester GL10 3EU

RSPB Members' Group based at: Gloucester (details from RSPB, The Lodge, Sandy, Beds SG19 2DL)

Annual reports

'Gloucestershire Bird Report', Filkins, Awre, Newnham

Books

Swaine, C M *Birds and Bird Watching in Gloucestershire.* Gloucestershire Naturalists' Society, 1969.

Swaine, C M. *Birds of Gloucestershire.* Alan Sutton, 1982.

Some recent peak counts from Cotswold Water Park

Great Crested Grebe	200
Mute Swan	210
Canada Goose	210
Wigeon	850
Teal	580
Mallard	1600
Pochard	3400
Tufted Duck	1200
Coot	5400
Lapwing	5230
Snipe	250
Black-headed Gull	10 000
Common Gull	5000
Lesser Black-backed Gull	1600

HEREFORD AND WORCESTER

The two halves of this county are divided by the Malvern Hills, with Worcester to the east drained by the River Severn, and Hereford to the west drained by the Wye which eventually joins the Severn near the river's mouth. In the extreme east, the county borders the conurbation of the West Midlands, but the bulk of the county is largely rural, typically with meadows, cattle, and woodland. It is, in the woods that many of the species associated with the area are to be found: Redstart, Pied Flycatcher, and Wood Warbler; while Buzzard, Hobby, and Sparrowhawk sail overhead. Although lacking dramatic birdwatching localities, the county is well provided with country parks and, in the extreme south-west, the edge of the Black Mountains creates added diversity with its Ring Ouzels and Red Grouse. Worcester's speciality bird, the Marsh Warbler (over 30 per cent of the British population nests in the county), is to be found scattered in sites of overgrown vegetation beside the county's waterways.

Birdwatching sites

UPTON WARREN (OS SO936677)
This reserve, the result of subsidence, is administered by the Worcestershire Nature Conservation Trust. The site consists of a series of pools, and reed and sedge swamp, with surrounding meadows and alder and willow carr. Birdwatching is varied and excellent at all times of the year. Breeding birds include Ruddy Duck, Great Crested Grebe, and Kingfisher. In the woodland areas, Treecreeper and Little Owl occur. This is one of the few sites in the county that attracts migrant waders, with Spotted Redshank, Wood Sandpiper, and Greenshank appearing annually. Access is from the A38 road south-west of Bromsgrove, with a car park and viewing point.

WYRE FOREST (OS SO759766)
This Nature Conservancy Council reserve protects some of the best examples of native mixed woodland in the area. Oak is the dominant tree species, but the richness and variety of the site make this a splendid spring and summer venue for the birdwatcher. The numerous old trees with twisted branches and natural cavities provide sites for the many hole-nesting species, including all the tits, Nuthatch, Redstart, and Pied Flycatcher. All the woodpeckers nest as do Tawny Owl and Woodcock. The forest is situated north of the A4117 road west of Kidderminster.

BARNT GREEN (BITTELL) RESERVOIRS (OS SP0174)
These three areas of water south of Birmingham (access via the A441) can easily be viewed from the road. The reservoirs have provided the bulk of the county's records for many species, particularly wintering wildfowl, with good numbers of Shoveler, Tufted Duck, and Pochard. A winter gull roost can contain several thousands of individuals, while the more natural margins are attractive to Snipe and Teal. The small amounts of vegetation are sufficient to encourage Siskin, Reed, and Sedge Warblers. Unusual observations have included Osprey, Peregrine, Purple Sandpiper, and Temminck's Stint.

MALVERN HILLS (OS SO7742)
This extensive ridge of hills, rising to over 400 metres (1300 feet) in height, divide the present county into two, and has been declared an Area of Outstanding Natural Beauty (AONB). The hills should be visited in spring or early summer to be appreciated to the full. A mixture of woodland in the valleys, bracken, and grass slopes, all topped with rocky outcrops provides a range of habitats that can be enjoyed from the numerous public footpaths throughout the area. In the woods, Redstart, woodpeckers, and Goldcrest occur, while, in the more open areas, Buzzard, Kestrel, and Raven can be seen. This is a favourite stopping point for migrant Ring Ouzels.

CLENT HILLS COUNTRY PARK (OS SO935800)
This open heath and grassland park, administered by the Hereford and Worcester County Council, provides some spectacular views of the surrounding countryside and holds sizeable populations of species such as Redstart, Tree Pipit, Meadow Pipit, and Yellowhammer. At migration times, the grassy slopes offer resting places for Wheatear, Whinchat, and occasional Ring Ouzel. Access is from the A491 road south of Stourbridge, and facilities include a car park and nature trail.

Tawny owl

rufous phase   grey phase

Yellowhammer

♀   ♂

Organizations in Hereford and Worcester
Herefordshire Ornithological Club (HOC), The Garth, Kington HR5 3BA
West Midland Bird Club (WMBC), 8 Bowstoke Road, Great Barr, Birmingham B43 5EA
Herefordshire and Radnorshire Nature Trust (HRNT), 25 Castle Street, Hereford HR1 2NW
Worcestershire Nature Conservation Trust (WNCT), Hanbury Road, Droitwich WR9 7DU
RSPB Members' Group based at: Worcester and Malvern (details from RSPB, The Lodge, Sandy, Beds SG19 2DL)

Annual reports
'Herefordshire Ornithological Club Annual Report', The Garth, Kington, HR5 3BA
'West Midland Bird Report', 8 Bowstoke Road, Great Barr, Birmingham B43 5EA

Books
Gilbert, H A and Walker, C W. *Herefordshire Birds*. Woolthorpe Naturalist and Field Society, 1954.

Harrison, G R, *et al*. *The Birds of the West Midlands*. West Midland Bird Club, 1982.
Harthan, A J. *The Birds of Worcestershire*. Littlebury and Co, 1947.
Lord, J and Munns, D J. *Atlas of Breeding Birds of the West Midlands*. Collins, 1970.

Woodcock

WEST MIDLANDS, WARWICKSHIRE AND LEICESTERSHIRE

Tufted duck

Birdwatching sites

SANDWELL VALLEY (OS SP0392)

Nestling within the junction of the M5 and M6 motorways, the Sandwell Valley is the ultimate oasis. The RSPB has established an educational centre at the site, together with observation hides, and a nature trail that includes the marshland which often contains several Snipe. Work carried out to construct islands and plant woods has been successful with nesting Little Ringed Plover, Whitethroat, and Yellow Wagtail. A small selection of wildfowl occurs each winter, and rarities, such as Stone Curlew and Caspian Tern, have been reported. Access is via the Hamstead road from the A4041 east of Bromwich.

SUTTON PARK (OS SP116964)

Only 6 miles from the very centre of Birmingham, the 900 hectares (2220 acres) of open heath and wood with small mill ponds attract large numbers of people during fine weather and at holiday times. Visits for birdwatching must be timed carefully to avoid periods when human disturbance is at its height. The park's major claim to fame must be the nesting in 1954 by a pair of Black-necked Grebes which successfully reared a single young. Of more regular occurrence is the Great Crested Grebe, and flocks of up to twenty have been noted. The open heath attracts breeding Skylark, Linnet, and Meadow Pipit, together with migrant Wheatear, Whinchat, and Stonechat. In winter, Great Grey Shrike, Siskin, and Crossbill can be seen. Access to the car park is off the A5127 near Sutton Coldfield Station.

WEST MIDLANDS

The urban core of Birmingham and its immediate surroundings is not normally thought of as aesthetically pleasing for birdwatching nor are there great numbers or variety of birds to be seen there. Records refer mainly to observations made at artificial sites, and the species of interest frequently include those, such as Black Redstart, which are present on industrial buildings. This is not to say that the gardens and parks, together with the scattering of other rural oases remaining within the concrete, do not give rise to birdwatching surprises. In one year (1981) the Metropolitan county provided a list of over 150 species, including White-fronted Goose, Long-tailed Duck, Quail, Iceland Gull, Short-eared Owl, Wryneck, and Waxwing.

Organizations in the West Midlands
West Midland Bird Club (WMBC), 8 Bowstoke
Road, Great Barr, Birmingham B43 5EA
Urban Wildlife Group (UWG), 11 Albert Street,
Birmingham B4 7UA
RSPB Members' Groups based at: Birmingham,
Coventry, Solihull, Stourbridge, Walsall, and
Wolverhampton (details from RSPB, The Lodge,
Sandy, Beds SG19 2DL)

Annual reports
'West Midland Bird Report', 8 Bowstoke Road,
Great Barr, Birmingham B43 5EA

Books
Harrison, G R, *et al. The Birds of the West Midlands*.
West Midland Bird Club, 1982.
Lord, J and Munns, D J. *Atlas of Breeding Birds of
the West Midlands*. Collins, 1970.

Little ringed plover

WARWICKSHIRE

Once a lush, wooded county, Warwickshire is now pre-dominantly rolling farmland – a mixture of arable and pasture. In some areas, the desire for increased mechaniza-tion and a more commercially viable approach has trans-formed the patchwork of small fields and hedgerows into a 'prairie farming' landscape. Today's woods are plantations, re-established in recent years following the virtual clear-felling of the county's timber. Some sites have always held timber, but little of the original forest structure remains.

The county is drained in a south-westerly direction via the River Avon and its tributaries which meander through the centre of the county. Resulting sand and gravel deposits have produced the inevitable string of excavations which, together with the reservoirs, provide the only permanent open water of any size. The Avon flood plain is rather narrow and largely well drained, but some areas of flood-meadow remain. The closeness of the West Midland's industry has resulted in a canal network that is well represented in Warwickshire and makes another feature on the landscape. With a county bird list well in excess of 250 species, Warwickshire does very well indeed, bearing in mind that it is positioned in the agricultural Midlands, remote from sea, mountains, or marshlands.

Birdwatching sites

ALVECOTE POOLS (OS SK252045)
This site results from mining subsidence and is owned by the National Coal Board, although it is managed as a reserve by the Warwickshire Nature Conservation Trust. In addition to several shallow pools and other wetland habitat, the site is well vegetated with willow and alder scrub and carr. Nearly 200 species of birds have been noted at what is the county's oldest nature reserve. Although there is some restriction of access, good views can be obtained from neighbouring roads east of Tamworth. There is a nature trail within the site for permit holders. Breeding birds include Great Crested Grebe, Pochard, Little Ringed Plover, Snipe, and Kingfisher. The shallow water is attractive to migrant waders and, in addition to large flocks of Lapwing and Snipe, occasional rarities, such as Black-tailed Godwit and Pectoral Sandpiper, have been recorded. Winter waterfowl include good numbers of Teal and Wigeon.

Rutland Water nature reserve, now in Leicestershire, is one of the largest artificial lakes in England. It is the most important birdwatching locality in the county with over 200 species recorded.

Just scattered trees now remain of the woodlands which once covered much of Warwickshire. It is now mainly farmland.

Organizations in Warwickshire
West Midland Bird Club (WMBC), 8 Bowstoke
   Road, Great Barr, Birmingham B43 5EA
Warwickshire Nature Conservation Trust
   (WARNACT), 1 Priory Road, Warwick
RSPB Member's Group based at: Coventry (details
   from RSPB, The Lodge, Sandy, Beds SG19 2DL)

Annual reports
'West Midland Bird Report', 8 Bowstoke Road,
   Great Barr, Birmingham B43 5EA

Books
Harrison, G R, *et al*. *The Birds of the West Midlands*.
   West Midland Bird Club, 1982.
Lord, J and Munns, D J. *Atlas of Breeding Birds of
   the West Midlands*. Collins, 1970.
Norris, C A. *Notes on the Birds of Warwickshire*.
   Cornish Brothers, 1947.

KINGSBURY WATER PARK (OS SP204970)

This Warwickshire County Council park is based upon a series of gravel pits, several of which have been back-filled and either grassed or allowed to develop into areas of reed or scrub vegetation. The area is used for a wide range of recreational activities, but part of the site has been designated as a nature reserve with a nature trail and observation hides. Access is well signposted from the A4097 north-east of Birmingham. Bird populations are very varied, including a selection of woodland species, migrant waders, and winter wildfowl. Gravel islands have encouraged the establishment of a Common Tern colony. Oystercatchers may well nest, as do several pairs of Shelduck. The wintering flock of Canada Geese can contain as many as 500 birds in late autumn, with small numbers of Bewick's Swans present in most winters.

HARTSHILL HAYES (OS SP315945)

This is a woodland site which is best visited in spring and early summer. Hartshill Hayes is a combination of Forestry Commission land and a country park administered by the Warwickshire County Council. An extensive network of public footpaths passes through the area. Access to the car park and nature trail is well signposted from the A47 road west of Nuneaton. This is part of the old Forest of Arden which once was very extensive in the county. Woodpeckers, owls, and warblers are all abundant, the latter, usually including a few breeding pairs of Wood Warbler. Redstarts also nest.

DRAYCOTE WATER (OS SP467692)

This 300-hectare (740-acre) reservoir was first flooded in 1968 and has now become one of the most important birdwatching sites in the county. Much of the area is artificial in its construction, with concrete banks and dams, and it is also very disturbed by various recreational activities. Overlooking the reservoir is a small country park run by the county council. For the visiting birdwatcher, this is a winter site, when disturbing activities are at a minimum and the wildfowl numbers are at a maximum. Some recent peak counts at the site are: Wigeon 500; Gadwall 30; Teal 250; Mallard 940; Pochard 600; Tufted Duck 875; Goldeneye 100. The site also provides a home for the main winter gull roost in the county – often, as many as 100 000 individual birds may be involved.

CLOWES WOOD (OS SP0973)

This is a mixed woodland site controlled as a reserve by the Warwickshire Trust for Nature Conservation. Access is via the B4102 road to Terry's Green, south of Birmingham. In winter, the wood attracts Fieldfare, Redwing, Siskin, and a range of other finches. In summer, as well as the usual warblers, this is one of the few sites in the county for nesting Wood Warbler.

STOKE FLOODS (OS SP374791)

Stoke Floods is a small wetland site on the very edge of Coventry, containing open water, floodmeadow, and reedbed. Managed as a reserve by the Warwickshire Nature Conservation Trust, the site is very close to the recently established Coombe Valley Country Park and, although it is far from rural in its outlook, the area can provide a good day's birdwatching. Access is via the A427 road east of Coventry. Among the variety of species to be seen are the birds of Warwickshire's largest heronry. In the mid 1800s, the site was used as a duck decoy, and records indicate that over 1500 duck were caught and killed in one winter with more than 100 trapped in a single operation.

LEICESTERSHIRE

Leicestershire is a county of contrast. High ground in the west of the county is very much based upon coal which, in some areas, comes close to the surface. On a high outcrop of granite sits Charnwood Forest which is one of the best woodland areas in the county – a county generally considered to have one of the lowest percentages of woodland cover in England. Flowing southwards through central Leicestershire are the Rivers Wreake and Soar which drain the low-lying plain. Two other major rivers, the Trent and the Welland, form the western and eastern boundaries respectively. The limestone highlands in the east hold a scattering of woods among the otherwise very open arable farmland that has lost many of its hedges. A few gravel pits and an extensive network of reservoirs provide the open water. Of these, two key sites are in the east within the old county of Rutland, but several smaller reservoirs are scattered around Leicester itself. A total of some 280 species has been recorded in the county.

Birdwatching sites

CHARNWOOD FOREST
Although the forest is now very divided, a significant amount of woodland and undisturbed open countryside with bracken slopes and rocky outcrops remains to make this very much a key feature within the county. The centre of the area is directly north-west of Leicester.

Within the forest are several reserves, including the **Swithland Woods** (OS SK538129) and **Bradgate Park** (OS SK523116) administered by the Bradgate Park Trust. The Leicestershire and Rutland Trust for Nature Conservation also has several reserves within the forest.

There is a scattering of reservoirs through this part of the county, one of the more interesting sites for the birdwatcher being **Cropston Reservoir** (OS SK5410). Birdwatching can be productive throughout the year, but, at peak holiday times, the forest can attract large numbers of people; then birdwatchers are best advised to confine their activities to the early part of the day before major disturbance occurs. Spring and early summer will always be the most productive. Bird life is varied: over open country there are Skylarks, Kestrels, Wheatears, Whinchats, and Meadow Pipits; in the woods are found woodpeckers, Nuthatches, and Wood Warblers; and on the water there is a range of wildfowl and grebes, with waders on the muddy edges.

EYE BROOK RESERVOIR (OS SP853964)
Until the construction of Rutland Water, this was probably the major birdwatching attraction in the county. Although some species have decreased in numbers, a wide selection of birds can still be observed here. Access is controlled by the Leicestershire and Rutland Ornithological Society and they have provided an observation hide overlooking the area. Adequate views across the 160-hectare (400-acre)

reservoir can, however, be obtained from the minor roads beside the site. Natural banks make the area attractive to a range of waterbirds, including such passage migrants as Black Tern, Curlew Sandpiper, Little Stint, and Ruff. In winter, it is well known for its flocks of Goosander but the numbers have been decreasing in recent years.

RUTLAND WATER NATURE RESERVE (OS SK8904)
Without doubt, this is now the most important birdwatching locality in the county producing, not only an impressive list of birds, but also providing excellent facilities for the visiting birdwatcher. This Anglian Water Authority reservoir is one of the largest man-made lakes in England, with a shoreline of almost 25 miles in length. There are parking areas at various points around the perimeter, all of which offer views across the water and can provide an excellent range of species. Rutland Water demonstrates well how an area can be zoned for multirecreational use. In addition to the area provided for the many water sports and activities, nearly 150 hectares (370 acres) at the easten end have been designated as a reserve that is managed by the Leicestershire and Rutland Trust for Nature Conservation.

The reserve is divided into three sections. The first, on the south-west shore, is open to the public at all times. Here there is an information centre, and observation hides overlook one of the bays that make up the reserve shoreline. The second, on the north-west shore, is a scientific area where no visiting is allowed except under the strictest control. At the final area, centrally situated on the western shore and approached via the village of Egleton, access is by permit only on certain days of the week. Here, there are several hides overlooking managed lagoons which were conructed before the reservoir was filled. They now have managed water levels to create ideal conditions for a wide range of species. The planting of thousands of trees and shrubs has added to the diversity of the site which, together with a woodland walk that takes in some areas of ancient trees on an overlooking hill top, has resulted in well over 200 species being recorded at the reserve.

Some maximum counts at Leicestershire reservoirs

	Eye Brook	Rutland	Cropston
Great Crested Grebe	353	966	27
Mute Swan	19	184	3
Canada Goose	350	694	194
Wigeon	1618	7239	290
Gadwall	17	1109	
Teal	358	1635	120
Mallard	848	2781	240
Shoveler	46	616	4
Pochard	232	838	36
Tufted Duck	469	3379	51
Goldeneye	36	303	15
Goosander	14	119	
Ruddy Duck	318	229	3
Black-headed Gull	17 500	25 000	4000
Common Gull	17 500	12 000	100
Herring Gull	1000	600	700

Rare birds at Rutland Water

In its short life (the first water was present in the reservoir in 1973) the Rutland Water reserve has produced an exciting array of rare and unusual species. The following list is just part of the reason why this is such a popular site.
Night Heron; Rough-legged Buzzard; Temminck's Stint; Pectoral Sandpiper; Red-necked Phalarope; Bridled Tern; Leach's Petrel; Ring-necked Duck; Velvet Scoter; Red Kite; Sabine's Gull; Mediterranean Gull; Red-throated Pipit; Collared Pratincole; Alpine Swift; White Stork; and Long-billed Dowitcher.

Organizations in Leicestershire

Leicestershire and Rutland Ornithological Society (LROS), 28 Oakfield Avenue, Birstall, Leicester LE4 3DQ
Leicestershire and Rutland Trust for Nature Conservation (LRTNC), 1 West Street, Leicester LE1 6UU
RSPB Members' Groups based at Leicester and Loughborough (details from RSPB, The Lodge, Sandy, Beds SG19 2DL)

Annual reports

'Leicestershire and Rutland Ornithological Society Annual Report', 28 Oakfield Avenue, Leicester LE4 3DQ

Books

Hickling, R. *Birds in Leicestershire and Rutland*. Leicestershire and Rutland Ornithological Society, 1978.
Mitcham, T. *The Birds of Rutland and its Reservoirs*. Sycamore Press, 1984.
Otter, J. *The Birds of East Leicestershire*. Loughborough Naturalists' Club, 1966.

imm.

Green woodpecker

♂

LINCOLNSHIRE

Populations of the Wash
Based upon the results of the 'Birds of Estuaries
Enquiry', some of the highest counts for the Wash
are:

Pink-footed Goose	3150
Shelduck	8660
Oystercatcher	14 820
Knot	67 500
Bar-tailed Godwit	3000
Redshank	6000
Brent Goose	2970
Wigeon	3680
Grey Plover	2000
Dunlin	39 500
Curlew	3200

Organizations in Lincolnshire
Lincolnshire Bird Club (LBC), 42 Wolsey Way, Glebe
Park, Lincoln LN2 4QH
Lincolnshire Naturalists' Union (LNU), 61
Woolthorpe Road, Colsterworth, Grantham
Lincolnshire and South Humberside Trust for
Nature Conservation (LSHTNC), The Manor
House, Alford LN13 9DL
RSPB Members' Group based at: Lincoln (details
from RSPB, The Lodge, Sandy, Beds SG19 2DL)

Annual reports
'Lincolnshire Bird Report', 42 Wolsey Way, Glebe
Park, Lincoln LN2 4QH

Books
Cornwallis, R K. *Supplement to the Birds of
Lincolnshire, 1954-1968.* Lincolnshire Naturalists'
Union, 1970.
Smith, A E and Cornwallis, R K *The Birds of
Lincolnshire.* Lincolnshire Naturalists' Union,
1955.

**Some recoveries of birds ringed in
Lincolnshire**
Bar-tailed Godwit – ringed in Lincolnshire in
September 1983, found dead in Mauritania in
November of the same year.
Guillemot – ringed as a nestling in Norway in July
1981, found dead on the Lincolnshire coast in
February 1983.
Dunnock – ringed in Lincolnshire in October 1983,
trapped and released in Belgium only eleven days
later.
Lesser Whitethroat – ringed in Lincolnshire in June
1983, found dead in Hungary in October 1983, the
first British ringed Lesser Whitethroat to be
recovered in Hungary.
Whitethroat – a bird ringed at Donna Nook in August
1980 was trapped and released at Gibraltar Point
in September 1982 and then found dead in
Morocco in April 1984.

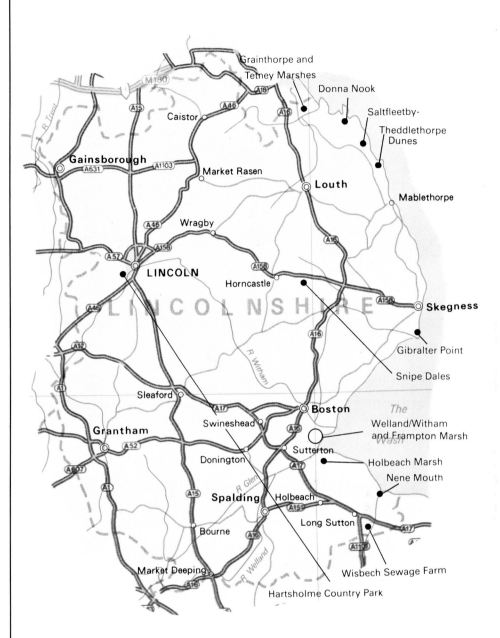

The vast expanse of Lincolnshire is dominated by a bulging
North Sea coastline stretching from the Wash in the south
to the mouth of the Humber in the north. This is a very
rural, intensively farmed county. Woodland is scarce,
hedgerows have been lost, and, in areas, the rich soils
provide a bountiful harvest of cereals or potatoes. Reclamation has taken place for centuries, including the draining of
the fens with their fertile black soils in the south and, more
recently, the reclaiming of the saltmarsh around the Wash
and near the entrance to the River Humber. In striking
contrast to the flat coastal areas is the Lincolnshire Wold
with its rolling landscape occupying the north and west of
the county. The southern half is drained by three rivers, the
Witham, Welland, and Nene, all of which enter the sea via
the Wash; in the north and west, drainage is northwards to
the Humber via the Trent and Ancholme. Lincolnshire is a

prime example of a county where the birdwatchers gravi-
tate towards the coast – here they find some of the more
'natural' habitats, the greatest concentration of birds, the
better chances of discovering a rare visitor, and the only
extensive wetland habitat in the county. Inland freshwater
sites are extremely few, widely scattered, and are mainly
small gravel pits or reservoirs – none has achieved any
major recognition as a birdwatching locality. The pre-
dominance of the coast, with its migratory birds and rare
visitor, is the reason for the list of over 320 species.

Birdwatching sites

THE WASH
This vast area of intertidal mud and saltmarsh that stretches
across the Norfolk/Lincolnshire border is one of the largest

in Britain and, ornithologically, may be the most important site in eastern England. No fewer than twelve species occur here in internationally important numbers while the populations of a further eight are nationally important. Migrant and wintering waders and wildfowl occur in huge concentrations that move to and from their feeding grounds with the daily changes in the tides. The numbers are so large that the birds often look like clouds of smoke as they wheel through the sky in a vast haze well out over the rich tidal mud.

The congregations of birds gather at specific points to sit out the high-tide period when feeding is impossible, and, because of the birds' complete dependence upon the tidal system, the visiting birdwatcher should study carefully the tide-table before any visit. The key period is the span of two to three hours before the high tide when the birds are slowly being moved by the rising water; then they start to pack together and flight to the security of the roost sites. It is in the winter months that the greatest spectacle occurs, but remember that, with easterly winds or low temperatures at this time of the year, the Wash can be a very cold place. There is interest at other times of the year, however, with nesting Ringed Plover and Little Tern on the shingle beaches and Redshank and Black-headed Gull on the saltmarsh. At migration time, in common with much of the east coast, the Wash can provide some spectacular migrations, together with occasional rarities. Perhaps as many as half (up to 40 000 individuals) of the British wintering Twite arrive each autumn to remain in scattered flocks feeding on the seeds on the sea wall and saltmarsh.

There are several access points for the birdwatcher, and this is an area that can provide a very full day's watching – indeed, one or two sites around the Wash can keep an enthusiast occupied throughout the day.

Three rivers flow into the Wash in the Lincolnshire section, the Nene, Welland, and Witham – the latter two flowing on either side of Frampton Marsh. All offer excellent birdwatching near their mouths.

Nene Mouth (OS TF4925) is the site where, many years ago, Sir Peter Scott set up his home to study the wildfowl of the washes; he lived in one of the lighthouses that still survive on the site today. Like so much of the birdwatching around the Wash, at this site it is possible to follow the public footpath on top of the sea wall. Follow the path on the west side of the river mouth.

Welland/Witham and Frampton Marsh (OS TF3637) are areas where some of the widest of the remaining saltmarsh is to be found, and it is no coincidence that here are reserves of the RSPB and Lincolnshire and South Humberside Trust for Nature Conservation. These reserves contain some of the most productive land for breeding Redshank and Black-headed Gull and, once again, there are public footpaths which follow the sea walls throughout.

The area around Holbeach, including **Holbeach Marsh** (OS TF4234), forms the central mass of the Wash and, within this very core, are some of the major wildfowl and wader roosts. On the extreme spring tides the birds pour over the sea wall to find secure places on the open farmland where they gather in compact groups, often turning the black, freshly ploughed fields into a distinct grey – so tightly are they congregated.

At **Gibraltar Point** (OS TF5558), a northern corner of the Wash, important wader roosts occur in autumn and winter but, to the birdwatcher, the site is better known for its bird observatory. The field station here provides residential accommodation throughout the year and is operated by the Lincolnshire and South Humberside Trust. Since its inauguration, the observatory has ringed over 107 000 birds of some 155 species. The National Nature Reserve at Gibraltar Point covers some 430 hectares (1060 acres) of coastal habitat stretching inland to include the grassland and marshes behind the dune system. Hen Harrier, Short-eared Owl, Snow Bunting, and Shore Lark can all be expected in addition to the wintering wildfowl and waders. It is for its spectacular migratory movements and occurrence of rare visitors that Gibraltar Point is best known – a movement of 10 000 Swallows on one day and 8000 on another; over 1000 Goldcrests among the bushes at one time; while several parties, totalling thousands of thrushes drop from the sky after a tiring flight across the North Sea. Rare birds cease to be rare when it is discovered that, among the birds trapped and ringed are fifty-six Barred Warblers, fifty-two Wrynecks, and twenty-two Icterine Warblers, together with single Actic and Subalpine Warblers.

winter

Knot

winter   summer

Duneland north of the Wash and near to Mablethorpe can be productive in birdlife.

THE COAST

North of the Wash, the Lincolnshire coast can be divided into two sections. South of Mablethorpe, the concrete sea walls and narrow sandy beaches mark where the coastline is being eroded and provide little of interest for the bird-watcher. Northwards, towards the Humber, the dunes and saltmarsh are more extensive and more productive.

The long stretch of Lincolnshire coast, referred to as **Saltfleetby-Theddlethorpe Dunes** (OS TF4890), covers some 500 hectares (1235 acres) and forms a National Nature Reserve administered in conjunction with the Lincolnshire and South Humberside Trust for Nature Conservation. Inland behind the dunes is a freshwater marsh with breeding Sedge Warbler, Reed Bunting, and Snipe, while, in the winter months, the extensive clumps of sea buckthorn provide food for the winter thrushes which, in turn, attract the wintering Merlin. The open sandflats provide feeding for a range of wader species.

Donna Nook (OS TF4299) is another coastal reserve operated by the County Trust, with an open lagoon and saltmarsh which together provide an impressive list of over 250 species, including a variety of common and rare migrants. Wintering coastal species include Shore Lark, Snow Bunting, Lapland Bunting, and Twite. Caution must be exercised at this site, however, because no access is possible when the red flags are flying to indicate that the firing ranges are in operation.

Grainthorpe and Tetney Marshes (OS TA3603) encompass a further expanse of sandflats, dunes, and saltmarsh on the southern shore of the Humber mouth. It is here that the RSPB has a 1300-hectare (3200-acre) reserve which contains one of Britain's largest Little Tern colonies. Visiting birdwatchers should note that access into the colony area is not permitted and they should confine themselves to the excellent views that can be obtained from the sea wall at high tide. Other breeding species are Shelduck, Oystercatcher, Redshank, and Ringed Plover, with wintering and passage flocks of Greenshank, Golden Plover, Bar-tailed Godwit, and offshore Common Scoter.

SNIPE DALES (OS TF3268)

Principally, this is a grassland site where extensive woodlands are being recreated. There is a good selection of breeding warblers, including the Grasshopper Warbler and Whitethroat while, in the scrubby areas, Linnet and Yellowhammer nest. Woodcock, Short-eared Owl, Heron, and Snipe are regular visitors. Access is off the A1115 near the junction with the A158 road.

HARTSHOLME COUNTRY PARK (OS SK945694)

This is a small country park operated by the City of Lincoln. Access is from the south of Lincoln off the A46 road to Newark. Facilities include a car park, and a nature trail which passes around the lake and woodland. Among several species, Nightingale and Kingfisher are regular.

WISBECH SEWAGE FARM

This once famous birdwatching site is on the border of Lincolnshire, Norfolk, and Cambridgeshire. It is described under the latter.

SHROPSHIRE

Shropshire lies firmly and centrally at the junction between England and Wales. The county is divided by the River Severn which meanders through the county's heart and upon whose banks sits the one major town – Shrewsbury. This is an extremely rural county which was bypassed by industrial development in the past, just as it is bypassed today by the tourists from the English Midlands heading for Wales. North of the Severn are the arable plains that extend eastwards into central England. Low lying, this area provides the only wetland of consequence, the meres and mosses in the extreme north on the Cheshire/Clwyd border. To the south of the river are the uplands that lead to the Welsh hills – the Clee, Long Mynd, and Clun Forest – where sheep rearing dominates. Far from the coast and lacking in diversity of bird habitat, Shropshire's bird list is rather restricted and contains only a little over 255 species.

Birdwatching sites

EARL'S HILL (OS SJ4004)

This Shropshire Trust for Nature Conservation reserve is principally a rocky and grassy hill that overlooks wooded valleys, slopes, and fast-flowing streams. Access is via the A488 at Pontesbury village and facilities include an information centre and nature trail. The visiting birdwatcher should concentrate on late spring/early summer when the visiting migrants have arrived and bird song is at its peak.

Among the resident woodpeckers, Treecreeper, Nuthatch, and tits, the breeding birds include summer visitors, such as Pied Flycatcher, Redstart, and Wood Warbler. Dipper and Pied and Grey Wagtails inhabit the streams while the more open areas can reveal the flashing glimpse of a Sparrowhawk or Merlin, or the relaxed flight of a Buzzard, Kestrel, or Raven.

SHROPSHIRE MERES

In the extreme north of the county, in the vicinity of Ellesmere and, to a lesser extent, near Whitchurch the series of water-filled hollows, known as 'The Meres' is to be found. Several of the lakes are natural, while others have been created by the extraction of peat – with the passage of time, they have acquired a natural appearance. The areas that have not been excavated, but still retain their peat upon which dense masses of moss have grown, are known locally as 'The Mosses'. Several sites have been declared reserves and are administered by the County Trust or County Council. Some are disturbed by recreational activities, but many still retain a peaceful existence and support breeding Heron, Great Crested Grebe, and Kingfisher. Migrant Black Terns are regular and, in the winter, this is the best area in Shropshire for concentrations of wildfowl, including up to fifty Goldeneye and a steadily increasing number of Ruddy Duck. Access is via the A528 road north-west from Shrewsbury.

Among the sites within the area, birdwatchers should consider visiting:
Colmere Country Park – a lake with woodland and grassland; **The Mere, Ellesmere** – a large lake with surrounding scrub. This site is likely to produce the most varied bird populations. The 'Meres Centre' contains information on all sites in the area; **Brown Moss** – a mixture of water, wood, and heath. Over thirty species of birds breed at this site; **Wenn Moss** – a typical example of an unexcavated raised peat bog.

SOUTHERN UPLANDS

A certain amount of variety in the countryside is immediately apparent. Some of the highest ground, over 500 metres (1645 feet), is dry moorland plateau where rocky slopes are interspersed with extremely poor hill grazing upon which the only agriculture attempted is sheep farming. These same sheep can provide conservation difficulties on the lower slopes. Down in the valleys are all that remain of the once widespread oakwoods; constant grazing has prevented regeneration and woodland is lost as the old trees die. Poor pasture land also exists, but many areas have now been established as conifer plantations. For the birdwatcher with a love of the hills and hillwalking, there are many suitable sites to visit.

Long Mynd (OS SO4294) is an extensive National Trust moorland reserve of nearly 2000 hectares (5000 acres) where the visitor will find the Shropshire Hills Information Centre. Here, further details of the region, its walks, and wildlife can be obtained. The bird of the Long Mynd is, without doubt, the Buzzard which sails over the slopes and edges of the deep-cut valleys, occasionally mobbed by a passing Raven. On the hilltops are Ring Ouzel, Wheatear, and Stonechat, while the heather provides a home for the Red Grouse. Dipper and Grey Wagtail inhabit the streams; woodpeckers (particularly

Shopshire Meres

Whitchurch

Ellesmere

Oswestry

Whittington

Market Drayton

Hodnet

Newport

Earl's Hill

Long Mynd

SHREWSBURY

Wellington

TELFORD

Oakengates

Ironbridge

Lydham

Church Stretton

Bridgnorth

SHROPSHIRE

Clun

Ludlow

Woofferton

Clun Forest

Wenlock Edge

The high ground of the Long Mynd, owned by the National Trust, is home for the soaring Buzzard.

Green) and flocks of tits occupy the woods. Among the breeding birds are several summer migrants including Redstart, Tree Pipit, and Spotted Flycatcher.

Clun Forest (OS SO2585) is in the extreme south-west of the county and, unfortunately, considerable areas are now swathed in conifer plantations. The remaining oak-woods contain nesting Redstart and Pied Flycatcher; the more open areas are sites for Meadow Pipit and Short-eared Owl.

Wenlock Edge (OS SO5595) The limestone ridges and slopes, together with the rough pastures and wooded valleys provide equally good habitats for all the typical bird species of south-west Shropshire.

Spotted flycatcher

imm.

Goldeneye

Organizations in Shropshire

Shropshire Ornithological Society (SOS), Arnsheen, Betley Lane, Bayston Hill, Shrewsbury SY3 0AS
Shropshire Trust for Nature Conservation (STNC), Agriculture House, Barker Street, Shrewsbury SY1 1QP

Annual reports

'Shropshire Bird Report', Church Cottage, Leebotwood, Church Stretton, Shropshire

Books

Rutter, E M *et al. A Handlist of the Birds of Shropshire*. Shropshire Ornithological Society, 1964.

Birds of prey in Shropshire

Although the variety of bird life in the county is rather poor, Shropshire can justifiably boast a good selection of birds of prey – certainly when compared with other inland English counties.
Honey Buzzard – a rare visitor; less than ten records.
Red Kite – with the continued growth of the Welsh breeding population, the number of records continues to increase.
White-tailed Eagle – no recent occurrences; less than ten records.

Montagu's Harrier – no recent occurrences.
Marsh Harrier – occasionally appears as a spring or autumn migrant.
Hen Harrier – small numbers are present in the county in most winters.
Goshawk – recorded annually, with a small breeding population now established in the south of the county.
Sparrowhawk – widespread and common; breeds.
Buzzard – widespread in the south of the county, occasionally recorded in the north; breeds.
Rough-legged Buzzard – occasional winter visitor.
Osprey – passage migrant with small numbers each spring and autumn probably reflecting the increasing Scottish breeding population.
Kestrel – widespread and common; breeds.
Red-footed Falcon – a rare visitor; less than ten records, one in 1982.
Merlin – recorded annually from moorland areas, but numbers decreasing, and breeding is rarely confirmed.
Hobby – recorded annually, particularly in spring; may breed.
Peregrine – up to ten individuals recorded in most years.
Gyrfalcon – no recent occurrences; less than ten records.

NOTTINGHAMSHIRE, DERBYSHIRE, AND STAFFORDSHIRE

Black grouse

Black-winged Stilts in Nottinghamshire

One of Nottinghamshire's major ornithological claims to fame is the only successful nesting of the Black-winged Stilt in Britain. In 1945, three pairs were discovered at the Nottinghamshire sewage farm – at that time a site well known for producing the occasional rare bird. The birds were seen on several visits, and eventually, two nests, each with three eggs, were discovered. It subsequently came to light that a local boy had collected a clutch of stilt eggs from a third nest in another part of the farm. The entire breeding attempt was almost doomed when flooding took place and submerged the eggs but, fortunately, urgent work lowered the water level and raised the nests. Eventually, three young fledged, two from one nest and one from the second. There has been one subsequent breeding attempt in Britain, in Cambridgeshire, but no young were reared although eggs were laid.

Organizations in Nottinghamshire

Trent Valley Bird-Watchers (TVBW), 330 Westdale Lane, Mapperley, Nottingham NG5 3GJ
Nottinghamshire Trust for Nature Conservation (NTNC), 2-12 Warser Gate, Nottingham NG1 1PA
RSPB Members' Group based at: Nottingham (details from RSPB, The Lodge, Sandy, Beds SG19 2DL)

Annual reports

'Birds of Nottinghamshire', 19 Woodlands Grove, Chilwell, Nottingham

Books

Dobbs, A. *The Birds of Nottinghamshire*. David & Charles, 1975.
Frost, R A and Herringshaw, D. *Birdwatching in the Dukeries and North Notts*. Private printing, 1979.

NOTTINGHAMSHIRE

Nottinghamshire is very much a central link between: the Lincolnshire Wolds and the flat lands to the east; the uplands of the southern Pennines in Yorkshire to the north; and via the coalfields of Derbyshire and the industrial areas to the south-west. Generally, it is a low-lying, rural county but there is industry where coal lies beneath the surface of the land or along the line of the Trent Valley. The river is dominated by five gigantic power stations, fed by coal from the Midlands' fields. Associated with this development have come the gravel pits and the resulting winter wildfowl populations. In the north, the famous Sherwood Forest can still boast some of the ancient timber that once covered much of the county; while the extreme south-east contains the beautiful Vale of Bevoir, claimed by many to be one of the most scenic areas of England. Some 300 species of bird have been recorded in the county.

Birdwatching sites

SHERWOOD FOREST

Sherwood Forest Country Park (OS SK6267) is a Nottinghamshire County Council park containing some of the finest examples of oak trees to be found in Britain. Such massive trees set in woodland clearings can give us a little of the flavour of ancient Sherwood. Access is via the A614 road west of Ollerton.

   Clumber Park (OS SK6274), nearly 1300 hectares (3200 acres) of National Trust parkland, is one of the 'Dukeries' and contains a lake, heathland, and a wood. Access is via the B6005 south-east of Worksop, and facilities include a car park, an information centre, and a nature trail.

   Typical 'Dukeries' parkland forms the basis of the County Council **Rufford Country Park** (OS SK6465). It is rather more formal and perhaps less attractive to the birdwatcher than the other sites in the area, but the park does contain a wildlife area with a lake. Access is via the A614 south of Ollerton.

   Hannah Park Wood (OS SK5977) is a small remnant of Sherwood Forest, owned by the Woodland Trust. The mixed woodland structure contains some high forest oak with a range of typical bird species. Access is via the B6005 road south of Worksop.

   On the border with Derbyshire, the limestone gorge of **Creswell Crags** (OS SK5374) contains a lake and wooded hillsides. Access is via the B6042 east of Creswell village.

   Bird populations within Sherwood Forest are varied, the distribution being very dependent upon the structure of the wood (mature trees, young trees, or a mixture), the amount of undergrowth, and the presence or absence of water. Summer visitors include a range of warblers, Spotted Flycatcher, Redstart, and Cuckoo; in winter, wildfowl, such as Canada Goose, Pochard, and Goldeneye, use the lakes, with parties of Redpolls, Siskins, and Crossbills in the woodland. Resident species include the woodpeckers, tits, Nuthatch, Treecreeper, Pied Wagtail, and a range of finches.

MARTIN'S POND (OS SK5240)

Owned by the Nottingham City Council and administered as a reserve by the Nottinghamshire Trust for Nature

Sherwood Forest still boasts some of the finest oaks in Britain, such as the massive 'Major Oak'.

Conservation, this is a very urban site and potentially very disturbed. In fact, it supports a good bird population with a full list of some 100 species of which over twenty breed in most years.

SOUTH NOTTINGHAMSHIRE GRAVEL PITS

The south of the county, in the valley of the River Trent, contains an extensive series of gravel pits. Several have been refilled with waste fly-ash from the power stations but many remain and, between them, they hold a sizeable population of winter wildfowl. Without doubt, the main site is the reserve at Attenborough, but other gravel pits worth a visit from the birdwatcher are Besthorpe, South Muskham, Hoveringham, and Gunthorpe.

   Attenborough Reserve (OS SK5234) is a Nottinghamshire Trust for Nature Conservation reserve of some 100 hectares (250 acres), based upon a series of disused gravel pits with access off the Nottingham-to-Long Eaton road. The site contains a car park, information centre, and observation hide. The reserve is a completely artificial site but the excavations were carried out long enough ago for the area to have become revegetated with a wide range of plants that attracts an impressive list of birds. Over 215 species have been recorded. Among the breeding birds, a small colony of Common Terns is established on the islands, while Grasshopper, Reed, and Sedge Warblers breed every year, and Garganey do so occasionally. Other summer visitors include Little Ringed Plover and Yellow Wagtail. In winter, large numbers of Pochard and Tufted Duck congregate on the water, with Water Rail, Green Sandpiper, and Jack Snipe on the muddy margins. Regular migrants, include Black Tern, Spotted Redshank, and Ruff, with unusual birds in recent years including Osprey, Red-backed Shrike, Little Crake, and Spoonbill.

DERBYSHIRE

Derbyshire exhibits some dramatic extremes in habitat and scenery. In the south, the low-lying Trent Valley [altitude only some 30 metres (100 feet)] above sea level is principally dairy country with little woodland, although the industry along the Trent itself has produced a string of worked-out gravel pits. Towards the east are the Derbyshire coalfields where industrial development, coupled with arable farming (and the consequent loss of woodlands) have created that area of Derbyshire where the human population is densest. Travelling north and west from the coalfields, woodland increases and the land rises as the foothills of the southern extremity of the Pennine Chain are encountered. The land rises steadily to over 600 metres (2000 feet) at the highest point on Kinder Scout. This is the area of the Peak National Park which is set almost entirely within the borders of Derbyshire. The county covers some 263 000 hectares (650 000 acres), the national park over 140 000 hectares (346 000 acres). Nearly 300 species of birds have been recorded within the county, of which some 110 nest each year.

Birdwatching sites

THE PEAK NATIONAL PARK

This extensive park, created in 1951, comprises almost the whole of northern Derbyshire and, within its boundaries, there is considerable diversity together with many opportunities for the visiting birdwatcher. The following sites are all worth considering:

Tideswell Dale (OS SK1574) – a fast-flowing river with surrounding woods; **Dovedale** (OS SK1450) – a famous beauty spot, perhaps best avoided at peak holiday times; **Goyt Valley** (OS SK0175) – moorland, stream and tree-fringed reservoir; **Tissington Trail** (OS SK1752) – woodland nature trail; **Upper Derwent Valley** (OS SK1789) – steep-sided, wooded valleys with reservoirs and moorland; **Manifold Trail** (OS SK0850, Staffordshire) – woodland valley, cliffs, and rocky river.

It is worth taking any opportunity to explore new sites or to devote extra time to the better-known localities. The park contains many information centres for all visitors, and a considerable amount of literature is available on the wildlife of the region. The following list is a broad indication of the different habitats and the range of species that can be expected:

open grassland/farmland/bracken slopes – Skylark, Lapwing, Curlew, Corn Bunting, Nightjar, Snipe, Black Grouse; *woodland* – Long-eared Owl, Pied Flycatcher, Redstart, Wood Warbler, Hawfinch, Sparrowhawk, Crossbill; *streams/rivers* – Dipper, Kingfisher, Grey and Pied Wagtails, Common Sandpiper; *high tops/moorland* – Red Grouse, Meadow Pipit, Curlew, Hen Harrier, Merlin, Twite, Golden Plover, Short-eared Owl; *rocky outcrops/quarries* – Kestrel, Jackdaw, Stock Dove, Ring Ouzel, Buzzard, Peregrine, Raven; *reservoirs* – gull roosts, Mallard, Tufted Duck, Teal, Red-breasted Merganser.

SPRING WOOD/STAUNTON HAROLD RESERVOIR (OS SK3824)

Access to this site is via the B587 road south of Melbourne. Viewing across the reservoir is possible from several points. Wintering wildfowl at the site include Pochard, Shoveler, Wigeon, and Goldeneye. The adjoining woodland is operated as a reserve by the Derbyshire Naturalists' Trust, and extends to the water's edge where an observation hide is positioned. Typical mixed woodland species include Lesser Spotted Woodpecker and Tawny Owl, while the surrounding scrub contains Whitethroat and Grasshopper Warbler.

DRAKELOW WILDFOWL RESERVE (OS SK2220)

This 9-hectare (22-acre) site is owned by the Central Electricity Generating Board, and is situated beside the Drakelow 'C' Power Station, within a loop of the river. Access is strictly controlled, and permits should be obtained from the CEGB in advance of a visit. The reserve is based upon disused gravel pits and includes a field centre, educational facilities, and several observation hides. Winter duck numbers are frequently in excess of 1000 individuals, while breeding birds include Little Ringed Plover, Reed and Sedge Warblers. In recent years, more unusual visitors have included Red-necked Grebe, Spotted Crake, and Temminck's Stint.

OGSTON RESERVOIR (OS SK3760)

Access is via the B6014 road east of Matlock. This is probably the county's most popular birdwatching reservoir. Not only has the site produced a good selection of bird species, but it has scenic appeal with a range of surrounding habitats. It was first created by the National Coal Board in 1958, and, since then, over 200 different species have been recorded. Recent observations have included Black-throated Diver, Shag, up to 200 Teal, Long-tailed Skua, and a range of migrant waders more normally associated with coastal localities.

Skylark

Organizations in Derbyshire
Derbyshire Ornithological Society (DOS), Brentwood, Burleigh Drive, Derby DE3 1AL
Derbyshire Wildlife Trust (DWT), Elvaston Castle Country Park, New Derby DE7 3EP
RSPB Members' Groups based at: Derby and High Peak (details from RSPB, The Lodge, Sandy, Beds SG19 2DL)

Annual reports
'Derbyshire Bird Report', Brentwood, Burleigh Drive, Derby DE3 1AL

Books
Frost, R A. *Birds of Derbyshire.* Moorland, 1978.

Some peak Staffordshire wildfowl counts			
	Aqualate	Belvide	Blithfield
Great Crested Grebe	-	36	161
Canada Goose	592	280	680
Wigeon	400	90	1135
Teal	150	291	727
Mallard	1850	1520	2062
Shoveler	380	570	82
Pochard	130	342	270
Tufted Duck	131	843	137
Goldeneye	-	100	90
Goosander	5	15	104
Ruddy Duck	137	425	630
Coot	308	2050	727

FOREMARK RESERVOIR (OS SK3323)

This is a new reservoir, created in the mid-1970s, with access from the A514 road south of Derby. Although it does not yet rival the established sites, there is clearly much potential with records of over 100 Goosander, Scaup, Red-necked Grebe, and up to ten Grey Plover – the largest party to be recorded in the county.

STAFFORDSHIRE

The southern part of Staffordshire is dominated by heavy industry where a finger of the county thrusts into the West Midland conurbation but, further north, there are marked contrasts. The very rural centre could be described as typical unspoiled English countryside with forests, heaths, and rich dairy farmland. Skirting the industrial spread of the 'Potteries' in the north-west is the open high country and moorland of the north-east which continue as far as the visually very striking valley of the River Dove that provides the border with Derbyshire. Staffordshire's most notable river is the Trent, flowing south-eastwards through the heart of the county gathering water from its main tributaries, the Sow and Blithe, en route. The damming of the latter has produced what is now one of Britain's most famous birdwatching localities, Blithfield Reservoir, which, together with some of the smaller artificial sites, provide the only sizeable areas of open water in the county. In most years some 110 species nest.

Derbyshire's reservoirs offer considerable birdwatching potential in a county where natural habitat has been lost in some areas.

Birdwatching sites

COOMBE VALLEY AND CHURNET VALLEY WOODS (OS SK0053)

Access to these RSPB woodland reserves, with their steep-sided valleys and fast-flowing streams, is via the A523 road east of Leek. Facilities include car park, information centre, observation hides, and a nature trail. Although visiting is possible and to be recommended throughout the year, spring and summer will always prove most productive for birdwatching. All three species of woodpecker, Sparrowhawk, Tawny and Long-eared Owls, Redstart, Wood Warbler, and Pied Flycatcher nest in the woodland; Dipper, Grey Wagtail, and Kingfisher beside the stream; and Tree Pipit and Woodcock in the glades. Mixed flocks of thrushes, tits, and finches occur in winter.

RESERVOIRS

There is a selection of reservoirs in the river valleys throughout the county, but two sites dominate the birdwatching scene:

Belvide Reservoir (OS SJ8510) was originally constructed in 1834 as a feeder reservoir for the Shropshire Union Canal but it was eventually leased to the West

Midland Bird Club as a reserve in 1977. The 120-hectare (300-acre) site contains, in addition to open water, areas of reedfen, open mud, and surrounding wet grassland. Observation hides have been constructed. Although access is controlled, viewing is possible from the surrounding public rights of way. Because of the undisturbed nature of the site, bird densities are very high, and as many as 5000 wildfowl may be present at any one time. Huge numbers of Swifts, Swallows, and martins congregate in the late summer, and a wide variety of migrant waders occurs. The impressive list of rare birds that have been recorded here includes Marsh Sandpiper, Whiskered Tern, and Golden Oriole. The reservoir is situated immediately south of the A5 road east of Cannock.

Blithfield Reservoir (OS SK0523) was first flooded in 1952. This 320-hectare (800-acre) reservoir has, quite justifiably, acquired the reputation of being one of the most important artificial sites for wildfowl in Britain. Situated north-east of Uttoxeter, viewing is particularly easy from the B5013 which crosses the site on a causeway. The West Midland Bird Club operates a permit access scheme on behalf of the Staffordshire Waterworks Company which allows use of the observation hides and walkways. Good views can be obtained from the surrounding roads and lanes. Much of the reservoir banking is 'natural' and, at times of low water, the exposed mud is particularly attractive to migrant waders. This is one of the country's main wintering areas for Ruddy Duck. Rarities have included Lesser Yellowlegs, Caspian Tern, and Richard's Pipit.

Tittesworth Reservoir (OS SJ9960) is very much an upland reservoir, set in striking scenery and surrounded by woods and rocky hillsides. Bird populations are not high, but viewing conditions are good with small numbers of wildfowl, grebes, Common Sandpiper, and Curlew. Access is via the A53 road on a minor road to Meerbrook.

Although **Aqualate Mere** (OS SJ7720) is not a reservoir, this shallow mere of some 60 hectares (150 acres) with its dense surrounding vegetation and expanse of reeds, is the fourth sizeable area of water in the county. Access is from the A518 road east of Newport but it must be noted that this is a private site. Of interest is a heronry of some fifty pairs and a good collection of winter wildfowl.

The huge heathland of Cannock Chase attracts a wide variety of birds.

CANNOCK CHASE (OS SJ9784)

Cannock Chase is a huge area of heathland, woodland, and bog which, in the late summer, is a blaze of purple heath. Nature trails, public footpaths, and visitor facilities are plentiful, but equally, at some times of the year, the more popular sites are crowded with visitors. The visiting bird-watcher should, however, always be able to find a remote spot from which to enjoy the abundant bird life of the region. Even the conifer plantations can provide excitements, for, among the Coal Tits and Goldcrests, there are regular parties of Crossbills, and the occasional Two-barred Crossbill has been reported. The broadleaved woodlands attract Tawny Owl, Nuthatch, Wood Warbler, and Hawfinch; the more open sites Yellowhammer, Whinchat, Grasshopper Warbler, and Nightjar. Wintering and migrant birds are less numerous, but Ring Ouzel, Merlin, and Great Grey Shrike can all occur.

TILLINGTON MARSHES (OS SJ9123)

A wetland reserve of the Staffordshire Nature Conservation Trust situated immediately north-west of the town of Stafford, this is a site of pools, meadows, and marshes in which public footpaths provide excellent birdwatching possibilities. Small numbers of duck winter, and breeding birds include Snipe, Redshank, and several warblers.

FORD GREEN RESERVE (OS SJ8950)

Within the City of Stoke-on-Trent, this very urban site is the result of subsidence producing marshy land that is susceptible to flooding. Access is from Ford Green Road in Smallthorne, and a selection of common species can be expected, including Sedge Warbler, Kingfisher, and Common Sandpiper.

DEEP HAYES COUNTRY PARK (OS SJ9653)

This is a County Council country park of freshwater areas that were once reservoirs, together with woods and meadows. Access is from the A53 road south of Langsdon. Facilities include an information centre, car park, and nature trail. Bird species include Tufted Duck, Kingfisher, and Reed Bunting, together with several woodpeckers, tits, and warblers.

Organizations in Staffordshire
West Midland Bird Club (WMBC), 8 Bowstoke Road, Great Barr, Birmingham B43 5EA
Staffordshire Nature Conservation Trust (SNCT), Coutts House, Sandon, ST18 0DN
RSPB Members' Groups based at: Burton, Lichfield, North and South West (details from RSPB, The Lodge, Sandy, Beds SG19 2DL)

Annual reports
'West Midland Bird Report', 8 Bowstoke Road, Great Barr, Birmingham B43 5EA

Books
Harrison, G R *et al. The Birds of the West Midlands*. West Midland Bird Club, 1982.
Lord, J and Blake, A R M. *The Birds of Staffordshire*. West Midland Bird Club, 1962.
Lord, J and Munns, D J. *Atlas of Breeding Birds of the West Midlands*. Collins, 1970.

LANCASHIRE, CHESHIRE, GREATER MANCHESTER, AND MERSEYSIDE

LANCASHIRE

With the creation of Merseyside and Greater Manchester, much of the industrial and heavily populated south of the county was lost. Although towns such as Burnley, Blackburn, Preston, and Lancaster remain, all linked by a canal system that was once the lifeblood of the area, Lancashire is now a more rural county. On the eastern border are the Pennine uplands with their vast tracts of heather moorland, much of it with limited access and providing an undisturbed area where upland species can breed successfully. At the southern end, where the Pennines disappear into the Greater Manchester area, the moorlands are more popular for recreational purposes.

From the uplands flow the rivers that drain the county in a westward direction, the Lune and the Ribble. En route to the Irish Sea, they flow through quiet farming valleys still well supplied with woods, copses, and hedgerows. In the far north, the limestone rocky scenery indicates the rugged grandeur of the Lakes that are just across the border.

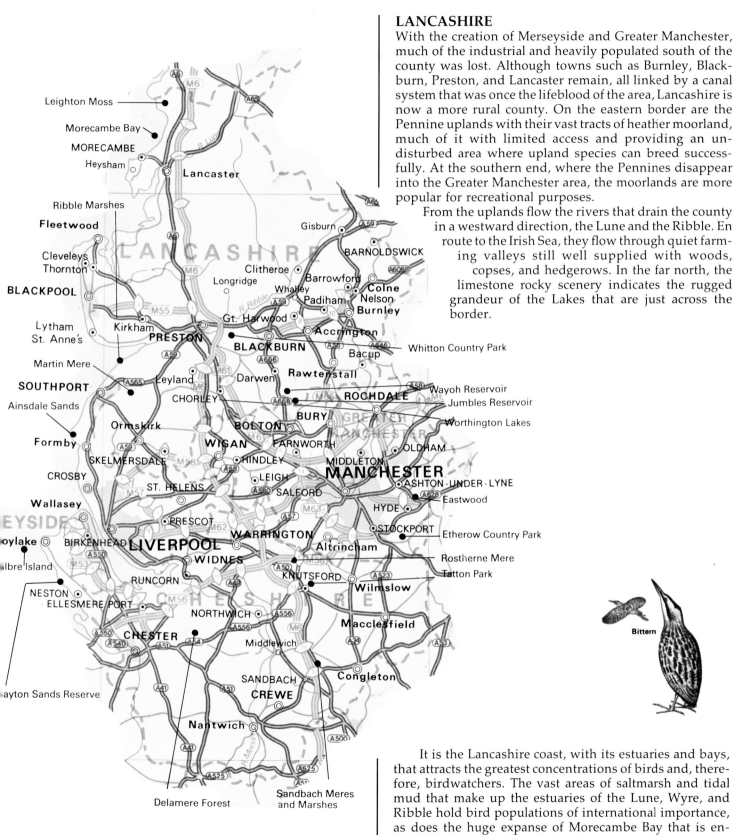

It is the Lancashire coast, with its estuaries and bays, that attracts the greatest concentrations of birds and, therefore, birdwatchers. The vast areas of saltmarsh and tidal mud that make up the estuaries of the Lune, Wyre, and Ribble hold bird populations of international importance, as does the huge expanse of Morecambe Bay that is enclosed within two arms, the extremities of which are marked by Fleetwood on the southern shore and Walney Island in Cumbria in the north. In excess of 320 species have been recorded in the county, of which near 130 breed each year.

The Ribble offers a variety of habitats for birds, especially near the coast.

Birdwatching sites

LEIGHTON MOSS (OS SD4775)

This large reed-swamp of some 130 hectares (320 acres) is owned by the RSPB and includes open meres and scrub of willow and alder. Access is from near Silverdale station north of Carnforth and east of the A6 road. Visitor facilities include a car park, an information centre, and observation hides. This is not only the key site for Bittern in the British Isles, but it is also probably the best site at which to view them. It would be quite unusual to spend a day birdwatching here and not catch a glimpse of this species. Other breeding birds include Bearded Tit, Reed, Sedge, and Grasshopper Warblers, Mallard, Teal, and Shoveler. In some years, Gadwall and Garganey also nest. Migrant species include a range of waders (particularly in autumn) as well as the occasional Marsh Harrier and Osprey. Black Terns are regular. In late summer and autumn, the reedbeds provide secure roosting sites for a range of species, dominated by the Starling, but including Swallow, Pied

and Yellow Wagtails. In winter, large concentrations of wildfowl are best seen at high tide when feeding areas on the nearby Morecambe Bay are covered.

MORECAMBE BAY (OS SD3567)

This is the largest area of continuous tidal mud in Britain. The bay totals some 51 000 hectares (126 000 acres) in area of which, at low tide, some 31 000 hectares (76 500 acres) consist of sand and mud – mud carried and deposited over the years by five major rivers that enter the bay. Our knowledge of the birds of Morecambe Bay was greatly enhanced when detailed studies were carried out in response to the suggestion that a huge tidal barrage should be constructed across the bay. It is these tides that govern the movements of the birds which, in turn, create the spectacle that birdwatchers come to see. Visiting birdwatchers should beware, however – tidal predictions in this area are often seriously affected by westerly winds which can make this a dangerous place.

There are many vantage points for watching birds on Morecambe Bay: several areas of coast road, particularly on the Cumbrian shore (the A5087), should be investigated; while, on the Lancashire side, information is available at the Leighton Moss RSPB reserve from where a visit can be arranged to the RSPB Morecambe Bay site and observation hide. Further south at Hest Bank is probably the best high-tide roost which is accessed from the A5105 road and railway crossing.

RIBBLE MARSHES (OS SD3720)

This is another vast coastal site, including some 3200 hectares (7900 acres) of saltmarsh and mudflats owned by the Nature Conservancy Council. There are no formal visiting facilities but good views of the high-tide roosts can be obtained from the coast road, access to which is by following the A565 north of Southport. Bird populations of

---

The waders and wildfowl of Morecambe Bay

The detailed studies of the bird populations of Morecambe Bay have produced some exciting counts, and the following information is based on the results of the 'Birds of Estuaries Enquiry'.
1 Species with winter population of **international** importance: Pink-footed Goose; Shelduck; Wigeon; Pintail; Oystercatcher; Knot; Dunlin; Bar-tailed Godwit; Curlew; Redshank; and Turnstone; in addition, Ringed Plover and Sanderling during their spring and autumn migrations.
2 Additional species with wintering populations of **national** importance: Teal; Mallard; Eider; Common Scoter; Goldeneye; Red-breasted

Merganser; and Grey Plover.

Morecambe Bay is, therefore, a most important site for at least twenty species of birds, but there are also Short-eared Owls that hunt the saltmarsh in winter, and Peregrines that prey on the wader flocks or perhaps on the parties of Twite seeking food among the creeks and gullies.

Some winter wader populations

	Morecambe	Europe and North Africa	Percentage at Morecambe Bay
Oystercatcher	38 000	470 000	8
Curlew	3900	110 000	4
Bar-tailed Godwit	7300	70 000	10
Redshank	4200	84 000	5
Turnstone	1500	11 500	13
Knot	65 000	435 000	15
Dunlin	45 000	830 000	5

Organizations in Lancashire

East Lancashire Ornithologists' Club (ELOC), 6 Lambeth Street, Colne BB8 7BL
Lancaster and District Bird Watching Society (LDBWS), 28 Manor Road, Slyne, Lancaster LA2 6LB
Lancashire Trust for Nature Conservation (LTNC), The Pavilion, Cuerdon Valley Park, Bamber Bridge, Preston PR5 6AX
RSPB Members' Groups based at: Blackpool, Lancaster, and Preston (details from RSPB, The Lodge, Sandy, Beds SG19 2DL)

summer   winter

Dunlin   winter

Annual reports

'Lancashire Bird Report', 31 Laverton Road, St Annes-on-Sea, Lancs FY8 1EW

Books

Hardy, E. *Birdwatching in Lancashire*. Dalesman, 1979.
Oakes, C. *The Birds of Lancashire*. Oliver & Boyd, 1953.
Spencer, K G. *The Status and Distribution of Birds in Lancashire*. Private printing, 1973.

Britain's first Collared Pratincole

To date, some seventy records of Collared Pratincole have been reported in Britain, but Lancashire can claim the first – albeit of somewhat uncertain date. According to Clifford Oakes in his book, *The Birds of Lancashire*, a Pratincole was shot near Ormskirk in 1807, preserved as a specimen by a gentleman named J Sherlock, and then sent to the Liverpool Museum. When K G Spencer compiled his notes on the status of the birds in Lancashire, he examined the specimen in the museum. He records the fact that there is some confusion about the date it was shot, considering it most likely to have been 18 May 1805 – two years earlier than Oakes recorded. He also gives the locality as being near Southport – not Ormskirk – so is this first British record now for the county of Lancashire or for the new county of Merseyside!

Morecambe Bay must be one of the most famous birdwatching sites in Britain but it can also be a dangerous place for visitors.

the Ribble estuary can be very high: up to 14 000 Pink-footed Geese; 70 000 Knot; 15 000 Oystercatcher; and 42 000 Dunlin. In addition, more unusual records have included Broad-billed Sandpiper, Bonaparte's Gull, and Rose-coloured Starling.

MARTIN MERE (OS SD4214)

Martin Mere is a Wildfowl Trust reserve created on reclaimed marshland of the River Ribble. Access is well sign-posted from the A59 road north of Ormskirk. Facilities include a car park, centre, a collection of pinioned birds, and observation hides. Although for the visiting bird-watcher, the spectacle of thousands of Pink-footed Geese, Wigeon, Pintail, and Teal during the winter months is without doubt the main attraction, a wide range of other species occurs, including concentrations of Ruff (up to 250), Black-tailed Godwit, and Golden Plover. In summer, when most of the wildfowl have departed, breeding birds include Red-legged Partridge, Little Ringed Plover, and Little Owl; while recent rarities have included Lesser Yellowlegs, American Wigeon, and White-winged Black Tern.

WAYOH RESERVOIR (OS SD7316)

Under an agreement with the North West Water Authority, this 50-hectare (124-acre) site is now a reserve managed by the Lancashire Trust for Nature Conservation. Situated some 5 miles north of Bolton, the reserve is best viewed from the public footpaths that give access to the site. Winter wildfowl include the diving ducks, principally Tufted Duck and Pochard, while, in summer, the surrounding scrubland attracts several breeding warblers.

WHITTON COUNTRY PARK (OS SD6627)

Old estate parkland on the outskirts of Blackburn has been converted into a country park by the Lancaster County Council. Access is via the A674 road west of Blackburn. The ornamental character of the parkland is offset by some natural woodland and open grassland. A good selection of bird species can be encountered.

CHESHIRE

From east to west, Cheshire ranges from the high ground of the southern Pennines through low-lying land with its mosses and meres, many of which have resulted from natural subsidence, until it rises again to the central Cheshire ridge. This ridge acts as a dividing line between the River Weaver flowing to the Mersey near Runcorn and the Gowy that enters the Mersey near Ellesmere Port. Beyond, the River Dee forms the western boundary from

Pintail

where the high land of Wales complements the Pennines in the east. In the north, Cheshire's industrial zone abuts with Merseyside and Greater Manchester, while much of the remainder of the county is pastoral farming. The once extensive woodlands have been lost to satisfy the demands of industry to the north and agriculture within – now only the higher ground holds examples of the formerly dominant mixed deciduous forests. The county has no true coastline, but the short frontages of the tidal Dee and Mersey estuaries, with their extensive saltmarsh and mud flats, attract large populations of wintering birds. Over 300 species have been recorded in the county.

Birdwatching sites

SANDBACH MERES AND MARSHES (OS SJ7260)
This complex of shallow pools (the result of subsidence) with its open water, muddy edges, reedbeds, wet grassland, and neighbouring wet woodlands is, in fact, made up of three reserves operated by the Cheshire Conservation Trust. They are known locally as 'The Flashes'. This is an excellent area for the birdwatcher at any time of the year and, although access is not possible, indeed not desirable, various viewing points and the wide range of species present, make this a particularly attractive spot.

The three reserves are **Elton Hall Flash, Foden's Flash**, and **Watch Lane Flash** – all clearly visible from the surrounding roads and car parks (access via A533 road south of Middlewich). Breeding species include Great Crested Grebe and Little Grebe, Little Ringed Plover, Pochard, Teal, Grasshopper and Sedge Warblers. In winter, Bewick's Swan, Pochard, Shoveler, and Pintail are all regular while, during migration, a wide selection of waders has been recorded, with several unusual species such as Pectoral and Upland Sandpipers.

DELAMERE FOREST (OS SJ5471)
At one time, an ancient forest covered this central ridge of Cheshire but now much of the area is swathed with Forestry Commission plantations. A forest trail is reached via the B5152 road at Delamere village, however, and this can produce a selection of species even if such specialities as the Nightjar have now deserted the area. Typical summer visitors include a range of warblers (a watch should be kept for Wood Warbler), Cuckoo, Redstart, and Tree Pipit, while resident species include Sparrowhawk, three species of woodpecker, Goldcrest, and Redpoll – in some years Siskin and Crossbill are abundant.

DEE ESTUARY
Much of the Dee and its birds fall within Merseyside and Clwyd, but the key area within Cheshire is the **Gayton Sands Reserve** of the RSPB (OS SJ2778). Viewing is best from the river front off the B5135 road at Parkgate. The reserve is made up of over 2000 hectares (5000 acres) of intertidal mud and saltmarsh, and it is one of Europe's most important sites for winter wildfowl. Birdwatching visitors should not venture out on to the saltmarsh because tidal conditions and the network of creeks and channels make this an extremely dangerous place. Species that occur in outstanding numbers include Shelduck, Pintail, Oystercatcher, Grey Plover, Knot, Bar-tailed Godwit, Redshank, and Dunlin. Considerable numbers of Water Rails occur in the shoreline vegetation and they are frequently forced into the open at high tides. In midwinter, Hen Harrier, Merlin, and Peregrine are regular occurrences.

ROSTHERNE MERE (OS SJ7484)
This is a National Nature Reserve operated by the Nature Conservancy Council, and, although public visiting is not possible without prior arrangement (there is an observation hide in memory of A W Boyd, a leading Cheshire ornithologist), there are many view points from the surrounding roads. Access is from Rostherne village, off the A556 road. In addition to spectacular numbers of wildfowl using the reserve as a daytime roost, the site also attracts night-roosting gulls, frequently exceeding 20 000 individuals, of which the majority are Black-headed (up to 17 000) and Herring (up to 6000). Recent population changes at the mere have included a dramatic rise in Canada Geese (now up to 600 birds) and Ruddy Duck (up to 100); a decrease in Mallard and Teal; and a small increase in Pintail, Pochard, and Goldeneye.

TATTON PARK (OS SJ7481)
The 400-hectare (1000-acre) park is run by the Cheshire County Council and is situated off the A5034 north of Knutsford. The park contains the large Melchett Mere which holds breeding Great Crested Grebe, Teal, and Mallard, together with large numbers of wintering wildfowl. The surrounding parkland attracts woodpeckers, finches, and tits. In recent years, records have included Black-throated Diver, Black-necked Grebe, and Red-breasted Flycatcher.

GREATER MANCHESTER
Created in 1974, Greater Manchester probably exhibits a wider range of habitats than would be expected, because the county is bordered by the Pennines to the east, the plains of Cheshire to the south, and the industrial regions

Some recent wildfowl counts			
	Mersey	Dee Gayton Sands	
Shelduck	6800	5745	5070
Wigeon	4850	750	745
Teal	11 050	2920	1530
Mallard	1120	4950	3340
Pintail	13 750	11 265	11 265
Oystercatcher	19	30 360	10 910
Ringed Plover	42	600	600
Grey Plover	186	1410	1330
Lapwing	5300	4320	400
Knot	260	28 390	17 750
Dunlin	21 000	22 000	22 000
Curlew	808	4655	3500
Redshank	890	3470	1400

Organizations in Cheshire
A total of twenty-three ornithological groups and clubs throughout Cheshire have combined to form the Cheshire Ornithological Association (COA), 30 Prince Edward Street, Nantwich CW5 5NW
Cheshire Conservation Trust (CCT), Marbury Country Park, Northwich CW9 6AT
RSPB Members' Groups based at: Stockport and Wirral (details from RSPB, The Lodge, Sandy, Beds SG19 2DL)

Annual reports
'Cheshire Bird Report', 33 Sharston Crescent, Knutsford WA16 8AF

Books
Bell, T H. *The Birds of Cheshire*. Sherratt and Son, 1962.
Bell, T H. *A Supplement to the Birds of Cheshire*. Sherratt and Son, 1967.

of Merseyside to the west. Within its 128 000 hectares (nearly 320 000 acres) the county can offer bleak uplands, densely wooded valleys, flooded meres, and city centres. Notwithstanding, it is a very urban/suburban county with small areas of open country/woodland and a few areas of high moorland. Water bodies are mainly few, small, and artificial but include flashes and meres in the west which are more typical of Cheshire. Approximately 110 species of birds nest each year.

Birdwatching sites

JUMBLES RESERVOIR (OS SD1473)
North of Bolton is a series of reservoirs of which this is one (access from the A676). The surrounding pastures and woodland produce a variety of bird life in addition to the wintering wildfowl and breeding Great Crested Grebes. Snipe and Common Sandpiper are regular.

EASTWOOD (OS SJ9797)
This is an educational reserve of the RSPB, with restricted access. It consists of mixed broadleaved woodland in a steep-sided valley with a fast-flowing stream and pools.

Grey Wagtail, Kingfisher, and Grey Heron frequent the stream, and Nuthatch, Great Spotted Woodpecker, Treecreeper, and Tawny Owl nest in the woodland. Wood Warbler and Blackcap are regular summer visitors; Siskin and Redpoll occur in winter.

WORTHINGTON LAKES (OS ST5810)
North of Wigan off the A5106 are three reservoirs on which it is possible to see a range of waterfowl and migrant waders.

ETHEROW COUNTRY PARK (OS SJ9690)
Under the control of Stockport Metropolitan Borough, this park of reservoir and pools, river and marsh, woods and valleys contains a wide range of bird species. Facilities include an information centre, nature trail, and observation hide. Within the park is the Compstall reserve of the Cheshire Conservation Trust with its range of waterfowl on the open water, including Goldeneye, Pochard and Wigeon; streams with Dipper and Grey Wagtail; and woods with Sparrowhawk, Buzzard, and a selection of warblers. In winter, Water Rail, Siskin, and Green Sandpiper occur. Access is via the B6104 road in Compstall.

Organizations in Greater Manchester
Manchester Ornithological Society, (MOS), 5 Church Cottages, Holmes Chapel Road, Chelford, Macclesfield SK11 9AQ
Lancashire Trust for Nature Conservation (LTNC), The Pavilion, Cuerdon Valley Park, Bamber Bridge, Preston, Lancashire PR5 6AX

RSPB Members' Groups based at: Bolton, Manchester, Oldham, Rochdale, Stockport, and Wigan (details from RSPB, The Lodge, Sandy, Beds SG19 2DL)
Annual reports
'Birds in Greater Manchester', 87 Gleaneagles Road, Heald Green, Stockport SK8 3EN

Books
Holland, P et al. Breeding Birds in Greater Manchester. Manchester Ornithological Society, 1984.

MERSEYSIDE
The ornithological interest of this Metropolitan County is very much oriented towards the coast and the estuaries of the Mersey and the Dee – for the Wirral peninsula falls within the county boundary and looks across both rivers. Further details are given under Cheshire and Lancashire.

Birdwatching sites

AINSDALE SANDS (OS SD2910)
Nearly 500 hectares (1235 acres) of sand-dunes and pine woodland here are controlled by the Nature Conservancy Council, but there are public access paths. This is a site where bird variety is very dependent upon the weather. In winter months following storms, the sea can be very productive with Red-throated Diver, Common Scoter, Guillemot, and Razorbill; while, on the beach, there is always a

selection of waders including Sanderling, Grey Plover, and Curlew. Rock and Meadow Pipits haunt the dunes. In the summer months, there are usually a few terns feeding offshore while, at migration time, unusual visitors have included Sooty Shearwater, Velvet Scoter, and Grey Phalarope.

HILBRE ISLAND (OS SJ1888)
Set in the mouth of the Dee estuary and reached at low tide by walking across the exposed sands from West Kirby, Hilbre Island is a mecca for birdwatchers, but visitors should exhibit caution. Over the years, this site has produced a wide range of species, some spectacular high-tide counts, and, at times of gales, some remarkable passages of seabirds. Several rarities have been recorded including Royal Tern, Lapland Bunting, and Honey Buzzard. Among the more regular avian visitors are Purple Sandpiper, Kittiwake, and Manx Shearwater.

Some peak wader counts on Hilbre

Oystercatcher	15000	Dunlin	7000
Ringed Plover	150	Bar-tailed Godwit	60
Grey Plover	36	Curlew	86
Knot	8000	Redshank	400
Sanderling	250	Turnstone	330
Purple Sandpiper	49		

Organizations in Merseyside
Liverpool Ornithologists' Club (LOC), 39 Ilford Avenue, Crosby, Liverpool L23 7YE

Merseyside Naturalists' Association (MNA), 47 Woodsorrel Road, Liverpool L15 6UB
Wirral Bird Club (WBC), 8 Park Road, Meols, Wirral L47 7BG
Cheshire Ornithological Association (COA), 30 Prince Edward Street, Nantwich CW5 5NW
Annual reports
'Cheshire Bird Report', 33 Sharston Crescent, Knutsford WA16 8AF
'Lancashire Bird Report', 31 Laverton Road, St Annes-on-Sea, Lancs FY8 1EW

Books
Hardy, E. The Birds of the Liverpool Area. Buncle, 1941.
Raines, R J. The Birds of the Wirral Peninsula. Liverpool Ornithological Society, 1960.

WEST AND SOUTH YORKSHIRE AND HUMBERSIDE

YORKSHIRE

England's largest county 'suffered' with the boundary reorganization in 1974. Not only was it subdivided into three administrative units, but Yorkshire also 'lost' territory to Durham, Cumbria, Lancashire, and the newly formed counties of Cleveland and Humberside. Yorkshire has immense variety; its long coastline with dramatic cliffs and broad sands contrast with the rolling valleys and high peaks. The old county of Yorkshire could boast an annual bird list approaching 300 species, with nearly 150 of them remaining to nest.

WEST YORKSHIRE

Birdwatching sites

AIRE VALLEY

The valley of the River Aire is extremely low lying before its confluence with the River Ouse and then on to the Humber. In addition, the extensive coal mining has resulted in considerable subsidence which has replaced much of the temporary flooding in the 'Ings' (a name bestowed on the flood levels by the Vikings) by permanent water areas of varying depth. Most are easily viewed from the surrounding roads.

Fairburn Ings (OS SE4527) is a Local Nature Reserve, owned by the National Coal Board but, through the North and West Yorkshire Councils, leased as a reserve to the RSPB. Access is via the A1 road at Fairburn village; facilities include car park, information centre, and observation hides. The area consists of shallow lakes, marshy depressions, and flooded pools, together with old mining spoil heaps now planted with a variety of trees to produce a mixed woodland of ash, alder, birch, and sallow.

The reserve is of importance for its wintering wildfowl, including Mallard, Teal, Shoveler, Pochard, Tufted Duck, Goldeneye, Goosander, and Whooper Swans. Common Terns nest, with Black Terns, Little Gulls, and a variety of waders occurring on passage. Autumn roosts contain Yellow and Pied Wagtails, Swallow, and martins. Breeding species include the common wildfowl together with Lapwing, Redshank, Snipe, Little Ringed Plover, and Great Crested and Little Grebes. A wide range of rarities has been recorded including Needle-tailed Swift, Laughing Gull, Ferruginous Duck, and Crane. Well over 150 species are recorded each year of which some sixty breed.

BRETTON COUNTRY PARK (OS SE2813)

This is a wooded parkland site with two large ornamental lakes providing a variety of bird species. Access is via the A637 road south of West Bretton village. The open nature of the park provides suitable habitat for Kestrels and even Curlews, while the thicker woodland sites attract woodpeckers, tits, and so on. Breeding species on the lake include Great Crested Grebe, Canada Goose, and Tufted Duck, with winter wildfowl increasing and including Goldeneye, Pochard, and Wigeon.

STONEYCLIFFE WOOD RESERVE (OS SE2716)

This is a mixed oak and birch woodland reserve of the Yorkshire Wildlife Trust and contains a good selection of typical woodland species. The area is best visited in the early morning in spring and early summer when bird song is at its height.

ECCUP RESERVOIR (OS SE3142)

Access is to the west of the A61 road north of Leeds. The surrounding woodland holds a selection of birds, but the main interest is the reservoir with its winter wildfowl. Up to 3000 Mallard and over 100 Goosander have been recorded. In winter, a substantial gull roost can include over 8000 Black-headed Gulls, 4000 Common Gulls and, in addition to Herring, Lesser, and Great Black-backed Gulls, such species as Mediterranean, Little, Iceland, and Glaucous Gulls are all recorded each year.

3rd year   imm

Gannet

adult

Organizations in Yorkshire

Yorkshire Naturalists' Union (YNU), c/o Doncaster Museum, Chequer Road, Doncaster DN1 2AE

Yorkshire Wildlife Trust (YWT), 10 Toft Green, York YO1 1JT

Annual reports

'Yorkshire Naturalists' Union Ornithological Report', 51 Red Scar Lane, Scarborough YO12 5RH

Books

Chislett, R. *Yorkshire Birds.* Brown, 1953.
Dickens, R F and Mitchell, W R. *Birdwatching in Yorkshire.* Dalesman, 1977.
Vaughan, R. *Birds of the Yorkshire Coast.* Hendon Publishing, 1974.'

Organizations and reports in West Yorkshire

Bradford Naturalists' Society (BNS), 4 Beckfoot Lane, Bingley BD16 1LX: 'Annual Report'

Castleford and District Naturalists' Society (CDNS), 31 Mount Avenue, Hemsworth, Pontefract WF9 4QE: 'Annual Report'

Huddersfield Birdwatchers' Club (HBC), 25 Thorpe Lane, Almondbury, Huddersfied HD5 8TA: 'Birds in Huddersfield'

Leeds Birdwatchers' Club (LBC), 6 Grove Road, Menston, Ilkley LS29 6JD: 'Annual Report'

Wakefield Naturalists' Society (WNS), 392 Dewsbury Road, Wakefield WF2 9DS: 'Birds Around Wakefield'

RSPB Members' Groups based at: Airedale, Huddersfield, and Leeds (details from RSPB, The Lodge, Sandy, Beds SG19 2DL)

SOUTH YORKSHIRE

Birdwatching sites

POTTERIC CARR NATURE RESERVE (OS SE5901)

Access to Potteric Carr is from Junction 3 of the M18 motorway. This Yorkshire Wildlife Trust reserve has been developed over the years to provide an attractive range of wildlife habitats, together with excellent facilities for the visiting birdwatcher. The habitat is very diverse, with open water, reedfen, wet grassland, willow scrub, and mature woodland; consequently, the bird life is also varied with nearly 200 species recorded from the site. In winter, it is the wildfowl on the open water that are the major attraction. Sometimes there are Pintail, Gadwall, or Goosander among the duck but, more uncommonly, a Jack Snipe can be located among the Snipe, or a visiting Bittern seen with the resident Grey Herons. Small numbers of migrant waders occur each spring and autumn, and summering Reed and Sedge Warblers nest in good numbers near the waters while Blackcap, Willow Warbler, and Whitethroat breed in the drier areas. Autumn finch flocks are very much features of the reserve, including Chaffinches, Linnets, Goldfinches, and Redpolls, and joined later in the year by the occasional Brambling or passing Great Grey Shrike.

LANGSETT RESERVOIR AND MOORS (OS SK2199)

North-west of Sheffield, South Yorkshire includes the edge of the Pennines and the High Peak – the Peak National Park. The number of bird species is limited, for this is predominantly rolling heather moorland with its specialized communities of Red Grouse, Golden Plover, Hen Harrier, Short-eared Owl, and the occasional Peregrine. The area contains many public footpaths – but also many private areas where access is strictly controlled. An up-to-date map should be consulted for public rights of way. The reservoirs are mainly steep sided and unattractive to many birds, although the surrounding woodland can be productive, and the rocky shore provides a habitat for Common Sandpipers and Grey Wagtails, with Dippers on the nearby streams. Mallard, Teal, and Tufted Duck all nest, while migrant waders can include Oystercatcher, Greenshank, and Green Sandpiper. Goosander and Goldeneye are both regular in winter at a time when gull roosts can exceed 8000 individuals. All the reservoirs in the area can be viewed easily from the road system reached via the B6077 road west of Sheffield.

WORSBROUGH COUNTRY PARK (OS SE3503)

Access to this park is via the A61 road south of Barnsley. The country park includes the local reservoir, as well as woodland and open country in the valley of the River Dove.

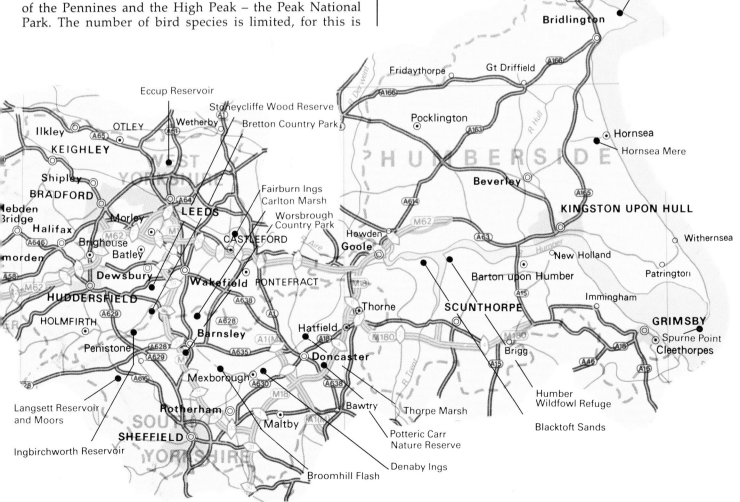

Kingfisher, Grey Heron, and grebes are all regular and there is a good chance of seeing a selection of waders from the observation hide which overlooks the reservoir's muddy margin in the south-west corner. Moorhen and Water Rail are likely to be seen here. In addition to the regular selection of tits, warblers, and finches, the woodland is home for Willow Tit and Lesser Spotted Woodpecker.

THORPE MARSH (OS SE5909)
This 20-hectare (50-acre) reserve is owned by the Central Electricity Generating Board and administered by the Yorkshire Wildlife Trust. Access is near Almholme north of Doncaster. The lake, pasture, and scrubland provide habitats for a range of species including regular Kestrel, Sparrowhawk, Barn and Short-eared Owls, while Curlew, Redshank, and Snipe are found on the damp grasslands.

DENABY INGS (OS SE5000)
This is a Yorkshire Wildlife Trust reserve situated east of Mexborough, with access via the A6023 road. It is a marshland site with standing water resulting from mining subsidence. Breeding birds include Pochard, Little Grebe, Little Ringed Plover, and Yellow Wagtail. In winter,

West Yorkshire's reservoirs provide a winter site for large numbers of gulls.

Whooper and Bewick's Swans are regular visitors. An observation hide provides views across open water.

CARLTON MARSH (OS SK3710)
Carlton Marsh is a small excavated marsh administered by the Barnsley Borough Council. Shallow water with surrounding rushes and willows attract several species, including Water Rail, Snipe, and Little Ringed Plover. Several warblers and occasionally a Whinchat nest. Access is off the B6132 road at Carlton, north of Barnsley.

BROOMHILL FLASH (OS SE4102)
This is another area of water resulting from mining subsidence and run as a reservoir by the Yorkshire Wildlife Trust with access via the B6273 road at Broomhill village. An observation hide provides viewing for a range of waterbirds that includes Yellow Wagtail, Grey Heron, and Green Sandpiper.

INGBIRCHWORTH RESERVOIR (OS SE2106)
Easily viewed from the perimeter, this reservoir is reached via the A629 road north-west of Penistone. Wintering wildfowl, passage waders, and congregations (in autumn) of Swallows and martins occur here.

Pink-footed goose

The dramatic cliffs of Flamborough Head are popular for observing the north-south seabird migration along the English coast.

HUMBERSIDE

The county is very much dominated by the Humber and its two tributaries, the Rivers Ouse and Trent which together flow into the broadening Humber mouth with its tidal expanses and final guardian at Spurn Head. Only in the north is there a variation from the low-lying character of the countryside – here the Yorkshire Wolds eventually give way to the North Sea at the dramatic Flamborough cliffs that extend northwards beyond the county boundary. Ornithologically, Humberside must accept a 'split personality' for, south of the river, the county is linked with the Lincolnshire birdwatchers; to the north, the Yorkshire ornithologists still record and report the bird observations to the limits of the old county boundary.

Birdwatching sites

FLAMBOROUGH HERITAGE COAST

For scenic beauty the coastline from Flamborough northwards is quite exceptional and, during the summer months, the cliffs are alive with nesting seabirds. Flamborough Head itself has now become an established site for observing the seabird migration that passes north and south along the English coast, and, together with many other places on the clifftops, it is an excellent spot to search for grounded migrants that have just completed a North Sea crossing.

Bempton Cliffs (OS TA1974) form an RSPB reserve with viewing points from which to observe the nesting seabirds; it is well signposted from Bempton village. The site is best visited between April and mid-July, after which the majority of the birds have departed. The most successful breeding species is the Kittiwake with well over 65 000 pairs nesting; but good numbers of Guillemot, Razorbill, and Fulmar all occur. Cliff-nesting Puffins are extremely difficult to count, but as many as 2500 individuals can be seen on one day. This is the site of Britain's only mainland Gannet colony, now numbering over 500 pairs. Apart from the seabirds, Bempton is an excellent locality at which to see Corn Bunting, Jackdaw, Rock Pipit, and Rock (Feral) Pigeon.

HORNSEA MERE (OS TA1847)

The large freshwater lake is fringed with reeds and surrounded by farmland and mixed woodland. It is an RSPB reserve with access from the B1242 road in Hornsea from where the Mere is clearly signed. The wintering wildfowl include several hundred Coot, Mallard, and Goldeneye, as well as Teal, Wigeon, Pochard, and Tufted Duck. The natural edge of the Mere attracts migrant waders and, in the surrounding fields and woodland, Wheatears, Whinchat, and several warblers occur regularly. This is one of Britain's most northerly localities for nesting Reed Warblers and, in most years, over 600 pairs nest. Yellow Wagtail, Little Gull, and Black Tern regularly congregate. The best viewing at the site is from the public footpath that follows the southern shore.

The new county of Humberside is dominated by the River Humber.

THE HUMBER

The river dominates the county; from the Ouse at Goole and the Trent at Scunthorpe, the combined flow cuts a broad swathe through the south of the county. Apart from major developments near Hull and Grimsby, the river is still remarkably unspoiled with several good birdwatching localities, and any area of tidal mud or saltmarsh can attract birds.

Blacktoft Sands (OS SE8423) is an RSPB reserve situated on the southern bank of the river at the confluence of the Trent and Ouse. The site is a large tidal reedbed with a saltmarsh fringe. Management work has created a series of lagoons overlooked by observation hides. Access to the reserve car park is via the A161 road and Ousefleet village east of Goole. Nesting birds include Reed and Sedge Warblers, Water Rail, Bearded Tit, Short-eared Owl, Reed

Bunting, and Grasshopper Warbler. On the newly constructed lagoons, recent colonists are Shoveler, Gadwall, Redshank, and Little Ringed Plover. Marsh Harriers have bred and occur in most summers, while Hen Harrier and Merlin turn up each winter. At times of migration, a range of waders is recorded, including occasional Avocet, Black-winged Stilt, and Little Stint. The lagoons now regularly function as a high-tide roosting site, and the visiting bird-watcher should check the tide-tables in advance. Recent rarities have included Penduline Tit, Hudsonian Godwit, and Wilson's Phalarope.

Humber Wildfowl Refuge (OS SE8724) The refuge was established to provide a secure feeding and resting site for the Pink-footed Geese that winter on the Humber each year, but many other wildfowl take advantage of the security. Large numbers of waders make use of the tidal mud. Because of the possibility of disturbance; access to the refuge is not permitted, but views across the site can be obtained from the surrounding roads, particularly at grid references SE864242 and 936263. This area is best visited in the late autumn or winter.

In addition to being a Yorkshire Wildlife Trust reserve, **Spurn Point** (OS TA4115) houses one of the longest-established British bird observatories. First operated in 1945, the accumulation of information relating to migration through the area is formidable. The structure of the land, with the peninsula following a north-south direction, produces some spectacular observable bird migrations, often involving tens of thousands of finches, larks, pipits, and thrushes heading southwards in late autumn. At the same time, many thousands of birds can make landfall after crossing the North Sea, and as many as 6000 Black-birds have been recorded on a single day.

Although Spurn will always provide the most spectacular birdwatching at migration times, there is interest here throughout the year. Access is via the B1445 road east of Hull.

Opposite: *Bempton Cliffs are good for observing nesting seabirds.*

Bird records from Flamborough Head
The following is a selection of records from just one year's observations at the Head:
Red-throated Diver – 164 on 12 February;
White-billed Diver – one flying north on 10 December;
Fulmar – 19 300 on 8 February;
Sooty Shearwater – 622 on 13 August;
Goshawk – one on 5 March and 12 November;
Red-necked Phalarope – one flying north on 29 October;
Arctic Skua – at least 3300 during the autumn migration;
Ross's Gull – one on 12 February and 10 December;
Alpine Swift – one on 10 July;
Thrush Nightingale – one on 5 June;
Rustic Bunting – one on 30 September.

Some peak counts from the Humber
The following species all occur on the Humber in numbers defined as nationally or internationally important:

Pink-footed Goose	2390	Knot	25 000
Shelduck	3233	Sanderling	200
Mallard	8400	Dunlin	18 850
Pintail	200	Curlew	2650
Ringed Plover	570	Redshank	5670
Grey Plover	830	Turnstone	390

Some recent recoveries
An important aspect of the Spurn Point observatory's migration studies is the ringing of migrant birds, and some recent recoveries indicate just some of the variety in the movements that occur.
Reed Bunting – ringed at Spurn in October 1983, recovered Sweden September 1984.
Meadow Pipit – ringed at Spurn in September 1984, recovered Belgium just seven days later.
Redstart – ringed at Spurn August 1981, recovered Strathclyde July 1983.
Kingfisher – ringed at Spurn October 1981, recovered West Yorkshire August 1983.

Organizations in Humberside
Lincolnshire Bird Club (LBC), 42 Wolsey Way, Glebe Park, Lincoln LN2 4QH
Lincolnshire Naturalists' Union (LNU), 61 Woolthorpe Road, Colsterworth, Grantham
Lincolnshire and South Humberside Trust for Nature Conservation (LSHTNC), The Manor House, Alford LN13 9DL
Yorkshire Naturalists' Union (LNU), c/o Doncaster Museum, Chequer Road, Doncaster DN1 2AE
Yorkshire Wildlife Trust (YWT), 10 Toft Green, York YO1 1JT

Annual reports
'Lincolnshire Bird Report', 42 Wolsey Way, Glebe Park, Lincoln LN2 5QH
'Yorkshire Naturalists' Union Ornithological Report', 51 Red Scar Lane, Scarborough YO12 5RH

Books
Chislett, R. *Yorkshire Birds.* Brown, 1953.
Smith, A E and Cornwallis, R K. *The Birds of Lincolnshire.* Lincolnshire Naturalists' Union, 1955 (with 1969 supplement).

Redpoll
♂ summer
♀ winter

NORTH YORKSHIRE

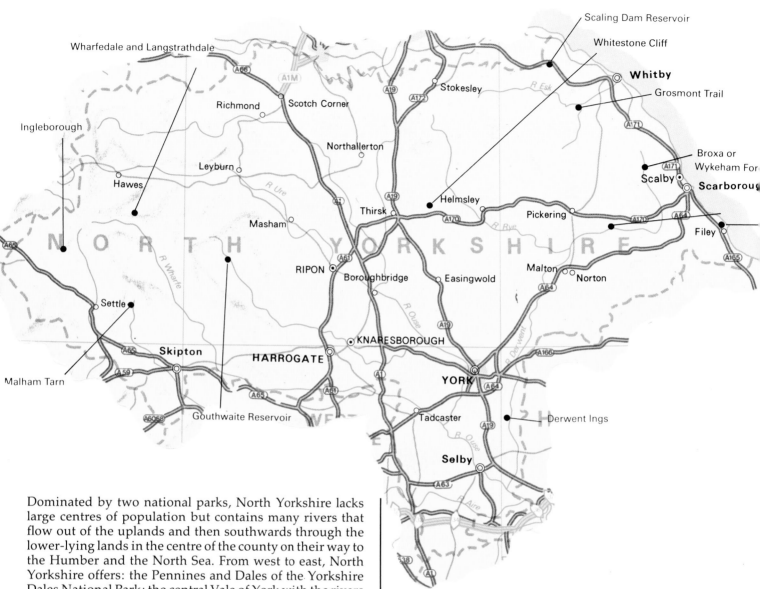

Wharfedale and Langstrathdale

Ingleborough

Scaling Dam Reservoir

Whitestone Cliff

Whitby

Grosmont Trail

Broxa or
Wykeham For

Scalby

Scarboroug

Filey

Richmond

Scotch Corner

Stokesley

Northallerton

Leyburn

Hawes

Helmsley

Thirsk

Pickering

Masham

RIPON

Boroughbridge

Easingwold

Malton

Norton

Settle

Skipton

HARROGATE

KNARESBOROUGH

YORK

Malham Tarn

Gouthwaite Reservoir

Tadcaster

Derwent Ings

Selby

Dominated by two national parks, North Yorkshire lacks large centres of population but contains many rivers that flow out of the uplands and then southwards through the lower-lying lands in the centre of the county on their way to the Humber and the North Sea. From west to east, North Yorkshire offers: the Pennines and Dales of the Yorkshire Dales National Park; the central Vale of York with the rivers Derwent, Swale, Ure, Wharf, and Nidd; and finally the uplands of the North York Moors National Park which reach the sea at the cliffs centred around Whitby. Ornithologically, the coastline is rather poor, lacking in estuaries and tidal mudflats, but compensated by the rocky beaches where seaweed-covered boulders attract wintering Turnstone and Purple Sandpiper, as well as providing nesting sites for Rock Pipit.

Birdwatching sites

DERWENT INGS (OS SE7044)
Nearly 6 miles of the River Derwent can flood across the surrounding grazing meadows to create attractive feeding for a wide range of wildfowl and waders. The extent and timing of the flood are obviously very dependent upon the prevailing weather, but it can be expected most regularly in the late winter. Access to the area is via the B1228 road south-east of York with views across the floods at Storwood, East Cottingwith, Ellerton, Aughton, and from the A163 at Bubwith in the south. At times of flood, counts can include: 250 Bewick's Swan; 1500 Mallard; 2000 Teal; and

5000 Wigeon. Whooper Swan and Canada and White-fronted Geese also occur, while occasional unexpected visitors have included Bittern and Crane; the Ruddy Duck now nests in the area.

GOUTHWAITE RESERVOIR (OS SE1269)
This reservoir is easily viewed from the road between Ramsgill and Pateley Bridge (north of the B6265) which runs on the southern shore. The northern end is most attractive to birds. Diving ducks, Pochard, Tufted Duck, Goldeneye, and Goosander are all regular, as are Grey Heron and Curlew, and there is a large gull roost in the winter. The surrounding area can produce Buzzard, Hen Harrier, and Great Grey Shrike in winter.

FILEY BRIGG (OS TA1280)
The Brigg is a small promontory north of the town of Filey, where the Scarborough Borough Council has established a nature trail and an observation hide with views across the

Organizations in North Yorkshire
Yorkshire Naturalists' Union (YNU), c/o Doncaster Museum, Chequer Road, Doncaster DN1 2AE
Yorkshire Wildlife Trust (YWT), 10 Toft Green, York YO1 1JT

Curlew

Harrogate and District Naturalists' Society (HDNS), 16 Beckwith Road, Pannal Ash, Harrogate HG2 0BG
Scarborough Field Naturalists' Society (SFNS), 4 Whin Bank, Scarborough YO12 5LE
Wharfedale Naturalists' Society (WNS), 17 Ben Rhydding Road, Ilkley LS29 8RL
York Ornithological Club (YOC), 8 North Parade, Bootham, York
RSPB Members' Groups based at: Whitby and York (details from RSPB, The Lodge, Sandy, Beds SG19 2DL)

Annual reports
'Yorkshire Naturalists' Union Ornithological Report', 51 Red Scar Lane, Scarborough YO12 5RH
Reports produced by the Harrogate and York Societies

Books
Chislett, R. *Yorkshire Birds.* Brown, 1953.
Vaughan, R. *Birds of the Yorkshire Coast.* Hendon Publishing, 1974.

cliffs and rocky shoreline. This can be a spectacular site for observing bird migration. There are good wintering populations of birds here, too, so that birdwatching in autumn, winter, and spring is worthwhile. Purple Sandpipers winter on the rocks, while offshore there are parties of Red-breasted Merganser and Eider often with accompanying Common Scoter or Long-tailed Duck. The beach is a likely site for Shore Lark, Snow, and Lapland Buntings. Unexpected visitors can include Grey Phalarope, Black Guillemot, and Barred Warbler.

NORTH YORK MOORS NATIONAL PARK
This national park contains England's most extensive heather moorland, divided by deep valleys that carry a host of rivers draining the area. The wild tops provide nesting sites for Red Grouse, Golden Plover, Curlew, and Dunlin which, together with the Skylarks and Meadow Pipits, support a small population of Merlin, Hen Harrier, and Peregrine. The contrast between the barren tops and the well-wooded vales provides a diversity that produces well over 100 nesting species in the area. Access is readily available to many areas of the park, but up-to-date literature (obtainable from the National Park information centre at Pickering Railway Station) should be consulted for car parking, public footpaths, and nature trails.

The North York Moors National Park provides a contrast between the wooded vales and the barren tops where Grouse and Curlew nest.

Reflecting the variety of plant life, the birdlife in this typical Yorkshire dale can also be wide ranging.

On the edge of the Hambleton Hills, and reached via the A170 road east of Thirsk, **Whitestone Cliff** (OS SE5183) is a section of the 90-mile Cleveland Way long-distance footpath. The present section passes through a variety of woodland habitat as well as providing views across the open escarpment to the west. Resident birds include Linnet, Yellowhammer, Coal Tit, and Kestrel; in summer Willow Warbler, Chiffchaff, Redstart, Wheatear, Spotted Flycatcher, and Wood Warbler are present.

Easily viewed from the A171 road, **Scaling Dam Reservoir** (OS NZ7412) is surrounded by moorland and conifer plantations. Rather surprisingly for an 'upland reservoir', this site has produced several rare visitors including Great White Egret, Terek's Sandpiper, and Temminck's Stint. At times, the reservoir is disturbed by boating activities, but several species of wildfowl nest and, in winter, there is a large gull roost.

The **Grosmont Trail** (OS NZ8105) is a well-laid-out nature trail within Eskdale, starting in Grosmont village west of the A169 from Whitby. There is a good selection of woodland and farmland species.

Broxa or Wykeham Forest (OS SE9694) is just one of several forest areas within the national park that can reward a visiting birdwatcher. Several woodland walks are well signposted and can produce a good selection of birds in spring and early summer. Look for Turtle Dove, White-throat, three species of woodpeckers, and Sparrowhawk. A late-evening visit may result in sight and sound of Nightjar.

YORKSHIRE DALES NATIONAL PARK
This is certainly one of Britain's most spectacular national parks, with rich limestone scenery and a remarkable diversity of plant life. On the open uplands are Black and Red Grouse, Dunlin, Golden Plover, Snipe, and Ring Ouzel. Lower down the slopes Wheatear, Stonechat, Curlew, and Meadow Pipit appear, with a wide range of woodland species in the vegetated valleys. In common with all national parks, the visiting birdwatcher can find many sites likely to produce a range of species, but it is advisable to consult the most recent information available in advance of any visit. Maps, literature, and information boards are available in all national parks. For a selection of bird species in a wide range of habitats, it is worth considering a visit to the following localities:

Ingleborough (OS SD7474) is reached via the A65 and B6255 roads to Ingleton village. The high ground will yield Golden Plover, Red Grouse, Ring Ouzel, and the occasional Peregrine. The peak is 724 metres (2382 feet) above sea-level.

Wharfedale and Langstrathdale (OS SD9079) are accessed via the B6160. This is a varied area which, although it is very popular with tourists, still has its quiet parts with a good selection of birds including Dipper, Common Sandpiper, and Grey Wagtail by the streams and, in early spring, both Goosander and Red-breasted Merganser may be encountered. The wooded valleys can hold Pied and Spotted Flycatchers, together with Redstart, Hawfinch, and Wood Warbler.

Malham Tarn (OS SD8966) is reached from Malham village. This National Trust reserve has been studied in very great detail. Breeding birds include Great Crested Grebe, Shoveler, and Tufted Duck; the surrounding woodland holds Marsh Tit, Redpoll, and Nuthatch; winter gull roosts exceed 12 000 birds; nearby hill tops provide nesting sites for Red Grouse, Dunlin, and Golden Plover.

CUMBRIA AND ISLE OF MAN

CUMBRIA

Britain's largest and probably most popular national park, the Lake District, dominates the county, and visitors to Cumbria are often unaware of the other interest that the county has to offer. The coastline stretches from the 'gooselands' of the Solway in the north, via the sandstone seacliffs with their nesting seabirds, to the broad expanse of tidal mud at Morecambe Bay in the south. To the north and east of the Lake District are the agricultural Solway Plain and the well-drained Eden valley, and then, in the far east, the land rises again as it reaches the high Pennines. Although human population is largely restricted to Carlisle and to the coastal industrial centres of Workington and Barrow-in-Furness, people have had a marked effect upon the Cumbrian countryside. Extensive sheep grazing has prevented the natural regeneration of the upland oak-woods, and areas that were once forested are now grass and bracken; large conifer plantations of imported trees, particularly Sitka Spruce (favoured for their rapid timber production), have been planted in giant blocks; and, in the

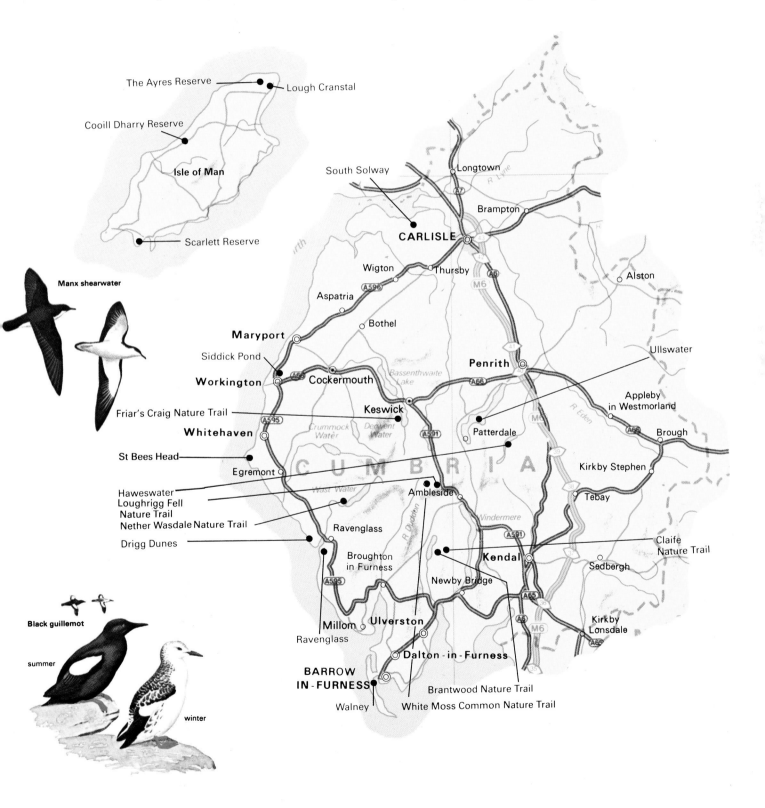

The Ayres Reserve — Lough Cranstal
Cooill Dharry Reserve
Isle of Man
Scarlett Reserve

South Solway
Longtown
Brampton
CARLISLE
Wigton — Thursby
Aspatria
Bothel
Maryport
Siddick Pond
Workington — Cockermouth
Bassenthwaite Lake
Penrith
Ullswater
Appleby in Westmorland
Friar's Craig Nature Trail
Keswick
Whitehaven
Crummock Water
Derwent Water
Patterdale
Brough
St Bees Head
Egremont
C U M B R I A
Kirkby Stephen
Haweswater
Loughrigg Fell Nature Trail
Nether Wasdale Nature Trail
West Water
Ambleside
Tebay
Drigg Dunes
Ravenglass
Windermere
Claife Nature Trail
Broughton in Furness
Kendal
Sedbergh
Newby Bridge
Millom
Ravenglass
Ulverston
Kirkby Lonsdale
Dalton-in-Furness
BARROW IN-FURNESS
Brantwood Nature Trail
Walney
White Moss Common Nature Trail

Manx shearwater

Black guillemot

summer

winter

west, the coalfields have now been converted to extensive open-cast mining operations. Over 230 species of birds are recorded in the county each year.

Birdwatching sites

LAKE DISTRICT

The 224 000 hectares (553 000 acres) that make up the national park contain a wide range of habitats, each with its own bird community – and each worthy of examination by the Lakeland birdwatcher.

The **fells and crags** comprise the real 'high ground' where Dotterels nest and occur as passing migrants; Buzzard, Peregrine, and Raven dominate. England's only nesting Golden Eagle is found in this habitat. Of the small birds, Ring Ouzel, Wheatear, Skylark, and Jackdaw all breed. Once the summer is past the bird numbers are low.

On the **heather moors**, once again, the birds are present in the summer months, with few, apart from the Red and Black Grouse, remaining during the winter. Curlew, Golden Plover, and Merlin all nest, the latter unfortunately in decreasing numbers. In wetter areas, Snipe, Redshank, and Lapwing all breed.

The native **Lakeland oakwoods** contain resident populations of Green and Great Spotted Woodpeckers, six species of tits, Nuthatch, Treecreeper, and an increasing number of Sparrowhawks. In the summer months, migrants include several warblers (including Wood Warbler), Redstart, Pied Flycatcher, Tree Pipit, and Cuckoo. Features of the winter are the large flocks of pigeons and Chaffinches.

The lower-lying open farmland of **the Dales** is favoured by Kestrel, Pied Wagtail, Swallow, and House Martin. In winter, mixed finch flocks, including Yellowhammer and Brambling, congregate where livestock are being fed.

Ring ouzel

The flast-flowing waters of **Lakeland streams** are home for Common Sandpiper, Dipper, and Grey Wagtail; with Goosanders finding nest sites in convenient nearby trees. On the open **lakes**, Red-breasted Merganser have colonized and Greylag Geese have been re-established. Mallard, Tufted Duck, and Great Crested Grebe all nest, but the upland lakes retain few birds in winter.

Visiting birdwatchers will find many sites worth investigating, but up-to-date information is best obtained from the nine or so information centres within the park. The following localities are all worth an examination:

The national park includes a short stretch of Cumbrian coastline, and it is at the northern end of this that **Ravenglass** (OS SD0898) and the **Drigg Dunes** (at the mouth of the Esk river) are to be found and where the main birdwatching interest is. This is a Local Nature Reserve that once held Britain's largest colony of Black-headed Gulls within the dune system. This is now greatly decreased, but other breeding birds of interest are Arctic, Common, Sandwich, and Little Terns, Ringed Plover, and Oystercatcher.

The southern shore of **Ullswater** (OS NY4219) near Silver Crag can provide a wide range of species including Wheatear, Whinchat, Common Sandpiper, and Dipper.

The southern shore of the Solway Firth near Bowness offers some good views across the mudflats which provide very rewarding birdwatching.

Organizations in Cumbria
Association of Natural History Societies in Cumbria (ANHSC), 8 Everest Mount, Westfield, Workington, Cumbria
Cumbria Trust for Nature Conservation (CTNC), Church Street, Ambleside LA22 0BU
RSPB Members' Groups based at: Carlisle and South Lakeland (details from RSPB, The Lodge, Sandy, Beds SG19 2DL)

Annual reports
'Birds in Cumbria', Garden Cottage, Sizergh Castle, Kendal LA8 8AE

Books
Mitchell, W R & Robson, R W. *Lakeland Birds.* Dalesman, 1974.
Wilson, J O. *Birds of Westmorland and the Northern Pennines.* Hutchinson, 1933.

Arrival and departure of summer migrants
The following dates are the earliest and latest to be reported in recent years:

Earliest	Latest
Swallow 28 March	1 December
Cuckoo 9 April	31 August
Swift 16 April	6 November
Spotted Flycatcher 24 April	6 October
Yellow Wagtail 26 March	13 October
Willow Warbler 31 March	8 November
House Martin 11 April	20 November
Wheatear 24 February	11 November
Ring Ouzel 19 February	11 October

Haweswater (OS NY4712) is one of the least visited of the 'waters', although the road along the southern shore provides views across the lake and of the Naddle woodlands above. Peregrine, Buzzard, and Raven can all be seen from this road, with the possibility of Black Grouse and Golden Eagle. Haweswater is also an important winter gull roost, with recent peak counts: 8163 Black-headed; 12374 Common; 28 Lesser Black-backed; 17 Herring; 3 Great Black-backed.

Among the walks within the park, the following **nature trails** are all worthy of exploration:
Brantwood (OS SD3195), 2½ miles by Coniston Water; Claife (OS SD3895), 1½ miles by Windermere; Friar's Crag (OS NY2622), 1½ miles by Derwent Water; Loughrigg Fell (OS NY3704), 2½ miles from Ambleside; Nether Wasdale (OS NY1404), 3½ miles by Wastwater; White Moss Common (OS NY3406), just under a mile by Grasmere.

ST BEES HEAD (OS NX9611)
This is an RSPB reserve with access from the St Bees beach car park. This is a sheer sandstone cliff with gorse- and grass-covered tops. The cliffs hold one of the largest seabird colonies on the west coast of England. A search among the 5000 or so breeding pairs of Guillemot, Razorbill, and Puffin could well produce a view of some of the few pairs of Black Guillemot which also nest – the only English breeding station. Other breeding species include Rock Pipit, Shag, Whitethroat, and Peregrine.

SOUTH SOLWAY (OS NY2761)
It is in Scotland that the Solway claims the major ornithological interest, but birdwatching on the southern shore can be equally rewarding. Some of the best views across the tidal mud are obtained from the coast road between Burgh-by-Sands and Bowness-on-Solway, although the shoreline as far as Skinburness can be productive. *Breeding:* Lapwing, Redshank, Snipe, Skylark, Meadow Pipit. *Autumn:* Bar-tailed Godwit, Knot, Shelduck, Grey Plover, Yellow Wagtail, Black Tern. *Winter:* Barnacle and Pink-footed Geese,

Oystercatcher, Scaup, Peregrine, Merlin, Short-eared Owl, Ringed Plover. *Spring:* Curlew, Whimbrel, Black-tailed Godwit, Common Tern, Little Tern, Pomarine Skua.

SIDDICK POND (OS NY0030)
Siddick Pond is a Cumbria Trust for Nature Conservation reserve, which is only 1 mile north of Workington and is easily viewed from the A596 road. It is a shallow, reed-fringed lake of some 20 hectares (50 acres), which is very close to the coast and attractive to a range of waterfowl. Over thirty-five species nest on the reserve each year while, in the winter, Whooper Swan and Goldeneye are regular visitors. In recent years, other sightings have included Long-tailed Duck, Red-necked Grebe, Wood Sandpiper, Iceland Gull, and Garganey.

WALNEY (OS SD1969)
Walney, close to Barrow-in-Furness, forms the south-western corner of the county and, although it is an industrial area, there are several good birdwatching sites in the locality.

The northern bay of **Duddon Estuary and Sands** is mainly sand rather than mud but, even so, bird populations are quite high with up to 8000 Oystercatcher, 6000 Dunlin, and 2000 Redshank. There is a small colony of nesting Little Terns on the estuary. Views across the sands are possible from roads on both sides.

Access to **Bardsea Country Park** is from the A5087 south-east of Ulverston. It is a mixed woodland site on the shore of Morecambe Bay holding an equally mixed selection of woodland and estuarine species.

At the southern end of **Walney Island** is a reserve of the Cumbria Trust for Nature Conservation. Facilities include car park, nature trail, and observation hides. The site is best known for its gull and tern colonies with particularly large numbers of Lesser Black-backed and Herring Gulls and smaller numbers of Great Black-backed. Among the other breeding species are the most southerly Eider on the English west coast. Large numbers of ducks and waders are present in the winter months.

Walney Bird Observatory is based on Walney Island and carries out detailed studies of the bird migration through the area. Considerable numbers of rare birds have been recorded which, in one year (1982), included an impressive list of warblers. In addition to the commoner species, Grasshopper, Sedge, Reed, Lesser Whitethroat, Whitethroat, Garden, Blackcap, Chiffchaff, and Willow, the bird observatory also reported: Paddyfield Warbler – one from 11-13 September, the first record for Cumbria; Melodious Warbler – two on 27 August; Barred Warbler – one on 16 September; Pallas's Warbler – two on 13 October; Yellow-browed Warbler – one from 8-9 November; Wood Warbler – one on 5 September.

ISLE OF MAN

Situated in the centre of the Irish Sea, approximately 34 miles from the Irish and English coasts, the Isle of Man is nearer to Scotland at only about 15½ miles from Burrow Head in Dumfries and Galloway. The spine of the island, rising to some 600 metres (over 1900 feet) is broken by a central valley that connects two of the major towns, Peel and the capital, Douglas. The extreme north and south are intensively cultivated. The main attraction for the bird-watcher is the coastline, much of it consisting of slate cliffs, but the extreme north at The Ayres and the south at Langness are tidal sandy beaches with dunes. Nearly 200 species of birds are recorded on the island each year.

There are numerous local birdwatching sites, among which are:

Scarlett Reserve (OS SC2566) – about 1¼ miles south-west of Castleton (seabirds); **The Ayres Reserve** (OS SE4303) – about 1¼ miles west of Bride village (terns); **Cooil Dharry Reserve** (OS SC3190) – access off coast road, A3, at Glen Wyllin (woodland birds); **Lough Cranstal** (OS NX4502) – access east of Cranstal off A16 (wildfowl).

A flavour of the variety of birds to be found is indicated by the following list:

Fulmar – nearly 2000 breeding pairs; Manx Shearwater – regularly seen offshore; Peregrine – up to nine breeding pairs; Black Guillemot – present off most of the coast throughout the year; Raven – over thirty pairs nest in most years; Chough – breeding population of some fifty-five pairs in most years.

Thrift in full flower among the salt marshes of the Solway Firth.

Buzzard, Peregrine, and Raven are the birds which typify the high fells of the English Lake District.

CALF OF MAN

The best known of the Isle of Man bird haunts is the small rocky island of some 250 hectares (600 acres) situated only about 500 metres off the south-west tip, the Calf of Man. Many of the seabirds to be seen around the coast of the main island nest on the Calf – indeed, this is the one site at which the Manx Shearwater still nests on the island that gave it its name. At one time, over 10000 pairs may have nested on the island but, following a rather rapid decline, the bird seems to have become extinct here shortly after the end of the eighteenth century. Confirmation that the species was nesting once again was obtained in 1967 when a single chick was discovered, and one or two pairs are now confirmed to breed in most years; the total population may be numbered in tens of pairs. It now appears that the Storm Petrel is landing on the island at night each summer but, as yet, breeding has not been established. Additional breeding species include the Raven, Chough, Hooded Crow and Short-eared Owl.

In most years, some thirty-eight species nest on the island and over 170 can be recorded. The Calf has been the site of a bird observatory since 1959 and, during this period, substantial amounts of data relating to bird migration through the area have been accumulated. Several rare species have been recorded, including Britain's first White-throated Robin in 1983. Over 100000 birds have been ringed on the island and, among the recoveries of interest, are Blackbird and Robin from the Netherlands, Redwing, Razorbill, and Spotted Flycatcher from France, and Goldcrest from Belgium.

Organizations in Isle of Man
Manx Ornithological Society (MOS), Ivie Cottage, Kirk Michael, Isle of Man
Manx Nature Conservation Trust (MNCT), Ballacross, Andreas, Isle of Man

Annual reports
'Peregrine' (The Manx Bird Report), Troutbeck, Cronkbourne, Braddan, Isle of Man
'Calf of Man Observatory Annual Repot', Manx Museum and National Trust, Douglas, Isle of Man

Books
Cullen, J P and Slinn, D J. *Birds of the Isle of Man.* Manx Museum, 1975.

DURHAM, CLEVELAND, AND TYNE AND WEAR

DURHAM

In the west of the county two rivers, the Tees and the Wear, flow from the high ground of the Pennines as rapid torrents, only to slow and meander as they drain the central mass of Durham, to leave the county again as they reach the North Sea via two very industrialized river mouths to the north and south. With the county boundary reorganization, Durham became a more rural county, and even the coalfields in the centre of the county have decreased and the waste tips are being reclaimed for agriculture. The mixed farming of the central valleys contrasts with the sheep farming on the poorer soils of the western hills. Compared with the concentrations of birds at the two estuaries to the north and south, the Durham coastline has relatively little to offer the visiting birdwatcher.

Birdwatching sites

WITTON-LE-WEAR (OS NZ1631)

Based upon a series of old gravel workings beside the River Wear, the Durham County Conservation Trust reserve lies just east of Witton village (access via the A68 road). The habitat consists of lakes, wet grassland, scrub, and some mature woodland. Facilities include a car park, nature trail, and observation hides. Summer visitors to the reserve include Tree Pipit, Grasshopper, Sedge, and Willow Warblers, Little Ringed Plover, and Common Sandpiper. In winter, the selection of wildfowl includes Goldeneye and Goosander, while Teal and Greylag Goose are present throughout the year. Dipper, Grey Heron, and Kingfisher are among the waterside birds.

CASTLE EDEN DENE (OS NZ4238)

This is a 200-hectare (500-acre) coastal woodland site controlled by the Peterlee Development Corporation, but including a National Nature Reserve. A range of resident woodland species including Bullfinch, Linnet, Goldcrest, and several tits, is augmented by both summer and winter visitors, and, at times, the unexpected migrant. Siskin and Brambling are regular in late autumn and, in some years, Great Grey Shrike and Waxwing occur. The river mouth provides a site for a small selection of waders.

HAMSTERLEY FOREST (OS NZ0930)

This Forestry Commission woodland still retains several areas of deciduous trees, and various nature trails and woodland walks have been developed to display the variety of the area. An information centre near Hamsterley village provides current details. In the conifer woods Crossbill, Siskin, Goldcrest, and Coal Tit all occur, with Pied Flycatcher, Redstart, and Wood Warbler in the hardwood trees. The fast-flowing stream attracts Dipper and Grey Wagtail.

UPPER TEESDALE (OS NY8428)

Here there is an extensive area of moors and dales, partly operated as a reserve by the Nature Conservancy Council, where access is confined to the public footpaths. Adjoining the site is the **Cow Green Reservoir** which can be viewed by leaving the B6277 road at Langdon. Goosander are regular visitors to the reservoir, while the open moorland attracts Red Grouse, Curlew, Black Grouse, Snipe, and Redshank.

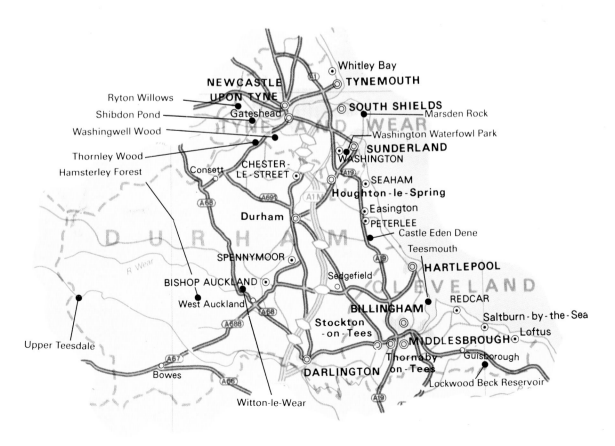

Organizations in Durham
Durham Bird Club (DBC), 6 Whitesmocks Avenue, Durham DH1 4HP
Durham County Conservation Trust (DCCT), 52 Old Elvet, Durham DH1 3HN

Annual reports
'Birds in Durham', 9 Prebends Field, Gilesgate Moor, Durham DH1 1HH

Books
Temperley, G W. *A History of the Birds of Durham*. Natural History Society of Northumberland and Durham, 1951.

Some interesting species in Durham
Golden Eagle – an occasional bird occurs in the west of the county, usually around the high fells, such

as Mickle Fell, near Newbiggin. These birds are presumably wanderers from the Cumbrian nesting areas.
Osprey – occurs regularly as a migrant to/from the Scottish breeding sites. Witton-le-Wear is a favoured locality.
Black Grouse – a popular area for seeing this species is by Langdon Beck in Upper Teesdale; over twenty birds may be present at the lek.
White-fronted Goose – occasional small parties of up to fifteen birds occur at Derwent Reservoir (west of Consett) and, when seen clearly, are usually noted to be of the Greenland race that normally winters in Ireland, Wales, or the west of Scotland.
Crossbill – flocks of over 100 individuals can be encountered late in the year in Hamsterley Forest. In the winter of 1982-83 they were joined

by an example of the Parrot Crossbill, a rare visitor from northern Europe.

Crossbill ♀
♂
juv.

CLEVELAND

Although Cleveland is dominated by the River Tees, its industrial mouth, and the urban areas of Hartlepool, Middlesbrough, Redcar, and Guisborough, the rather small county of Cleveland does hold some variety. In the south, the northern edge of the North York Moors National Park is just within the county boundary – so Red Grouse is included on the list of breeding birds; in the north is the farmland and Wynyard Forest before the county gives way to the agricultural region of Durham. For the birdwatcher,

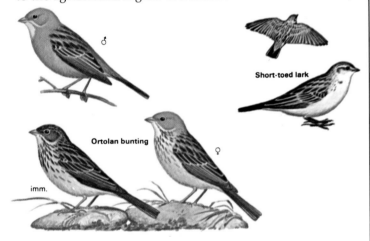

Short-toed lark

Ortolan bunting

imm.

♂

♀

however, it is the Teesmouth area that, in spite of its developments and great losses in bird habitats, still provides the greatest variety and concentration of birds. Over 225 species can be expected in the county each year, with nearly 100 of these breeding.

Birdwatching sites

TEESMOUTH
Birdwatching possibilities in this area include the docks and port at Hartlepool, together with the Hartlepool promontory which is probably the most productive site at which to watch migrant seabirds; the beach south of Seaton Carew as far as North Gore at the very mouth of the Tees is a good site for Common and Velvet Scoters. South of the river, South Gare and the Coatham Sands towards Redcar produce Snow Bunting and Sanderling, with other waders roosting at high tide. Away from the coast, most interest is on the north side of the river with a series of marshes – Cowpen and Saltholme; and the Seal Sands and nearby Reclamation Pond.

LOCKWOOD BECK RESERVOIR (OS NZ6714)
Easily viewed from the A17 road east of Guisborough, the reservoir, with its surrounding woodland, provides a mixed bird community including both winter wildfowl and resident woodland species.

Rare birds in Cleveland in 1983
Each year the birdwatchers of Cleveland manage to amass a considerable number of records including several rare birds; 1983 is perhaps as typical as any in this way.
Little Egret – Dorman's Pool in June, third county record; White-rumped Sandpiper – Dorman's Pool in July/August, ninth county record; Wilson's Phalarope – Reclamation Pond in September, tenth county record; Ross's Gull – Seaton Carew in February, fourth county record; Short-toed Lark – Saltholme in April, third county record; Subalpine Warbler – South Gare in September, third county record; Ortolan Bunting – Hartlepool in August, seventh county record; Little Bunting – Hartlepool in September/ October, fourth county record.

Organizations in Cleveland
Teesmouth Bird Club (TBC), 43 Hemlington Road, Stainton, Middlesbrough TS8 9AG

Cleveland Nature Conservation Trust (CNCT), Old Town Hall, Mandale Road, Thornaby TS17 6AW

Annual reports
'County of Cleveland Bird Report', 48 The Green, Norton, Stockton, Cleveland

Books
Stead, P J. *The Birds of Tees-side*. Natural History Society of Northumberland and Durham, 1964.
Grainger, P D. *Birdwatching in Clevelandia*. Gordian Print, 1985.

Little Auks in 1983
In February 1983 a spectacular northward movement of Little Auks was recorded off the north-east coast of England:
Whitburn: 49 on 3rd, 1101 on 7th, and 3500 on 11th; Hartlepool: 233 on 6th, 151 on 7th, 68 on 8th, 17 on 9th, 1000+ on 11th, and 58 on 12th; South Gare: 10 on 6th and 87 on 7th.

A tide-line survey for dead bodies in late February located 117 dead Little Auks on the Cleveland coast. The numbers recorded in 1983 are probably only surpassed by those in 1895 when 'thousands' of birds occurred throughout the British east coast, and the movement of birds off Teesmouth in January of that year is reported to have lasted for two weeks.

Some recent peak counts from Teesmouth
Shelduck 2300; Wigeon 675; Teal 2150; Mallard 850; Goldeneye 440; Oystercatcher 680; Ringed Plover 850; Golden Plover 670; Grey Plover 300; Lapwing 4800; Knot 7100; Sanderling 480; Dunlin 4050; Bar-tailed Godwit 260; Curlew 670; Redshank 1750; Turnstone 250; Black-headed Gull 4000; Common Gull 2550; Herring Gull 1150; Great Black-backed Gull 2085; Kittiwake 660; Sandwich Tern 1330.

Nesting seabirds in summer are the highlight of a walk along the clifftops at Marsden Rock.

TYNE AND WEAR

Birdwatching sites

SHIBDON POND (OS NZ1963)
This is a subsidence pond with surrounding marsh and scrub, operated as a reserve by the Durham County Conservation Trust. Essentially, it is an urban reserve on the outskirts of Newcastle. The habitat range is such that species as varied as Water Rail, Grasshopper Warbler, Yellow Wagtail, Lesser Whitethroat, Goldeneye, and Shelduck all occur. Access is via the B6317 road at Blaydon.

MARSDEN ROCK (OS NZ3965)
This cliff-top walk on the outskirts of South Shields provides excellent views of nesting Kittiwake and Fulmar; the offshore rock is an important site for Cormorants. Each summer the RSPB establishes a viewing post overlooking the rock. In the late autumn, offshore birds include migrant terns, skuas, and Gannets, and an occasional Peregrine turns up in the winter.

WASHINGTON WATERFOWL PARK (OS NZ3156)
This is a Wildfowl Trust park/reserve, with car park, visitor centre, and observation hides. Access is well signposted from Washington New Town. In addition to the usual extensive Trust collection of waterfowl, the site also includes a reserve on the banks of the River Wear. Shallow lagoons attract a wide range of winter wildfowl as well as waders and other waterbirds.

RYTON WILLOWS (OS NZ1565); WASHINGWELL WOOD (OS NZ2159); THORNLEY WOOD (OS NZ1760)
These three reserves are run by the Gateshead Metropolitan Borough Council. Access is from the villages of Ryton, Sunniside, and Swalwell respectively. All three sites offer a wide range of species, and a spring or early summer visit could expect to produce Tawny Owl, Sparrowhawk, Hawfinch, Water Rail, Wood Warbler, and Grey Wagtail. Winter wildfowl include Goldeneye and Goosander, with Siskin, Redpoll, and Brambling in the woodland areas.

Shelduck

juvs.

Organizations in Tyne and Wear
For details of societies and reports *see* Northumberland and Durham.
RSPB Members' Groups based at: Newcastle and Sunderland (details from RSPB, The Lodge, Sandy, Beds SG19 2DL)

NORTHUMBERLAND

The high ground of Northumberland is in the north and west, with the granite of the Cheviot Hills on the border with Scotland and the northern end of the Pennine chain. It is here that the 113000 hectares (280000 acres) of the Northumberland National Park have been established, and the Pennine Way, one of England's long-distance footpaths, starts its journey southwards. Here, in the high ground of the west, are the grouse moors, hillsheep farming, and forestry plantations. Eastwards, the land drops towards the coastal plain and southwards to the Tyne valley, an agricultural area drained by a series of rivers flowing eastwards to the North Sea – the Pont, Wansbeck, Coquet, Aln, and Tweed (on the border with Scotland). Each river produces its own small estuary which, together with the islands (Holy, Farne, and Coquet), make up major features of the Northumberland coast. Much of the county's natural woodland has been lost but, deep in the river valleys, important areas of oak, ash, and mixed deciduous woodland remain. Areas of open water are few – some mining subsidence and some artificial reservoirs – the most important of which is the recently completed Kielder Reservoir, the largest artificial lake in Britain. This now forms part of the Border Forest Park, but the construction of the reservoir (6 miles in length) is so recent that the full impact upon the bird populations has still to be realized. Nearly 240 species are recorded in the county each year.

Large numbers of seabirds breed on the Farne Islands off the coast of Northumberland.

Birdwatching sites

THE COAST

As with so many coastal counties, the birdwatchers of Northumberland tend to concentrate on the coastal localities for their viewing, seeking the greater variety and the possibility of a rare visitor that such sites provide. It is worthwhile birdwatching almost anywhere along the coast from Amble northwards. Over 500 Ringed Plover, 800 Purple Sandpiper, and 1300 Turnstone regularly winter on the Northumberland beaches, and offshore are the islands with their important seabird colonies. The shoreline is well known for its Eiders (over 2000 nests are reported each year) which congregate in the harbours and estuaries at the end of each breeding season. In winter, divers and grebes are regular. Various areas are worth a visit, including **Alnmouth, Castle Point, Seahouses, Budle Bay**, and the **Tweed Estuary** – in all cases, there are opportunities for cliff-top or beach walks. Two coastal ponds are certainly worth investigating: **Creswell Ponds** (OS NZ2894) off the A1068 road at Ellington; and **Holywell Pond** (OS NZ2317) on the A192 road on the border with Tyne and Wear.

FARNE ISLANDS

These important seabird islands are owned by the National Trust and they allow visitors to go to two of them. Details should be obtained from the information centre in Seahouses, from where summer boat trips to the islands can be

Organizations in Northumberland
Northumberland and Tyneside Bird Club (NTBC), 27
  Edrington Grove, Chapel House, Newcastle-
  upon-Tyne NE5 1JG
Natural History Society of Northumbria (NHSN),
  Hancock Museum, Barras Bridge, Newcastle-
  upon-Tyne NE2 4PT
Northumberland Wildlife Trust (NWT), Hancock
  Museum, Barras Bridge, Newcastle-upon-Tyne
  NE2 4PT

Annual reports
'Birds in Northumbria', 32 Manners Gardens,
  Seaton Delaval, Whitley Bay NE25 0DW

Books
Galloway, B and Meek, E R. *Northumberland's
  Birds*. Transactions of the Natural History Society
  of Northumbria, 1978-83.

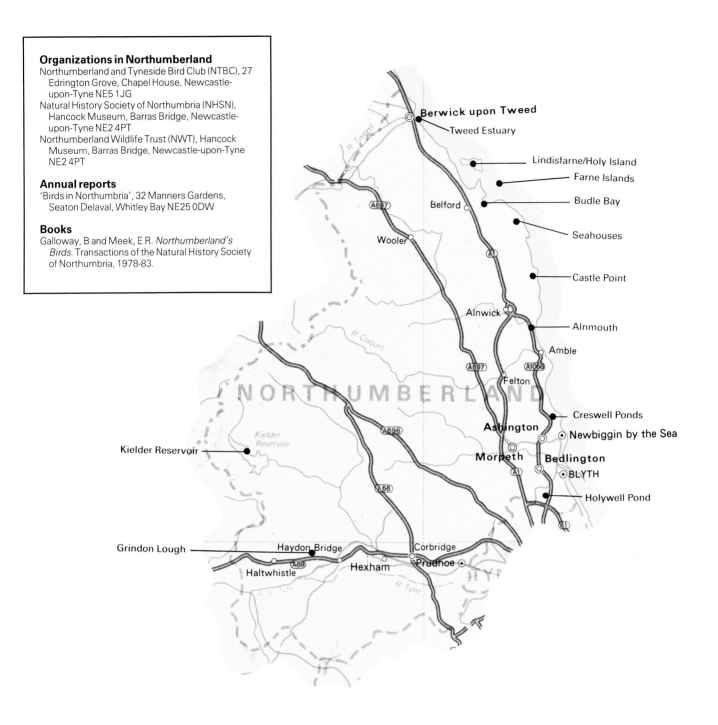

Greylag goose

Notes on some specialities of Northumberland

Black-necked Grebe – there is a regular breeding locality for this species within the county. In a good year, as many as five pairs may rear over fifteen young.

Greylag Goose – the regular wintering flock at Lindisfarne can often number over 6000 birds, with additional parties of over 1000 in the Tweed valley.

Merlin – although decreasing, this species is still reasonably common as a nesting bird with nearly 100 regularly used sites although only 25 per cent of these may be occupied in any one year.

Roseate Tern – up to forty pairs breed on the offshore islands but, in common with the British population, numbers are decreasing. This is the most southerly, regularly used nesting locality on the English east coast.

Waxwing – although numbers vary greatly each year, the Waxwing is an annual winter visitor to the coastal area. It is most frequently recorded in November/December, with some birds remaining throughout the winter until early spring.

Twite – up to 100 winter each year on the Coquet estuary.

arranged. The numbers of breeding birds on these islands are impressive:
Fulmar 120 pairs; Cormorant 340 pairs; Shag 620 pairs; Eider 1700 nests; Oystercatcher 30 pairs; Ringed Plover 20 pairs; 'large' gulls 1000 pairs; Kittiwake 4500 pairs; Sandwich Tern 4000 pairs; Roseate Tern 15 pairs; Common Tern 200 pairs; Arctic Tern 4000 pairs; Guillemot 6000 pairs; Razorbill 40 pairs; Puffin 14000 pairs. At migration times, the islands can often produce the unexpected, with up to 1000 Goldcrests on a single day, or the occasional Bluethroat or Pallas's Warbler.

LINDISFARNE/HOLY ISLAND (OS NU0943)

This is an extensive Nature Conservancy Council reserve of dunes, saltmarsh, and tidal mudflats. The causeway to the island is not passable at high tide. This is the only site in Britain where the pale-bellied Brent Goose winters – all the others are in Ireland. Although the normal wintering population is only some 600 birds, at times the flock can number over 1000 individuals. Other winter visitors occurring in large numbers are Wigeon (over 30000), Eider (over 2000), Knot (over 9000), Dunlin (over 14000), and Bar-tailed Godwit (over 4000). Several other species, including Long-tailed Duck and Whooper Swan, occur in larger numbers than at any other English wintering site. Breeding birds are rather few – perhaps the inevitable consequence of this being such a popular tourist area – but the list of species to occur as migrants is most impressive. In one year, the following birds were all recorded: Marsh Harrier, Rough-legged Buzzard, Wryneck, Citrine Wagtail, Pallas's Warbler, Yellow-browed Warbler, Radde's Warbler, and Red-breasted Flycatcher.

Eider

1st winter

♂

Comparatively few birds breed on Lindisfarne, perhaps because it is popular with visitors when the causeway becomes passable at low tide.

NORTHUMBERLAND NATIONAL PARK

To gain the maximum benefit from a visit to the park, up-to-date literature should be obtained from the information centres. The park is based on the extensive grandeur of the Cheviot Hills with their varied habitats ranging from the high heather moorlands and rocky crags to the valley woodlands, farmland, and natural lakes. On the immediate western boundary is the Forestry Commission's **Border Forest Park** – largely coniferous trees but retaining some of the native species in the valleys. The bird life is varied: on the tops are Dunlin, Curlew, Golden Plover, Merlin, and Short-eared Owl; in the woodlands Redstart, Wood Warbler, and Pied Flycatcher.

Lindisfarne/Holy Island in the distance boasts a large Nature Conservancy Council reserve.

Grindon Lough (OS NY8067) is a Northumberland Wildlife Trust's shallow lake reserve of some 90 hectares (220 acres), and is noted for its winter wildfowl populations which include Pink-footed, Bean, and Greylag Geese and Whooper Swan although numbers are never large. The reserve is easily viewed from the road reached via the A69 road at Haydon Bridge.

Set in beautiful Northumberland countryside, Kielder Reservoir offers some good birdwatching.

The Pennine Way, one of England's long-distance footpaths, begins its journey southwards from the Northumberland National Park.

Kielder Reservoir (OS NY7087) is a Northumbrian Water Authority reservoir on the edge of the National Park. It offers a car park and information centre, together with a growing variety of bird life as the reservoir comes to maturity. Surrounded by woodland, this is a splendid locality for some good birdwatching and spectacular scenery.

WEST, SOUTH, AND MID-GLAMORGANSHIRE, AND GWENT

THE GLAMORGANS

This, the most industrialized area of Wales was divided into three separate counties in the boundary reorganization of 1974 but, ornithologically, it is still viewed as a whole with the production of a 'Glamorgan Bird Report'. Although the image of South Wales, with its major towns such as Cardiff, Barry, Port Talbot, and Swansea, is one of intense industrial development associated with the coal mines, well over half of the county is farmed. In addition, the extreme north includes sections of the Brecon Beacons National Park [rising to nearly 1000 metres (3300 feet)] and other upland sites are now heavily used for commercial forestry. Much of the county is open upland hills although often there is ribbon-development housing, mining, and light industry in the valleys which fall away to the lowlands in the coastal zone – the Gower Peninsula in the west and the so-called 'Vale of Glamorgan' in the east. The contrast between the two areas, upland and lowland, is emphasized dramatically by a marked climatic difference. The uplands are bleak windswept, wet, and cold, similar to much of upland Wales, with their heather moors and grazing sheep. The coastal lowlands are drier, more sheltered, and distinctly milder – to the extent that some elements of the vegetation is reminiscent of southern Europe. Where the coast has not been developed, there are cliffs, bays, sanddunes, and river estuaries from the Burry Inlet in the west to the Rhymney estuary in the east. Freshwater areas are in short supply – a few reservoirs in upland valleys which contrast with the Welsh oakwoods that fill the dry valleys, and a small number of lowland pools as at Oxwich on the Gower and Kenfig south of Port Talbot. At the end of 1984, the Glamorgans could boast a bird list of exactly 300 species with some 110 nesting annually.

West Glamorgan and its birdwatching sites

For birdwatching, the most important area of the county is the **Gower Peninsula**, a headland thrusting out to form the southern arm of Carmarthen Bay and containing almost as much variety of habitat and ornithological interest as the rest of Glamorgan combined.

BURRY INLET (OS SS5295)

Apart from the boundary estuaries with England, the Burry Inlet holds more wildfowl and waders each winter and on migration than any other Welsh estuary. The largest concentrations are to be found between Whitford Point and Loughor, and are easily viewed by access from the B4295 road. Several species occur here in internationally or nationally important numbers. Some recent peak counts are:

Wigeon 2230; Pintail 1160; Shoveler 250; Oystercatcher 16000; Ringed Plover 150; Grey Plover 700; Knot 7000; Sanderling 220; Dunlin 7500; Curlew 2000; Black-tailed Godwit 60; Bar-tailed Godwit 500; Redshank 550; Turnstone 800.

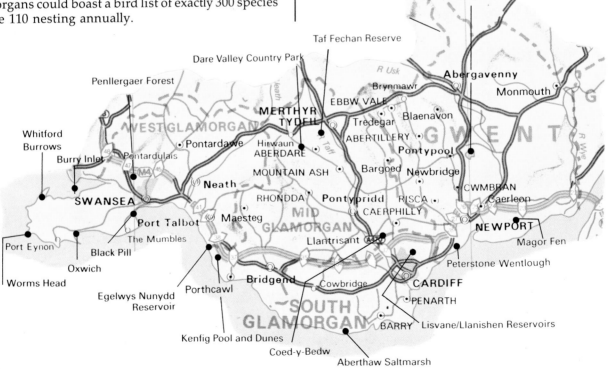

WORMS HEAD (OS SS4187)

Whereas much of the northern shore of the Gower is the tidal mud of the Burry Inlet, Worms Head island signals the western limit of the southern shore which is a complete contrast. Cliffs, with their nesting seabirds and grassy summits, lead eastwards to coastal dunes and marshes fringed with woodland and broad sandy beaches. On Worms Head itself, breeding birds include Guillemot, Razorbill, Fulmar, Kittiwake, Cormorant, and Shag, with perhaps a small number of Puffins. In addition to the breeding birds, this has become a well-established site for seawatching, and Manx Shearwaters, several species of terns, gulls, and skuas can all be recorded flying past offshore. In late autumn, this is an excellent area to watch for the movements of small birds during the mid-morning migration period.

OXWICH (OS SS5086)

This is a Nature Conservancy Council reserve on the southern shores of the Gower, with a mixture of marshes and reedbed, saltmarsh, and dunes; it is well protected on either side by tree-covered headlands. The reserve contains two nature trails reached via the car park off the A4118 west of Swansea: one is a shore trail taking in the dunes and beach; the other a woodland trail passing through forests of oak and ash. The reserve includes pools with reedbeds where both Sedge and Reed Warblers nest.

WHITFORD BURROWS (OS SS4393)

Here there is another coastal reserve with an observation hide overlooking part of the Burry Inlet from which many of the shorebirds can be seen. Although it is owned by the

A variety of seabirds, such as Kittiwake and Fulmar, breed among the cliffs and caves of Worms Head.

National Trust, the headland of saltmarsh and sand-dunes is leased to the Nature Conservancy Council. There is public access to the information centre via minor roads west of the B4271 at Llanrhidian to Llanmadoc. In addition to the regular Burry Inlet species, Golden Plover, Purple Sandpiper, and Spotted Redshank, can also be seen at this site.

BLACKPILL (OS SS6290)

At the coast on the western outskirts of Swansea, Blackpill has become famous for a single species, the Ring-billed Gull. The beach at Blackpill is a regular site for roosting flocks of gulls and, in 1973, a bird that was eventually identified as Britain's first Ring-billed Gull, a North American species, was seen among a large flock of Common Gulls. Less than three months later, a second bird was discovered at the same site, with a third before the year was out. Since then, there has been a steady string of records from many British localities. Within eight years, a total of thirty-seven birds had been recorded, many at Blackpill, and, by the end of 1984, some 348 individuals had been noted in Britain with many more in Ireland. The numbers seen at Blackpill indicate that this is still one of the key localities for the species, with the following numbers reported each year:

1973	3	1977	2	1981	1
1974	3	1978	5	1982	11
1975	5	1979	2	1983	7
1976	2	1980	0	1984	9

The search for Ring-billed Gulls on Blackpill beach inevitably leads to the discovery of other interesting gull species, with the following annual totals:

	1982	1983	1984
Iceland Gull	1	7	6
Glaucous Gull	1	1	6
Mediterranean Gull	25	17	28

Worms Head has become established as a site for sea watching.

PENLLERGAER FOREST (OS SS6249)
This is a Forestry Commission site with walkways through mixed woodland and beside the river. Access is via junction 47 off the M4. A good range of species, best seen in spring and early summer, includes woodpeckers, tits, Kingfisher, and so on.

Grey phalarope

Organizations in Glamorgan
Cardiff Naturalists' Society (CNS), National Museum of Wales, Cardiff CF1 3NP
Gower Ornithological Society (GOS), 203 Penybanc Road, Ammanford, Dyfed SA18 3QP
Glamorgan Trust for Nature Conservation (GTNC), Glamorgan Nature Centre, Fountain Road, Tondu, Bridgend CF32 0EH
RSPB Members' Groups based at: Cardiff and West Glamorgan (details from RSPB, The Lodge, Sandy, Beds SG19 2DL)

Annual reports
'Glamorgan Bird Report', 37 Penhill Road, Llandaff, Cardiff CF1 9PR
'Gower Birds', 14 Bryn Terrace, Mumbles, Swansea SA3 4HD

Books
Heathcote, A *et al. The Birds of Glamorgan.* Cardiff Naturalists' Society, 1967.
Morrey Salmon, H. *A Supplement to the Birds of Glamorgan.* Cardiff Naturalists' Society, 1974.

Unusual divers and grebes at Lisvane/Llanishen
Total records in Number of records at South Glamorgan Lisvane/Llanishen

Red-throated Diver	17 7
Black-throated Diver	9 5
Great Northern Diver	26 17
Red-necked Grebe	15 9
Slavonian Grebe	28 17
Black-necked Grebe	26 20

Bird notes of interest for Glamorgan
Sociable Plover – the first record for Wales was at the Neath estuary in October 1984.
Marsh Harrier – the species has started to summer at two sites in the county, Oxwich and Crymlyn Bog.
Little Whimbrel – a bird at Sker Farm in September/October 1982 was the first to be recorded in Great Britain and Ireland.
Marabou Stork – two birds in 1982 are apparently the only recorded examples of this escape from captivity being seen in the wild in Britain.
Peregrine – the species breeds in the county every year with up to ten pairs attempting to nest. Unfortunately, the species is very vulnerable to egg collectors in south Wales and, in 1982, only three young were reared; none in 1983; and only a single young in 1984.

The varied habitat of Gwent attracts a wide range of birds.

EGLWYS NUNYDD RESERVOIR (OS SS7984)

A Glamorgan Trust for Nature Conservation reserve, access to the reservoir is via the Exit 38 on the M4 south of Port Talbot. The site is of interest to the visiting birdwatcher for its winter wildfowl which includes flocks of diving duck, and, because of the proximity of the coast, the frequent occurrence of storm-driven birds such as Scaup, Grey Phalarope, and Leach's Petrel.

Grey wagtail ♀
♂

Red-necked grebe

summer

Slavonian grebe

summer

imm.

Pied flycatcher

♀

♂

South Glamorgan and its birdwatching sites

LISVANE/LLANISHEN RESERVOIRS (OS SS1881)

These reservoirs are easily viewed from the B4562 road south of Cardiff. Although the main interest is the winter wildfowl, particularly congregations of Tufted Duck and Pochard, with a few Shoveler, Scaup, Ruddy Duck, and Goldeneye, this is a regular stopping point for small numbers of freshwater waders, with annual records of Little Ringed Plover, Little Stint, Greenshank, and Green Sandpiper. Unusual observations have included Arctic Skua, Mediterranean Gull, and Firecrest.

ABERTHAW SALTMARSH (OS ST0465)

This is a Glamorgan Trust for Nature Conservation reserve with easy access from minor-road car parking on the B4265 immediately to the east of the power station. Predominantly, it is a saltmarsh, but the reserve includes a pebble storm beach. The reserve is favoured by birdwatchers as a migration study area, and spring and autumn visits are usually the most successful.

COED-Y-BEDW (OS ST1282)

This mixed woodland valley reserve is run by the county trust; it is reached via the B4262 road west of Taff's Well. It is preferable to visit the site in spring or early summer when the reserve is at its most attractive and bird song is at its height. Among the more familiar resident and summer visitors, the reserve holds populations of Woodcock, Grey Wagtail, Pied Flycatcher, Green and Great Spotted Woodpeckers.

The Black Mountains are home for the Ring Ouzel and Ravens.

Mid-Glamorgan and its birdwatching sites

KENFIG POOL AND DUNES (OS SS8081)

This Mid-Glamorgan County Council reserve has acquired the reputation of being one of the most important birdwatching localities in South Wales. The varied habitat within the 800-hectare (2000-acre) site includes pools, reedbeds, dunes, grassland, and rocky coast, and attracts a wide selection of bird species including several national rarities. Facilities for the visiting birdwatcher include a car park in Kenfig (west of B4283, north of Porthcawl), an information centre, and observation hides. This is a site for all-the-year birdwatching although the winter, with its Bewick's and Whooper Swans, its range of duck species, hunting Short-eared Owl, and Merlin, will always provide the greatest variety. Migrant waders and terns are regular, as are breeding Sedge, Reed, and Grasshopper Warblers, while the Cetti's Warbler appears to be taking the first steps towards colonizing the site. Among recent rare birds recorded are:

Purple Heron – April/May 1984 and May 1983; Ring-billed Gull – December 1984; Firecrest – December 1984; Red-breasted Flycatcher – November 1984; Red-crested Pochard – August/September 1983; Spoonbill – October 1983; Alpine Swift – April 1983; Aquatic Warbler – August 1983.

TAF FECHAN RESERVE (OS ST0307)

This is a small, but varied, steep river-valley reserve controlled by the Merthyr Borough Council. The habitat includes woodland, scrub, and river, with some grassland. Access is from the A470 road immediately north of Merthyr.

The river attracts Grey Wagtail, Dipper, and Kingfisher; the woods in summer hold Pied Flycatcher, Redstart, and Wood Warbler; while, at all seasons, Buzzard, Raven, and Sparrowhawk occur.

DARE VALLEY COUNTRY PARK (OS SN9702)

This is an extensive site of over 300 hectares (740 acres), based upon a valley once mined for coal but now landscaped and including a series of nature trails. The park has a car park and information centre with access from the A4059 west of Aberdare. The mixture of river, lake, and wood provides habitats for a selection of species including Grey Wagtail, Dipper, and Kingfisher; Yellow Wagtail and Teal; Buzzard, Kestrel, and Green Woodpecker.

GWENT

The north and north-west of Gwent contain the uplands and the industry. The county boundary passes through the Black Mountains which form part of the Brecon Beacons National Park while, just to the south, is the eastern limit of the South Wales coalfield, with the industrialized valleys interspersed with high moorland. Separating the uplands from the flat alluvial lands of the coast is the undulating central core of Gwent formed largely of agricultural land – principally stock farming with grass fields, hedges, and small copses. Well over half the county is under agriculture or used for rough grazing, with at least 10 per cent of the remainder made up of woodland, including the Wye Valley in the east which lies within the boundary of the Forest of Dean. Three rivers dominate Gwent: the Ebbw near the western boundary; the Usk rising in the Welsh mountains to the north and draining much of central Gwent until finally flowing into the Bristol Channel at Newport; and the Wye which, together with its tributaries, form the eastern boundary. Over 250 species have been recorded in Gwent, nearly 200 of which are noted each year and some 115 nest annually.

Birdwatching sites

SEVERN ESTUARY

The tidal mud, from the estuary of the Usk eastwards to the county boundary, attracts considerable numbers of birds in winter. Many of these are spread throughout the entire estuary but, at high tide, the roosts on the Gwent coast contain nearly 25 per cent of all the birds. The key wader roosting site is at the mouth of the Usk by the power station, but the saltmarsh and tidal mud that can be viewed from the several villages accessed from the B4245 road south of the M4 (Exit 23) can produce birds at various localities. During the 'Birds of Estuaries Enquiry' in the mid-1970s, the following maximum counts were obtained for the Gwent coast:

Oystercatcher 60; Lapwing 2970; Ringed Plover 1220; Grey Plover 480; Golden Plover 3000; Turnstone 350; Curlew 590; Redshank 700; Knot 13200; Dunlin 23500; Mallard 510; Teal 340; Wigeon 210; Shoveler 160; Shelduck 600; Herring Gull 430; Common Gull 500; Black-headed Gull 12500.

Peterstone Wentlouge (OS ST2686) is probably the prime site on the Gwent coast, with its promise of large numbers of birds and frequent sightings of rare or unusual species. This is a Gwent Trust reserve of saltmarsh, mud-flats, and flood meadows. Access is from the B4239 road from which much of the area can be viewed. The main importance of the site is the wintering flocks of waders that feed on the tidal mud (commonest being the Knot and Dunlin), but a good selection of wildfowl also occurs and small migrants can include large parties of Swallow, Field-fare, and Redwing. Regular winter visitors are Peregrine, Merlin and Short-eared Owl. Among the more unusual arrivals have been Avocet, Mediterranean and Ring-billed Gulls, Bee-eater, and Dartford Warbler.

MAGOR FEN (OS ST4286)
This Gwent Trust reserve is a first-rate example of a remnant fen habitat of the kind that was once widespread in the old county of Monmouthshire. It is a mixture of meadows, pools, and reedbeds – all extremely wet. A small car park and an observation hide are reached from Magor village (access via Exit 23 on the M4) and a short nature trail passes through the reserve. Breeding species include Reed

Bunting, Grasshopper Warbler, an important county colony of Reed Warbler, Yellow Wagtail, and Water Rail. The reserve achieved national fame on 29 October 1981 when an American Bittern was discovered and it remained at the site until February 1982. During this period, the bird was seen by thousands of visiting birdwatchers from every corner of Britain. The following year, another rare heron, Gwent's first Night Heron, was recorded on the reserve.

WYE WOODLANDS
The deep valleys of the River Wye cut through some splendid mixed deciduous woodland on the county's eastern border. Oak, ash, and lime all create a varied habitat, and there are conifer plantations, too. There are several parking areas, reserves, and forest walks. Visiting birdwatchers should be on the lookout for Buzzard, Sparrowhawk, Peregrine, Crossbill, Pied Flycatcher, Wood Warbler, and a host of other species.

BLACK MOUNTAINS
Part of the Brecon Beacons National Park, these uplands provide the rather limited, but none-the-less exciting birdwatching associated with high moorland country. The fast-flowing streams and rivers fringed by oakwoods give the variety necessary to attract species such as Common Sandpiper, Dipper, Grey Wagtail, Wood Warbler, and Redstart. On the high tops, Red Grouse, Ring Ouzel, and Raven are to be found.

LLANDEGFEDD RESERVOIR (OS ST3399)
Only completed as recently as 1963, this reservoir has become established as a major site in Wales for wintering wildfowl. A series of nature trails circles the reservoir, including the steep hills and woods which surround the site. Access is via a minor road east of Pontypool. Some recent peak counts include:

Wigeon 2000; Mallard 675; Pochard 330; Tufted Duck 50; Goosander 40; Coot 320; Lapwing 750; Snipe 28; Black-headed Gull 13500; Common Gull 10000; Lesser Black-backed Gull 1000.

The countryside surrounding the Black Mountains contrasts strongly with the high moorlands of the uplands themselves.

Organizations in Gwent
Gwent Ornithological Society (GOS), 20 High Cross Drive, Newport NP1 9AM
Gwent Trust for Nature Conservation (GTNC), 16 White Swan Court, Monmouth NP5 3DR

Annual reports
'Gwent Bird Report', 17 Castle Park Road, Newport, Gwent

Books
Ferns, P N, *et al. The Birds of Gwent.* Gwent Ornithological Society, 1977.
Ingram, G C S and Morrey Salmon, H. *The Birds of Monmouthshire.* Newport Museum, 1963.

Short-eared owl

DYFED

The 568000 hectares (1400000 acres) that are the county of Dyfed are made up of the old counties of Cardigan, Carmarthen, and Pembroke – ornithologically, however, all three retain a certain degree of independence. The county contains a varying mixture of habitat: a very long coastline with high rocky cliffs, sand-dunes, and muddy estuaries; an extensive river system running through deep Welsh valleys; one complete national park and part of a second with associated long-distance footpaths; some of the high Cambrian Mountains; and the oldest rocks in south Wales. The county's shape and form have been sculpted by the glaciers of past ice ages, which cut the deep valleys and left the lowlands which, today, are given over to farming. On the upland heaths and moors, sheep grazing predominates, with remnant woodland (principally oak) now confined to the steep valley sides where felling has been difficult or impossible. Even here, regeneration of trees is made difficult by the ever-present grazing sheep. The same deep valleys have provided the scarce freshwater lakes that are now augmented by artificial reservoirs in valleys that were once wooded and occupied by fast-flowing rivers. These same rivers give us limited, but ornithologically important marshes and flood areas; here, winter some of the scarce Greenland population of the White-fronted Goose.

An outline description of Dyfed would not be complete without mention of the Pembrokeshire islands, off the very south-west tip of the county, all with their important ornithological histories.

Over 270 species of bird are recorded in the county each year.

Birdwatching sites

PEMBROKESHIRE COAST NATIONAL PARK
The national park occupies almost 170 miles of the Dyfed coastline and its immediate hinterland, stretching from Cardigan in the north to beyond Tenby in the south. The Pembrokeshire coast long-distance footpath runs the entire length, and provides excellent opportunities for birdwatching at various localities along its route. Within the park, the coastal habitat includes the offshore islands which face the rocky cliffs, the tidal estuary of the Cleddau river which enters the sea at Milford Haven, and a range of saltmarsh. The hinterland includes areas of fresh water, heath, and wood. Apart from Ramsey, the islands are reached by boat from Dale.

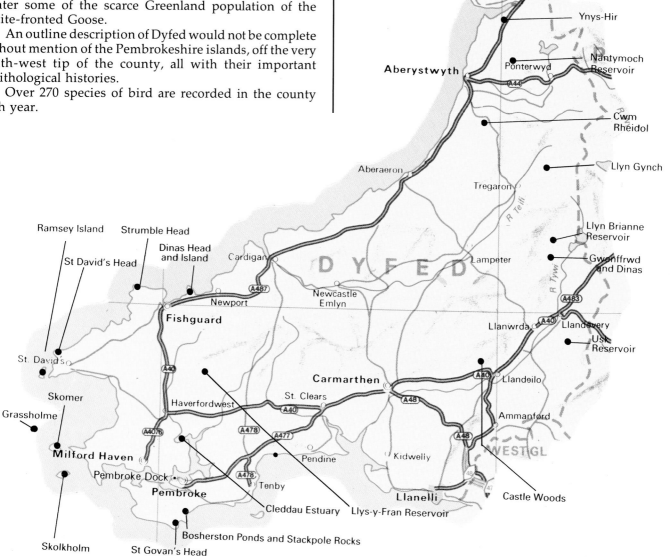

Ramsey Island (OS SM7024) is a 200-hectare (500-acre) island reached by boat from St Justinian's, west of St David's. In addition to an impressive colony of grey seals on the beaches, the island holds many breeding seabirds (mainly Guillemot, Razorbill, and Puffin) as well as Chough and Rock Dove. In winter, Purple Sandpipers occur regularly. The open, grassy surface of the island provides little of interest in the way of breeding birds but, as the island is only about a mile off the Welsh mainland, wandering birds frequently cross to it and, in the autumn, parties of Buzzard, together with occasional rare visitors such as Tawny Pipit and Buff-breasted Sandpiper, are recorded.

Skokholm (OS SM7305), which is the site of Britain's very first bird observatory, is now a West Wales Naturalists' Trust reserve. Although the breeding seabirds are not as spectacular as on Skomer, the island does contain sizeable populations of Manx Shearwater (perhaps as many as 40000 pairs) and Storm Petrel (up to 7000 pairs). From their burrows on Skokholm, Manx Shearwaters, ringed during experiments on bird navigation, successfully returned to their nest sites from central Europe and North America. Other shearwaters ringed on the island have been found dead on the coast of Australia. Recent unusual sightings have included Woodchat Shrike, Red-breasted Flycatcher, Melodious Warbler, and Little Swift.

Skomer (OS SM7209) is a National Nature Reserve administered by the West Wales Naturalists' Trust. The number of visitors allowed to go to the island on any one day is limited but, once on it, a nature trail allows views of a most spectacular seabird colony. Recent estimates of breeding pairs include:
Manx Shearwater 60000; Storm Petrel 500; Fulmar 350; Kittiwake 2520; Great Black-backed Gull 100; Lesser Black-backed Gull 14500; Herring Gull 2940; Razorbill 2500; Guillemot 2000; Puffin 7000.

Ramsey Island where, in winter, Purple Sandpipers occur regularly.

Other breeding species include Cormorant, Shag, Oystercatcher, and Chough. In recent years, a rare Little Shearwater has been discovered on the island calling from within one of the burrows. Other unusual records have included Pectoral Sandpiper, Hoopoe, Ortolan Bunting, and Black-and-white Warbler.

Small numbers of various seabirds nest on **Grassholm** (OS SM5909) island but, without doubt, the main interest is in the Gannet colony – the second largest in Britain and the third largest in the world — numbering in excess of 20000 pairs. In complete contrast to the marked rise in Gannet numbers (only twenty pairs in 1860) is the decline in Puffins; the present colony of only one or two pairs compared with at least 100000 pairs in the late 1800s. The island is owned by the RSPB.

The various **headlands** within the national park provide excellent birdwatching with good vantage points from which to look for passing seabirds, as well as breeding birds on the cliffs and clifftops. All are readily accessible as part of the coast path. **St Govan's Head** (OS SR9693) includes the reserve at **Bosherston Ponds** and **Stackpole Rocks** (OS SR9894). **Dinas Head and Island** (OS SN0040) is one of the most interesting circular walks on the coast, and includes the 3 miles around the 'island'. **Strumble Head** (OS SM9039) is an ideal vantage point from which to watch the movement of seabirds in and out of Cardigan Bay. **St David's Head** (OS SM7227) is the most westerly point of the Welsh mainland. Throughout the year, the headlands produce views of Fulmar, Peregrine, Raven, Stonechat, Buzzard, Chough, and Gannet. In summer, Manx Shearwater, Razorbill, Guillemot, and, if conditions are suitable, the occasional glimpse of a Storm Petrel. At migration time, a range of summer warblers, Wheatear, and flycatchers may make landfall, while offshore, Arctic and Great Skuas will chase the passing terns.

The Western Cleddau has a wildfowl sanctuary.

The **Cleddau Estuary** (OS SN0011) and its tidal mud can be viewed from many sites, including the wildfowl sanctuary established along the reaches of the Western Cleddau, which supports the largest variety in the entire estuary. Key species are Ringed Plover, Curlew, Canada Goose, Knot, and Wigeon. The most productive access points are from the villages of Hook, Llangwm, Cosheston, and Lawrenny.

CASTLE WOODS (OS SN6123)

This reserve is an old mixed deciduous woodland operated by the West Wales Naturalists' Trust. The combination of woodland and wet meadows in the wide valleys produces a good selection of birds on a relatively small site – some 28 hectares (69 acres). Three species of woodpecker, Redstart, Wood Warbler, and Pied Flycatcher all nest, with regular visits from Sparrowhawk, Buzzard, and Raven. The reserve is reached via the A40 or B4300 roads west of Llandeilo.

YNYS-HIR (OS SN6896)

Ynys-Hir is an RSPB reserve situated on the Dyfi estuary. Access is via the A487 road just south of Eglwysfach village. In addition to a car park and information centre, the reserve contains five observation hides. The habitat is diverse: deciduous and coniferous woodland; farmland with grazing sheep; bracken slopes overlooking river, gorge, and peat bog; with freshwater marsh and saltings associated with the river estuary. The oakwoods contain nesting Pied Flycatcher, Redstart, Wood Warbler, Nuthatch, Great and Blue Tits, Great and Lesser Spotted Woodpeckers. Goldcrest and Coal Tit occur in the conifers and Sedge and Grasshopper Warblers in the marsh. Buzzard, Kestrel, and Sparrowhawk breed, and a few pairs of Nightjars and Shelduck nest on the hillsides. Red-breasted Merganser and Common Sandpiper nest beside the river. During the winter months, Merlin, Hen Harrier, and Peregrine regularly hunt the reserve, while wintering wildfowl include Wigeon, Teal, and a small flock of White-fronted Geese.

Organizations in Dyfed
West Wales Trust for Nature Conservation (WWTNC), 7 Market Street, Haverfordwest, Dyfed

Raven

Annual reports
'Carmarthenshire Bird Report' and 'Pembrokeshire Bird Report', 7 Market Street, Haverfordwest, Dyfed

Books
Ingram, G C S and Morrey Salmon, H. *A Handlist of the Birds of Carmarthenshire.* West Wales Naturalists' Trust, 1954.
Ingram, G C S, *et al. The Birds of Cardiganshire.* West Wales Naturalists' Trust, 1966.
Saunders, D. *A Brief Guide to the Birds of Pembrokeshire.* Walters, 1976.

Some rare birds in Dyfed in 1984
Surf Scoter (North America) – at Burry Point 6-7 October.
Crane (north and central Eurasia— – two near Pembry 23 December 1983 – 29 January 1984 (one found shot on 28 January).
Baird's Sandpiper (North America) – at Dale 15 September-1 October.
Lesser Yellowlegs (North America) – at Bosherston Ponds 7-22 October.
Ring-billed Gull (North America) – up to four at Aberystwyth 1 March-3 April.
Pallas's Warbler (south and central Asia) – at Strumble Head 31 October.
Rose-coloured Starling (south-east Europe) – at Castlemartin 1 July.

A walk along one of a number of nature trails around Llys-y-Fran reservoir offers good access to a variety of habitats.

CWM RHEIDOL (OS SN6979)

There is a 2½-mile nature trail that circles the reservoir which provides water for the Rheidol power station, maintained by the Central Electricity Generating Board. Access is via the A4120 east of Aberystwyth. This is a good place for a selection of winter wildfowl.

GWENFFRWD AND DINAS (OS SN7446)

About 3 miles north of the village of Rhandirmwyn there is an RSPB reserve. The site consists of hillside oakwoods with bracken slopes and exposed rocky outcrops. The rivers and streams are bordered with ash and alder, while the higher ground is predominantly heather moorland. A series of footpaths and nature trails passes through the reserve's varied habitats. Among the birds of prey, Buzzard, Sparrowhawk, and Kestrel nest, while Red Kite are often seen overhead in spring. Nestboxes in the woodland area are occupied by Pied Flycatcher, Redstart, Great and Blue Tits. Other nesting species include Wood Warbler, Green and Great Spotted Woodpeckers, Woodcock, Tawny Owl, Blackcap, and Nuthatch in the woods; Grey Wagtail, Common Sandpiper, and Dipper along the rivers; and Tree Pipit, Whinchat, Red Grouse, Meadow Pipit, and Wheatear in the more open areas.

RESERVOIRS

Usk reservoir (OS SN8228) spans the border with Powys. Access is via minor roads west of the A40 at Trecastle. There are suitable viewing points and pathways for birdwatching, especially on the northern edge of the water. A good selection of winter wildfowl may be seen on the water while typical woodland species occupy the surrounding trees.

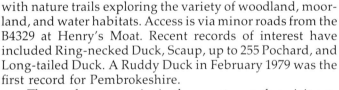

The area around **Llys-y-Fran reservoir** (OS SN0324) has been developed as a country park by the Dyfed County Council, with nature trails exploring the variety of woodland, moorland, and water habitats. Access is via minor roads from the B4329 at Henry's Moat. Recent records of interest have included Ring-necked Duck, Scaup, up to 255 Pochard, and Long-tailed Duck. A Ruddy Duck in February 1979 was the first record for Pembrokeshire.

Three other reservoirs in the county worth a visit are: **Llyn Brianne Reservoir** (OS SN8050); **Nantymoch Reservoir** (OS SN7588); **Llyn Gynoh** (OS SN8064).

POWYS

The county of Powys (formerly Montgomery, Radnor, and Brecon) is the central upland mass of Wales. Stretching from the English border in the east, it is limited by the Black Mountains and the Brecon Beacons in the south on the very edge of the Welsh coalfields; the Cambrian Mountains and the edge of the Snowdonia National Park in the west; and the Berwyn Mountains in the north. The mountains of Powys lack rocky crags and cliffs; these are rounded upland hills of red sandstone with damp peat bogs. Natural waters are few, but several upland reservoirs have been created by damming the deep valleys of fast-flowing rivers such as the Vyrnwy and Claerwen. Powys has no coastline, but just 'touches' salt water at the very innermost edge of the Dyfi estuary. Covering nearly 508 000 hectares (1 255 000 acres), the county is only just a little smaller than Dyfed, the largest of the Welsh counties, but it has a human population of only some 110 000. Powys is the most sparsely populated of all the English and Welsh counties. Indeed, the county can boast more sheep than people, for the upland character of the terrain is ideal for hill grazing, relieved only by the forestry plantations of non-native conifers. On the steep slopes of the valleys, however, some of the native oak-woods have survived.

Birdwatching sites

BRECON BEACONS NATIONAL PARK

As there are in all national parks, here there are many walks and visitors' areas to interest birdwatchers. Habitats range from the sheep-grazed moors, with their nesting Red Grouse and Golden Plover, to the dividing valleys, with their fast-flowing streams and nesting Grey Wagtail and Dipper, and the woodlands where Pied Flycatcher and Redstart breed. Up-to-date information is available from several centres within the park.

Talybont Reservoir (OS SO1019) is a reserve of the Brecknock Naturalists' Trust situated south of Talybont village off the B4558 road. There are good views of the entire area from the roadside. The main interest is wintering wildfowl, but migrant waders are regular arrivals in small numbers, and this is probably the most productive bird-watching reservoir in the county. Three species of swans occur in winter, with Goldeneye and Goosander regularly present. The nearby woodland attracts Redpoll and Siskin.

East of the B4560 road south of Talgarth, the shallow **Llangorse Lake** (OS SO1326) attracts a good selection of birds. The lake is easily viewed and very undisturbed.

LAKE VYRNWY (OS SN9821)

This is an RSPB reserve, under an agreement with the Severn-Trent Water Authority, and set within the Berwyn Mountains. In addition to the lake itself, the site includes extensive areas of heather moorland, plantations of conifers, deciduous woodland, meadows, and scrub. Facilities for the visiting birdwatcher include car park, information centre, nature trails, and observation hides, all reached from the B4393 at the southern end of the lake. Goosander, Grey Wagtail, Common Sandpiper, Dipper, and Kingfisher nest by the lake and rocky streams. The woodland of oak, beech, rowan, and birch holds Nuthatch, Treecreeper, Green and Great Spotted Woodpeckers, Sparrowhawk, Chiffchaff, and a selection of warblers; while the pure oak-woods are favoured by Redstart, Wood Warbler, and Pied Flycatcher. Crossbill and Siskin nest in the conifers. Raven, Buzzard, Merlin, and Hen Harrier frequent the moorland where Wheatear, Ring Ouzel, Curlew, and Golden Plover all breed.

ELAN VALLEY AND RESERVOIRS (OS SN9065)

Several reservoirs have been created in the valleys of the Elan and Claerwen. They are all reached via minor roads

Pen-y-Can, the highest point in the Brecon Beacons.

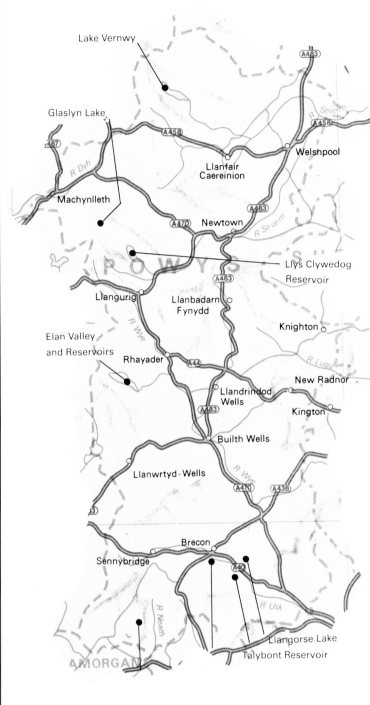

Goosander

Above: *Talybont reservoir is of birding interest mainly in the winter.*

Opposite: *The countryside west of Rhayader offers wildfowl and a variety of woodland and moorland birds in late spring.*

west of the B4518 west of Rhayader: **Craigh Goch Reservoir; Penygarreg Reservoir; Garreg-ddu Reservoir; Cabancoch Reservoir; Claerwen Reservoir.**

Wildfowl numbers on all these sites are relatively low, but the surrounding woodland and moorland can be very productive for birds in late spring and summer. Wood Warbler, Pied Flycatcher, Redstart, Whinchat, and Wheat-ear all nest; while Buzzard, Peregrine, and Sparrowhawk are regularly seen.

LLANIDLOES LAKES AND RESERVOIR
North of Llanidloes, the B4518 road passes the **Llyn Clywedog Reservoir** (OS SN9386), and beyond, via minor roads, **Glaslyn Lake** and moorland (OS SN8395). Birds to look for in this quiet undisturbed region of the county are Red Grouse, Wheatear, Golden Plover, Raven, Buzzard, and Ring Ouzel. Red Kite are regularly seen. A summer visit to the region can reveal over fifty species – a respectable total for an upland Welsh site.

Organizations in Powys
Herefordshire Ornithological Club (includes Radnorshire) (HOC), The Garth, Kington, Herefordshire HR5 3BA
Montgomeryshire Field Society (MFS), Cartref, Y Cefn, Trewern, Welshpool SY21 8SZ
Brecknock Naturalists' Trust (BNT), Chapel House, Llechfaen Brecon, Powys
Herefordshire and Radnorshire Nature Trust (HRNT), 25 Castle Street, Hereford HR1 2NW
Montgomeryshire Trust for Nature Conservation (MTNC), 7 Severn Square, Newtown, Powys
RSPB Members' Group based at: Radnor (details from RSPB, The Lodge, Sandy, Beds SG19 2DL)

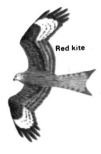

Red kite

Annual reports
'Herefordshire Ornithological Club Annual Report' (includes Radnorshire), The Garth, Kington, Herefordshire HR5 3BA
'Montgomery Bird Report', 7 Severn Square, Newtown, Powys

Books
Ingram, G C S and Morrey Salmon, H. *A Handlist of the Birds of Radnorshire.* Herefordshire Ornithological Society, 1955.
Massey, M E. *Birds of Breconshire.* Brecknock Naturalists' Trust, 1976.

The Red Kite in Wales
In the early years of the twentieth century, the Red Kite population in central Wales fluctuated from as many as twelve pairs in the first decade to an all-time low of only three pairs in 1922. Breeding pairs could still only be counted in single figures by the end of the 1950s for, although considerable effort was put into protecting the breeding birds (twelve young were reared in 1954), the breeding population showed few signs of increasing. Success was achieved from the early 1960s onwards, with changing public opinion adding support to overcome the still-present problems of persecution in various forms, together with the problem of general disturbance, and so on. A significant increase has taken place throughout the 1960s, '70s, and '80s.

	breeding pairs	young reared		breeding pairs	young reared
1960	10	10	1961	13	6
1962	11	6	1963	14	4
1964	14	7	1965	17	11
1966	15	11	1967	22	11
1968	19	12	1969	24	16
1970	24	17	1971	22	16
1972	26	19	1973	26	14
1974	27	12	1975	28	24
1976	29	18	1977	28	17
1978	32	22	1979	30	18
1980	29	27	1981	32	21
1982	38	23	1983	33	24

By 1983, in addition to the thirty-three breeding pairs, a further thirteen pairs were present, many of them nest building or repairing nests but not actually laying eggs. Unfortunately, the species is still subject to the attentions of egg collectors.

GWYNEDD AND CLWYD

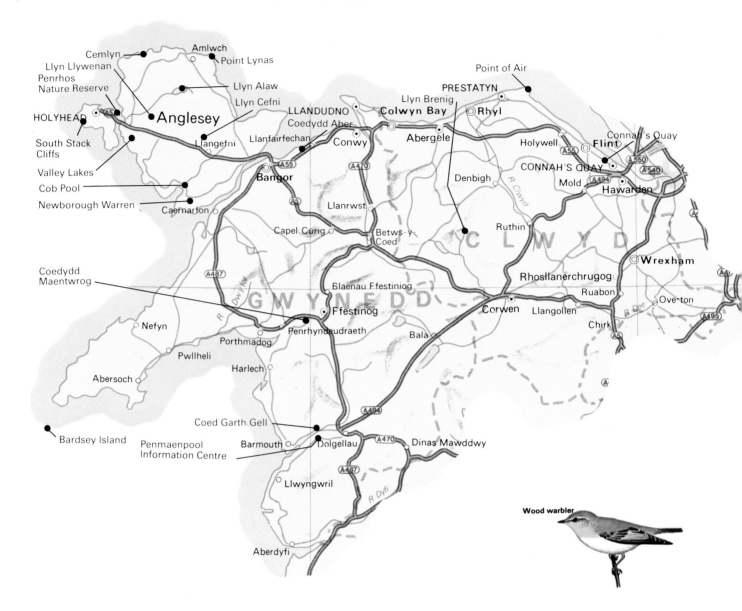

Wood warbler

GWYNEDD

Comprising the old counties of Anglesey, Caernarvon, and Merioneth, Gwynedd consists of three distinct sections: the Snowdonia National Park which covers over 50 per cent of the county; the Lleyn Peninsula, stretching out into the Irish Sea to culminate in the famous bird island of Bardsey; and the island of Anglesey, with the offshore bird islands of the Skerries to the north, and Holy Island to its immediate west. Human interference with this part of Wales has been limited by the harsh climate of the uplands where the rugged peaks can offer little more than limited sheep grazing, while the lower-lying areas of marshes and rather poor soils have not lent themselves to intense agricultural developments. Woodland is scarce; many of the deciduous trees have been felled to create grazing pastures or have been replaced by the faster-growing conifers. Gwynedd can boast a long and, at times, very rugged coastline, stretching from the high cliffs at the Great Orme's Head in the north, via rocky headlands, dunes, and marshes to the gentler reaches of the Dyfi estuary in the south. Well over 200 species are recorded in the county each year, to which can be added an impressive annual total from Bardsey Island.

Birdwatching sites

BARDSEY ISLAND (OS SH1224)
Thrusting out into the Irish Sea, Bardsey with its lighthouse well known as an attraction for night-migrating birds, is an ideal locality for the study of bird migration. The Bardsey Bird and Field Observatory has now been operating for over thirty years, during which time it has accumulated a vast quantity of data, relating not only to the migrations across the Irish Sea, but also to the breeding birds of the island. Access is by boat from Pwllheli, and there is accommodation on the island but this must be booked in advance. Over fifty species breed in most years, including some 3000 pairs of Manx Shearwaters, small colonies of Storm Petrels and Shags, occasional pairs of Peregrines and Ringed Plovers, nearly 100 pairs of Oystercatchers, up to seven pairs of Choughs and Little Owls, and twenty-five pairs of Wheatears.

The island's list of spring and autumn migrants is impressive. Over 275 species have been recorded on Bardsey, including vagrants from North America, southern Europe, and Asia. Regular migrants can occur in huge numbers, with counts of over 5000 Willow Warbler, 33 000 Chaffinch, 20 000 Redwing, and 2500 Whitethroat. The Bardsey lighthouse has attracted over 115 different species, many of them occurring every year and often in large numbers. Over a thirty-year period, more than 13 000 individual birds unfortunately were killed by striking the light at night, including over 4000 Redwing, 1400 Sedge Warbler, and 1600 Starling. The occurrence of some species on the island is surprising bearing in mind that Bardsey is offshore. There are more records of Melodious Warbler than of Corn Bunting; only one record of Nuthatch compared with three of Grey-cheeked Thrush; fourteen records of Kingfisher compared with seventeen of Yellow-browed Warbler.

SNOWDONIA NATIONAL PARK
From the west coast to the very peak of Snowdon itself, the national park contains mountains, moors, valleys, and lakes. Cold, windswept, and inhospitable in the winter, the summer sees a marked change in climate, and the scenic grandeur attracts large numbers of visitors. Birdwatchers will find a wide range of species in the variety of different habitats. Many reserves have been established within the park, and current information can be obtained from the numerous National Park Centres.

In the valley oakwoods, the species to be encountered include woodpeckers, Wood Warbler, Pied Flycatcher, and Redstart, with Tawny Owl and Sparrowhawk particularly common. Kingfisher, Dipper, and Grey Wagtail occur near the streams while, on the open moors and mountain tops, Buzzard, Golden Plover, Merlin, and Short-eared Owl all occur. This is the one part of Wales where inland-nesting Choughs are found, and Peregrines are increasing in parallel with the rise in the British population. There are many areas worth investigating but, among the existing reserves are: **Coedydd Aber** (OS SH6672) – rocky valley with mixed woodland; **Coedydd Maentwrog** (OS SH6541) – oak woodland; **Yr Wyddfa** (OS SH6353) – upland lakes, rocks, and crags; **Penmaenpool Information Centre** (OS SH6918) – estuary, saltmarsh, and freshwater marsh; **Coed Garth Gell** (OS SH6819) – oak and birch wood with river gorge and glades.

CONWAY ESTUARY AND GREAT ORME
These very different but closely situated localities can provide the variety necessary for a good day's birdwatching at many different times of the year. The Conway Estuary is best viewed from the south of the A55 road where roadside observation points provide excellent opportunities for watching a range of waders and wildfowl, particularly in winter and early spring. On Great Orme there is a nature trail, covering some 3 miles, from which it is possible to observe the breeding seabirds, including Fulmar, Kittiwake, Guillemot, Razorbill, and Shag. On the heather and cropped grassland clifftops, Wheatear and Dotterel are both regular passage visitors while, in the gorse clumps, Linnet, Whitethroat, Stonechat, and Cuckoo all breed.

The birch and oak woodland of Coed Garth Gell reserve is well worth a visit.

ANGLESEY

The island provides a good selection of birdwatching sites. Indeed, it is quite possible for a visitor to spend two weeks on Anglesey and still not exhaust its potential. The coastline has rocky cliffs and islands with breeding terns and Black Guillemot; the saltmarsh and mudflats offer refuge to parties of wintering waders; and there are extensive dunes and open sands. Inland, Anglesey can boast woods, lakes, and bird-rich farmland. Barn Owls are common, and many waterfowl inhabit the secluded pools.

Newborough Warren (OS SH4067) is a series of pools, saltmarsh, and sand-dunes operated as a National Nature Reserve by the Nature Conservancy Council. Facilities include a public observation hide from which a range of wildfowl and waders can be seen. Access is via the A4080 road near Newborough.

South Stack Cliffs (OS SH2082) are operated as a reserve by the RSPB. The cliffs are located on the western tip of Anglesey near Holyhead, with access via the A5 and the village of Tyn-y-nant. There is a car park and an information centre at Ellin's Tower from where excellent views of the cliffs and the birds can be obtained. In addition to the cliffs and offshore stacks, the reserve includes maritime heath with associated gorse and bracken. This is a good site at which to view Peregrine, together with nesting colonies of Guillemot, Razorbill, Puffin, Kittiwake, and Shag, as well as Raven, Jackdaw, Stock Dove, and a few pairs of Chough. Stonechat, Linnet, Wren, and Whitethroat, as well as many migrant warblers, are to be found on the heath, and passing seabirds are regularly noted offshore.

The North Wales Naturalists' Trust reserve of **Cemlyn** (OS SH3393) consists of small pools and shingle banks where breeding terns and gulls should not be disturbed when nesting. Other interesting features of the site are passage waders and wintering wildfowl. Shelduck nest in the rabbit warrens, and the range of other breeding birds includes Red-breasted Merganser and Redshank. Both Golden and Grey Plovers are common in winter. A North American Blue-winged Teal arrived in 1983. Access is via minor roads north of the A5025 at Tregele.

Llyn Alaw (OS SH3987) is a Welsh Water Authority reservoir of some 1000 hectares (2500 acres), situated west of the B5111 south of Amlwch. The site includes a reserve area at the north-east end where there are restrictions of access. Otherwise, there are car parks, an information centre, and an observation hide. The water has surrounding areas of mixed woodland. The site is worth visiting at

South Stack Cliffs on Anglesey are an RSPB reserve where Peregrine, a variety of seabirds, and birds typical of upland heaths can all be found.

all times of the year but, when people are fishing, the birds are often confined to the undisturbed sections. The natural edges of the reservoir attract a range of migrant waders, including Little Stint, Curlew Sandpiper, and Spotted Redshank while, in winter, both Whooper and Bewick's Swans occur, with occasional White-fronted and Pink-footed Geese. Among recent counts have been some of the largest to be recorded in North Wales: 715 Mallard; 186 Tufted Duck; ninety-three Pochard; and thirty-seven Goldeneye.

Other birdwatching sites on Anglesey worth visiting are: **Penrhos Nature Reserve** (OS SH2780) – access from the A5 on Holy Island; the **Cob Pool** (OS SH4168) – viewed from the A4080 near Malltraeth; **Point Lynas** (OS SH4893) – access from the A5025 and east of Amlwch; **Llyn Cefni** (OS SH4477) – access from B5111 north of Llangefni; **Llyn Llywenan** (OS SH3481) – access from B5109 north of Bodedern; **Valley Lakes** (OS SH3278) – a series of lakes south of the A5 and the town of Valley.

BARMOUTH BAY AND BROAD WATER

These are two sites on the Gwynedd west coast reached via the A493 and providing a selection of species associated with tidal mud and saltmarsh. The Broad Water is a large, shallow, tidal pool. Birds are attracted to the pool to roost and feed in response to tidal movements.

Organizations in Gwynedd
Cambrian Ornithological Society (COS), 21 Benarth Court, Glan Conwy, Colwyn Bay LL28 5ED
North Wales Naturalists' Trust (NWNT), 376 High Street, Bangor LL57 1YE

Annual reports
'Cambrian Bird Report', 9 St David's Place, Llandudno LL30 2UE

Bonelli's warbler

'Bardsey Observatory Report', Department of Zoology, University of Leeds LS2 9JT

Books
Breeze Jones, E and Thomas, G E. *Birdwatching in Snowdonia*. John Jones, 1976.
Hope Jones, P. *The Birds of Merioneth*. Cambrian Ornithological Society, 1974.
Hope Jones, P and Dare, P. *Birds of Caernarvonshire*. Cambrian Ornithological Society, 1976.
Roberts, P. *The Birds of Bardsey*. Bardsey Bird and Field Observatory, 1985.

Recent records of rare birds in Gwynedd
Pied-billed Grebe – Aber Ogwen, November-December 1984.
Little Egret – Mochras, May 1984.
Black Duck – a male appeared at Aber in February

1979 and was still present at the end of 1984. During its stay, the bird crossbred with Mallard and produced up to eight hybrids in a season.
Surf Scoter – Llanfairfechan, December 1983 to April 1984.
Black-winged Stilt – Bardsey, April 1984.
Broad-billed Sandpiper – Malltraeth, June 1984.
Bonaparte's Gull – Bardsey, November 1984.
Forster's Tern – Penmon, September-October 1984.
Bee-eater – Bardsey, July 1984; South Stack, August 1984; Tyn-y-Croes September 1984.
Subalpine Warbler – Bardsey, May 1984.
Bonelli's Warbler – Bardsey, August 1984.
Little Bunting – Bardsey, April and October-November 1984.

CLWYD

Stretching from the foothills of Snowdonia and the Berwyn Mountains, Clwyd nestles between the high ground in the west and the lowland marshes of Cheshire in the east. The southern shore of the Dee estuary, on the border with England, usually holds populations of birds to excite the birdwatcher (for details *see* CHESHIRE), but there is little else of interest on the coast. Apart from a collection of lakes and reservoirs in the west, freshwater is scarce and important bird sites few.

Birdwatching sites

POINT OF AIR (OS SJ1284)
Owned by the Welsh Water Authority, and a reserve by agreement with the RSPB, this area of dunes, shingle, and saltmarsh forms the very entrance to the Dee estuary.

Llyn Llywenan on Anglesey, contrasts markedly with the earlier cliff scenery, and shows the variety of scenery to be found in a confined area.

Access is via the A584 and the village of Talacre. Visiting birdwatchers should avoid disturbing the high-tide roosts and nesting birds.

The mudflats are rich feeding grounds and attract up to 20000 waders which gather on the shingle spit at high tide in winter. Commonest species are Oystercatcher, Knot, Dunlin, and Redshank, and good numbers pass through in spring and autumn with a particularly noticeable passage of Dunlin, Ringed Plover, and Sanderling in May. Up to 1000 waterfowl winter in the area, the most numerous being Mallard and Shelduck, but Teal, Wigeon, Shoveler, Pintail and Red-breasted Merganser are always present. Although the Little Tern no longer nests on the shingle area, flocks of terns still gather at high tide in the autumn. In winter, the same spit attracts Snow Bunting, Twite, Greenfinch, and the occasional Lapland Bunting or Shore Lark.

CONNAH'S QUAY (OS SJ2870)
This reserve was created by the Central Electricity Generating Board and is managed by the Deeside Naturalists' Society. The site consists of marshes, pools, and scrub, with an information centre and observation hides. Access is via the A548 from Queensferry. It attracts wintering wildfowl, there is a high-tide wader roost, and the occasional bird of prey, particularly hunting Merlin, Peregrine, Hen Harrier, and Short-eared Owl, may be drawn to the site. During the autumn migration, impressive collections of Black-tailed Godwit and Spotted Redshank have been recorded.

LLYN BRENIG (OS SH9758)
Llyn Brenig is a Welsh Water Authority reservoir north of the A5 road at Cerrigydrudian. This upland site has surrounding moorland and forest attracting a small but varied bird population.

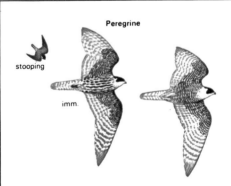

Organizations in Clwyd
Clwyd Ornithological Society (COS), 48 Fford Pentre, Carmel, Holywell, Clwyd CH7 1PZ
Deeside Naturalists' Society (DNS), 38 Kelsterton Road, Connah's Quay, CH5 4BJ
North Wales Naturalists' Trust (NWNT), 376 High Street, Bangor, Gwynedd LL57 1YE

Annual reports
'Cambrian Bird Report', 21 Benarth Court, Glan Conwy, Colwyn Bay LL28 5ED
'Clwyd Bird Report', 48 Fford Pentre, Carmel, Holywell, Clwyd CH7 1PZ

Books
Birch, J E, *et al. The Birds of Flintshire*. Flintshire Ornithological Society, 1968.

DUMFRIES AND GALLOWAY, BORDERS, FIFE AND LOTHIAN

DUMFRIES AND GALLOWAY

Dumfries and Galloway consists of the counties of Dumfriesshire, Kirkcudbrightshire, and Wigtownshire. From the rugged hills in the north, with their nesting Golden Plover, Curlew, and Hen Harrier, the region is drained southwards by numerous rivers flowing through fertile lowlands to reach the northern arm of the Solway Firth via marshlands and estuaries with their winter flocks of wildfowl and waders. Further to the west, the river mouths are divided by steep cliffs and headlands which eventually form the south-west corner of Scotland at the Mull of Galloway. None of the region's rivers is particularly long – from east to west, the Esk, Annan, Nith, Urr, and Cree – but their steep valley sides still contain some remnants of the once widespread native woods of oak, ash, and hazel.

Birdwatching sites

CAERLAVEROCK (north shore of Solway)

The Solway is not only one of the largest expanses of intertidal mud and saltmarsh in Britain, it also contains some of the most dramatic wintering populations of swans, geese, ducks, and waders. It is certainly among Britain's best-protected sites for these species, and there is a 5500-hectare (13600-acre) National Nature Reserve at **Caerlaverock** (OS NY0365) which includes the Wildfowl Trust refuge at **Eastpark** (OS NY0565). With its observation hides and raised towers, this is a site for spectacular winter birdwatching. The numbers of birds present are huge and, in conservation terms, their populations are very important indeed, with the entire breeding population of Barnacle Geese from Svalbard (Spitzbergen) wintering in the area. Access on to the mudflats can be dangerous, for the rising tide quickly

Loch Trool in the old county of Kirkcudbrightshire demonstrates the more rugged scenery found in the northern parts of Dumfries and Galloway.

fills the creeks and gulleys. Visiting birdwatchers need not (and should not) take risks, however, because excellent views of the species can be obtained at Eastpark and on the surrounding farmland. Access to the reserve is via the B725 road at Bankend.

GALLOWAY FOREST PARK

This vast area of some 66000 hectares (163000 acres) stretches across the border with Strathclyde and contains a variety of mountains, bogs, treeless hills, fast-flowing streams, lochs, and forests. Guides to the area are available from many centres in the park and these highlight the numerous trails and walks which demonstrate well the diversity of habitat in the area. In addition to the well-organized access points, the visiting birdwatcher can expect to discover many new sites with just a little exploration. The A712 road crosses the south of the park, and many minor roads enter the area eastwards from the A714 north of Newton Stewart. As well as the trails for the more active visitor, the park offers several forest drives which explore some of the more exciting areas. The extensive afforestation that has taken place clearly influences the scenery and the wildlife, but there is still much to see: the Red Grouse and Golden Plover of the moorland; the Short-eared Owl and Whinchat of the young plantations; the Goldcrest and Siskin of the more mature woodland. Where areas of original deciduous wood remain, Tree Pipit and Wood Warbler still occur. Although they are by no means common, sightings of Golden Eagle, Raven, and Golden Pheasant can be made.

WOOD OF CREE (OS NX3870)

This is an RSPB reserve on the east bank of the River Cree north of Newton Stewart; access is via the A75 and minor roads through the village of Minnigaff. This is one of southern Scotland's largest deciduous woodlands, and the

Organizations in Scotland
Royal Society for the Protection of Birds, Scotland (RSPB), 17 Regent Terrace, Edinburgh EH7 5BN
Scottish Ornithologists' Club (SOC), 21 Regent Terrace, Edinburgh EH7 5BT
Scottish Wildlife Trust (SWT), 25 Johnston Terrace, Edinburgh EH1 2NH

Annual reports
'Scottish Bird Report', 21 Regent Terrace, Edinburgh EH7 5BN
'Scottish Birds', Journal of the Scottish Ornithologists' Club

Books
Baxter, E and Rintoul, L J. *The Birds of Scotland*. Oliver & Boyd, 1953.
Duerden, N. *Scottish Birds*. Jarrolds, 1975-76.
Hardy, E. *A Guide to the Birds of Scotland*. Constable, 1978.
Knowlton, D. *The Naturalist in Scotland*. David & Charles, 1974.
Lees, A B. *Scottish Birds*. James Pike, 1975.
Richmond, K. *A Regional Guide to the Birds of Scotland*. Constable, 1968.
Thom, V M. *Birds in Scotland*. Poyser, 1986.

selection of species likely to be encountered in late spring and early summer is excellent. In addition to the wood itself, the area includes the floodplain immediately adjoining the river, together with open moorland and many fast-flowing small streams that pour their water into the Cree. Woodland breeding species include Redstart, Tree Pipit, Wood Warbler, Woodcock, Pied Flycatcher, Buzzard, and Sparrowhawk; with Mallard, Teal, Snipe, Curlew, Oyster-catcher, Common Sandpiper, Dipper, Grey and Pied Wag-tails along the river and streams.

KEN-DEE MARSHES (OS NX6376 and 6969)

Within the general area there is an RSPB reserve. Viewing is best from the main roads on both sides of Loch Ken and the River Dee (A713 and A762), as well as from the numerous minor roads in the area. Visiting birdwatchers should be particularly cautious when parking.

In addition to the loch and river, the area consists of extensive floodplains with surrounding farmland and mixed woods. The site is famous for the wintering Greenland population of the White-fronted Goose, sometimes numbering 500 individuals. Other species of note include Greylag Goose, Wigeon, Pintail, Teal, Mallard, Shoveler, Goosander, and Whooper Swan. Several birds of prey occur in the area with Merlin, Kestrel, Sparrowhawk, Peregrine, and Buzzard all regular. Breeding birds include Redshank, Great Crested Grebe, Teal, Shoveler, Goosander, Grasshopper Warbler, Redstart, and Willow Tit.

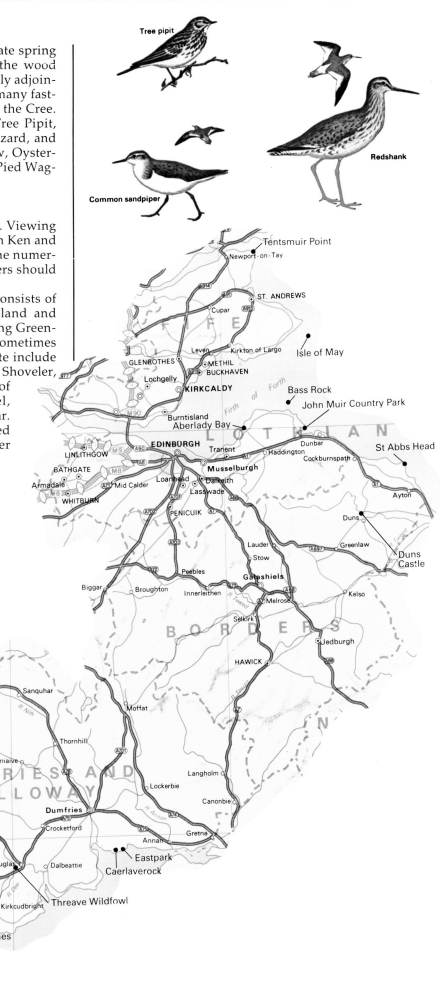

THREAVE WILDFOWL REFUGE (OS NX7461)

This is a National Trust for Scotland reserve on the banks of the River Dee and overlooking a series of islands and marshes south-west of Castle Douglas on the A75 road. There are good views of the area from the observation hide beside the railway line, as well as from various places on the surrounding roads. In addition to White-fronted and Grey-lag Geese, the site has attracted vagrant Snow Goose, Bean Gooose, and Lesser White-fronted Goose. Wintering grebes also occur.

Vast colonies of nesting seabirds can be seen among the spectacular cliffs of the reserve of St Abbs Head on the Berwickshire coast.

MULL OF GALLOWAY (OS NX1530)

The Mull is an RSPB reserve of rugged granite cliffs at the very headland of a peninsula stretching to the south-west corner of Scotland. Access is via the B7041 road from Drummore. The cliffs hold small colonies of breeding sea-birds, including Guillemot, Razorbill, Kittiwake, Black Guillemot, Shag, Cormorant, Fulmar, and the larger gulls. For the birdwatcher, April to June is the best period for visiting but, as well as observing the breeding birds, it is worth watching for passing birds offshore. These can include Gannet, Manx Shearwater, and the occasional Peregrine.

Some peak counts at Caerlaveroc/Solway	
Whooper Swan	125
Pink-footed Goose	15 000
Greylag Goose	680
Barnacle Goose	10 500
Shelduck	2300
Pigeon	2700
Pintail	2400
Shoveler	150
Scaup	750
Goldeneye	200
Red-breasted Merganser	110
Ringed Plover	1400
Golden Plover	10 000
Grey Plover	500
Knot	21 500
Sanderling	15 000
Black-tailed Godwit	130
Bar-tailed Godwit	7000
Curlew	6500
Greenshank	100
Turnstone	600

Other regularly recorded species include Bewick's Swan, Teal, Gadwall, Pochard, Tufted Duck, Purple Sandpiper, Spotted Redshank, and Whimbrel. As many as twenty-four species of waders can be recorded in a single season and up to seventeen species of wildfowl seen on a single visit. These large concentrations frequently attract the attention of Peregrines, several pairs of which breed in the high ground of the region and move to the lowland coastal areas for the winter. Here, they are often joined by Merlin, Hen Harrier, Sparrowhawk, and Short-eared Owl.

Organizations in Dumfries and Galloway
Scottish Ornithologists' Club (SOC) branches at: Dumfries, New Galloway, and Stranraer (details from SOC, 21 Regent Terrace, Edinburgh EH7 5BT)

Annual reports
'Scottish Bird Report' (covers all Scotland) Scottish Ornithologists' Club, 21 Regent Terrace, Edinburgh EH7 5BT

Books
Gladstone, H S. *The Birds of Dumfriesshire*. Witherby, 1911.
Service, R. *The Birds of Kirkcudbrightshire*. Maxwells, 1884.
Thom, V M. *Birds in Scotland*. Poyser, 1986.

BORDERS

The Borders region consists of the counties of Roxburghshire, Selkirkshire, Peeblesshire, and Berwickshire. It stretches from the Cheviot Hills and the border with Northumberland in the south, to the hills of Pentland, Moorfoot, and Lammermuir in the north, and is divided by the River Tweed and its tributaries which eventually reach the North Sea at Berwick. Much of the region was once open sheepgrazed grassland but now it is increasingly clothed with coniferous forests. Deciduous woodland and large expanses of open water are scarce. Although the rocky coastline is short, it boasts the highest cliffs of eastern Scotland and, ornithologically, it is probably the most important part of the Borders, for this coastline holds seabird populations of international worth.

Birdwatching sites

ST ABBS HEAD (OS NT9168)

Without doubt, the greatest attractions at this National Trust for Scotland/Scottish Wildlife Trust reserve are the vast colonies of nesting seabirds which, together with the dramatic cliff scenery, provide an unforgettable spectacle. Most numerous are Kittiwake, with over 19 000 nesting pairs, and Guillemot, with more than 7000 pairs; but, among the others, are 260 pairs of Razorbills, 125 pairs of Shags, 1500 pairs of Herring Gulls and smaller numbers of Fulmar, Cormorant, Puffin, and Lesser Black-backed Gull. It is possible to walk to the main breeding area from St Abbs (access via B6438) but there is also a small car park near the reserve. As well as its breeding colonies, St Abbs is an excellent site for observing offshore migrations of seabirds in addition to the spring and autumn vagrants that have crossed the North Sea. Divers and grebes are regularly seen offshore in winter months, with marked autumn passages of Sooty and Manx Shearwaters, Great and Arctic Skuas, and Iceland and Glaucous Gulls. Among the windblown migrants, Wryneck, Black Redstart, Firecrest and Red-breasted Flycatcher occur frequently; but more unexpected visitors also turn up: a male American Wigeon on Mire Lake, St Abbs in October 1983 would perhaps have been more likely on the west coast of Scotland; a Rose-coloured Starling feeding in a garden at St Abbs in June 1983; and a Dartford Warbler singing on the head in May 1983 was the first record for Scotland.

DUNS CASTLE (OS NT7755)

A Scottish Wildlife Trust reserve of woodland, open country and loch. Access is via the A6105 road at Duns. There is a good selection of woodland species, including tits, Pied Flycatcher, and a range of warblers.

The Isle of May, in the mouth of the Firth of Forth in Fife, is the home of one of Britain's longest-established bird observatories.

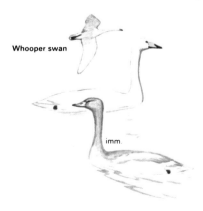

Whooper swan

imm.

Species of interest in Borders	Organizations in Borders
Mute Swan – some fifty pairs breed in the region with approximately 200 non-breeding birds in the lower Tweed valley.	Scottish Ornithologists' Club Borders Branch (SOC), The Tubbs, Dingleton Road, Melrose, Roxburghshire TD6 9QP
Pink-footed Goose – wintering flocks occur at over eight regular sites, but the birds are most numerous at West Water Reservoir (north of Peebles) where over 19 000 have been recorded.	**Annual reports** 'Borders Bird Report', 143 Eskhill, Penicuil, Midlothian EH26 8DE
Greylag Goose – over 5000 winter in the region. Black Grouse – decreasing numbers, but display leks in the north contain up to eleven males.	**Books** Brady, F. *The Birds of Berwick-upon-Tweed and District.* Private printing, 1975.
Black-headed Gull – there are widespread colonies in the region, with at least 12 000 pairs nesting, the largest colony holding over 9000 pairs. Robin – on autumn migration, concentrations of over 800 birds have been recorded at coastal localities.	Thom, V M. *Birds in Scotland.* Poyser, 1986.

Bass Rock is best known for its Gannet colonies.

FIFE

At just over 130000 hectares (320000 acres), Fife is the smallest of the Scottish regions. It is unique among them in that it is based upon a single county, Fifeshire. This is very much a coastal region with the Firth of Tay to the north, Firth of Forth to the south, and the North Sea coast in the east terminating at Fife Ness, a well-known migration watchpoint. Although this is a coastal county, the Lomond Hills provide the high ground that contrasts with the dramatic estuaries of the Tay and Eden. This is one of Scotland's more urban regions, but the once-extensive coal mines have now gone, and reclamation, together with the creation of reservoirs, have added to Fife's diversity. Some 200 species of bird are recorded in the region each year.

Birdwatching sites

TAY-EDEN ESTUARY
These two sites can provide some exciting birdwatching throughout the year, but it is the winter concentrations that give the greatest variety. Access for birdwatching can be gained from many points, including the A91 north of St Andrews, the B946 west of Newport-on-Tay, minor roads north of the A914, and minor roads east of A913 at Newburgh.

TENTSMUIR POINT (OS NO5027)
This Nature Conservancy Council reserve consists of foreshore, sand-dunes, and scrubby woodland. The bird populations are closely associated with the Tay to the north

Shag

Some peak counts on the Eden Estuary

Mallard	800		
Teal	850	Grey Plover	770
Wigeon	1750	Golden Plover	1700
Eider	1650	Curlew	600
Red-breasted		Black-tailed Godwit	210
Merganser	140	Bar-tailed Godwit	2000
Shelduck	2000	Dunlin	5000
Oystercatcher	5200	Knot	3500
Lapwing	1500	Sanderling	120
Ringed Plover	710	Redshank	2200

In addition, good numbers of Pintail, Scaup, Goldeneye, Goosander, and Ruff all occur. The Firth of Tay can hold more spectacular concentrations with flocks of Pink-footed Goose (6000) and Greylag Goose (2000) using the estuary as a roosting site. Eider counts have exceeded 12 000 individuals, and often contain a number of large parties of as many as 100 ducklings, while Oystercatcher, Bar-tailed

Godwit, Dunlin, and Redshank all occur regularly in numbers of more than 1000.

Organizations in Fife
Scottish Ornithologists' Club St Andrews Branch (SOC), St Anthony's Rest, Star of Markinch, Fife KY7 6LE
Fife Bird Club (FBC), 6 Foulden Place, Dunfermline KY12 7TQ
RSPB Members' Groups based at: Dunfermline and Kirkcaldy (details from RSPB, The Lodge, Sandy, Beds SG19 2DL)

Bird reports
'Fife and Kinross Bird Report', 133 Duddingstone Drive, Kirkcaldy, Fife

Books
Boase, H. *Birds of North Fife*. Private printing, 1964.

and the Eden to the south. In addition to the more familiar species, Eider congregate in large numbers and Common Scoter and Red-breasted Merganser regularly appear off-shore.

ISLE OF MAY (OS NT6599)

This small, 57-hectare (140-acre) island in the very mouth of the Firth of Forth is not only a Nature Conservancy Council reserve, but also houses one of Britain's longest-established bird observatories. Founded in 1934, the observatory has accumulated an extensive collection of migratory data: thousands of birds have been ringed; and many rare and unusual birds have been recorded. The breeding birds on the island have undergone a dramatic change; from 8000 nesting pairs of terns and a very few gulls, the situation altered dramatically, with an increase in gull numbers to 34000 Herring Gulls and 5000 Lesser Black-backed Gulls and a dramatic decline in the tern population so that, now, they have virtually disappeared. In contrast, Puffins have increased from a very small number in the 1950s to over 8000 by the early 1980s; Shags from six pairs in the 1930s to 1000 in the 1980s. Access to the island is by boat from Crail, Anstruther, or Pittenweem but this is very dependent upon the prevailing weather conditions. The bird observatory does have limited accommodation on the island (21 Regent Terrace, Edinburgh). In recent years, the Isle of May has added two species to the British list of birds. In September 1950, an Isabelline Shrike from southern Asia was watched on the island and, although this was the very first, in the following thirty years a further fourteen were recorded elsewhere in Britain. In October 1954, a Siberian Thrush from eastern Asia was trapped and ringed during migration studies on the island.

LOTHIAN

The region comprises the old counties of East, Mid- and West Lothian. Between the Lammermuir Hills in the east to the Pentlands in the west, Lothian region slopes from south to north towards the shores of the Firth of Forth, where there are the extensive sands in the east and then the coastlands of Edinburgh to Queensferry. All the region's rivers flow northwards – the Tyne, Esk, and Water of Leith. Much of the human population is centred around Edinburgh while the remainder of the region is remarkably rural – fertile and intensively farmed near the coast; acidic and barren in the hills. The historic oakwoods have gone, replaced by artificial coniferous forests or sheep grazing. Upland reservoirs provide open stretches of fresh water, generally lacking in birds, while, offshore, a series of small islands in the Firth attracts colonies of breeding seabirds.

Birdwatching sites

ABERLADY BAY (OS NT4780)

This extensive, 580-hectare (1430-acre) Local Nature Reserve is owned by the East Lothian District Council, and comprises a vast stretch of open bay, mudflats, sand-dunes, and salt marsh. The reserve is famous for its flocks of wintering Pink-footed Geese which feed on the surrounding farmland but which, at low tide, roost well out on the mud far from the shore and the A198 road. The road provides excellent views across the reserve, and access into it is restricted. The goose flock can peak at as many as 8500 birds, and the 'Pink-feet' can be joined by the occasional Bean, White-front, Greylag, and Brent. An impressive list of over 225 species has been recorded, with over fifty of these breeding each year, including Eider and Shelduck. Among the recent observations of rare birds have been two Broad-billed Sandpipers in May/June 1983 and 1984; Ring-billed Gull in October 1983 and 1984; two White-rumped Sandpipers in August 1983; Grey Phalarope in October 1983; Mediterranean Gull in May 1983; and Richard's Pipit in November 1983.

BASS ROCK (OS NT6087)

If weather permits, boat trips to the Bass Rock are possible from North Berwick during the summer months. Among the breeding seabirds, it is the spectacular Gannet colony that attracts the most attention. At the time of writing, the colony contains over 18000 nesting pairs compared with only some 4000 to 5000 pairs in the 1940s. The birds have been known to breed on the island since the fourteenth century. Other breeding seabirds occur in small numbers and include Kittiwake, Puffin, Guillemot, Razorbill, Shag, and Fulmar. It is, however, the Gannet that dominates the scene, and, with a scientific name of *Sula bassana*, the association between the bird and the rock is complete.

JOHN MUIR COUNTRY PARK/TYNE ESTUARY (OS NT6480)

From this East Lothian District Council park (access via the A1087), it is possible to walk towards the estuary and thus encounter a range of habitats, including cliffs, estuarine mudflats, and sandy beaches. Autumn and winter provide the greatest number of birds but the site is well worth a visit at any time. In winter, many species of wildfowl and wader occur, including a regular flock of Whooper Swans, with divers and grebes usually to be seen offshore. Kestrel and Sparrowhawk are regularly seen, with the occasional Peregrine and Merlin sighted over open country. To get the best out of a visit, the birdwatcher should try to be there at high tide.

Red-breasted merganser

> **Organizations in Lothian**
> Scottish Ornithologists' Club Edinburgh Branch (SOC), 13 Henderson Row, Edinburgh EH3 4DH
> RSPB Members' Group based at: Edinburgh (details from RSPB, The Lodge, Sandy, Beds SG19 2DL)
>
> **Annual reports**
> 'Lothian Bird Report', 13 Henderson Row, Edinburgh EH3 4DH
>
> **Books**
> Nash, J K. *The Birds of Midlothian.* Witherby, 1935.

CENTRAL AND STRATHCLYDE

CENTRAL

The region comprises the old counties of Stirlingshire, Clackmannanshire, and part of Perthshire. From the tidal inner estuary of the Firth of Forth, with its refineries and industry around Grangemouth, and its wintering populations of Pintail, Knot, and Curlew, the Central region stretches north and west until it reaches the peaks and ridges that make up the Grampian mountains. From Ben Lomond and Ben More to Ben Vorlich, the region includes remnants of the Caledonian forest, old oaks, grouse estates, and hill sheep farming. In the south, Central presents a gentler, more rolling prospect, with peat bogs and fells and the occasional massive tip of colliery waste. Although the area is well supplied with bodies of fresh water, the larger upland lochs of the region are deep, steep sided, very cold, and generally lacking in bird interest. It is the smaller lochans and their associated peat bogs that attract a range of breeding birds, including several species of duck as well as colonies of gulls and occasional Greenshank or Wood Sandpiper.

Birdwatching sites

LOCH LOMOND (OS NS3598)

At the extreme south-east corner of this, the largest freshwater lake in Britain, is the National Nature Reserve

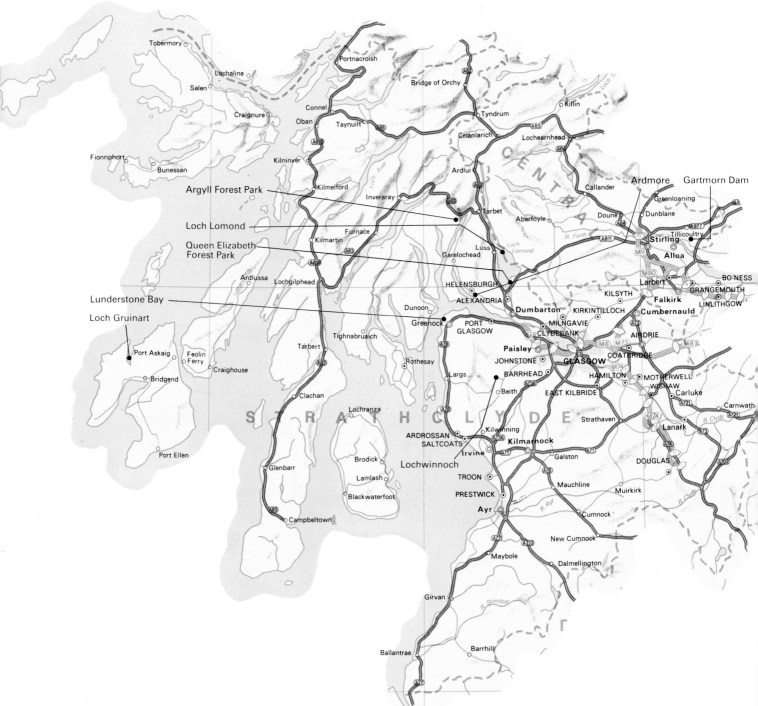

The freshwater Loch Lomond is a National Nature Reserve which, for the birder, is mainly of interest in the winter.

administered by the Nature Conservancy Council. Access to the Loch is via the A82 road on the western shore or via the B837 and B829 on the wilder, less accessible eastern shore. The northern section of the Loch is steep sided and rugged although it is edged with some excellent woodland, particularly on the eastern shore near Inversnaid. At the southern limit, the Loch opens into a wider expanse of water containing several small islands and, of particular interest to the visiting birdwatcher, marshes and shallow water where the River Endrick flows into the Loch. In the summer months, the bird interest is mainly away from the Loch itself and among the surrounding woods and marshes. Breeding birds include Grasshopper Warbler, Woodcock, Redstart, Long-eared Owl, and Capercaillie. On the Loch shore (and the small islands that may be visited by boat from Luss) are nesting Red-breasted Merganser and Common Sandpiper, while Grey Herons regularly feed in the area. Small numbers of migrants are recorded each spring and autumn, including the occasional rarity, such as the Pectoral Sandpiper from North America. It is the winter months that provide the main bird interest on the Loch; Whooper Swan and Greylag Goose occur regularly with occasional parties of White-fronted Goose from the Greenland breeding grounds.

QUEEN ELIZABETH FOREST PARK

East of Loch Lomond and the mass of Ben Lomond, the forest park stretches beyond the town of Aberfoyle and is crossed by the A821 and several minor roads. Within the forest are numerous sites of interest to the birdwatcher. In the west, much of the land is treeless, open, and exposed. On the highest peaks and crags, Raven, Ptarmigan, and occasional Golden Eagle are to be found while, on the slightly lower slopes, Curlew, Meadow Pipit, and the occasional Hen Harrier and Merlin nest. The greatest variety of woodland within the park is found in the east where both Green and Great Spotted Woodpeckers now occur, together with Goldcrest, Wren, and Tree Pipit. The lochs and waterways attract Dipper, Grey Wagtail, Goosander, and small numbers of Goldeneye and Wigeon. Information on the Forest Park is best obtained from the David Marshall Lodge (NN520015) above the town of Aberfoyle; here there is current literature relating to many aspects of the park's interest.

GARTMORN DAM (OS NS9294)

This is a reservoir under the control of the Clackmannan District Council with access via the B9140 road east of Alloa. Facilities include a visitor centre and observation hide. Although the variety of wildfowl is not large, Whooper Swan and Greylag Goose are regular visitors, and counts of over 2000 duck, comprising some six species, are frequent.

STRATHCLYDE

Strathclyde comprises the old counties of Ayrshire, Lanark-shire, Renfrewshire, Dunbarton, Argyll, and Bute. Centred around the Clyde estuary, this vast region of Western Scotland embraces an unusual coastline of indentations, islands, and peninsulas. Offshore are remote areas: Tiree, Mull, Jura, Arran, and Bute. In the north, Strathclyde has mountains and peat bogs, rocky cliffs and sandy dunes, deep sea lochs and fast-flowing, clear-water rivers. By contrast, the south includes the urban areas of Greenock, Glasgow, Motherwell, Kilmarnock and Ayr. Less rugged, the south of Strathclyde has more rolling hillsides and grazing sheep although, in common with many similar sites in Britain, there is an increasing amount of forestry.

Birdwatching sites

LOCH GRUINART (OS NR2767)

This RSPB reserve was established on the Isle of Islay with one major objective: to farm the land in such a manner that it will be attractive to the vast congregations of wintering geese that use the island. The entire reserve of over 1200 hectares (3000 acres) includes, not only the grassland, but also moorland, saltmarsh, and the tidal loch together with some small areas of woodland. The B8017 road passes through the reserve and provides good views for the visiting birdwatcher, although care should be taken not to block the road with a parked car.

This is the most important feeding and roosting site in the world for the Greenland race of the Barnacle Goose. These birds are present on the island from October to April each year and, at times, can number as many as 20000, often accompanied by large numbers of the Greenland White-fronted Goose. Hen Harrier, Buzzard, and Short-eared Owl breed, and regular sightings are made of Golden and White-tailed Eagles. Peregrine and Merlin are usually seen throughout the year. Other breeding species include Teal, Lapwing, Redshank, Snipe, and Curlew with many other waders and wildfowl in the winter months. Chough are present on the island and are regularly seen on the reserve.

LOCHWINNOCH (OS NS3558)

This RSPB reserve is reached via the A760 road east of the town of Lochwinnoch. Facilities include a visitor centre, car park, nature trails, and observation hides. The reserve is centred around a shallow loch and an area of sedge and reedgrass marsh. There are small areas of boundary wood-land. Breeding birds include Great Crested and Little Grebes, a colony of Black-headed Gulls, Sedge and Willow Warblers, Reed Bunting, and several duck – Mallard, Shoveler, Pochard, and Tufted Duck. Wildfowl numbers increase in winter and include Greylag Goose, Whooper Swan, Wigeon, Pochard, Teal, Goldeneye, and Goosander. Small numbers of waders occur, with Lapwing, Snipe, and Redshank often joined by a range of migrant species when exposed mud develops on the loch edge at migration time. Kestrel and Sparrowhawk are present throughout the year, together with an occasional Peregrine.

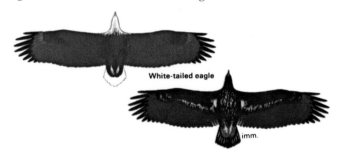

White-tailed eagle

imm.

Fast-flowing, tree-lined rocky streams surrounded by moors are typical of the northern parts of Strathclyde.

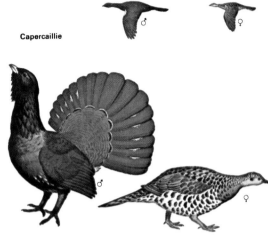

Capercaillie

Mull is one of the more remote areas of Strathclyde.

ARDMORE (OS NS3178)

Ardmore is a Scottish Wildlife Trust reserve with views across the tidal mud of the Clyde estuary. Access is via the A814 road on the north shore of the Clyde to a car park and nature trail. The Clyde estuary attracts large numbers of wintering birds, including a massive gull roost (predominantly Black-headed) of over 35000 birds. Among the other populations are: Pintail 130; Shelduck 1000; Eider 2500; Goldeneye 400; Red-breasted Merganser 150; Turnstone 200; Oystercatcher 3500; Curlew 700; Redshank 8000; Dunlin 4000.

LUNDERSTONE BAY (OS NS2173)

This birdwatching site on the banks of the outer Clyde is immediately adjacent to the A78 road. Although it is very popular with visitors in the holiday season, birdwatchers

A gull nest with eggs on the island of Mull.

will find much to interest them early or late in the day and during the winter months. A range of wildfowl and waders occurs, with large concentrations of gulls at all times, and terns and Gannets flying offshore in the summer.

ARGYLL FOREST PARK

Britain's oldest forest park was created in 1935 and is situated on the north bank of the Clyde. The park is crossed by numerous roads, including the A880, A83, and A815, and current literature and information are obtainable from the various forest offices in the area. There is a broad spectrum of habitats which includes: the upland areas with their Buzzard, Raven, Hen Harrier, Red Grouse, Twite, and occasional Golden Eagle; the forestry woodland which attracts Crossbill, Capercaillie, Siskin, Sparrowhawk, and Black Grouse; and the mixed deciduous woods with their populations of Willow and Wood Warblers, four species of tits, numerous Jays, and less frequent Magpies.

Organizations in Central
Scottish Ornithologists' Club Stirling Branch (SOC), 4 Archers Avenue, Stirling FK7 7RJ

Organizations in Strathclyde
Argyll Bird Club (ABC), SMBA, Dunstaffnage, Argyll
Scottish Ornithologists' Club Ayr Branch (SOC), Rowantree Cottage, Culzearn Country Park, Maybole KA19 8LD
Scottish Ornithologists' Club Glasgow Branch (SOC), 18 Rowland Crescent, Newton Mearns, Glasgow G77 5JT
RSPB Members' Groups based at: Ayr, North Ayrshire, Glasgow, Hamilton, Helensburgh, and Renfrewshire (details from RSPB, The Lodge, Sandy, Beds SG19 2DL)

Annual reports
'Argyll Bird Report', 4 Achagoil, Minard, Inveraray, Argyll
'Ayrshire Bird Report', 11 Kirkmichael Road, Crosshill, Maybole KA19 7RJ
'Clyde Area Bird Report', Paisley Museum, High Street, Paisley, Renfrew

Books
Hogg, A. *Birds of Ayrshire*. Glasgow University, 1983.
Gibson, J A. *An Atlas of Renfrewshire Vertebrates*. Renfrewshire Natural History Society, 1970.
McWilliams, J M. *The Birds of the Firth of Clyde*. Witherby, 1936.

TAYSIDE AND GRAMPIAN

TAYSIDE

Tayside comprises the old county of Angus and part of Perthshire. From the North Sea coast between Montrose and Carnoustie in the east, to Rannoch Moor in the west; from the Grampian Mountains in the north to the foot of the Ochil Hills and Loch Leven in the south, the Tayside region is one of contrasts. In the north, the grouse estates, forestry, and livestock predominate while, in the south, there is arable farming with a scattering of fruit farms. The bird life of Tayside is as varied as the countryside, ranging from seabirds nesting on the cliffs, to wintering waders on the tidal mud; Osprey on the upland lochs; wild geese on the lowland waters; and a complete range of woodland species exploiting the mixed forests of oak, elm, and hazel in the valleys and pines in the uplands.

Birdwatching sites

MONTROSE BASIN (OS NO6957)

The basin is an Angus District Council/Scottish Wildlife Trust reserve immediately inland from Montrose and surrounded by three main roads: A92, A934, and A935. Observation hides provide views across the tidal mud which fills the basin at low tide and through which the South Esk flows to the North Sea. This is a site for autumn and winter birdwatching: Mute Swan 250; Greylag Goose 500; Pink-footed Goose 500; Shelduck 350; Mallard 500; Wigeon 3500; Eider 500; Oystercatcher 1800; Ringed Plover 250; Dunlin 2000; Knot 4000; Redshank 2600; Curlew 1000.

SEATON CLIFFS (OS NO6641)

This Scottish Wildlife Trust reserve is not suitable for breeding seabirds, but the cliffs hold nesting populations of House Martin and, offshore, it is possible to watch Eider, Guillemot, Fulmar, and Kittiwake. During the winter, the water's edge is a favourite haunt for Purple Sandpiper, and wind-blown migrants are regular in the autumn months.

KILLIECRANKIE (OS NN9162)

There are two reserves in this area. The National Trust for Scotland has a summer visitor centre with walks that pass

Loch Leven has two bird reserves.

through a wooded gorge; and the RSPB has a woodland and heather moorland reserve. Both sites are reached via the A9. The oakwoods contain a mixture of associated birch, ash, elm, and alder, and rise steeply on banks above the River Garry until they reach a plateau of farmland, above which a further steep rise leads to the heather moorland. On the high ground and cliffs, Buzzard, Raven, Kestrel, Curlew, and Black Grouse all nest; on the wooded slopes, Green and Great Spotted Woodpeckers, Crossbill, Wood Warbler, and Redstart all occur. On the river fringes are found Common Sandpiper, Dipper, and Grey Wagtail.

LOCH OF THE LOWES (OS NO0544)

This Scottish Wildlife Trust reserve, reached via the A923 east of Dunkeld, is best known for its nesting Ospreys, but the reserve contains a range of habitats, and facilities include a visitor centre and observation hide. Although the reserve is more interesting during the spring and summer, the Loch holds up to 1000 Greylag Geese and other wildfowl in the winter. The surrounding woodlands contain Treecreeper, Redstart, Spotted Flycatcher, Grasshopper and Wood Warblers. Goldcrest, Siskin, and Long-tailed Tits are regular, and the occasional Capercaillie is seen. This is an important site for Scottish grebes: in the nineteenth century, the Great Crested Grebe nested in Scotland for the first time. More recently, a pair of Slavonian Grebes has nested.

LOCH OF KINNORDY (OS NO3653)

This is an RSPB reserve beside the B951 road west of Kirriemuir. The Loch has developed into a freshwater marsh with varying amounts of open water, and it is bordered by extensive willow and alder scrub. Facilities include a car park and observation hides. Among the breeding birds are Mallard, Teal, Shoveler, Tufted Duck, Gadwall, and a recent colonist, the Ruddy Duck. There is a large and noisy colony of Black-headed Gulls and, around the fringes of the site, are nesting Sedge Warbler, Reed Bunting, and Redshank. Sparrowhawk and Long-eared Owl are regular and, among the annual migrants, are Greenshank and Ruff. In the winter, the Loch is used as a roost by Greylag Geese and hunted by Hen Harrier and Short-eared Owl.

Organizations in Tayside
Scottish Ornithologists' Club Dundee Branch
(SOC), 6 Park Road, Invergowrie, Dundee DD2
5AM
Angus Wildlife Group (AWG), 2 McGregor's Land,
Kirriemuir DD8 4HQ
Perthshire Society of Natural Science, (PSNS),
Parkhill, Arnbathie, Perth PH2 7PL
RSPB Members' Group based at Dundee (details
from RSPB, The Lodge, Sandy, Beds SG19 2DL)

Annual reports
'Angus Bird Report', 4 Dunrossie Crescent, Tayock,
Montrose DD10 9LT
'Perthshire Bird Report', Perth Museum, George
Street, Perth

Books
Boase, P. *Birds of Angus*. Private printing, 1962.
Boase, P. *Birds of North and East Perth*. Private
printing, 1961.
Crighton, G M. *Birds of Angus*. Private printing,
1976.

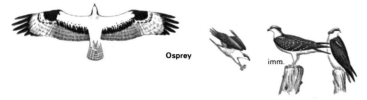

Osprey   imm.

VANE FARM/LOCH LEVEN (OS NO1501)

There are two reserves at the site – the Nature Conservancy Council's Loch Leven reserve; and the Vane Farm reserve of the RSPB. The Loch attracts some impressive numbers of wintering wildfowl: Whooper Swan 250; Greylag Goose 5000; Pink-footed Goose 10000; Mallard 2500; Teal 500; Wigeon 1000; Shoveler 500; Pochard 1000; Tufted Duck 2500; Goldeneye 500; Goosander 250; Mute Swan 250.

The entire Loch covers an area of over 1600 hectares (4000 acres) and contains several islands on which at least six species of duck nest: Tufted Duck, Mallard, Wigeon, Shoveler, Gadwall, and Shelduck. The best views across the Loch are from the RSPB reserve on the B9097 east of the M90. Vane Farm has an observation room fitted with binoculars and telescope as well as an additional observation hide on the Loch shore. In addition to the water habitat, the reserve includes areas of mixed farmland, birch woodland, and heather moorland together with rocks and cliffs. Willow Warbler, Spotted Flycatcher, and Tree Pipit are common.

LOCH OF LINTRATHEN (OS NO2855)

This is a Scottish Wildlife Trust reserve surrounded by minor roads leading off from the B951. It is a site for winter birdwatching for, although the loch is very deep, it is visited by many wildfowl. The Mallard flock can be as numerous as 3000, the largest concentration in Scotland. Greylag Geese use the site as a roost, leaving the surrounding farmland and concentrating at dusk; as many as 5000 have been recorded. Smaller numbers of other wildfowl include Whooper Swan, Teal, Pochard, Wigeon, Goldeneye, and Goosander.

Rannoch Moor is a wild and remote place in the far west of Tayside.

RANNOCH FOREST (OS NN5755)

This area of remnant Caledonian pine forest is operated as a Nature Reserve by the Forestry Commission. Access is via the B846 road which follows the northern shore of Loch Rannoch. Capercaillie and Black Grouse are abundant in the area, while other interesting species include Siskin, Scottish Crossbill, Redstart, Spotted Flycatcher, and Tree Pipit.

GRAMPIAN

The region comprises the old counties of Banffshire, Aberdeenshire, Kincardineshire, and part of Moray. From the Cairngorm mountains in the west, and the Grampian mountains in the south, the region extends through fertile valleys and a coastal plain to a lengthy coastline facing north and east. Many rivers, originating in the high country, flow through the region: the Dee, Don, Spey, and Lossie; but Grampian lacks a major estuary. Variations include high sea-cliffs with colonies of nesting birds, to sandy dunes and beaches with open vistas and apparently endless skies contrasting with the high tops where frosts and snow can be present throughout the year, and the slightly lower moorland slopes with the grouse estates. Over 220 species are recorded in the region each year, of which as many as 140 may nest.

Birdwatching sites

ST CYRUS (OS NO7464)

This is a coastal reserve operated by the Nature Conservancy Council; it includes sand-dunes, beaches, and sea cliffs. Access is via the A92 road north of Montrose, but some of the reserve is closed to visitors when the Little and Arctic Terns are nesting. In addition to the fifty or so species that nest on the reserve, the visiting birdwatcher is likely to discover a range of migrants during the late autumn. Offshore, skuas, divers, and shearwaters are regularly seen, and there is a colony of Fulmars nesting on the cliffs. Small birds are not numerous but, among the breeding species, are Stonechat and Grasshopper Warbler.

SANDS OF FORVIE AND YTHAN ESTUARY (OS NK0227)

This is an extensive [over 1000 hectares (2500 acres)] Nature Conservancy Council reserve that is worth visiting throughout the year. Access is via a car park on the A975 road north of Newburgh. The reserve holds high populations of many ground-nesting birds and, for this reason, access is restricted to footpaths and to the foreshore, although views across the ternery can be obtained from the observation hide. Recent estimates of breeding populations: Eider 2100 pairs; Common Tern 465 pairs; Little Tern 48 pairs; Sandwich Tern 1670 pairs; Arctic Tern 200 pairs. Kittiwake and Fulmar also nest.

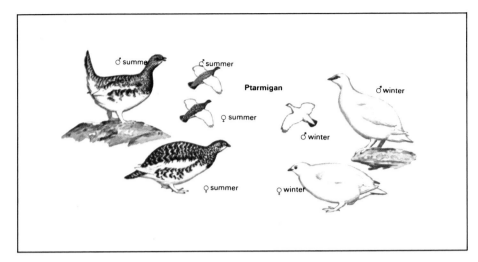

Peak wader counts on the Ythan Estuary

Oystercatcher	610	Knot	260
Ringed Plover	220	Sanderling	250
Golden Plover	2000	Dunlin	375
Grey Plover	40	Bar-tailed Godwit	95
Lapwing	1900	Curlew	630

Some unusual records from Grampian in 1984

Blue-winged Teal (North America) – one at Fraserburgh/Strathbeg in September.
King Eider (Arctic) – one at Ythan in May-June.
Surf Scoter (North America) – four in Spey Bay during the year.
Black-winged Stilt (southern Europe) – one on the coast in October-November.
Marsh Sandpiper (south-eastern Europe/Asia) – one at Lossiemouth in April.
Wilson's Phalarope (North America) – one at Cotehill Loch in September.
Snowy Owl (Arctic) – one in Cairngorms in June-October.
Alpine Swift (southern Europe) – one at Greg Ness in October.

Organizations in Grampian

Scottish Ornithologists' Club Aberdeen Branch (SOC), 24 Seafield Gardens, Aberdeen AB1 7YB
Aberdeen University Bird Club (AUBC), Department of Zoology, University of Aberdeen, Tillydrone Avenue AB9 2TN
RSPB Members Groups' based at: Aberdeen and Moray (details from RSPB, The Lodge, Sandy, Beds SG19 2DL)

Annual reports

'North-East Scotland Bird Report', 17 Rubislaw Terrace, Aberdeen AB1 1XE

Books

Thom, V M. *Birds in Scotland.* Poyser, 1986.

The lower moorland slopes of Banff have grouse estates and dramatic skies.

In autumn and winter the estuary attracts large numbers of waders and wildfowl, including as many as 10000 Pink-footed Geese and flocks of Greylag Goose, Eider, and Whooper Swan. Sanderling occur regularly and Common and Velvet Scoters are seen offshore. Following gales in the North Sea, the estuary mouth can provide shelter for a range of seabirds not normally found close inshore, including shearwaters and divers.

FOWLSHEUGH (OS NO8879)

This is an RSPB sea-cliff reserve, with access via the A92 road south of Stonehaven with a small car park in Crawton. Views of most of the breeding species (visits should be confined to April-June) can be obtained from various points on the cliff-top path. Recent estimates suggest populations of breeding pairs may be: Fulmar 270; Shag 20; Kittiwake 30000; Herring Gull 400; Guillemot 20000+; Razorbill 4000+; Puffin 150; Jackdaw 50.

LOCH OF STRATHBEG (OS NK0759)

The Loch of Strathbeg is a large, shallow loch, separated from the sea by wide sand-dunes and bordered by freshwater fen, saltmarsh, woodland, and farmland. Because access is across Ministry of Defence property from the A952 road at Crimond, it is necessary to obtain a permit from the RSPB in advance (The Lythe, Crimonmogate, Lonmay, Fraserburgh, AB4 4UB).

Facilities include a car park, visitor centre, and

observation hides. The reserve is best known for the major concentrations of wintering Whooper Swan, Tufted Duck, Pochard, Goldeneye, and Greylag and Pink-footed Geese. This is also a well-known staging post on the goose migration, with varying numbers every spring and autumn. Breeding birds include Eider, Shelduck, Tufted Duck, Water Rail, and Sedge Warbler.

GLENMUICK (OS NO2585)

Glenmuick is a vast mountainous area operated as a reserve by the Scottish Wildlife Trust under an agreement with the Balmoral Estates. This is a summer site for the birdwatcher – high in the Grampian Mountains – hunting ground for the Golden Eagle. Up-to-date information is obtainable from the visitor centre where current literature should be consulted. Access is south of the A93 road at Ballater, to the Spittal of Glenmuick. Look out for Ptarmigan, Red Grouse, and Golden Plover.

MUIR OF DINNET (OS NO4399)

This is a Nature Conservancy Council reserve consisting of areas of open water, marshland, and woodland. Access is via the A93 and the town of Dinnet. Some 140 species have been recorded in the area, over seventy of which breed each year. Woodcock and Redpoll are particularly common and, in autumn/winter, as many as 8000 Greylag Geese and 2000 Pink-footed Geese have been recorded. Goldeneye are present throughout the year, with breeding Black Grouse and wintering Hen Harrier and Merlin.

HIGHLAND AND WESTERN ISLES

The region comprises the old counties of Caithness, Sutherland, Ross and Cromarty, Nairnshire, Inverness-shire, and parts of Moray and Argyll. Covering over 2 250 000 hectares (5 557 500 acres) this region represents more than one-third of the land area of Scotland, but it has a human population of only about 145 000, that is, less than 2 per cent of the Scottish population. This sparsely populated wilderness forms the northernmost area of mainland Britain. In the west are large numbers of islands, sea lochs, and peninsulas; in the east, by contrast, the straight coastline is broken by the Firths of Moray, Cromarty, and Durnoch. The north coast stretches bleak and rugged from John O'Groats to Cape Wrath. These towering north-coast seacliffs, with mile after mile of spectacular scenery, edge an area made up of vast tracks of 'barren' moorland and mountains which are relieved only by the fertile farmland in the south-east, countless freshwater lochs, and areas of ancient woodland. Only the recently arrived stands of commercial forestry vary the landscape. In the extreme south, the uplands include the

Cairngorm mountains and Ben Nevis but the region is split diagonally from Loch Linnhe at Fort William, via Loch Lochy and Loch Ness along the Great Glen fault, to Inverness.

Countless rivers lace the region and, ornithologically, the most famous is the Spey, centred around Aviemore. It is here that conservation and the tourist industry have come into direct conflict on the remote mountain tops and slopes as land is developed for winter sports. Forestry, sporting estates, and livestock dominate the Highland region, and it is only in the east that mixed farming is in evidence.

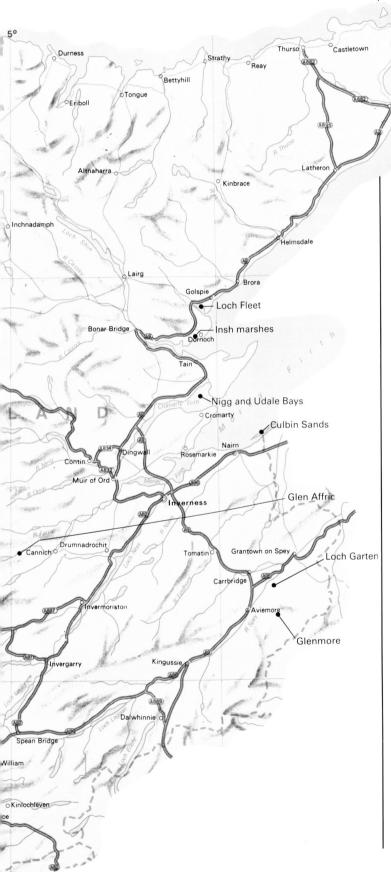

Birdwatching sites

GLEN AFFRIC (OS NH2424)

This is a Forestry Commission native pinewood reserve. Access to the site is via the A831 road at Cannich. A woodland trail passes through the area. Visiting birdwatchers should look for Scottish Crossbill, Black Grouse, and Capercaillie in the woods; Goosander on the loch; and Dipper and Grey Wagtail by the river. On this site, as on all Highland sites, it is always worth keeping an eye on the sky for, throughout the Highland region, birds of prey are to be seen regularly soaring on rising air currents.

LOCH FLEET (OS NH7796)

Loch Fleet is a Scottish Wildlife Trust reserve which is easily viewed from the A9 road north of Dornoch. At migration time, the area attracts many waders, but it is best known as a wintering site for Long-tailed Duck, Eider, and Common and Velvet Scoters.

BALRANALD (OS NF7070)

This is an RSPB reserve on the coast of North Uist. Access is via the A865 and minor road to Goular. The reserve consists of rocky coast, sandy beaches, a dune system, and the machair marshland that is a feature of the Outer Hebrides. The 650 hectares (1600 acres) of the reserve contain an unusually high population of breeding wildfowl and waders, the highest density of any British site. In recent years, forty-five species have nested on the reserve, with the following estimates of breeding pairs: Mallard 60; Gadwall 5; Tufted Duck 23; Teal 14; Shoveler 17; Wigeon 1; Oystercatcher 100; Redshank 90; Ringed Plover 77; Dunlin 54; Corncrake 14; Arctic Tern 155; Common Gull 60; Twite 9; Corn Bunting 60.

In addition, an occasional pair of Red-necked Phalarope breeds, and Fulmar, Black Guillemot, and Eider nest along the coast. A small offshore island holds populations of Shag, Cormorant, and Puffin. Marked spring sea passages can include several Pomarine Skuas in early May, with regular observations of petrels and shearwaters.

HANDA (OS NC1348)

The island of Handa is managed as a reserve by the RSPB and it is possible to stay on the island by contacting the RSPB Scottish Office, 17 Regent Terrace, Edinburgh, EH7 5BN. Access is via Tarbet reached from the A894 from where visits can be arranged. The island is rough pasture with peat bogs and small lochans surrounded by high cliffs

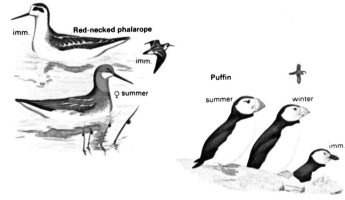

White-tailed Eagles have been successfully reintroduced into Rhum.

and sandy bays. Some thirty species nest on the island, including: Red-throated Diver 3 pairs; Arctic Skua 19 pairs; Great Skua 38 pairs; Shag 200 pairs; Eider 20 pairs; Puffin 430 pairs.

In the winter months occasional Golden Eagles wander across from the mainland, and Barnacle Geese are regularly seen.

NIGG AND UDALE BAYS (OS NH7873 and 7367)

These are two tidal bays at the very mouth of the Cromarty Firth. The viewing is best from the B817 and B9175 roads on the north shore, and the B9163 on the southern. The Cromarty Firth is an important wintering site for wildfowl and waders: Mute Swan 300; Whooper Swan 150; Pink-footed Goose 1200; Greylag Goose 500; Wigeon 10000; Goldeneye 600; Red-breasted Merganser 400; Oyster-catcher 3000; Ringed Plover 200; Curlew 2000; Bar-tailed Godwit 1500; Redshank 2000; Dunlin 2600; Knot 2000.

ISLE OF RHUM (OS NM3797)

Rhum is a large, mountainous island operated as a reserve by the Nature Conservancy Council. Access is by steamer from Mallaig, reached via the A830. Nature trails are pro-

Crested tit

Barnacle goose

vided but some areas are closed to visitors. The island has become famous as the site of the successful reintroduction of the White-tailed Eagle into Britain. Over seventy eaglets have been introduced from Norway and, after acclimatization, released on to the island. From 1983, breeding attempts have been recorded, and a single young was successfully reared in 1985. The other breeding bird of note is the Manx Shearwater; a colony of more than 130000 pairs uses the loose soil on the high slopes for nesting burrows. Other breeding birds on Rhum include Black Guillemot, Merlin, Peregrine, and Red-throated Diver. The planted woodlands attract a range of species less typical of the area: Robin, Dunnock, Song Thrush, Wren, and Chaffinch.

CULBIN SANDS (OS NH9057)

This is an RSPB reserve on the shore of the Moray Firth, east of Nairn. Behind the reserve is the largest sand-dune system in Britain, now largely planted with commercial woodland. The reserve itself consists of sandflats, shingle bars, and saltmarsh, and, although small numbers of breeding birds include Oystercatcher, Ringed Plover, Redshank, and some Little Terns, it is the flocks of wintering waders and wildfowl that are of most interest.

INSH MARSHES (OS NH7799)

The RSPB reception centre and car park, together with observation hides and a nature trail, are reached via the B970 road south of Insh. The reserve is based upon the flood plain of the upper River Spey, bordered by birch and juniper woodland. At times of winter floods, there are large flocks of waterfowl. Breeding birds include Wigeon, Mallard, Teal, Tufted Duck, Shoveler, Redshank, Snipe, Curlew, and Water Rail. Whooper Swans winter, and Grey-lag and Pink-footed Geese appear on migration. Among the more unusual visitors are Ring-necked Duck, Wood Sand-piper, and Spotted Crake. There is a large colony of Black-headed Gulls. Birds of prey are seen throughout the year; Hen Harriers are particularly numerous while Osprey, Peregrine, and Sparrowhawk are regularly recorded.

LOCH GARTEN (OS NH9718)

This RSPB reserve is well signposted from the B970 road east of Boat of Garten. The reserve contains the site where Britain's best-known pair of Ospreys nest and they can be viewed with powerful binoculars and telescopes from the 'George Waterston Osprey Hide'. This is normally open from late April to late August. Loch Garten reserve contains a very important remnant of the once-extensive Caledonian Scots Pine forest, as well as lochs, bogs, and dry, sandy moraines. The reserve also holds characteristic breeding communities of Crested Tit, Scottish Crossbill, Caper-caillie, Black Grouse, Redstart, and Siskin. The lochs attract Little Grebe, Teal, Goldeneye, Water Rail, Goosander, and Greylag Goose.

GLENMORE (OS NH9810)

Over 2500 hectares (6175 acres) of forest park have been established by the Forestry Commission with access via a minor road from the B970 at Coylumbridge. Literature about the park can be obtained at the forest office. Birds to be encountered in the area include Scottish Crossbill, Crested Tit, Capercaillie, Black Grouse, Siskin, Gold-crest, Dipper, Grey Wagtail, Common Sandpiper, and Goosander.

With its remnants of Caledonian pine forest, the Beinn Eighe mountain reserve is only opened to the public during the summer.

BEINN EIGHE (OS NG0061)

This site comprises nearly 5000 hectares (12350 acres) of Nature Conservancy Council mountain reserve with remnants of Caledonian pine forest. The site is only open to visitors in the summer months when access to the visitor centre and car park is via the A832 road beside Loch Maree. Bird populations of the open country include Red Grouse, Golden Eagle, Buzzard, and Merlin. In the woodlands, the populations are low, but include Tree Pipit, Coal Tit, and Siskin.

INVERPOLLY (OS NC1312)

Inverpolly is another large Nature Conservancy Council reserve, covering nearly 11000 hectares (27000 acres) of mountain, moor, wood, and shore. Access is via the A835 at Knockan, where a visitor centre can provide current literature and trail guides. A minor road to Inverpolly starts at Drumrunie. The diversity of habitat produces a range of species exceeding 100 in most years. On the open moorland Wheater, Ring Ouzel, Greenshank, and Stonechat all nest; in the woodland Treecreeper, Long-eared Owl, and Spotted Flycatcher occur; Red-breasted Merganser and Goosander can be seen by the lochs, while there are Shag, Fulmar, and Black Guillemot at the coast.

Some important breeding species of the Highland region

Almost all of the whole British population of the species set out below nest in the Highland region. The numbers are estimates of the number of breeding pairs:

Red-throated Diver	1000	Dotterel	80
Black-throated Diver	100	Greenshank	900
		Rock Dove	?
Slavonian Grebe	75	Fieldfare	10
Common Scoter	100	Redwing	70
Goldeneye	35	Crested Tit	800
Golden Eagle	450	Twite	10 000
Osprey	30	Scottish Crossbill	?
Ptarmigan	?	Snow Bunting	20
Corncrake	500		

Some peak winter bird counts on the Moray Firth

Red-throated Diver	150
Great Northern Diver	75
Greylag Goose	1200
Pink-footed Goose	500
Shelduck	500
Wigeon	2600
Pintail	100
Scaup	100
Long-tailed Duck	5600
Common Scoter	3500
Velvet Scoter	600
Goldeneye	400
Red-breated Merganser	150
Oystercatcher	4000
Knot	4000
Bar-tailed Godwit	1600
Redshank	1700
Dunlin	3500

Organizations in Highland

Scottish Ornithologists' Club Inverness Branch (SOC), Ashton Farm Cottage, Inverness, IV1 2NM

Scottish Ornithologists' Club Thurso Branch (SOC), Mill Cottage, Olrig, Castletown, Caithness KW14 8SN

East Sutherland Bird Group (ESBG), An Sithean, Bonar Bridge, Sutherland IV24 3AW

Annual reports

'Caithness Bird Report', 7 Duncan Street, Thurso, Caithness

Books

Angus, S. *Sutherland Birds.* Northern Times, 1983.
Knowlton, D. *The Naturalist in the Hebrides.* David & Charles, 1977.
Nethersole-Thompson, D and Watson, A. *The Cairngorms: their Natural History and Scenery.* Collins, 1974.

Golden eagle

imm.

ORKNEY AND SHETLAND ISLANDS

North Hill

Noup Cliffe

The Barony

Marwick Head

Birsay Moors and Cottasgarth

The Loons

Finstown

Orkney Islands

Stromness

Kirkwall

Hobbister

St Mary's

Copinsay

North Hoy

Burwick

Shetland Islands

Hermaness

Haroldswick

Gutcher

Belmont

Lumbister

North Fetlar

Mid Yell

North Roe

Ulsta

Hillswick

Toft

Sullom

Sandness

Voe

Scalloway

Lerwick

Quarff

Noss

Lock Spiggie

Sumburgh

ORKNEY

Separated from the Scottish mainland by the Pentland Firth, the county of Orkney is made up of about seventy islands of which some twenty are inhabited. Much of the landscape is now treeless, but remnants of the native birch, hazel, and rowan remain in some of the deeper gullies. Although much of the land is farmed under the crofting system, it is patchworked with lochs and moorland. The sea and its seabirds dominate Orkney, and the varying coastal features of high cliffs and sandy beaches provide for a wide range of birds. Over 320 species have been recorded in the islands, of which nearly 100 breed. The Orkneys are well supplied with RSPB reserves, and all the following sites are under the management of the Society.

Birdwatching sites (mainland)

BIRSAY MOORS AND COTTASGARTH (OS HY3719)
Access to the site of low undulating moorland with heather, blanket bog, marshy areas, and streams is via the B9057

Black-throated diver

Summer

Black-throated diver

Winter

road. The reserve contains a high density of nesting Hen Harriers and Merlins, with ground-nesting Kestrels. There are small colonies of Great and Arctic Skuas, as well as four species of gulls, Golden Plover, Dunlin, and Curlew. Stonechat, Wheatear, and Short-eared Owl also nest.

COPINSAY (OS HY6101)
Copinsay is a small island reserve off the mainland coast. It was established as a memorial reserve to the late James Fisher. There are cliff-nesting colonies of Kittiwakes, Guillemots, Razorbills, Shags, Fulmars, Puffins, Black Guillemots, and Cormorants. Other nesting species of interest include Corncrake, Rock Dove, Twite, Arctic Tern, and Raven.

HOBBISTER (OS HY3806)
The heather moorland, low sea-cliffs, and sandy beaches are reached via the A964 road. Breeding birds on the moorland include Hen Harrier, Merlin, Short-eared Owl, Red Grouse, Curlew, Snipe, and Twite. On the cliffs, there are Fulmar, Raven, Kestrel, and Black Guillemot. Outside the breeding season, the coast attracts divers, grebes, and marine ducks.

THE LOONS (OS HY2524)
This is an area of marshland reached via the B9056 road west of the A967. The area contains a high density of nesting ducks and waders, and during the winter months, it provides a refuge for a small flock of Greenland White-fronted Geese.

MARWICK HEAD (OS HY2224)
Access to Marwick Head is via the B9056 road. Here there is the largest and most spectacular seabird colony on mainland Orkney. Among the breeding birds are 35000 Guillemots and 10000 Kittiwakes, together with Fulmar and Razorbill.

The remote and rocky shoreline of the small island of Papa Westray off the north-east corner of Westray in the Orkneys.

Birdwatching sites (islands)

NORTH HILL (OS HY4953) (Papa Westray)
The reserve is at the northern end of the island and contains a very large colony of Arctic Terns together with Arctic Skua, Eider, Ringed Plover, Oystercatcher, Dunlin, Wheatear, Corncrake, Black Guillemot, Guillemot, Razorbill, Shag, and Rock Dove.

NORTH HOY (OS HY2201) (Hoy)
During the summer the moorland provides a home for nesting Great and Arctic Skuas, Red Grouse, Golden Plover, and Dunlin. Birds of prey are common on the reserve, and the cliffs hold a wide range of nesting seabirds.

NOUP CLIFFS (OS HY3950) (Westray)
The cliffs guard the north-west corner of the island, and contain the second largest colony of nesting seabirds in Britain: 70000 Guillemots, 4000 Razorbills, 70000 pairs of Kittiwakes, together with Puffin, Shag, and Fulmar.

Notes on some selected species in Orkney
Red-throated Diver – approximately 100 pairs nest.
Gannet – a single colony, on Sule Stack, contains over 4000 pairs.
Whooper Swan – passage birds peak at over 1800 in November.
Hen Harrier – as many as 100 pairs may nest on the islands.
Arctic Skua – over 1000 pairs nest, the majority on Eday.
Great Skua – over 1600 pairs nest, the majority on Hoy.
Glaucous Gull – up to sixty individuals may be seen each year, mainly from January to May.

Arctic skua

light phase

dark phase

imm.

Kittiwake – although the numbers are declining, the island supports nearly 125 000 breeding pairs.
Arctic Tern – over 33 000 pairs nest in more than 200 colonies; over 7500 pairs on Papa Westray.
Rook – nesting first recorded in the 1870s; population now over 1350 pairs.

Great Auk in Orkney
As a breeding bird in Orkney, the Great Auk was apparently confined to Fowl Craig on Papa Westray. In the summer of 1812, a female was killed with a stone while incubating an egg. The following year a male was killed at the same site, and this bird is preserved as a specimen in the British Museum. Although there are later records from the island of St Kilda – the most recent British occurrence was from that island in 1840 – the Papa Westray birds represent the last recorded British breeding for the species before it became extinct.

Gamebirds in Orkney
Red Grouse – well established with nesting birds present on seven islands, and wintering flocks of up to forty individuals.
Ptarmigan – one bred on Hoy; now extinct, with the last bird shot in the mid-nineteenth century.
Black Grouse – attempts were made to introduce the species in the mid-nineteenth century, but

failed.
Red-legged Partridge – attempts were made to introduce the species in the mid-nineteenth century, but failed.
Grey Partridge – several introductions have been attempted, the latest on Shapinsay in the 1970s; the success is uncertain.
Quail – one or two recorded every year, usually in late spring.
Pheasant – first introduced in the late 1850s, it is now well established and nests on several islands.

Organizations in Orkney
Orkney Field Club (OFC), 24 Hillside Road, Stromness KW16 3AH

Annual reports
'Orkney Bird Report', 34 High Street, Kirkwall KW15 1AZ

Books
Booth, C *et al. The Birds of Orkney.* The Orkney Press, 1984.

Lesser grey shrike

SHETLAND ISLANDS

The 100 or so remote, and once inaccessible, islands that make up the Shetlands are over 90 miles north of John O'Groats but the coming of a major industry has made them easier to reach. The discovery of North Sea oil has resulted in a massive oil terminal at Sullom Voe and this has led to a considerable improvement in the communications to this most northerly part of the British Isles. The islands have heather moorland, craggy mountains, and croft farmland, but they are dominated by the sea and by seabirds. Bird migration forms a significant part of the islands' importance for ornithology for here is a birds' crossroads set between the coasts of Scandinavia, Iceland, and Britain. Over 340 species have been recorded in Shetland, of which over eighty breed in most years.

Birdwatching sites

FAIR ISLE (OS HZ2172)

The 'ultimate' birdwatching locality in Britain, Fair Isle has been a mecca for the student of bird migration for many years. There is accommodation on the island: details from 21 Regent Terrace, Edinburgh EH7 5BT. Fair Isle is situated in the open sea between the Orkneys and the Shetlands, and each year gathers a remarkable set of records for rare migrants, apparently from all corners of the globe. Well over 300 species have been recorded from the island, with nearly 200 noted in any one year. Breeding seabirds abound and, with the correct weather conditions, migrants may descend upon the island in their thousands, but there may be just one or two from Asia or North America. The following species were recorded in 1984: Red-footed Falcon (southern Europe); Lesser Golden Plover (North America); Great Snipe (north-eastern Europe); Short-toed Lark (southern Europe); Olive-backed Pipit (Asia); Red-throated Pipit (Arctic); Thrush Nightingale (eastern Europe); Red-flanked Bluetail (Asia); Lanceolated Warbler (Asia); River Warbler (eastern Europe); Paddyfield Warbler (Asia); Subalpine Warbler (southern Europe); Arctic Warbler (north-eastern Europe); Lesser Grey Shrike (southern Europe); Rustic Bunting (north-eastern Europe); Little Bunting (north-eastern Europe); Yellow-breasted Bunting (north-eastern Europe); Black-headed Bunting (south-eastern Europe).

NORTH FETLAR (OS HU6091)

Access to Fetlar is by ferry from Yell or Unst. The RSPB reserve is in the north of the island and comprises moorland and high sea-cliffs with small lochs and sandy beaches. This is the site of the famous nesting by the Snowy Owl and, although female birds still remain on the island, no male has been seen for several years.

There are many rare breeding birds on Fetlar, and visiting birdwatchers should take great care to avoid disturbing them. Among the more interesting are Manx Shearwater, Storm Petrel, Merlin, Whimbrel, Red-necked

Puffins seem to stand guard over the cliff ledges along the southern end of the Fair Isle in the Shetlands. Fair Isle is Britain's 'ultimate' birding spot.

Organizations in Shetland
Shetland Bird Club (SBC), 3 Lighthouse Buildings,
  Breiwick Road, Lerwick

Annual reports
'Shetland Bird Report', 3 Lighthouse Buildings,
  Breiwick Road, Lerwick
'Fair Isle Bird Observatory Report', FIBOT, Fair Isle,
  Shetland

Books
Tulloch, B and Hunter F. *A Guide to Shetland Birds.*
  Shetland Times, 1979.
Williamson, K. *Fair Isle and its Birds.* Oliver & Boyd,
  1965.

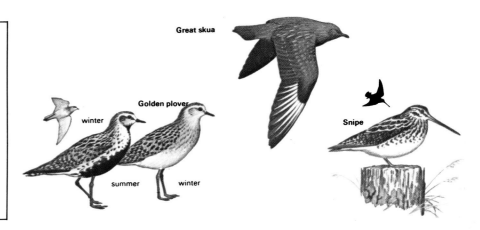

Phalarope, Arctic Tern, Great and Arctic Skuas, six species of gulls, Raven, and Twite.

HERMANESS (OS HP6016)

This Nature Conservancy Council reserve forms the northernmost point of the island of Unst and the British Isles. This is one of Britain's most important seabird sites – with several miles of inhabited cliffs, backed by moorland containing an equally impressive bird population. Over 8000 pairs of Gannets nest and, since 1970, they have been joined each year by a lone Black-browed Albatross from the southern oceans. Among the other breeding birds are 5000 pairs of Kittiwakes, 10000 Fulmars, 16000 Guillemots, 2000 Razorbills, and 5000 Great Skuas.

LOCH SPIGGIE (OS HU3717)

This is an RSPB reserve on Mainland Shetland reached via the B9122 road. Loch Spiggie is large and shallow, and was formed as sand-dunes accumulated and dammed a shallow bay. The main interest at the site is the wintering Whooper Swans, Greylag Geese, and Pochard. Spring and autumn migrants often make landfall.

LUMBISTER (OS HU4891)

This RSPB heather-moorland and peat-bog reserve is situated on the western side of the island of Yell. Breeding birds include Red-throated Diver, Raven, Merlin, Curlew, Snipe, Golden Plover, Dunlin, Arctic Tern, Great and Arctic Skuas.

NOSS (OS HU5540)

This uninhabited island is a reserve of the Nature Conservancy Council, with acces via Lerwick and the island of Bressay. Gannet, Guillemot, and Kittiwake nest in profusion, and other breeding birds include Eider, Great Skua, and Great Black-backed Gull.

Esha Ness on the mainland of the Shetland islands looks westwards out into the Atlantic Ocean.

NORTHERN IRELAND AND THE REPUBLIC OF IRELAND

Compared with mainland Britain, the bird life of Ireland is poor in many ways, and especially so in relation to woodland species. There is, for example, a marked shortage of owls and woodpeckers. There are also fewer active birdwatchers in Ireland, but interest and involvement are growing rapidly and an extensive network of important bird reserves has been established.

The importance to ornithology rests with the large populations of seabirds using the many offshore islands and sea-cliffs that face the Atlantic ocean; the country's large number of undrained loughs, bogs, and marshes, particularly in the centre and west of the country; the profusion of wintering sites for the breeding birds from the Greenland and Iceland nesting grounds; and landfall for the large numbers of wind-blown and drifted migrants that

have crossed the North Atlantic either unaided or on board a ship. Although recent years have seen the completion of several surveys of Irish birds, there is still much to be discovered by the exploring birdwatcher.

Birdwatching sites

CASTLECALDWELL FOREST, County Fermanagh
This is an RSPB reserve at the western end of Lower Lough Erne with access via the A47 road. The reserve contains a large coniferous forest together with willow and alder scrub and reedswamp on the lough shore. Islands in the lough are particularly important for the breeding population of Common Scoter which numbers up to eighty pairs. Other breeding birds include Red-breasted Merganser, Mallard, Tufted Duck, Sandwich Tern, Lesser Black-backed Gull, and Grey Heron. Corncrake, Long-eared Owl, Water Rail, and Sparrowhawk all nest.

GREENCASTLE POINT, County Down
The Point is situated on the north shore of Carlingford Lough and is easily viewed from the village of Greencastle. Nesting Common, Arctic, Sandwich, and Roseate Terns occur.

LOUGH FOYLE, County Derry
Access to this RSPB reserve is by various minor roads from the A2 between Ballykelly and Eglinton. It is a site for the winter birdwatcher, for the complex mixture of mudflats, shell ridges, and mussel beds attracts a wide range of species. The beds of eelgrass throng with more than 20000 Wigeon, 1000 Teal, and nearly 1000 Brent Geese of the pale-bellied form. On the surrounding fields 1200 Whooper and 300 Bewick's Swans occur, together with small numbers of grey geese. Equally impressive are the waders:

8000 Curlew, 3000 Bar-tailed Godwit, and 2000 Oyster-catcher. Many passage migrants are recorded, and winter-ing birds of prey can include both Peregrine and Gyr Falcon.

RATHLIN ISLAND, County Antrim
The cliffs at the western end of the island hold large numbers of breeding seabirds including Guillemot, Razor-bill, Puffin, Black Guillemot, Fulmar, Shag, and Kittiwake. Peregrine, Raven, Buzzard, and Chough all nest on the island and it has been proved that Manx Shearwater have bred in recent years. Access is by boat from Ballycastle.

WEXFORD WILDFOWL RESERVE, County Wexford
South of Wexford on the N25 road, this joint reserve of the Irish Wildbird Conservancy and the Department of Fisheries and Forestry is one of the most important winter-ing areas for wildfowl in Ireland. The area is known as 'the Slobs', and can attract more than 6600 Greenland White-fronted Geese. Consequently, it is the principal wintering site for this species, holding over half the world's popula-tion. The reserve has an information centre and observa-tion hides. At any one time there can be as many as 15500 wildfowl on the site with the following peak counts: Mallard 2500; Teal 1300; Wigeon 1750; Pintail 1000; Shoveler 100; Scaup 300; Tufted Duck 200; Pochard 100; Shelduck 200; White-fronted Goose 6600; Brent Goose 600; Bewick's Swan 200; Oystercatcher 1600; Lapwing 5000; Golden Plover 7000; Black-tailed Godwit 1250; Curlew 1000; Bar-tailed Godwit 1000; Redshank 750; Dunlin 3000.

SALTEE ISLANDS, County Wexford
Access to these islands is from Kilmore Quay. Formerly a famous bird observatory, the Saltee Islands recorded many rare and unusual visitors. Fewer birdwatchers now visit the

Magpie

Organizations in Ireland
Irish Wildbird Conservancy (IWC), Southview, Church Road, Greystones, County Wicklow
Northern Ireland Ornithologists' Club (NIOC), 1 Upper Cavehill Road, Belfast BT15 4EZ
Ulster Trust for Nature Conservation (UTNC), Barnett's Cottage, Barnett's Demesne, Malone Road, Belfast
RSPB Members' Groups based at: Antrim, Bangor, Belfast, Enniskillen, Larne, Limavady, and Lisburn (details from RSPB Northern Ireland, Belvoir Park Forest, Belfast BT8 4QT)

Annual reports
'Irish Bird Report' published in *Irish Birds*, the journal of the Irish Wildbird Conservancy
'Northern Ireland Bird Report', 22 Marlborough Drive, Carrickfergus, County Antrim

Books
Deane, C D. *Handbook of the Birds of Northern Ireland. Belfast News*, 1954.
Hutchinson, C. *The Birds of Dublin and Wicklow.* Irish Wildbird Conservancy, 1975.
Merne, O J. *The Birds of Wexford.* Irish Tourist Board, 1974.
RSPB. *Birds Around Belfast.* RSPB, 1981.
Ruttledge, R F. *Ireland's Birds.* Witherby, 1966.
Ruttledge, R F. *A List of the Birds of Ireland.* National Museum of Ireland, 1975.
Stapleton, L. *Birds of Clare and Limerick.* Limerick, 1975.
Whilde, T. *Birds of Galway and Mayo.* Irish Wildbird Conservancy, 1977.

North American Birds in Ireland 1983-84
Lesser Golden Plover – Cork and Galway, July-September 1983.
Least Sandpiper – Cork, August 1984.
Baird's Sandpiper – Wexford, October 1983 and September 1984; Waterford, September 1984.
Stilt Sandpiper – Wexford, August 1983.
Spotted Sandpiper – Cork, October 1983.
Bonaparte's Gull – Dublin and Kerry, February and March 1983.
Laughing Gull – Cork and Dublin, January and June 1984.
Forster's Tern – Dublin, Wicklow, and Derry, January, September, and December 1983.
Belted Kingfisher – Clare, October-December 1984.
American Robin – Offaly, June 1983.
Black-and-white Warbler – Derry, September 1984.
Northern Parula – Cork, October 1983.
Blackpoll Warbler – Cork, October 1984.
Yellow-rumped Warbler – Cork, October 1983.
Northern Waterthrush – Cork, October 1983.
Rose-breasted Grosbeak – Cork, October 1983.
White-throated Sparrow – Antrim, December 1984.

In addition there were numerous records of the following species during the two years: American Wigeon; Ring-necked Duck; Surf Scoter; White-rumped Sandpiper; Semipalmated Sandpiper; Buff-breasted Sandpiper; Long-billed Dowitcher; Lesser Yellowlegs; Wilson's Phalarope; and Ring-billed Gull.

islands, but rare birds are still recorded, with Tawny Pipit, Yellow-browed Warbler, Woodchat Shrike, Red-breasted Flycatcher, and Little Bunting in 1983. Approximately 250 species have been recorded on the islands and, of these, forty-seven nest.

CAPE CLEAR ISLAND, County Cork
Still active as a site for the study of bird migration, Cape Clear is reached via Baltimore on the Irish mainland. Hostel-type accommodation is available on the island, but must be booked in advance from 46 The Glen, Boden Park, Dublin 16. The site has achieved international fame for the movements of seabirds that take place offshore in the autumn months, at which time rare visitors are often recorded. Breeding birds include Black Guillemot and Chough.

SLIGO BAY, County Sligo
Bounded by the N59, N4, N15, and several minor roads, Sligo Bay can be viewed from several different areas. The bay consists of three separate estuaries: the rivers Ballysadare, Garavague, and Drumcliff, divided by narrow peninsulas. On the northern shore, up to 1000 Barnacle Geese spend the winter, but other visitors include: Brent Goose 2000+; Wigeon 2000; Oystercatcher 800; Dunlin 1000; Curlew 500; Bar-tailed Godwit 400.

AKERAGH LOUGH, County Kerry
Just north of Tralee on the L105 road, the Lough has achieved international fame for the large numbers of North American vagrant waders that have occurred there in the autumn. Among these have been three additions to the Irish list: Solitary Sandpiper in 1958; Baird's Sandpiper in

1962; and Stilt Sandpiper in 1968. More importantly, depending upon water levels, the site can attract as many as 3500 Teal, 10 000 Lapwing, and 4000 Curlew.

LOUGH DERRAVARAGH, County Westmeath
There are many loughs in central Ireland that are worth visiting in winter, and Lough Derravaragh is one. Access is via the T10 road north of Mullingar. In some winters, as many as 9000 wildfowl may be seen on the lough, including over 5000 Pochard, 2000 Tufted Duck, 600 Mallard, and 200 Teal. In November, the concentration of Coot may exceed 3000 and, later in the winter, small numbers of Whooper Swan also occur.

The visiting birdwatcher should also take time to explore the following loughs: **Lough Kinale, County Longford; Lough Sheelin, County Cavan; Lough Oughter, County Cavan; Lough Iron, County Westmeath.**

RIVER SHANNON
The basin of the River Shannon stretches from Lough Allen, County Leitrim, via Lough Bofin, County Roscommon; Lough Ree, County Longford; and Lough Derg, County Tipperary to the mouth of the river from Limerick to Kerry Head. Winter birdwatching can be productive at many sites along the river, but the greatest concentrations occur in the estuary itself, including up to 15 500 wildfowl and 67 500 waders. Some of the commonest species are: Teal 2500; Wigeon 10 000; Shelduck 1000; Lapwing 5000; Golden Plover 2500; Curlew 3250; Black-tailed Godwit 8500; Bar-tailed Godwit 1250; Redshank 3250; Knot 2500; Dunlin 29 500.

Birdwatching is a relaxing pastime in County Kerry and its islands.

COUNTY KERRY ISLANDS
These are two small island reserves of the Irish Wildbird Conservancy. Little Skellig holds over 20000 pairs of breeding Gannets and over 1000 pairs of Kittiwakes. Puffin Island holds some eleven breeding species including 10000 Puffins 20000 Manx Shearwater, and large numbers of Storm Petrel. Raven and Chough also nest. Landing is not permitted, but boat trips around both islands can be arranged from Portmagee west of the N70 road.

ILLAUNMAISTER, County Mayo
This is another Irish Wildbird Conservancy reserve off the Mayo coast. It is well known for its wintering Barnacle Geese and breeding colony of 5000 Puffin.

INDEX

Numbers in *italics* refer to illustrations